THE HISTORY OF
CHRISTIAN THEOLOGY

Volume 1: The Science of Theology

Editor: Paul Avis

THE HISTORY OF CHRISTIAN THEOLOGY

Volume 1: The Science of Theology

Editor: Paul Avis

Gillian R Evans
Alister E McGrath
Allan D Galloway

Marshall Pickering, Basingstoke

Wm. B. Eerdmans Publishing Co., Grand Rapids

First published 1986 by Marshall Morgan & Scott Ltd,
Marshall Pickering,
3 Beggarwood Lane, Basingstoke, Hants., United Kingdom
A subsidiary of the Zondervan Corporation
and
Wm. B. Eerdmans Publishing Co., 255 Jefferson Ave. SE,
Grand Rapids, Mich. 49503

British Library Cataloguing in Publication Data

Evans, G. R.
  The science of religion.—(The History of Christian theology; v. 1)
  1. Theology — History
  I. Title   II. McGrath, Alister E.
  III. Galloway, Allan D.   IV. Series
  230'.09   BR145.2

ISBN 0-551-01382-6

Library of Congress Cataloging-in-Publication Data

Evans, G. R. (Gillian Rosemary)
  The science of theology.

  (The History of Christian theology)
  Includes index.
  1. Theology — History.   I. McGrath, Alister E.,
1953-   . II. Galloway, Allan Douglas, 1920-
III. Title. IV. Series.
BT21.2.E93 1986   230'.09   86-19645

ISBN 0-8028-0195-1

THE HISTORY OF CHRISTIAN THEOLOGY

The History of Christian Theology aims to provide an extended introduction to religious thought in the Christian tradition from an historical perspective. It presents the unfolding of Christian thought in its various departments: doctrine, ethics, philosophical theology, the study and interpretation of the Bible, interaction with the sciences and with other religions. The various volumes of the *History* will eventually constitute a set of fundamental resource books of wide usefulness in religious education and in ministry. The approach aims to combine clarity of presentation and ease of reference with academic integrity and theological depth.

Editor

THE SCIENCE OF THEOLOGY

The present volume in *The History of Christian Theology* concerns the nature of theology itself. *The Science of Theology* unfolds the Church's changing understanding of the discipline of theology from the dawn of the Christian era to the present day. It examines the philosophical foundations and commitments underlying developments in doctrine, ethics, biblical interpretation, etc, through the centuries. *The Science of Theology* focuses on the methods, norms and sources of theology rather than on doctrine or practice. In the first part, Gillian R. Evans describes the foundation period of Christian theology in the patristic age and its impressive flowering in the Middle Ages. In the second part, Alister E. McGrath explores the philosophical assumptions behind Reformation theology and Protestant orthodoxy up to and including the Enlightenment. In the final part Allan D. Galloway outlines the various developments in nineteenth- and twentieth-century theology that have created the present situation of Christian theology. *The Science of Theology* provides the essential background to the most critical question confronting contemporary theology: What are we doing when we do theology, and how should we set about it?

Editor

CONTENTS

PART I

PATRISTIC AND MEDIEVAL THEOLOGY

1

CHRISTIANS AND ROMANS

1. THE NEW TESTAMENT AND PHILOSOPHY

The Roman author Varro, 'a man universally informed' as the playwright Terence calls him, wrote forty-one books on 'human' and 'divine' subjects. Much of his work is lost, but his account of the three kinds of religion he found among his contemporaries was sufficiently striking and apposite for Augustine of Hippo (354–430) to repeat it in his *City of God*. There was

1. a literary or 'poetic' theology concerned with the worship of the gods of myth and legend;
2. the official religion of the State which was designed to promote good citizenship ('civil' theology);
3. and a 'natural theology' concerned with questions of interest to philosophers who wanted to know how the world began and what sustains it.

Reason and Revelation
The last of Varro's divisions – as Augustine realised – presented a challenge to Christian thinkers as the others did not. Christianity had no place for pagan gods; Christians were prepared to die rather than call the Emperor divine; but 'natural theology' dealt with questions which were also important for Christians. Augustine was impressed by the success some of the philosophers had had in coming close to Christian truth by the exercise of their reason, and without the aid of the revelations God had provided in the Bible.

For Augustine himself the relationship between the application of reason to the study of the world and the understanding Christianity had of it was never simple, and perhaps never fully resolved. It has presented a challenge to Christian thinkers in every age, as the science and philosophy of the day has seemed to question the assertions of faith. And yet it has appeared an indispensable aid. The Carolingian scholar Johannes Scotus Eriugena had no doubt that philosophy and theology were one. 'What is philosophy but the study by which God, the supreme and principal cause of all things, is both humbly worshipped and looked for by reason?'

The Greek and Hebrew Heritage

The usefulness and the challenge of philosophy first presented itself through the contact of early Christianity with Greek thought. Judaism was not fundamentally a philosophical religion but a practical one. Its keynote was the Law. The Talmud is not a treatise on abstract questions of ethics, but a collection of examples of hypothetical and moral problems capable of being resolved as though they were actual cases. The Old Testament gives a picture of a Creator, a God who guides the world and watches over his chosen people, giving them the Law, leading them, punishing them, receiving them back. He is not beyond naming, or even seeing. He is hidden from our sight by his majesty, rather than by his intrinsic invisibility.

Under the influence of the Greeks, their language well-adapted for philosophy and their love of the intellectual and abstract, the transcendence of God came to be increasingly accentuated. The Jewish tradition could not easily find a place for a notion of a God such as the Platonists described, so high as to be beyond being itself. God's very name is 'I Am' (Exodus 20). Nevertheless, something of its influence was felt; God's name, instead of being that by which he reveals himself so that he can be called, came to be thought of as something so holy that mentioning it ought to be avoided. The Old Testament shows an increasing tendency to personify Wisdom in a Greek way, and to think of it as 'creative' (Job 28:12ff.; Proverbs 8:22ff.; Ecclesiasticus 24:1ff.). Later Judaism makes room for angels as ministers of God (Tobias 12:15; I Enoch 20:1ff.). In these and a number of other ways, the adoption of the Greek language and some Greek habits of thought by communities of Jews in the Greek-speaking areas of the Roman Empire resulted in the importation of fresh nuances of meaning, fresh ideas, new emphases. When the sayings of Jesus were first written down, more than thirty years after his death, they had long been current in Greek.

Hellenist Christians

The first Christians did not regard themselves as adherents of a new religion, but as holding to the true Judaism in their recognition of Jesus as the Messiah. But amongst their number were some Hellenists whose underlying assumptions were those of the Greek philosophical tradition. Conflict arose and they were expelled from Jerusalem. In Acts 11:19–20, Luke describes how they travelled 'as far as Phoenicia and Cyprus and Antioch', preaching to the Jews, and a few, 'men of Cyprus and Cyrene', preached to the Greeks. The influence of their preaching was largely free of that emphasis upon the Law which we find among the Christians who stayed behind in Jerusalem.

Paul of Tarsus

These missionaries were joined by Paul of Tarsus. He was brought up in a Greek city, but he was a philosopher neither by inclination nor by training, with only a limited command of the ideas of Greek thinkers. Paul mentions the famous paradox of the Cretan who says that all Cretans are liars (Titus 1:12), so that it is impossible to tell whether he is telling the truth, but mentions it as though he thought it not a philosopher's puzzle but a statement about the Cretan character. This apart, there are no more than hints of the influence of Greek thought in his letters: the discussions of conscience and natural law in the second chapter of Romans, and of natural goodness and self-sufficiency in Philippians 4, have a Stoic flavour, and there are Platonic undertones about the discussion of immortality in 2 Corinthians 3–4. However, in exploring the implications of Jesus' life on earth and his crucifixion and resurrection, Paul has little use for philosophy.

Early Christian Writings

Elsewhere in the New Testament echoes of Plato are to be heard – in Hebrews and especially in the opening of John's Gospel – but they are distant echoes. The New Testament was not written by philosophers. Nor, for the most part, were the works of the Apostolic Fathers: the *Didache*, Clement's *Epistle(s)*, the Epistle of Barnabas, the seven letters of Ignatius of Antioch, the letters of Polycarp to Philippi, the *Shepherd of Hermas*, Papias, and various fragments. Clement, for example, wrote c.AD 94 from the Church of Rome to the Church of Corinth. There are elements of Greek thought in his letter, but of a kind which must have been commonplace at that time. For example, he believes, that our knowledge and intellect come through a process of divine illumination. Through Christ, he says, we are to gaze into the heights of heaven. 'Through him we see as if in a mirror' (2 Cor. 3.18) 'the spotless . . . face of God; through him the eyes of our hearts have been opened; through him our minds which were darkened and insensible leap up to the light; through him God willed that we should have a taste of immortal knowledge' (*Ep. to Cor.* xvi).

Clement's first concern was with the practical running of the Churches and with the spiritual well-being and growth of Christians, just as Paul's had been. Overt philosophising was a sophistication for which, as yet, the young Church had neither time nor urgent need. Its writers made use of ideas which had some common currency (though perhaps not always with an awareness of their source), as opposed to making a systematic attempt to set out Christian teaching in terms acceptable to a philosopher.

The beginnings of a Systematic Theology
The attempt to be philosophically and theologically systematic did not come all at once, even when doctrinal differences began to appear among Christians and stimulated Christian thinking. The Docetists, for example, denied the reality of Christ's human nature and his suffering, because it seemed to them impossible that God himself should have become a mortal and suffering being. They held that he had merely presented an appearance of these things in Christ. This matter raised questions about first principles. It was above all a Platonist's reservation, based on a concept of God as transcendent above his creation, immutable, incapable by his very nature of lowering himself.

Ignatius of Antioch (martyred c.AD 115), wrote impassioned letters to the Churches prior to his execution in a desire to restore unity to the Church. He insists on 'the virginity of Mary and her child-bearing and likewise the death of the Lord.' These three mysteries were revealed, he says, by a star of astonishing brightness which shone at the birth of Jesus. Ignatius was no Hellenist. He aims to persuade by the fire of his conviction and the power of his eloquence, not by reasoned argument. But he saw that certain of the philosophers' assumptions threatened Christian belief in the reality of Christ's humanity.

It was a Jew, Philo of Alexandria, a contemporary of St. Paul, who first tried to reconcile the differing viewpoints of the philosophers and believers in the God of the Jews and Christians. He was prompted by the circumstances of his own life, the practical necessity of finding principles of reconciliation in a Greek-speaking and highly educated community of Alexandrian Jews where enlightened Jews were also philosophers.

After his death Christian apologists following his lead, continued trying to interpret Scripture in the light of philosophy. The philosophical problems raised as a result of this, and of attempts to reason heresy out of existence, run as continuous threads through the work of Christian writers throughout the Middle Ages and beyond.

The centuries during which Christian doctrine was reaching its first detailed formulation were also centuries of evolution for Platonism. The philosophers confronting the Christian apologists who came after Philo did not have at their disposal a fully developed philosophical system. They were engaged in much the same tasks of clarification and classification as their opponents, and the friction between the two developing systems of belief furthered the philosophers in their thinking, as well as making considerable difference to the direction of Christian doctrine. These encounters encouraged both sides to emphasise certain principles at the expense of others and to see certain issues in a different light.

For both parties, the debate was far from being merely academic. Philosophy involved more than a set of scientific opinions and moral rules. It satisfied, for the educated pagan, deeper ethical needs. It was both a speculative study directed towards the highest Good and the First Cause of all things, and a way of life involving man's every action. The encounter between Christianity and philosophy was to a certain extent an encounter between two theologies.

2. THE RELIGIONS OF THE EMPIRE

Syncretism

It was Imperial policy in the later Roman Empire to try to unify the religious diversity of the Empire by imposing an official religion in every town. Unity of worship was a civic matter, not a personal one. The individual worshipper could put his trust in whatever gods or system of thought he preferred, provided he had no objection to taking part in unified public worship on official occasions. Even the most scrupulous and intellectually fastidious of pagan philosophers had little difficulty in living in the syncretistic world of late Roman paganism, whatever his opinions on ethical and metaphysical questions. Local worshippers were able to carry on with their own traditions, their devotion to the local deities undisturbed. Communities from other parts of the Empire might settle locally, still maintaining loyalty to their own gods, those lesser deities of trees and stones, the familiar *daemones*, their source of comfort since childhood. Late Roman paganism was accommodating. It accepted new gods into the pantheon without displacing the old. A nominal equivalence was declared between, for example, Zeus and Jupiter, Hera and Juno, but it was of no very pressing importance which identity should engender religious zeal in the worshipper. Indeed, the greater gods of the Roman Pantheon soon came to have chiefly literary existence.

Mystery Religions

Some of the oriental religions sat uneasily among the jostling crowd of gods. Cybele and Serapis, Mithra and Mazda, all presented their worshippers with a mystery. The heart of these cults lay in the initiation into secret rites and the revelation of hidden truths. They excluded the uninitiated. The cults were not compatible in spirit with the comfortable domestic religions of simple country people, the showy religion of public and civic ritual. They had an intensity – most notably in the state of ecstasy into which Dionysius' or Bacchus' worshippers would whip themselves – which was not to be found elsewhere among the pagans. Nevertheless, some accommodation could be arrived at. Cybele the Great Mother, with her consort Attis, the god of vegetation, was represented by Venus and Adonis, or as Demeter or Ceres with Dionysius or Sabazius from the Graeco-Roman Pantheon. Mithra could be thought of as the Sun God, the Unconquered, *Sol Invictus*.

Jews and Christians

Something of this intensity and exclusivity was to be found in different ways among Jews and Christians. These alone stood out relentlessly against the prevailing syncretism. The Jews refused to allow Yahweh to be equated with Zeus or Jupiter. In his account of the wars which ended with the fall of Jerusalem in AD 70, the Jewish historian Josephus – whose sympathies were with the Roman side – gives only a few grudging paragraphs to the religion of the Jews, but he says enough to show that it remained uncontaminated by the practices of others. The Christians, too, kept themselves apart. The earliest Christian writings outside the New Testament are concerned not with the place of Christians in the wider pagan world, but with strengthening small Christian communities. Clement's *First Epistle* is concerned with problems of division within the Church; the *Didache* considers instruction before baptism and the way in which services should be conducted: *Hermas* looks at the problem of repentance: Ignatius writes on the unity of the Church; Polycarp examines the sin of avarice; Barnabas asks how the Old Testament is to be interpreted.

The exclusivity of Jews and Christians made them unpopular with rulers intent on maintaining the all-embracing rationale of Roman paganism and resulted in persecution. But their existence also challenged the philosophers, who recognised a rapidly developing and sophisticated system of Christian thought and belief which rivalled their own.

3. A CLASSICAL EDUCATION: PHILOSOPHY AND RHETORIC

The Empire of the first century AD based the education of its young men upon a Roman model which was, in its turn, modelled upon a Greek ideal. The Greek notion of *paideia* embraced both education and culture. It involved a training of mind and body which would fit the individual for his place in a society of considerable political, artistic and literary sophistication. This view of the individual as having a place in a larger whole was of a piece with the Greek world picture. Greek thinkers had looked for laws within the universe, which would govern not only the regular movements of the heavenly bodies, the structure of natural objects, and even chance and change on a cosmic scale, but also the events of human lives so that everywhere the same principles could be found in operation. The ultimate laws of thought and action would thus create a harmony between the individual, and the whole to which the individual belongs. In their development of mathematics and the theory of music the Pythagoreans made much of this repeated patterning in the whole and in the part, in microcosm and macrocosm.

Plato proposed in the *Republic* an ideal state in which the philosopher would be king. The Romans took a different view. The Greeks had produced active citizens, politically aware, potential statesmen who were also thinkers and writers. The Romans put the civic virtues first. Accordingly the emphasis of Roman education fell upon oratory rather than philosophy. Philosophy was studied because it taught the young orator to think clearly and provided him with matter for his discourses, but the end in view was that he should be able to argue a case in a court of law, make political speeches and praise famous men in a well-turned eulogy – this last of particular importance in the later Empire.

Quintilian (born c.AD 35–40), was the first state-paid professor of rhetoric in Rome, his *Institutio Oratoria*, in twelve books, was perhaps the most complete manual of oratory produced by the ancient world. Quintilian advises that the pupil should begin with Greek, because Latin is in more common use; a preference must be given to Greek at first if the boy is to become equally proficient in both. This tells us something of interest both about the actual status of the Greek language amongst educated Romans, and about the position which was thought to be desirable for it. There was already a dichotomy of language between East and West, the Greek-speaking and the Latin-speaking Empire. This was to have profound long-term effects upon the development of Christian philosophy, because Latin is a language naturally more concrete than Greek. Christian thinkers of the West had to stretch its vocabulary and make it express ideas which did not come easily to it.

In one other respect Christian philosophy was marked by the training advocated by Quintilian. He is insistent – as educators were to be throughout the Middle Ages – on the importance of moral as well as intellectual training. He wanted to form the whole man so as to make him a powerful speaker and a good citizen. This vision of man as he ought to be was set out succinctly a century later by Aulus Gellius (c.AD 123–169), in a passage in his *Attic Nights*. He describes how in Athens he and his fellow philosophy students used to hold regular philosophical dinners, 'entertainments which we young men used to hold at Athens at the beginning of each week', and how, after they had eaten, they would discuss philosophy and 'profitable and delightful conversations' ensued.

Aulus Gellius describes the kind of man he hopes will be produced by this system of instruction. He is to be a man in all the ways which distinguish a man from the animals. His *humanitas* is not, says Gellius, what the Greeks call *philanthropia*, friendliness and good feeling towards all men without distinction, but what the Greeks call *paideia*, thorough instruction (*eruditio* and *institutio*) in the liberal arts, the sense in which it is used by Varro and Cicero. He is to be a man of skills and information, a cultivated man, but also a man of the world. That is not quite the Christian ideal, but the underlying emphasis on the connection between sound thinking and moral uprightness was taken over by Christian teachers in the forming of both the minds and the lives of young Christians in succeeding centuries.

FOR FURTHER READING

Dodds, E. R., *Pagan and Christian in an Age of Anxiety* (Cambridge, 1965).
Nock, A. D., *Early Gentile Christianity and its Hellenistic Background*, revised ed. (New York, 1964).
Nock, A. D., *Conversion* (Oxford, 1933).
Schürer, E., *The History of the Jewish People in the Age of Jesus Christ*, 2nd ed. (revised G. Vermes and F. Millar, Edinburgh, 1973).

2

PHILOSOPHERS AND GNOSTICS

1. PLATONISTS AND MIDDLE PLATONISTS

The Greek philosophical heritage was already very complex when Christianity began. The Middle Platonism of the first Christian centuries combines elements of Stoicism, parts of Aristotle's teaching, scraps from a number of philosophical systems. However certain governing principles had become common currency as a result of Plato's teaching and these gave the thought of the day a predominantly Platonic character, albeit flavoured with Stoicism and Aristotelianism.

Proclus' *Alcibiades* opens with comments on three topics which had consistently been a focus of debate:

1. the nature of being;
2. the problem of the presence of both good and evil in the world;
3. the idea of a scale or hierarchy of excellence in which all things have their proper place:

'The most valid and surest starting-point for the dialogues of Plato, and practically for the whole of philosophical consideration is, in our opinion, the discerning of our own being. If this is correctly posited, we shall in every way, I think, be able more accurately to understand both the good that is appropriate to us, and the evil that fights against it . . . Of the things that are, as it is natural for each one to differ in being, so also their perfection varies in different cases, according to their descent in the scale of being.'

These topics and their ramifications set the agenda not only for philosophers but also for Christian thinkers.

The World of Thought and the World of Matter

Plato distinguished two worlds, the world we perceive by our senses and the world we know intellectually, and which consists of ideas. The two, he perceived, are joined by some participation of one in the other, but they are quite different in kind. Above these two worlds stands God, so remote from the worlds we know that he cannot properly be said even to 'be'.

The Soul: Spirit or Matter

In this universe where what is in the mind is more real than what is obvious to the senses, the human soul was held by some Greek thinkers (notably Aristotle) to be a rarefied but still material thing, a suspension of fine particles of matter. Plato took a higher view of it, insisting on the immortality and immateriality of the soul in his *Phaedo*. His master, Socrates, was probably the first to envisage the soul as a personality, the moral and intellectual identity of a man, an agent which knows and acts in each human body. Aristotle preferred to see it as that which gives form to the body, which makes it 'actual' and individual, and not merely a shapeless lump of matter. For both there is a duality in man, a sense that the soul is somehow trapped or imprisoned within a body which is alien to it, an idea which had a long-term influence in Christian thought, and which still persists.

Plato's high view of the soul had a further implication which created difficulties for Christian thinkers. Plato held the view that virtue is knowledge. A being such as the soul which belongs to the world of ideas must be an intellectual and rational being. It cannot be possible for it to lack virtue without ceasing to be itself. Sin is at best folly, at worst, culpable ignorance, but in any case it involves an absence or dormancy of intelligence. Wrongdoing is, therefore not, as the Christians see it, an act of rebellion and defiance, but rather a bewilderment and weariness of the soul. That came to be seen by Augustine as a consequence of sin.

Middle Platonists

Only fragments survive of the work of most of the Middle Platonist thinkers. The Neoplatonist Porphyry later made a list of them: Severus, Cronius, Numenius, Gaius, Atticus and others. Their teaching survives principally in the popular accounts of Plutarch of Chaeronea (AD 50–120), Maximus of Tyre, and Apuleius, the author of *The Golden Ass*.

There appears to have been as much variety in their opinions as in their sources. Antiochus of Antioch (c.130–68 BC) helped to halt a drift away from Plato's doctrines towards a sophisticated scepticism about the possibility of knowing anything at all to be true. He taught that Ideas lie within the divine Mind and are used by the Creator as patterns or forms for created things. He was out of sympathy, however, with the notion that intelligence and the senses are entirely different from one another, and he therefore minimised Plato's emphasis upon the separateness of the worlds of matter and spirit.

On the other hand, Plutarch, a pupil of Ammonius of Alexandria, who taught more than a century after Antiochus' death, in the last years of the first and the beginning of the second century AD, made much of their difference. He insisted upon the simplicity and unity and freedom from 'otherness' of the Supreme Being, and the consequent need for intermediaries between God and men. These he believed to be the *daemones*, angelic spirits who are capable of passing from the transcendent realm to the realm of earth.

By contrast again, Apuleius, who taught outside the Academy Plato had founded, presented a version of Platonism in which Stoicism and Aristotelianism were freely mixed.

The achievement of the Middle Platonists was on the whole not original. Interest centred instead upon the masters of the past, the Stoics celebrating Heraclitus the physicist as their founder, the Epicureans Democritus the atomist. The Platonists themselves did not have the full corpus of Plato's writings but only the more popular of his dialogues.

Not all the Middle Platonists can be said to be syncretists. Atticus, a younger friend of Plutarch, rejected the synthesis of Plato and Aristotle, because he thought Aristotle wrong. But for the most part it was the mingling of ideas in Middle Platonism which gave it its stimulating qualities as far as Christians were concerned. Philosophers like these, in the habit of juggling apparent incompatibles were well-fitted to enter into the debates with Christians which began to work upon Christian thinking at the end of the first century AD.

2. STOICS

The most influential among the Stoics were the Romans Seneca (c.3 BC–AD 65); Epictetus (c.AD 60–c.AD 100); Marcus Aurelius (AD 121–80).

The Stoics contributed their conviction than man is held within a divine providence which takes care of him, but which also determines his actions.

1. God is both a beneficent providence and a lawgiver. The universe is perpetually engaged in securing certain ends by natural means.
2. Human freedom, the Stoics argued, consists in learning to live within events which cannot be prevented and circumstances which cannot be changed, in such a way that there is no chafing and the bonds are not felt. Man's end is the attainment of an inner freedom which makes him independent of what happens to him.
3. He uses his will to reach it.
4. It is a perfection which will bring him tranquillity and perpetual happiness.
5. That is an end in itself.
6. It is an essentially rational and intellectual achievement (all passion is condemned). It carries with it that virtue Plato thought to be inseparable from clarity of mind and reasonableness, and which is the sole good in man's life (health, happiness, possessions are of no account).
7. We are all, says Epictetus, portions of divinity imprisoned in an earthly body.

Stoicism came to include a good deal of Platonism through the work of Panaetius (a friend of the younger Scipio and an influence on Cicero) but it was not a system which found Plato's theory of ideas congenial. It was fundamentally a materialist doctrine, in which the material is itself divine.

3. ARISTOTELIANS

From Aristotle the Middle Platonists drew a knowledge of logical method, and an interest in causes and ends and purposes, in the physical world and beyond it.

Good and Evil
The presence of both good and evil in the world suggested to some thinkers that there must be two principles or sources of things which are utterly opposed and therefore eternally in tension with one another. Speusippus, one of Plato's pupils, thought so, and so did a number of the followers of Pythagoras. Aristotle denied that it was possible for opposites to act on one another. Christianity, too,

had to find a solution to the problem of evil and to give a place to Satan which accorded with a doctrine of God which made him at the same time the sole Author of all that exists and wholly good.

Those philosophers who rejected the 'two-principle' explanation insisted (as did the Platonist Plotinus and a different group of Pythagoreans) that everything is reducible to one great Principle. He knows, and the only object of his knowledge is himself. He is pure intelligence at work. In Plato's *Republic* a different characteristic of the First and Highest is emphasised: the idea of the Good is elevated above all other ideas. But wherever the emphasis is placed, the One is always thought of as beyond disturbance or distress, eternally tranquil, untouched by the corruptible material things of the world. Here too, Christians were looking at a problem which concerned the philosophers. Can a God of unimaginable height and greatness really care about the world? Can he involve himself with it in any way? Can he possibly have become man?

Matter and Spirit

In the hierarchy of things which the philosophers envisaged as lying beneath the single or dual First Cause there must, it seems, be a point where these abstractions become concrete, indeed material. The problem of the relation between the natural and the 'supernatural' caused difficulty because it seemed to involve a transition from one order of being to another. Aristotle himself had difficulty in thinking of anything as not somehow material. He explained the way things move in terms of a power which becomes an act, a potential which is realised (*dynamis – energeia*). Matter is what it is potentially capable of becoming.

This idea had a long-term influence but the usual view of the Middle Platonists got over the difficulty of the transition in a different way. Plato's picture, as his followers interpreted it, involves a process of streaming outwards and downwards from the One. Plotinus calls this process 'emanation'. The further things are from the beginning the more numerous they are. The One becomes plural by means of the Dyad, or principle of 'otherness'. If we pile up a series of geometrical points we still have only one geometrical point, but if we separate them along a dimension or line which makes them 'other than' one another, we get a series of points, a plurality ($1 \times 1 \times 1 = 1$, but $1 + 1 + 1 = 3$). The mathematically based conception of the universe favoured by Platonists and Pythagoreans was also helpful to Christians. In the twelfth century Thierry of Chartres was able to make use of the difference between multiplying 1×1 and adding 1 to 1 to show how God could be three Persons and one God, and at the same time the author of creation which is separate from him, although he is its source, and which is plural, while he remains One.

The Good Life
As to ethics: Aristotle, like Plato, put the good high in the scheme of things. He holds that reason must always be superior to the irrational. These two principles give him a system in which the virtuous man subordinates passion to reason, and where the highest activity of the good man is the contemplation of God himself. From this concentration upon those faculties in which he most closely resembles God man gains pleasure. He is also progressively purified of the lower tendencies in his nature, irrationality and the downward tug of the beast in him. These ideas are also common to many of the Platonists and they have a place in the Hermetic tradition. They find their way into Christian ethics in the form of an emphasis upon taking delight in God, and upon controlling unworthy desires.

Problems of Reconciliation
In the details of his picture of the universe, as well as in some of his fundamental principles, Aristotle was not always easy to reconcile with Plato. In the *De Dogmate Platonis* Apuleius looks at the idea that the divine triad is made up of soul, intellect and God. He holds that the supreme God and all other gods are transcendental, so that there can be no direct contact between the gods and man. So high is God that he is not only free of the web of suffering (*nexus patiendi*) but also of the web of doing and begetting (*nexus gerendi*) in which all created things are entangled. Beneath God himself the *daemones* come; they are indispensable to this theology because they are able to hear the prayers of men; indeed they are much involved in the affairs of men. They are to be identified with the multitude of gods the pagans worship, who can be pleased by songs and theatrical performances, influenced by offerings, flattered and cajoled. He writes of them at length in his *De Deo Socratis*.

Aristotle thought that since three elements are inhabited by living being, water by fish, earth by plants, air by 'footed' animals, it is inconceivable that the fourth element should be empty. The angels or *daemones* or lesser gods are the obvious candidates for the habitation of fire, although Apuleius preferred to place them in the air.

Albinus, too, sees God as a transcendent being, so high that he stands even above intelligence, and is the 'cause' of active intelligence, but he, too, has difficulty in reconciling some of Aristotle's ideas with Platonic principles. He accepts as beyond question that the Forms or Ideas are the thoughts of God but he does not make it clear whether he believes them to be causes. He is sure at any rate that the God who 'thinks' the world into being did not create matter.

4. GNOSTICS

There was a popular rival account of the origin of things to that of the philosophers in the second century. The Gnostic alternative was to tell a creation story in which powers and abstract forces are given names and carry out actions which are prompted by desires. They behave as though they were persons, yearning, for example, for incorruptibility, or moved by hopeless passion for an unattainable beloved. The creation narrative becomes an elaborate myth, allowing for adaptation or addition to meet any objection. Treated as an allegory, it is capable of satisfying educated and uneducated alike. It was attractive to those Christians who found parts of the Old Testament hard to accept. The Manichees of Augustine's day two centuries later had exactly this appeal for him, and kept him for nine or ten years a more or less devout Gnostic.

The Ophites

Irenaeus of Lyons (c.AD 130–c.200) describes the teaching of one of the many Gnostic sects, the Ophites, in his treatise *Against all Heresies*. It was as Bishop of Lyons that he wrote against the heretics and his particular concern was for the way Gnosticism was misleading the faithful. The Ophites call the Supreme Being 'Man' or 'Light', and believe that he dwells in Bythos. His Thought is called 'Son of Man' or 'Second Man', and is the male principle. The Holy Spirit is the female principle. (There is some warrant for this idea in the Septuagint version of Genesis 1.2.) Illuminated by the First and Second Man, the Holy Spirit produces another male principle, Christ. He is caught up with her into the true Church, the incorruptible Aeon. Some of the light which was shed on the Holy Spirit overflows, and falls down as dew. As it drops into the waters beneath it forms a body from them, the hermaphrodite Sophia. She rises out of the water, to avoid drowning, and the heavens are formed from her body. She leaves her body behind, and returns to her mother, the Holy Spirit.

But in the meantime she has given birth to Ialdabaoth. It is he who possesses a yearning for incorruptibility. He is the first of seven offspring of Sophia, each an angelic power, who creates a heaven over which to rule. Their mother, Sophia, governs the eighth heaven which is her body.

From the Triad with which the cosmic process began have come a succession of inferior powers, subject to change and stress. These angelic beings are capable of jealousy and resentment, just like Zeus and his children in the Greek Pantheon. The six younger powers revolt against Ialdabaoth, who, to defend himself, begets a son Nous, in the form of a serpent. Nous believes himself to be the Supreme Being. He joins with the other powers in creating man, and we enter history with the story of Adam and Eve. The course of Biblical history is portrayed as a struggle between Ialdabaoth and his mother Sophia.

The Appeal of Gnosticism

At its face value, this tale, and all the many versions of it which were held by other Gnostic sects, can scarcely be said to compare well with the Old Testament account in dignity or simplicity. Yet its appeal to minds familiar with the legends of the gods is apparent enough, and Christian and pagan alike knew them well. There is a comfortable fallibility about these beings which makes sense of the apparent muddle of a world full of sin and evil.

This was the great strength of the Gnostic account. It provided an explanation for the problem of evil which did not compromise the goodness of the Supreme Being. It made it possible to set the Triad above the noise and dust of battle, a source only of the most distilled good, and make Sophia (an emanence from the heights with a corporeal aspect, a compound being) the source of those powers who came to blows. It made evil comprehensible in terms of emotions every reader could recognise and understand: envy and resentment and a greed for power among the gods. It made it possible to picture two opposed and almost equal powers in the universe, perpetually at war. It eliminated the need to find a place for evil in a universe created by a single omnipotent and entirely good Creator, by conceding that the Creator was not omnipotent, nor his servants either. This was not, in itself, a shocking thought. Many thinkers of the day who held a high doctrine of the goodness of the Supreme Being and attributed to him Beauty and Truth and Justice in their supreme realisation, were content to think him less than omnipotent, for power has to do with action and activity is not an attribute of the Supreme Being. Plato's Creator is such a God. He works within an existing framework of laws, and he is content to take matter as he finds it.

Gnosticism was, in some of its many forms, a viewpoint which could be and was held by Christians. Its influence was as pervasive within Christianity as that of the philosophers whose ideas Christian apologists incorporated.

5. THE CREATION OF THE WORLD

The burning questions of the second century AD concerned the origin of things. Was the world created or did it exist from eternity? If it was created, who or what brought it into being, and why? How was it done? If there was a Creator was he all-powerful, or were other powers able to interfere with his work? Did he have helpers, a team of creators perhaps, working under him? Does he take an interest in the world now that he has made it? Can he control what takes place in it? If he is both good and powerful, how is it that anything can go wrong in the world? Where did evil come from and what is it? Why is it so strong a force in the world?

Jewish and Christian thinkers encountered these difficulties for themselves when they tried to interpret the opening chapters of Genesis. The Platonists were made aware of them by Plato's account of the matter in the *Timaeus*. Gnostic sects offered an answer of their own. The problem of origins was common ground for Christian and pagan thinkers alike. It was the first stage of a comprehensive investigation into ends as well as beginnings. If it could be established how things began, the events which ensued might be expected to fall into place, and some understanding of the purpose of the universe might be hoped for.

The Old Testament View

The Old Testament gives an account of the creation of the world by a single Being, acting, it appears, of his own free will, requiring no assistance, and completing creation according to an orderly plan in six days. A number of details are left obscure by the brevity of the narrative, particularly concerning the state of things when the act of creation began. It is not clear whether the Creator found some primal matter ready to hand, or whether he had to create it from nothing; nor is it clear what was his method of fashioning his creatures. Both these points were potential areas of controversy because the philosophers had a number of theories about the relation of God and matter.

Plato's Creator

The single work of Plato to be transmitted in a Latin version which was available throughout the Middle Ages was the *Timaeus*, with Calcidius' commentary of the first half of the fourth century. One reason why it did not drop out of sight was that it dealt with these interesting matters. Plato's account corresponded at many points with that of Genesis. Setting aside the ancient myths (the egg from which the world was hatched, for example), and the notion of a more or less spontaneous development from a mass of formless matter or from chaos, according to laws of necessity or chance, he postulated a Creator. This was a divine Being with a design, an Intelligence which was also a craftsman.

But Plato's Creator works with pre-existing matter and form like a human craftsman with clay and a diagram which acts as his pattern. He is not the ultimate source of the whole system. Plato believed that the world itself is a living being, and that its life, the soul of the world (*anima mundi*) inhabits living creatures in a series of divine sparks. The stars, too, are its living fragments. Something might be made of this by interpreting the references to the 'gods' in the Psalms (Ps. 95.3; 97.9, for example) to mean angels or even the elect among men who have that about them which is Godlike. But the attempt to identify the world soul with the Holy Spirit remained highly controversial because it implied that God is not above created things but part of them. The problems of reconciling the Genesis account with that of Plato gave rise to a long series of work on the Six Days of Creation up to the end of the Middle Ages and beyond. We shall continue to pursue these questions in the next chapter.

FOR FURTHER READING

Chadwick, H., *Early Christian Thought and the Classical Tradition* (Oxford, 1966).
Grant, R. M., *Gnosticism and Early Christianity* (London, 1959).
Jonas, H., *The Gnostic Religion* (London, 1958).
The Cambridge History of Later Greek and Early Mediaeval Philosophy, ed. A. H. Armstrong (Cambridge, 1970), Part 1.

3

PHILO: A JEWISH PHILOSOPHER

Philo of Alexandria (c.20 BC–c.AD 50) was the first writer to attempt to give a comprehensive account of Genesis – and much else in the Old Testament besides – in the light of the teaching of the philosophers.

He was born of a rich and influential Jewish family, and was himself a leader in the Jewish community, but like many of his family and friends, he was a Hellenised Jew who knew little or no Hebrew. The community at Alexandria was one of the largest of the Jewish settlements after the Dispersion. Philo himself says that they occupied two of the five regions of the city and numbered nearly a million. The city itself was mainly Greek in language and culture; indeed it had now taken the place of Athens as the centre of learning of the Greek world. The Jews themselves had become so fully Greek in language, and to a lesser extent in thought and customs, too, that the Septuagint was made to meet a pressing need for an Old Testament in Greek. The exchange went in both directions. The poet Juvenal speaks of some Greeks who have become converts to Judaism.

Philo's response to Genesis was therefore both that of a Jew and that of an educated Greek. He approved of the education of the day, the *Encyclia* or comprehensive training in literature, rhetoric, mathematics, music and logic which he had himself received. He enlarges in several of his works on its value as a training for the mind. The young soul, he says, cannot be united with philosophy until it has been prepared by its encounters with the humbler school subjects. He adopts positions in his writings which clearly show the influence of his philosophical training. From the Stoics, for example, he takes the doctrine that there are four passions: grief, fear, desire and pleasure; he adopts the Stoics' sevenfold division of bodily functions into the five senses, speech and reproductive power, and their fourfold classification of material things into inorganic matter, plants, animals and reasoning beings.

Finding Words

Philo and the Septuagint alike encounter some difficulty in rendering the principles of Judaism in terms of the Greek vocabulary of words and ideas. Translated into Greek, Semitic notions are subtly modified. The 'I am that I am' of Exodus 3:14 is rendered by ὁ ὤν in the Septuagint, with its associations with a Platonic Supreme Being juxtaposed to the personal God of the Hebrews. To call the Wisdom of Solomon *Sophia* was to evoke a Greek concept of wisdom. *Angelos*, in its Hellenistic usage, makes the angel an intermediary between God and the world who makes a bridge between a transcendent Being and a world with which he can have no direct contact. The Hebrew notion of Law can be approximated and no more to the *Nomos* which in Stoicism is an aspect of the *Logos*.

If Philo was not a pioneer in trying to bridge the gap between Greek philosophers and Jews, he set about the task far more systematically than anyone had yet done. He found the allegorical method of interpretation indispensable. He could thus set the legend of Deucalion beside Noah's Flood without implying that Noah was another name for Deucalion in the way that Zeus was another name for Jupiter. He could rescue Old Testament stories from the absurdity they might otherwise have in the eyes of some of the Greeks, and show that the inspired text contained nothing which, if rightly understood, could be regarded as unworthy of God. He could construct a synthesis of the Genesis account of creation and that of the philosophers.

Philo does not set Genesis and the philosophers side by side on the same footing. He believed that the Greeks were directly indebted to Moses for their ideas, that they were to be regarded as commentators rather than innovators. But the teaching of the philosophers enabled him to clear his mind on several points where Genesis is not explicit and to build up a picture of a God and his work which educated Jews would find acceptable.

In the treatise *That God is Unchanging*, for example, Philo addresses himself to the passages in the Old Testament where God's anger is spoken of. The anger we feel in ourselves is an emotional reaction, a sign that we are changeable beings. God does not change his mind, says Philo, nor does he feel anger. He is, like the Supreme Being of the Platonists, immutable and impassible, self-sufficient, neither needing the world he has made, nor disturbed by its affairs.

The same emphasis is to be found in Origen's book *On First Principles*. Philo was insisting upon a notion which had to be established if the Supreme Being of the philosophers was to be equated with the Yahweh of Scriptures. He explains that when the Bible speaks of God's anger it does so in order to convey figuratively to the reader that God carries out remedial and educative work for the good of his creatures; it is a work, not of vengeance for sin, but of goodness and generosity; it is a misfortune not to experience so loving a punishment. God's 'anger' shows us his providential care in action, the way in which he takes charge of the affairs of his world.

Creation

Why did this simple and self-sufficient Being create anything at all? In an anticipation of later Platonism, Philo, like Augustine, sees creation as an overflowing of divine benevolence. The giver is not diminished by his act of creation, but some diminution takes place in his creatures as the succession of beings which streams out from him in unbroken lines becomes increasingly remote from his Being. In framing his theory of grades of being, Philo again anticipates the Neoplatonists.

Philo sees no objection to the view that God was assisted by subordinate powers in his work of creation. If such beings – among the lowlier of the angels – were responsible for making the mortal part of man, then two major difficulties disappear at once. Firstly, these intermediaries are able to make contact with matter and mould it, as the Platonists thought the Supreme Being could not do, so transcendent was he. And, secondly, the work of these inferior angels explains the presence of evil in creation.

Philosophers and Gnostics alike widely believed that matter was not the creation of the good God. It was already there for him and his angels to use. (Philo does not insist upon the creation of the world from nothing.) It is a short step to associating evil with matter. In employing matter, the angels introduced the possibility that there might be evil in the created order. This view of matter as a mass existing before the world was made, also resolves a third difficulty. If it may be regarded as finite in quantity, as Philo believes, then we may postulate that all the matter available was used up in creation, and so there cannot be more worlds than this one.

It is clear that, like Clement and Origen, Alexandrian thinkers of succeeding generations, Philo was not uninfluenced in these arguments by the dualism which underlay the Gnostic explanation: the division between good and evil powers which corresponds to the division between matter and spirit. Like many Gnostics and Platonists, he thought of the soul as dwelling in the body as if in a tomb or a prison, or as if it were in exile there. If it was to rise to the spiritual and eternal world of the mind where it belongs, and from which it has fallen, it must free itself from bodily entanglements, such as the pleasures of the senses. The good man will therefore live a life of abstinence and strict self control, as Porphyry was to recommend in his treatise *On Abstinence from Animal Food*.

Philo's Theory of Knowledge

In his theory of knowledge, Philo is indebted to the philosophers.

1. The plans or patterns of all created things are, he believes, the ideas in God's mind, God's thoughts.
2. The human mind is made in the image of God, and it has a capacity to receive some shadow of the Ideas in the divine Mind, that is, to know, if imperfectly, realities beyond itself.
3. Education prepares the mind for philosophy, and philosophy, in turn, prepares the mind for the higher wisdom revealed to it in Scripture.
4. The truth thus attained cannot be communicated fully in human language, for no creaturely language is adequate to the task, but language can help the individual progress in his understanding.

Nous and Logos

Philo's conception of the Divine Mind, the Logos, combines Greek and Jewish elements into something which foreshadows the Christian thinking of future generations. From the Jewish tradition he takes the Creator 'Word of God' who made the heavens in Psalm 32.6; from the Greek he takes that connection of the 'Word' with 'Reason' which provides a link between the mind of God and the minds of created rational beings. In the writings of the Stoics he would have found the term *Logos* used, a legacy from Heraclitus. The Stoics interpreted the *Logos* as an all-pervading Reason, but they were still some way from a conception which will fit Christian requirements.

The first notion which may be regarded as the seed of the Logos doctrine was that of *Nous*, first proposed by Anaxagoras in the fifth century BC. He conceived of the world as at first a confused mingling of a multitude of pairs of opposites. *Nous* is the uncompounded divine Reason, which separated them, and put them in order.

Plato postulated the existence of such a *Nous* when he saw that his doctrine of Forms made little sense without it. He put forward his theory of Forms in the *Phaedo* and the *Republic*, and he himself saw some of its limitations by the time he wrote the *Timaeus*. In his later works Forms take a subordinate place. The greatest difficulty they raise is that of the way in which they can meet the material world. If they are not active, they can have no initiative to join themselves to Matter. In his later writings, Plato added an Efficient Cause to the system to explain how the Forms can affect Matter. This Efficient Cause can be identified with the divine *Nous*. The function of the *Nous* is set out most clearly in the *Philebus* where the four divisions of reality are described as the unlimited not-being, or Matter; the limit (perhaps the Form?); the combination of the two (the world as we see it, the world of Becoming); and the One who made the combination: *Nous*, or universal Intelligence. Plato never speaks of this supreme intelligence as the Logos, but its shape and purpose are clear.

The term Logos itself perhaps gained currency through the Stoics' use of it. Philo's Logos is the Idea of Ideas, the first-begotten Son of an uncreated Father, a second God, both the pattern upon which all things were made, and the means by which they were made. He is also God immanent within his creation. Through him God is able to reveal himself to beings from whom he would otherwise be unimaginably remote. He is, however, not himself the Supreme Being, as Philo is anxious to emphasise. Only those who are not far along the road of understanding would mistake him for God. But this second and ghostly 'God' may be all that the majority of men can hope to know of the God whose image he is.

FOR FURTHER READING

Daniélou, J., *Philon d'Alexandrie* (Paris, 1958).
Goodenough, E. R., *Introduction to Philo Judaeus*, 2nd ed. (Oxford, 1962).
Wolfson, H. A., *Philo*, 2 vols. (Cambridge, Mass., 1947).
Chadwick, H., 'Philo and the Beginnings of Christian Thought', *CHLGEMP*, Part II, 1.

4

THE BEGINNING OF
CHRISTIAN PHILOSOPHY

1. JUSTIN MARTYR

Irenaeus of Anntioch (martyred at Rome before AD 117) took the view that it is best to avoid enquiring into the causes of things. He preferred simply to refer every question to the Bible. Nevertheless, he himself can be shown to have made use of a philosophical handbook in much the same way as Plutarch. His attitude shows the difficulty in which Christian writers already found themselves by the second century if they wanted to follow Irenaeus' advice: that of freeing themselves from a classical intellectual tradition whose assumptions permeated the thought of the day. The first self-confessed 'Christian philosopher' to see no difficulty here at all – indeed, to encourage a syncretism – was Justin Martyr.

From Philosophy to Christianity
Justin Martyr was born near Samaria in the middle of the second century. At Ephesus, he began a philosophical pilgrimage which was to make him a Christian despite himself. He attached himself first to a Stoic tutor, then to a Peripatetic, then to a Pythagorean, who encouraged him to study mathematics, and finally to a Platonist, whose explanations he found satisfactory. But one day, while he was walking on the seashore, he met an old man who undermined his confidence in the Platonist solutions to certain difficulties, and led him to a Christian view. He explained to Justin what it was that he had been consistently seeking in all his journeyings, and thought he had found at last. He believed that the way to wisdom lay through right reasoning and philosophy, and that happiness was to be found by this means alone. 'Philosophy is the knowledge of that which is and the cognition of the truth; happiness is the reward of this knowledge and wisdom.' The old man showed him the difference between a knowledge of God and a knowledge

of material things which are perceived by the senses. He led him to see that he had not aspired highly enough in his thinking. 'And suddenly', Justin relates, 'a fire was lit in my soul, and a love of the prophets and of those men who are friends of Christ flooded me; and so, turning over in my mind what he had said, I discovered this "philosophy" alone to be safe and profitable.'

Justin became a Christian, then, because Christianity seemed to him to compare favourably with all the philosophies of the day – to be, indeed, the best philosophy. It was superior to Platonism because it enabled the believer to reach a higher wisdom, to make even better use of his reason, to attain a more perfect happiness. He remained a philosopher, with an optimistic confidence in the powers of human reasoning. He became a pioneer among Greek apologists, attempting to refute both attacks against Christians and the objections of the Jews, so as to show that Christianity is the best and only true philosophy.

The longest of Justin's works, in which he describes his conversation with the old man, was a dispute with the Jew Trypho in which Justin takes his part of Christian philosopher. He is also the author of an *Apology* addressed to the Emperor Antoninus Pius, and of a second *Apology*, intended as a supplement to the first. The Platonism which permeates his writings is of an eclectic sort, not only because he himself had held to so many schools of thought, but also because of the eclectic nature of contemporary Middle Platonism.

Reason: The Logos

For him the Logos is the key to the Christian use of philosophical methods and principles. The Logos is Reason. God acts according to reason and does nothing in vain. It follows that everything is capable of explanation in rational terms. Justin is confident that the truths of faith can be demonstrated to all reasonable beings, and that anyone who will not accept them is prejudiced or has misheard, God is transcendent, beyond time and space, impassible, immutable, incorporeal; he can be given no name. Nevertheless, by using his reason, man can serve him as he should.

Genesis and Plato

Justin has little difficulty with the reconciliation of Genesis and the *Timaeus*. He sees that both portray the cosmos as a created thing, dependent on the will of the Creator. It is something which comes after God, and lacks his attributes. From our own observation we are aware that it decays. Justin is not concerned to establish that

God created the world *ex nihilo*, and so it is not necessary for him to contend with the problem of the origin of matter and form which occupies so many later Christian thinkers when they discuss the Six Days of Creation, and which is often so sensitive an index of their philosophical background.

Some conflicts

Nevertheless, Justin is aware that 'the teachings of Plato are not in all respects similar to those of Christ'.

1. The Platonists, for example, teach that the soul possesses immortality by its inherent nature, rather than as God's gift.
2. They subordinate the Logos to the Father, making an inequality in the Godhead from the Christian point of view.
3. The Spirit or Pneuma is to many Platonists no more than a natural energy or a grace.

Justin found it necessary to defend this departure from Platonic orthodoxy on the part of the Christian philosopher because it caused offence.

A Higher Philosophy

Justin's *Apologia* explains the Christian position in terms which are designed to present it as a higher philosophy, with which no reasonable man can quarrel, rather than as a system of beliefs which happen to coincide at some points with pure philosophy and with which philosophers may therefore feel in sympathy. He writes:

> If on some points we teach the same things as the poets and philosophers whom you honour, and on other points are fuller and more divine in our teaching, and if we alone afford proof of what we assert, why are we unjustly hated more than all others? For while we say that all things have been produced and arranged into a world by God, we shall seem to utter the doctrine of Plato; and while we say that there will be a burning up of all, we shall seem to utter the doctrine of the Stoics; and while we affirm that the souls of the wicked, being endowed with sensation even after death, are punished, and that those of the good being delivered from punishment spend a blessed existence, we shall seem to say the same things as the poets and philosophers.

It is important to Justin that Christian philosophy should not seem to draw strength from these coincidences of teaching, but rather be shown to be their source, so that all philosophy depends upon the reasonable revelations of the Christian God.

In a work whose authenticity has been questioned, Justin (if it is he) adopts the standard Christian thesis of the day that the Greek philosophers had studied the Old Testament. He points out that the Greek writers themselves show how ancient Moses is. The Bible provides a means of assessing what the philosophers say. Justin is able, on this basis, to point to Plato's self-contradiction on the one hand, and to his knowledge of the truth of God's eternity and of his judgement on the other. The recentness of the revelation of himself which God made in the Incarnation is a little embarrassing here, but Justin speaks of the community of the Logos throughout eternity. He is able in this way to emphasise both the newness of what the Gospel has to say, and the antiquity of the Old Testament whose prophecies it fulfils.

All this is in many respects so familiar that it is easy to lose sight of the originality of much of what Justin has to say. He seems not to have been influenced by Philo, nor to have used St. John's Gospel. He had to think out for himself these positions which later became commonplaces.

2. CLEMENT OF ALEXANDRIA

Clement of Alexandria was probably born an Athenian, of pagan parents, about AD 150. He had a philosophical education, but he was also taught by a succession of Christian teachers, the last of whom, Pantaenus, had been a Stoic philosopher before his conversion. Clement's own philosophical background is compounded of Plato and Stoic ethics and Aristotelian logic – much the mixture which made up contemporary Middle Platonism all about him. Clement was not himself a professional philosopher, but rather an educated layman who saw a need to make a contribution to the contemporary debate among Alexandrian Christians: some of whom advocated something close to Gnosticism as the only tenable position for an educated man.

Clement had read Philo. He does not mention Justin, but he praises his pupil Tatian. He saw that in an age of philosophers, Christian apologists must address themselves to philosophical problems in philosophical terms, if they are to win converts among educated men. He regarded the study of literature and philosophy as a practical way of going about preparing the soul to receive divine revelation. The skills of the logician are helpful in thinking clearly

– and are in addition an essential weapon to use against the Devil who is the inventor of fallacies.

Clement himself composed, or rather planned, a trilogy consisting of first a *Protreptikos*, or 'exhortation to the study of philosophy', then a *Paidagogos*, or 'Tutor' concerned with training in holy living, and a *Didaskalos* or 'Teacher'. The last was never written. Instead, Clement composed his *Miscellany* or *Stromateis*, a form he chose in imitation of the *Attic Nights* of Aulus Gellius. Here there is a good deal of obscurantism and allusiveness; he intends his reader to make an effort to reach the truth. But in the *Paidagogos* all is plain and straightforward. He describes the work of the divine Pedagogue in converting men to himself, educating them and inviting them to salvation. All this he does out of love for mankind, and he will do it for everyone who seeks the truth, for all such are children who need to be taught in the eyes of God. God teaches by reward and by punishment, but always in love, and for the same end. This Pedagogue has worked through revelation by the Law and the Prophets.

Like Justin and Philo he takes it that the Greeks drew upon the Old Testament in framing their philosophy. Thales thought that water was the first cause of all things, and Anaxagoras believed that Mind was supreme over matter; both were indebted to Moses for the realisation that God is the first cause. In the same way, Aristotle perceived that faith is superior to knowledge and Epicurus understood how faith works in the mind, and the Stoics and Plato, too, learned from Moses.

Reason Applied to Revelation

Real philosophers do not wrangle, says Clement. Contentiousness is a recent phenomenon of philosophy. The way to discover truth is not by argument, but simply by asking questions of the Scriptures. God will give knowledge to the honest enquirer 'through the true illumination of logical investigation'. The enquirer proceeds by defining his terms. 'What better or clearer method . . . can there be than discussion of the term advanced . . . so that all who use the same language may follow it?' Once the terms are agreed we may proceed to see what may be deduced 'from points admitted'. 'The philosophers concede that the first principles of all things are indemonstrable', and that by demonstration we may arrive from this beginning at 'belief in points disputed'. The philosophical method Clement proposes is, then, one of steady advancement from the obvious to the mysterious.

Some Gnostic Notions
It is also an ascent – and here there is more than a touch of
Gnosticism about Clement. He holds that human nature possesses
an adaptation for perfection, which only the 'gnostic' or man of
'knowledge' attains. Adam cannot have been created already perfect,
or he could not have sinned. But he could not have been created
imperfect, because of God's perfection as a Creator. It must therefore be the case that God made him 'adapted to the reception of
virtue'. It is his intention that we should be saved by our own efforts
to make the best of our rational powers. We have an aptitude for
virtue and wisdom, which means a movement towards it, and this
we must make for ourselves. Some men apply themselves
wholeheartedly to learning and others do not. Those who do, attain
gradually to that resemblance to God which is the image in which
God made them. 'Let us then receive knowledge, not desiring its
results, but embracing itself for the sake of knowing.'

It is in this modified way that Clement is prepared to use Gnostic
ideas and concepts. He is in some sympathy with the more 'philosophical' version of the Valentinians, for example. The Valentinians
held that the Supreme Being is the Perfect Aeon, the *proarche*, the
Propater, Bythos, invisible, incomprehensible, eternal and unbegotten. Associated with him is *Ennoia*. From them is born *Nous*,
and *Aletheia*. *Nous* alone can comprehend the greatness of the
Father. *Nous* is also *Monogenēs*, *Patēr*, *Archē ton panton*. From him
emanate *Logos* and *Zoē*, Word and Life, and from them Man and
Church (*Anthrōpos* and *Ecclésia*). These form the archetypal
Ogdoad. There is myth here, but of a more dignified and abstract
sort than many Gnostic systems purveyed. Taken as allegory, this
account of things was not entirely out of keeping with the allegorical
method used by Clement and Philo before him in the interpretation
of Scripture.

Nevertheless, there are three elements in Gnosticism of which
Clement strongly disapproves. He cannot accept the rejection of the
God of the Old Testament (and the concomitant disapproval of all
bodily goods. He is against the Gnostic condemnation of marriage,
for example). He held, as the Gnostic did not, to the notion of
divine fear and punishment. And he insists on the freedom of the
will. 'We have heard by the Scriptures that self-determining choice
and refusal have been given by the Lord to men.'

Clement was an optimist. All in all, he cannot see any insuperable
difficulty in the way of philosopher or Gnostic if he wishes to become
a true Christian. It is simply a matter of his adjusting his perspective
so that he can see with the aid of the divine illumination God has

already given him, the truth of the Christian faith. He had high hopes of the ultimate salvation of a great many, if not all mankind.

3. ORIGEN

Origen (c.186–255) attempted something new. This giant among the theologians of the early Christian centuries tried to construct a comprehensive refutation of the teaching of the Gnostics and a systematic treatment of the differences between Christians and philosophers. He replaced Clement's cheerful confidence that, given goodwill and an open mind on the part of unbelievers, the differences could be shown to be minimal, with a sense that here was potential danger to the truths of faith. The differences must be emphasised, not glossed over. With a similar sense of the importance of defining what was uniquely Christian, he made the allegorical method of interpreting Scripture which Philo had used, and which the Gnostics had adapted to their own purposes, serve the needs of Christians.

Origen was born in Egypt, probably at Alexandria, with its libraries and its secular university and its numerous teachers of philosophy. Origen was given the best Christian education to be had, in the school of the vigorous Christian Church there. He distinguished himself and Bishop Demetrius made him a master in the school when he was seventeen. He seems to have seen his task clearly from the first. He set about mastering all learning, so as to arrive at the heights of theological truth step by step. In order to answer the questions raised by the non-Christians among his students, he attended the lectures of the local philosophers – Ammonius Sacca, for example, the teacher of Plotinus. He travelled, visiting Rome and Palestine.

Controversy
His career at Alexandria was irreparably damaged when he allowed himself to be ordained priest during his stay at Caesarea. It was not uncommon for promising young men to be seized in this way and subjected to forcible ordination. Angry at his defection, his own bishop condemned him; he was degraded from the priesthood. His works, too, became a centre of controversy, although they had been much admired at first. Origen remained a figure about whose orthodoxy there was serious doubt. Jerome disapproved of him; Epiphanius of Salamis (c.315–403) included extracts from Origen in his 'medicine-chest for the cure of all heresies'. Origen

was condemned by Justinian and the fifth Ecumenical Council of 553.

As a result, much of his work did not survive in Greek. The Latin translation of his book *On First Principles* made by Rufinus, the late fourth-century opponent of St. Jerome, bears the marks of the translator's wish to improve Origen's orthodoxy. Rufinus states frankly that he has made alterations to what he regards as corrupt passages. Jerome took a fiercer view that these were not textual corruptions but errors on Origen's part.

The difficulty arose because Origen was a pioneer. He was the first to formulate a number of doctrinal principles. He had to find technical terms for Christian notions. Above all, he had to find a means of keeping Christian ideas distinct from those of pagan philosophy in areas where there was common ground – and where some rapprochement was admittedly necessary in order that Christians should be able to win over educated pagans. The problem was to effect a meeting of minds without compromise, and without sacrificing any of the essential points of Christian doctrine.

Reason and Revelation: the Teaching Word
Origen was an educator. Like Clement, he saw the process by which the human mind made its way from secular learning to the higher truths of theology as the very process of redemption, God as the Teacher, and himself and other interpreters of the Bible as aiding the process as well as they could. He was certain that the Bible is divinely inspired. It is sometimes difficult to understand, but that is a sign that it contains most profound mysteries. It is God's textbook for the learning soul.

Accordingly, Origen made the interpretation of Scripture his first concern. At the beginning of the book he wrote against the philosopher Celsus he apologises because here he has set aside for a time the work of exposition on which he ought to have been engaged in order to deal with philosophical errors.

Origen believed that the Word which inspired the text of Scripture, Christ himself, gave it unity and coherence – that he is himself its unity. He also provided a series of graduated steps within the text, so that the beginner could read books such as Esther, Judith, Tobit, where the mysteries are less profound, and work his way gradually to the books which are harder to understand. Christ himself leads the reader on, sometimes without his realising it. The soul experiences the kiss of the Logos on the lips as in the Song of Songs. The role of the interpreter is thus a humble one, for Christ himself does most of the work.

Principles of Bible Study
Nevertheless, it is possible for him to provide the reader with a firm
grasp of certain foundation principles, and to teach him a method
of analysis, so that he will be able to progress more rapidly. The
principles are these:

1. The Bible is a unity.
2. Nothing in it is redundant, or anything less than the divinely
   inspired Word of God.
3. It contains a "progressive" revelation (an idea also to be found
   in Irenaeus).

1. The first of these principles presents considerable practical
difficulties to the interpreter. The Bible seems at first sight a huddle
of Semitic writings. Only by allegorical interpretation can it be made
to appear in all its unity and integrity and to yield up the timeless
truth it contains. Origen wanted in particular to reconcile the Gospel
of John with the accounts given in the Synoptic Gospels. Celsus the
philosopher knew of Christians who included only the Synoptics.
Origen's method was to make much of the symbolism of numbers,
and the interpretation of Hebrew proper names, so as to show how
one figure or event prefigures another and the whole Bible forms a
nexus of interrelated events. By taking Scripture as a whole in this
way, he argued, it was possible to check one interpretation against
another and ensure that nothing was merely invented. This method
was to provide a foundation for the system of mediaeval
interpretation.
2. The second principle made it necessary to pay scrupulous
attention to the grammatical oddities found in the text of Scripture.
In 'ascends up' the 'up' would seem to be superfluous, but we
cannot think that it is if the Word of God has been dictated as we
believe. Origen devised explanations for the special properties of
Scriptural language. His influence in the Middle Ages set in train a
sequence of works which attempted to resolve such difficulties.
3. The third principle, that revelation is progressive, poses difficulties of another kind. Scripture may be read as itself making a
progressive revelation; or we may regard the progressive revelation
as taking place within the individual believer. Origen portrays him
first as knowing only that Christ was crucified. He himself shares
his humiliation. Then, by Bible study day and night, by chastity,
by good works, by a complete dedication of himself to Christ, he
gradually advances, until he experiences the Second Coming within
himself. This view makes the coming of the Kingdom of God an

interior matter, not an event in history. If we take the former view, that the Old Testament prefigures the Incarnation in a historical way, Origen would like us to understand the first coming of Christ as only one stage in God's revelation of himself. The Second Coming is now in progress, in the missionary work of taking the Gospel to the world under the direction of the Holy Spirit.

There is a further alternative possibility here: that the Second Coming may be that fuller knowledge of God which will be given to believers in the life to come. In all these possibilities, Scripture holds a central place.

This is the high view of Scripture from which Origen approaches the task of demonstrating its truth to two kinds of believer in error, the Gnostic and the philosopher. His principal work against the Gnostic was the *Periarchon* or *De Principiis*. In it he tried to make Gnosticism not merely obviously heretical, but also clearly superfluous. He proposes in his preface to examine the rational grounds for statements about doctrine which rest upon authority, and to discuss principles for which there is no authority.

Problems of Language: describing the Trinity
He objects to the Gnostic position on two grounds: they misunderstand the nature of God and they have a false picture of the world he created. As he wrote about the nature of God, Origen began to develop his doctrine of the Trinity. He wanted to insist first of all – against the muddled pluralism of much Gnostic teaching, and the underlying dualism which makes good and evil two distinct first principles – that there is only one God. His doctrine remained obscure on the subject of the Holy Spirit. He gives the Spirit equal rank with the Father and the Son, but it is not clear whether he believed him to belong to the created Order. But with regard to the Son he is insistent that he was not created, but begotten before all worlds and that his suffering, death and resurrection were real historical events. However, the Son is not himself that which God the Father is. We should pray *to* the Father, *in* the Spirit and *through* the Son, but we should not pray *to* the Son.

This attempt to make a distinction clear by the use of prepositions is one of many experiments with theological language in the early Christian centuries which linked theology closely with contemporary work on the philosophy of language.

The World and Matter
Origen's second area of dispute with the Gnostics concerns the creation of the world. The first difficulty is to define 'world' in a

manner which will make it clear where the difficulty lies. Origen is able to find half a dozen meanings for the term which may confuse the issue: *Kosmos* may mean the earth together with its inhabitants; it may refer to the heaven and earth which will pass away (1 Cor: 7.31); Jesus refers to yet another world when he says 'I am not of this world'; the term may be applied to the spheres of the moon and the sun and to the outer fixed sphere. Origen wants to define the world as including everything which is above the heavens or in the heavens or upon the earth or in the 'lower regions'. For the purposes of the debate with the Gnostics, it is the matter in the world which is significant, for there, they claim, lies the root of evil.

Origen makes a departure here from the position of Philo and Justin and Clement of Alexandria. They are all ambiguous about the origin of matter, and Philo inclines strongly to the view that it existed before God made the world. 'I cannot understand how so many distinguished men have supposed it to be uncreated, that is, not made by God himself, the Creator of all things, but . . . the result of chance', says Origen. This firm, commonsense tone is found in Origen's account of the creation in general. He sees the Creator's achievement in modest terms. God's power is not infinite, says Origen; he created as large a number of intelligent beings as he could control, and as much matter as he could reduce to order. That is why God is said to have created all things by number and measure. He made what his providence could manage.

Matter and Evil

The source of evil cannot lie in matter, if matter is indeed so uncontroversial a thing, made by the Creator as the stuff of his subsequent creations. The philosopher Celsus had argued that evils 'are not caused by God, but inhere in matter and dwell among mortals'. Certainly they are not caused by God, says Origen, 'but in our view it is not true that "the matter which dwells among mortals" is responsible for evils. Each person's mind is responsible for the evil which exists in him, and this is what evil is.' Evil lies, then, in rational natures, rational beings which do not behave in a rational manner.

Intellectual Respectability

When Celsus wrote seventy years before Origen, he could assume with confidence that the majority of Christians were not educated men, and that his own philosophy was altogether a more sophisticated account of the world than theirs. In Origen's day many Christians were the intellectual equals of pagans and shared with them a common educational background so that they could answer them back on their own terms. This was Origen's intention in writing his *Contra Celsum*.

He does not mention Clement but it is clear that he had read him; he builds, too, on the notion put forward by Justin and his pupil Tatian, and by Theophilus and Athenagoras, that since Moses and the prophets can be shown to be earlier than the Greek philosophers they must therefore have been the source of their learning. He argues from a position of strength, in possession not only of the original version of the teaching of the Greeks which is preserved in the Bible, but also of the teaching of the Greek thinkers themselves. So wide-ranging and eclectic was the Middle Platonism of the schools of Alexandria that if Celsus takes a view characteristic of the Stoics, Origen has no difficulty in countering with a notion found in thinkers of another school. The exercise was a familiar one, the very stuff of philosophical debate. Cicero had employed a similar tactic in his book *On the Nature of the Gods*. But Origen saw a means here of making Christianity not only convincing to the pagan philosopher, but also respected as a philosophy in itself.

Divine Condescension

Celsus' principal objection to Christianity is easily disposed of. He says that it is recent, a turning from the ancient doctrine which all philosophers accept, that God is manifested in different forms in the world (the Stoic view) and that the deities the people worship in town and country are intermediate between the highest Being and man (the Platonic tradition). There are, says Celsus, many gods and many faces of God, so that it makes no difference whether we worship Zeus or Yahweh. Origen's conviction that the philosophers drew on Moses make the philosopher's argument form antiquity look weak.

The one God, whose Son became Incarnate and is able to cleanse the unworthy and make them fit for himself, is the educator who is in process of restoring his rational creatures to the state in which he intended them to live. That is why he speaks sometimes in the Bible in terms which suggest to Celsus that he is, for example, subject to human passions, threatening and blustering against his people. 'The Logos speaks like this,' Origen answers, 'because he assumes, as it were, human characteristics for the advantage of men'. The Logos is coming down to our level in his revelation of himself. It is exactly what a human adult does when he is talking to small children. He says 'what is appropriate to the weakness' of those he speaks to, and what is 'of advantage for the conversion and correction of the children'. 'So also the Logos of God seems to have arranged the Scriptures, using the method of address which fitted the ability and benefit of the hearers'.

4. ATHANASIUS

Athanasius was born in Alexandria about 296. He was given the sound education the city's schools afforded, both in secular learning and in Holy Scripture. As a young man he attracted the attention of Bishop Alexander, who made him his companion and secretary. In 319 Arius, priest in one of the palaces of Alexandria, and popular with his parishioners, was accused of teaching that Jesus was neither truly God nor truly man. Despite being condemned for his views in 321, he persisted in his teaching, citing Origen and others – with some justice – as authorities who had taught that the Son was subordinate, or inferior, or secondary in some way to the Father. The matter came to a head at the Council of Nicaea in 325, where it was determined that *homoousion*, 'of the same substance' should be adopted as a technical term to describe the essential unity of Father and Son. Everyone present, except the extreme Arians, subscribed to this. On Alexander's death, Athanasius succeeded him as bishop but was deposed and exiled in 335.

Theological Semantics
Athanasius' teaching is principally concerned with rebutting the Arian heresy. As he saw it, Arianism was merely a form of gnostic or pagan error, for the Gnostics and pagans too had ranks of divinities and semi-divinities. The Son is no more than a creature and certainly less than Almighty. In his *Contra Arianos* he puts this view forcefully:

> If God is Maker and Creator, and creates his works through the Son, and we cannot but regard things which came to be as having existence through the Word, is it not blasphemous, since God is the maker, to say that his craftsman, his Word and Wisdom 'once was not'? For then the Word . . . is adventitious, alien, essentially unlike . . . If the Word is not eternally with the Father, then the Trinity is not eternal; there was first a unity which later has become a trinity by addition . . . And, what is worse, the Trinity is found to be disparate, consisting of alien and different natures and substances . . . It may conceivably receive further addition

ad infinitum . . . it may diminish; for clearly what is added may be subtracted.

The objection here is, however, at root a matter of philosophy not Gnosticism: it is educated pagans whom Athanasius blames for leading the Arians astray – even if inadvertently. The Arians, he says:

> should take their questions to the Greeks who taught them – for it was they, not the Scriptures, who invented the term 'unoriginate' (*ageneton*). If they do this, they will discover that the term has all sorts of meanings, and that will make them realise that, even on ground of their own choosing, they do not know how to frame their questions properly. I have acquainted myself on their account with the various meanings of the word . . . 'unoriginate' is not only unscriptural; it is necessary, too, to be careful of its puzzling variety of meanings . . . it is an invention of the Greek [philosophers] who have no knowledge of the Son.

Half-understood philosophy lies at the bottom of the Arian contention that Jesus was not both fully God and fully man.

Athanasius' doctrine of creation and the fall of man also shows the influence of contemporary philosophy; he frames his ideas by explaining where they differ from the teachings of the philosophers. Thus he rejects the Stoic notion of a spontaneous generation of the world, the Platonic idea of pre-existent matter, and the Gnostic notion of a 'demiurge' who is the Father's agent of creation, but not himself the Father's equal. Then he puts forward the Christian view.

1. 'God made the whole order of things'; he 'brought it into being out of nothing'. He is good, and could not therefore begrudge anything to anyone; he did not begrudge existence to any creature, and so he made everything out of nothing, through his own Word, Jesus Christ.
2. He made man rational and gave him free will. He knew that a free will could choose evil as well as good, and so he placed man in the Garden of Eden where he could be protected.
3. When Adam sinned, 'the transgression of the commandment' had the effect of turning man back to his natural state, 'so that having come into being out of non-existence' he began to 'suffer disintegration into non-existence'. For if Adam and Eve's 'natural condition was once non-existence, and they were

summoned into being by the presence and loving-kindness of the Word, it followed that when men were deprived of the knowledge of God and turned back to non-existence (since evil is not-being, good is being) they should for ever be deprived even of being . . . that is, that they should disintegrate and remain in death and destruction'.

This account again draws upon philosophical principles; and its logic is especially forceful to the philosophically trained students of Athanasius' day.

Taking Stock
We have come some way since Justin; Christian doctrine by the time of Athanasius was readily expressed in terms which were comprehensible to, and in some cases supplied by, the philosophers. Debates about its exact formulation turned upon points raised by the contrast of assumptions in the Christian system and the systems of the philosophers. Christian apologetic was obliged to take account of the work of the philosophers because heretics and unbelievers alike made use of it. All this was to some extent a result of the influence of the Greek language upon the habits of thought of the day. A language's capacity for expressing philosophical ideas fosters or retards philosophical thinking in those who speak it. But the mediaeval evolution of Christian thinking was to depend predominantly upon the work of theologians who wrote and thought in Latin.

FOR FUTHER READING

Bigg, C., *The Christian Platonists of Alexandria*, 2nd ed. (Oxford, 1913).
Chadwick, H., *Early Christian Thought and the Classical Tradition* (Oxford, 1966).
Chadwick, H., *Origen Contra Celsum* (Cambridge, 1979).
Meijering, E. P., *Orthodoxy and Platonism in Athanasius*, 2nd ed. (Leiden, 1974).
Osborn, E. F., *The Philosophy of Clement of Alexandria* (Cambridge, 1957).

5

THE LATIN WEST

1. TERTULLIAN

Deriding the Philosophers
The first Latin writer to place Christianity and philosophy side by
side and try to judge their respective merits was the North African
Tertullian (c.160–225). He took a very different view from Justin.
In book after book he derided the philosophers for the errors of
their doctrine and for their presumptuousness. The philosophers,
he says, have furnished the heretics with false ideas and spurious
authorities:

> Valentinus . . . was of the school of Plato . . . the god of
> Marcion . . . came of the Stoics. And the doctrine that the soul
> dies is maintained from the Epicureans. And the denial of the
> restoration of the body is taken from the united school of all the
> philosophers. And where matter is made equal with God, there
> is the doctrine of Zeno. And where anything is alleged concerning
> a god consisting of fire, there comes in Heraclitus.
>
> The same matter is turned and twisted by the heretics and by
> the philosophers. The same questions are involved: Whence
> comes evil? And why? And whence man? And how? And . . .
> where does God come from? Wretched Aristotle, who taught
> them the art of dialectic, cunning in building up and pulling
> down, using many shifts in his sentences, making forced guesses
> at the truth. Away with those who have brought forward a Stoic
> and a Platonic, and a Dialectic Christianity.

Not only is philosophy misleading; it is also unnecessary. Philosophy served a purpose before the birth of Christ, but 'there is no
need of curious questioning now that we have Christ Jesus, nor of

enquiry now that we have the Gospel', he says. Athens and Jerusalem have nothing in common.

Intellectual Discipline

Tertullian was brought up in Carthage; the son of a proconsular centurion, he was given the orator's education of the day, with its emphasis on the use of language to convince and persuade and the smattering of philosophy the rhetorician was thought to need. He was converted at some time before 197. Until middle age, Jerome tells us, he remained a presbyter of the Church, but towards the end of his life he joined the Montanists. These ascetics expected the outpouring of the Holy Spirit upon the Church at any moment; the first signs of it, they believed, were to be seen in their own prophets. The movement was a generation old when Tertullian joined it. It had by now begun to place an emphasis upon a discipline of life which Tertullian found lacking in the Church of his day, and this was undoubtedly what attracted him to the Montanists. They seemed to him closer to the primitive Christians than the members of the Church he saw about him.

Forceful, decisive, Tertullian was impatient with intellectual curiosity. He thought it a characteristic of Gnosticism to require answers to obscure and irrelevant questions. He found that this habit of questioning made it difficult, if not impossible, to talk to heretics on the basis of arguments drawn from Scripture. Heretics are only too ready to use for their own purposes what he regards as the property of the Christians. To appeal to the Bible only causes them to ask more questions, and what is more it implies that they have a right to use it.

The Challenge of Heresy (Marcion)

Despite himself, Tertullian was obliged to touch on philosophical problems when he wrote against the heretics. It was impossible to discuss creation without some reference to the philosophers' views, or to define the divine nature without taking account of their thinking. That is to say, it was impossible given the teachings of contemporary Gnostics and heretics who themselves made use of it and could be rebutted only in such terms as they themselves chose to use. Tertullian's opponent Marcion was a rich merchant of Asia Minor who had settled in Rome and begun to form a community of disciples. His views caused such offence that he was excommunicated in 144; afterwards he continued his work, setting up small communities all over the Empire. So large a threat did he appear that a number of orthodox churchmen spoke and wrote against him, including Irenaeus. His communities posed a greater threat to orthodoxy, taken collectively, than any other heretics of the end of the second century.

Marcion taught that the Old Testament and the New were quite distinct. The New Testament teaches the love of God; the Old Testament depicts a God of law. The Creator-God of the Old Testament has nothing to do with the God revealed by Christ in his teaching and in his incarnate person. Marcion's dualism was not identical with that of most Gnostics: he had no taste for mythology, but he contributed a doctrine which was to be taken up by later generations of dualist heretics who compounded together Gnostic and Marcionite ideas. This approach to the Bible ran counter to the current of orthodox exegetical method that had now been running strongly for some generations and which interpreted the New Testament by the Old and the Old by the New.

First Principles

The greater part of Tertullian's book against Marcion is concerned with Scripture, as he defends the integrity of the Bible. His first few points are, however, treated philosophically. He attacks the very idea that there may be two first principles. 'The principle, and after that the whole dispute, is a matter of number, whether two Gods may be admitted', he says. He defines God as a Platonist might, as a single Supreme Being, unbegotten, not made, without beginning or end. He insists that a 'duality' of Gods is logically nonsense. It would be more consistent with logic to speak of a plurality of Gods, for if number is compatible with the substance of Deity, the richer it is in number the better; an infinite multitude of gods would then be better than two.

Natural Theology

Tertullian also sets out for the Marcionites' benefit the evidence God has provided in the natural world so that we may learn what he is like from what he has made. The evidence tells us much that is incompatible with Marcion's contention that the Creator is not the God of love. It is characteristic of a God of love that he should make himself known, and this is how he has done it. The evidence is external to God – the world is not itself God – but it is not 'extraneous'; it is a reliable index for us, for all things are God's. More, it is a worthy witness; there is no need to suggest that the God to whom it bears witness is merely a demiurge.

Marcion prompts Tertullian to examine the divine attributes, too, to show by philosophical principles why his goodness must be perpetual and an unbroken web underlying everything which exists, and why he must be rational. At last he clears his way, at the beginning of Book II, 'to the contemplation of the Almighty God, the Lord and Maker of the Universe'. 'His greatness . . . is shown in this, that from the beginning he made himself known; he never hid himself but always shone out brightly.'

Technical Terms

Tertullian contributed several of the Latin-derived technical terms of theology which are still in use. His rhetorician's training suggested to him that in Psalm 2.4–9, for example, where the Father appears to be conducting a dialogue with the Son, something like a play is taking place. There are *dramatis personae*. The word *persona* thus seemed an appropriate term to describe the Father and the Son in their communication with one another. Tertullian's use of the term *persona* gave a character to the notions of Father and Son which had not been present before.

2. HILARY OF POITIERS

The Latin West produced one great theologian in the generation before Augustine. Hilary of Poitiers, like Athanasius, devoted the greater part of his energies to the campaign against the Arians. As a result, he was exiled to Phrygia (356–60) and while he was there he wrote his book against the Arians, the *De Trinitate*.

It opens with an account of his conversion. He had a strong conviction that men were not born for mortality like beasts; the God who made them could not have given them life with the intention of taking it away from them: he must have had some unimaginable happiness in store. This idea greatly attracted Hilary. He began to burn with a desire to know what God was like. He reasoned that he must be a being beyond the understanding of the pagans: one, eternal, omnipotent and unchanging. These principles became clearer as he compared the opinions of various philosophers. In his reading he came at length upon the statement of Exodus 3:14: 'I am that I am'. He was 'utterly astounded' at the justice of this description, at how well it was possible to state the essence of the Deity in human language. There was more to be discovered about the infinity and beauty of God. Hilary began to conceive a hope of salvation. He read John's Gospel and his confidence increased. He was converted.

Human Language for God
Hilary goes on to describe the mystery of the Trinity in the same
'human language' (*humana sermo*). His task was not made easier by
the fact that he was attempting to do so in Latin. His account is
not easy to read; nor is it always clear. He was finding his way.

3. AUGUSTINE AND THE NEOPLATONISTS

When he was twenty Augustine (354–430) had a poor opinion of
Christianity. He had just arrived at Carthage from his home town
of Thagaste to study rhetoric. (Calcidius, the commentator through
whose work Plato's *Timaeus* was transmitted to the mediaeval West,
was perhaps the most famous of the masters to teach there in the
first half of the fourth century.) Mixing with his fellow-students,
Augustine learned of a number of alternative religious and philosophical systems; he and his friends took an interest in religion very
much like that which their modern counterparts might take in
politics; they tried out philosophies and discarded them; they
debated their differences; they enjoyed a freedom and a sense of
intellectual discovery which seemed at that time to Augustine to be
lacking in Christianity. But late fourth century Carthage was not the
Alexandria of Philo, Clement and Origen. Latin-speaking, without
access to much of the philosophical writing of the preceding
centuries, Augustine and his fellow-students had to find their own
way to an understanding of the finer points of philosophy.

Schools of Philosophers
Unaware of the consensus to which the philosophers had by now
begun to come, Augustine speaks of the *scholae dissentientes* of the
philosophers, the diverse beliefs they held about the nature of the
gods; he encountered the notion that the soul was a fallen mind
trying to ascend again to its first condition as the spiritual creature
it was intended to be; he learned of the role of fate and of providence
in men's lives as various schools of philosophers saw it; he heard
various accounts of the creation of the world. 'They all disagree!'
he exclaims.

Philosophy and Religion
His engagement with these controversies was not merely intellectual.
Philosophy, as it had for many century by century, satisfied religious
needs. Seneca, a Stoic of the first century AD, describes the change
it brought about in him. 'I realise', he says, ' . . . that I am not

only being made a better man; I am being transformed.' Augustine
was to experience a philosophical 'conversion' like Seneca's when,
in the course of his studies at Carthage, he read Cicero's lost book
Hortensius. 'That book contains an exhortation to philosophy' which,
he says, 'changed my outlook' (*mutavit affectum meum*). He was
consumed by a desire to pursue wisdom.

Appreciating the Bible

In his search he turned, not to the writings of the philosophers, but
to the Bible. He found it disappointing, crude stuff in comparison
with the *Tulliana dignitas*, the Ciceronian eloquence of the *Hortensius*. There were as yet few alternatives open to him. Augustine's
Greek was poor. It seems unlikely that he ever learned to read it
with ease, and it was not until 386, shortly before his conversion to
Christianity a decade later that someone presented him with some
books of the 'platonists' in Latin and he was able to make of
philosophy something more than a vague longing to attain 'wisdom'.
In his youth he found the Old Testament hard to take seriously.
Not only in its language, but in its portrayal of characters and events
it seemed to be far from the rarefied concept of Wisdom which he
had found in the *Hortensius* and which had excited and uplifted
him. Even at the time when he wrote the *Confessions*, many years
later, when he had come to admire and respect Scripture, he had
some difficulty over the behaviour of the patriarchs.

The Manichees

In reaction against the apparent absurdities of the Old Testament
story, he turned to a sect of latter-day Gnostics which had been
founded in the third century by the Persian prophet Mani. Mani
drew together the threads of the existing Gnostic tradition so
successfully that his influence spread rapidly through the Empire.
By the eighth century followers of Mani were to be found as far
East as China. Mani believed that God spoke through his Word
directly to the soul, illuminating it, so that those he had enlightened
could see him. Augustine's notion of the intellectual and rarefied
nature of spiritual discernment, his 'philosophical' idea of Wisdom,
made him receptive to these teachings.

We can discover something of what Augustine himself later recognised as his reasons for becoming a Manichee from a letter *On the
Profit of Believing* which he wrote in 391. He had led a friend of his
to the Manichees, and he was anxious to free him from his allegiance
to them and make him a Christian. Looking back, it seems to him
that the Manichees appealed to his intellectual vanity. They offered

him a way to Wisdom and the knowledge of God by the exercise of his reason; 'Who would not be attracted by such promises,' says Augustine, 'especially the mind of a young man who wanted to discover the Truth, and moreover a proud and loquacious mind?' The Manichees mocked the Old Testament. They made him feel that he belonged to a select body of discriminating individuals.

The Problem of Evil

More, the Manichees offered a solution to a problem which had long been troubling Augustine and which, if we may trust the *Confessions*, formed the connecting thread of his philosophical explorations up to the time when he became a Christian. They explained the origin of evil in terms which appealed to Augustine, who felt a deep war within himself between his soul and his body. The Manichee point of view seemed to combine many of the advantages of the Christians' and philosophers' explanations: God is good, and incapable of evil; good is opposed to evil; man is a mixed being, a fallen but potentially good soul in a body which acts as a prison and a punishment. Man's task is to see his way to the good again. The good God helps him by enlightening his mind. By the illumination thus thrown upon his understanding the believer comes to see the cosmic scale of the problem which he experiences within himself in microcosm. The evil is eternally pressing upon the good and trying to reduce its area of jurisdiction. The two natures of good and evil were separate from the beginning, and have always been opposed. The good is not aggressive, and unless it realises its danger it does not seek to meet the evil with active opposition. The human soul is a fragment of the divine substance of the good, which must learn to be uncomfortable in its prison, to strive to free itself and to war against the evil power.

Augustine became disillusioned with the Manichees only after nine years of optimism that they would in the end answer all his questions. When their leader Faustus at last came to Carthage and he was able to put his remaining difficulties to him, Augustine found him unable to resolve them – indeed, he proved a disappointingly ill-read and unimpressive figure. In 383 Augustine set out for Rome, to further his career and to make a fresh start.

Augustine and Platonism

Augustine continued to associate with the Manichees in Italy, more out of habit than conviction; he dabbled a little in philosophy. He was depressed and unable to see his way clearly. Within a year he won the post of master of rhetoric at Milan, and there he met a circle of philosophers who were able to offer him books and conversation of a higher order than anything he had met before. Zenobius, Hermogenianus, Manlius Theodorus, seem to have met from time to time as an informal philosophical society; they saw themselves as leaders of a philosophical renaissance, no mere Neo-platonists, but *platonici*, real Platonists.

Platonism had been revived in Italy by the work of two Greek academicians of the third century: Plotinus and his pupil Porphyry. It is in connection with these and other influences on Augustine which require discussion in their own right, that we shall pursue our treatment of his thought.

Plotinus

Plotinus (c.204–268) was a pioneer, but he left his papers in confusion. His pupil Porphyry produced a more or less systematic philosophy out of his teaching, editing the *Enneads* in six books of nine essays each. Porphyry (c.232–305) was himself a writer, and in Augustine's day it was he rather than Plotinus who was respected as an original thinker. Plotinus seemed to Augustine's contemporaries like Plato reborn, his teaching almost indistinguishable from that of the master.

Plotinus' six *Enneads* do not constitute a formal step-by-step exposition of Plotinian doctrine. The whole system of Plotinus is subsumed in each treatise. He saw a tension at every point between the perpetual emanation from the divine and the endless aspiration of those things which had streamed out from God to return to him.

Porphyry

Porphyry himself, educated first in Athens and later (after he had met him in Rome) a pupil of Plotinus, made enemies. Much of his considerable literary output was destroyed, and his major work, an attack on Christianity, was publicly burned, first by the Emperor Constantine (d.337) and then, in Augustine's lifetime, by Theodosius (d.395). But he contributed to Christian thinking a notion of a possibility of heightened spiritual experience.

Porphyry gave his energies as a writer to providing simple aids for students as well as to the great problems of the universe and the nature of man. His *Isagoge*, or introduction to the study of logic, became a classic, because it proved to be an excellent preliminary handbook for those about to begin on Aristotle's logical works.

Marius Victorinus

The translator who made these ideas accessible to Latin-speakers, Marius Victorinus, was, like Augustine, an African by birth and a rhetorician by profession. He taught at Rome under the Emperor Constantius, writing books on school subjects, grammar, rhetoric and logic and commentaries on Cicero and Aristotle. He seems to have seen, more than a century before Boethius, a need to make Greek works available to an increasingly Latin-speaking world. It was he who translated the 'books of the Platonists' which at last gave Augustine an opportunity to read the philosophers for himself.

In extreme old age he became a Christian (before 358) and before he died he had made a substantial contribution to the Arian controversy from the point of view of a Christian philosopher. His theological writings were designed to defend Athanasius' position and to show in philosophical terms why the Son must be regarded as consubstantial with the Father.

Ambrose

Augustine was brought to a pitch of weary sophistication by his encounters with the philosophers in Milan before his conversion. He had been disillusioned again and again by the sects he had followed, and which had made him promises. Here were cultivated men whose highest achievement, the result of profound reflection, was a grand disillusionment with the possibilities of reasoning.

Bishop Ambrose captured him for Christianity at last by his preaching. Augustine heard him give a series of sermons on the six days of creation. He was able to explain one or two of the passages in Genesis which had seemed particularly puzzling. The Manichees had provided answers which now appeared vain, so that Ambrose's suggestions filled a gap. Ambrose made use of the work of the Greek Fathers who had pioneered the work of reconciling Christianity and Neoplatonism: especially Philo and Origen. He provided allegorical accounts of passages in Genesis which, taken literally, had long seemed crude and unsophisticated to Augustine. He brought him to see the possibilities of a Christian philosophy.

4. AUGUSTINE'S CHRISTIAN PHILOSOPHY

Against the Academics

After his conversion Augustine retired with a group of friends and some of his family to Cassiciacum, to live the life of a Christian philosopher. He had been forced by illness to give up his post as professor of Rhetoric, and he had always wanted an opportunity to spend time with like-minded friends exploring great questions at leisure. During what proved to be a period of only a few months in the autumn of 386 the friends talked to some purpose, and Augustine was able to write several books on the underlying philosophical principles of Christian truth.

One of these works was the *Contra Academicos*. Augustine had only comparatively recently mastered the possibilities of philosophy to his own satisfaction, and he saw no need to give it up when he became a Christian. On the other hand, the greatest of the pagan philosophers clearly had only part of the answer to questions which Christianity resolved entirely. In the *City of God* which he was to begin a quarter of a century later, Augustine took a kindly view of the Platonists, as the philosophers who had achieved most by human reason. He points out that Plato saw God, as the Christians do, as the cause of all that exists, the ultimate reason of which human reason is a shadow or image, the end or purpose of all things.

He came to believe that since the very word philosopher means 'lover of wisdom' and Wisdom is God himself, then the philosopher is *ipso facto* a lover of God. Not all philosophers are lovers of true wisdom, but some of them have come close to Christian truth. Plato and his modern disciples have a notion of God close to the reality and therefore their thought is comparatively sound and helpful to the Christian.

The 'academics' who adapted Plato's philosophy into a system of negative criticism are another matter. Augustine's first task when he became a Christian, then, was to show the weaknesses in their negative approach to the discovery of truth, and to set out the principles of a truly Christian philosophy – the philosophy by means of which Plato had come so close to the truth.

Augustine's Theory of Knowledge

Augustine is perhaps nowhere so much a Platonist as in his epistemology. He was sure, from introspective analysis of his own mind and its workings, that the mind knows three things about itself with absolute certainty: that it understands; that it exists, and that it lives. It knows, too, by an active watchfulness, what the bodily senses perceive. Indeed, it animates the body; it is the life of the body. And when it uses the bodily senses to perceive, it sets them in motion and operation. Augustine has observed that each of the senses responds to a corporeal stimulus of a specific type. We cannot see with our ears or hear with our eyes. In handling those impressions which the senses give us, we cannot be confident that we 'know' what they seem to be telling us. The world of corporeal things is shifting and deceptive. More reliable is knowledge that is intuitive. We know mathematical laws 'simply by recognising them inside ourselves without reference to any material object'. Sense-experience may confirm our impression, but we 'know' already that two and two make four. Highest of all is the knowledge we have of God, for he is a thing known which makes itself known, a knowledge which comes to us, and thus, although he so far transcends our powers of grasping him that perhaps we cannot be said to know him at all, yet nevertheless he is that which we know best and most certainly. The soul brings about its own sensations and its own intellectual knowledge, but here is a knowledge which gives itself to the soul.

Augustine's theology owed much to the philosophers in those areas where their work had already begun to help form Christian doctrine. In particular, he worked out in the dialogues he wrote at Cassiciacum a Christian view of the idea of future blessedness (*De Beata Vita*). He arrived at a theory of evil in which evil is seen as itself nothing, but rather a turning from the good by the wills of rational beings. He understood the nature of God and the doctrine of the Trinity in terms which owed a great deal to the thinking of the philosophers, with certain essential Christian modifications, such as the insistence, which occupies him for a great deal of the *De Trinitate*, upon the equality of the Persons. And, in the *De Trinitate* and elsewhere, he developed a theory of language. He wrote at length on the way in which God reveals himself to men by signs.

FOR FURTHER READING

Brown, P. R. L., *Augustine of Hippo* (London, 1967).
Chadwick, H., *Augustine* (Oxford, 1986).
Evans, G. R., *Augustine of Evil* (Cambridge, 1983).
Gilson, E., *The Christian Philosophy of St. Augustine* (London, 1961).
Portalié, E., *A Guide to the Thought of St. Augustine* (London, 1960).
Warfield, B. B., *Studies in Tertullian and Augustine* (London, 1930).

6

THE END OF THE ROMAN WORLD

1. THE DECLINE OF PHILOSOPHICAL TRAINING IN THE WEST

When in the first century AD Quintilian composed his *Institutio Oratoria* he defined the orator as one who has a genuine title to the name of philosopher. In Augustine's day education was still designed to produce orators, and orators were agreed to need at least a smattering of philosophy. A century later the emphasis had shifted, in the changed world of a Roman Empire overrun with barbarians. The Ostrogoths in Italy, the Visigoths in Spain and southern Gaul, the Vandals in north Africa, the Burgundians in Gaul and Francia, the Anglo-Saxons in England, had more need of civil servants than of men who could make political speeches or act as advocates in law-courts. Quintilian's textbook was lost (except for a few fragments which appear to have been known in the twelfth century) until the end of the Middle Ages. The educational pattern which had filled the minds of educated men throughout the Empire with philosophy was modified, as philosophy lost its familiar vehicle. The study of grammar, with the aid of Donatus' textbooks and readings in the Roman poets became the normal scheme of education. Grammar still had a good deal of rhetoric about it; literary grace and a good Latin style were still taught. But the elements from the other *artes* which had been thought necessary began to drop away from the syllabus, and with them the more advanced study which had included philosophy.

As institutions, the schools suffered throughout the Empire. In Carthage they were closed altogether for a time. In Italy the patronage of the Emperor Theodoric, a rarity among barbarians in his interest in the culture of his conquered people, enabled the schools to survive.

Cassiodorus
Cassiodorus was one of the last generation to receive a training in rhetoric and philosophy of the old sort. He entered the service of the Emperor Theodoric in 507. He tried to establish a school at Rome, so that Rome might rival the Alexandria of Clement and Origen. But he was forced to fall back upon the plan of founding a school in the monastery he began at Vivarium, and to which he retired in 540. Knowledge of Greek was becoming so rare in the West that Cassiodorus, trying to provide texts for his monks at Vivarium, thought it best to stock their library with Latin works, or Greek works in Latin translations.

He is the author of an encyclopaedia, the *Institutiones*, in the first draft of which he lists the works in the library at Vivarium: Donatus and Fortunatianus on grammar, Cicero's *De Inventione*, Boethius' translation of Porphyry's Isagoge or introduction to logic, the *Categories* and *De Interpretatione* of Aristotle, Quintilian – texts of the schoolroom, for the most part, of a plain and solid kind. He had a strong sense of the need to salvage books and learning if the ancient culture of Greece and Rome was to survive. But he was not ambitious to do more than preserve and pass on the existing corpus and provide handbooks to help students master it.

2. BOETHIUS

The Relationship of Philosophy and Theology
The *Isagoge* of Albinus, who taught at Smyrna in the second century AD, was not the only philosophical introduction available in his day (Irenaeus used one like it), but it helped to establish a form of handbook indispensable to later Christian scholars. In it he made an attempt to explain how the departments of philosophy were related to one another. Albinus divides philosophy into physics, ethics and logic, after Xenocrates perhaps, or Aristotle.

He proposes another division, too, inspired by Aristotle's distinction of 'theory' and 'practice'. Theology is regarded as the first branch of 'theoria', the study of the divine, or that which is unmoved. This division, like the first, was to have a currency for many centuries and considerable importance in the thinking of the later Middle Ages.

The most influential transmitter of this idea was to be the Roman consul Boethius (c.480–524). In the *De Trinitate* he explains that physics, or natural science, is the study of objects in the created world which move and change and are concrete; theology is the study of that which is truly abstract and does not move or change. Between lies mathematics, which 'abstracts' from concrete objects those properties in which they resemble the unchanging and immovable. It deals, for example, in triangles and other geometrical figures which are never found in the world in exactly their perfect form, but which the mind can conceive of in their perfection by an exercise of intellectual abstraction. In this way, Boethius emphasises the hierarchical nature of knowledge, and the range of philosophy at its grandest, from the study of the created world to the study of the Creator. He makes theology merely a department of philosophy. And he encourages mediaeval scholars to ask themselves 'to what branch of philosophy' a subject belongs, as was usually done by the master in a short introduction or *accessus* when he began a series of lectures on a text.

In this way, the question of the relationship between philosophy and theology became a lively issue. Teachers of theology were obliged to defend their subject, as we shall see them doing in the thirteenth century and beyond.

Translating Greek Philosophers

Cassiodorus was not the only Roman of the day to see the need for a programme of preservation of the best texts of standard works. Bishop Victor of Capua produced a new edition of the Bible in 547, with corrected spelling; Bishop Maximian of Ravenna (d.556) revised Jerome's version of the Old Testament. A rich layman near Cumae revised Augustine's book on the Trinity. But the most ambitious of all was Boethius (c.480–524). He intended to translate the whole of Plato's and Aristotle's works into Latin, and more. He succeeded only in part. Those works he did translate and comment upon provided mediaeval scholars for half a millenium with almost all their materials for the study of logic and their only substantial textbook on arithmetic. It was perhaps in this rather pedestrian way that he made his chief contribution to the transmission of Greek philosophical ideas to the Christian Latin West.

The Consolation of Philosophy

His most popular work has always been the book he wrote in the condemned cell, awaiting execution on a charge of treason. *The Consolation of Philosophy* contains nothing that is distinctively Christian, and his writing without reference to the Christian God in such circumstances seemed to many of his readers, from at least as early as Carolingian times, a strong indication that he was not himself a Christian. But the book was read, and it influenced Christian thinking, on Providence and Fortune in particular. It gave a place to the notion of a capricious power who brought the confident crashing from the Pinnacle of Fortune and it kept within the conception of Providence certain elements familiar to Greek thinkers. But above all, because it is shot through with Neoplatonic assumptions, it did something to keep the system in the minds of mediaeval scholars when they had no direct access to Neoplatonic writings.

Boethius on Theology
Perhaps Boethius' most original contribution to the advancement of Christian philosophy, however, lay in his five 'theological tractates'. These are concerned with a series of problems of Christian philosophy. The *De Trinitate* is an attempt to consider afresh certain difficulties raised by Augustine when he himself wrote on the Trinity. It includes at the beginning Boethius' division of philosophy into its theological, mathematical and physical branches, which was to prove so stimulating to thinkers of the twelfth century. In the *Contra Eutychen* Boethius discusses the problem of the application of Aristotle's *Categories* when we are talking of God, a problem again raised by Augustine, but set out more economically and with greater technical exactitude by Boethius. He emphasises that attributes of God which in another being would be qualities or accidents are substantial in God. God's goodness and justice are inseparable from his being. The *De Hebdomadibus*, or *Quomodo Substantie* is an essay in axiomatic method. Boethius sets out nine rules, or self-evident principles, and poses a problem for his readers, which he promises can be solved by the application of these axioms and a certain amount of intellectual effort. His commentators later disagreed about the precise application of the axioms.

Boethius was the last of the Latin authors of the ancient world to write on these matters at such a level. Writers in Greek, on the other hand, continued to have access to the works of both Christian and pagan Platonists.

3. THE CAPPADOCIANS

The Alexandrians were so steeped in philosophical notions drawn from the schools in which they were trained, and so confident of the philosophers' debt to Moses, that they were inclined to take it for granted that pagan philosophy contained elements of Christian truth. Three thinkers born in Cappadocia, Basil of Caesarea, Gregory Nazianzen and Gregory of Nyssa, made distinctions more firmly than the Alexandrians had been able to do between philosophical principles which they found to accord with Christian revelation, and those which it showed to be false. They built upon Origen's work, but there were many points at which he had left questions unanswered. In particular they were anxious to establish – against common Greek belief – that the cosmos was not eternal, but had been created at the beginning of time. They insisted upon the humanity of the human soul, against the view of many of the Greek philosophers that the soul is divine. They argued against the notion that the body is something evil from which the soul must escape.

These were classic differences between philosophers and Christians, which had begun to emerge as key principles to be settled if a satisfactory synthesis was to be achieved. They troubled Augustine. But in subsequent centuries they continued to be pressing among the Greeks, in a way they were not among the Latins. The divorce of the two languages was also in some measure a divorce of cultures and concerns, so that the areas of common interest in the Greek and Latin worlds became different.

4. PROCLUS

Proclus was perhaps the last of the Greek Platonists to exert a substantial influence upon the development of Christian thought. This younger (411–85) contemporary of Augustine brought together in an orderly way in his *Elements of Theology* what he regarded as the essentials of the Platonic system of thought. He arranged his material under headings, each of which is either a self-evident truth or a truth which can be seen to follow from a previous axiom.

The Reasonableness of the Truth: Demonstrative Method
This method of demonstrating the truth so that all reasonable beings must see it and accept it was based upon that outlined in Aristotle's *Posterior Analytics*. It had been worked out in practice as a way of treating the subject-matter of geometry by Euclid in his *Elements*, but it had never been tried before for theology. If the demonstrative method worked for mathematical subjects, it was because the truths of mathematics are recognised intuitively, and not by learning from the evidence of the senses. The method ought to work better still for theology. Theological truths are of a higher order still, and can be known, even more than mathematical ones, by recognition of their truth with the aid perhaps of divine illumination.

Some of Proclus' Propositions were collected in a compilation known as the *Liber de Causis*, which came into the West at the end of the twelfth century under the name of Aristotle. This was at a time when the recently translated *Posterior Analytics*, and the *Elements* of Euclid, and a new perception of the possibilities of Boethius' use of the axiomatic method in the *De Hebdomadibus*, were all encouraging an interest in the uses of demonstrative method. In this oblique way, Proclus made his contribution to the development of philosophical method in philosophy. (He was more directly influential through the work of Pseudo-Dionysius. He made him see the importance of hierarchy. In Proclus' *Elements* much is made of the way in which one thing proceeds from or is dependent upon another.)

Paradox
He also took pleasure in the antitheses and paradoxes implicit in Neoplatonic thought; he helped to make them clear by setting them out crisply in his axioms, and again, he brought them to the attention of Pseudo-Dionysius. He contrasts unity and plurality, cause and effect, the procession out from God and the desire of all creation to return to him, eternity and time, limit and infinity. In the light of these oppositions, he explores the paradoxical relations within the Godhead, and the relations between God and his creatures in which many of them are exemplified.

5. PSEUDO-DIONYSIUS

Pseudo-Dionysius (c.500) was believed by his mediaeval readers to be the Dionysius the Areopagite who was converted by St. Paul at Athens (Acts 17:34). His writings were first mentioned in the early sixth century by Severus of Antioch, and they were attributed to the Areopagite at least as early as 533. The intention of their author was to bring together Christianity and philosophy in a grand synthesis. He did not want to be regarded as a pioneer. He insisted that what he taught was to be found in the Christian tradition. He was indebted to Proclus, but also to his own predecessors among Greek-speaking Christians who had tried to achieve a similar synthesis in terms which seemed appropriate in their own day – the Alexandrians and the Cappadocian Fathers who had followed up their work in the fourth century.

God the Cause
Pseudo-Dionysius saw more clearly than any of his predecessors
how integral to the structure of the universe was the unity in trinity
of the Godhead. The divine, he explains, is something in itself; it
is also an efficient cause; and it is a final cause to which the 'effects'
return by participating in it. This abstract and conceptually sophisticated doctrine of creation makes the early efforts of a Philo or a
Clement seem unduly preoccupied with mechanical details, but it
owes much to their efforts to identify and express the difficulties,
and still more perhaps to Proclus' account of Causes.

Negative Theology
In his *Mystical Theology* and *Epistle V* Pseudo-Dionysius considers
God in his first aspect, as that which he is, the unchanging One,
inaccessible to our knowledge. It is here that Pseudo-Dionysius
introduces 'negative theology', the notion that no affirmation can
be made properly of God, because we can say nothing in human
language of what he truly is. The *De Divinis Nominibus*, 'On the
Divine Names', is concerned with the way in which God causes the
effect of the created world. The *Ecclesiastical* and *Celestial Hier-
archies* and *Epistle IX* look at God as Final Cause, that to which
creation is eternally returning by an ascent from signs in the world
we perceive with our senses, to signs we perceive intellectually, and
so up towards God himself. Here again Proclus can be seen in the
background.
    The notion of a 'negative' theology appealed strongly to later
mediaeval mystics, who strove to lose themselves in contemplation
of a transcendence so great that nothing can be said of it at all.

The Sacramental Principle
Dionysius made a contribution, too, to the development of a
theology of the sacramental, in his doctrine that corporeal things
have an inherent power which they derive from the harmony or
sympatheia which binds the universe together. This theurgy had
been made little of by earlier Christian thinkers, perhaps because it
was easy to confuse with magic and the invocation of demons which
pagans had always indulged in. But it establishes the essential principle of the sacramental, that through objects in the created world
it is possible to call effectively upon God's aid.

Dionysius and the Philosophers
Pseudo-Dionysius was an exception among Christian thinkers of the
Greek world of the fifth and sixth centuries in his attitude to the

philosophers. There was a widespread turning against Platonism and Aristotelianism alike, partly over the residual difficulties about the beginning of the world, the soul and evil. John Philoponos (b.475/80), a pupil of the philosophical school at Alexandria, for example, wrote 'On the Eternity of the World against Proclus' (*De Aeternitate Mundi contra Proclum*) circa 529, the year when Justinian closed the Athenian academy. He wanted to reveal the weaknesses in a system he saw as essentially polytheistic and inclined, in its teaching on theurgy at least, to lapse into magic and demonology.

The Use of Aristotle (Maximus the Confessor)

To more than one writer, however, the Aristotelian logic seemed to offer a way out of a difficulty. It made it possible to give a hard edge to the system of Proclus and Pseudo-Dionysius.

Maximus the Confessor (c.580–662) an aristocrat and Imperial Secretary to the Emperor Heraclius, became a monk and apologist in Africa, working against the heretics there. His writings were many and varied, ascetic, doctrinal, some concerned with liturgical matters and some on problems of exegesis. His own belief was that the whole of history makes sense only in the context of the coming of Christ. In his Incarnation Christ made man divine (*theosis*) and thus restored him to the image of God in which he was made, but which had been damaged by original sin. Man's sin consisted in a desire for pleasure; that was why it was necessary for Christ to suffer pain in order to make good the damage. Maximus was himself something of a mystic, with a taste for 'negative theology' and a belief in the power of abnegation to bring a man to union with God.

Maximus wrote commentaries on the works of Pseudo-Dionysius which show him to have believed that Dionysius was St. Paul's convert. He approved of his attempt to bring together philosophy and Christianity. Nothing is said by chance by this blessed man, he claims, but all is learned and fitting and holy. Dionysius employed symbols so that he might increase our understanding, just as Scripture itself uses figurative expressions to help human understanding. Maximus drew up tables to explain diagrammatically the structure of the Dionysian universe, with the descent and progression of all things from God.

In his remarks on the *De Divinis Nominibus*, Maximus draws out the implications of Dionysius' teaching for the use of Aristotelian logic. Human wisdom draws its notion of probabilities from what the senses perceive and from there it makes its demonstrations. Syllogisms possess a power of convincing, a compelling necessity for rational minds, which is indispensable in persuading men of the truth of Christian doctrine. Logic, in other words, is built into the universe by the Creator.

6. JOHN SCOTUS ERIUGENA

Maximus was read in the Middle Ages, but a far more effective transmitter of Pseudo-Dionysian thought was the Irishman John Scotus Eriugena (c.810–877). He was made head of the palace school in Paris by the Frankish ruler Charles the Bald and he was involved in two major theological controversies of the day: the dispute which was opened by Godescalc of Orbais' writings in defence of an extreme predestinationism, and that which was begun by Paschasius Radbertus on the subject of the Eucharist. He was a philosopher as well as a controversialist. In the *De Praedestinatione* he wrote against Godescalc he discusses the relationship between philosophy and theology: 'What is it to write of philosophy but to expound the laws (*regulae*) of true religion, by which God, the Supreme and First Cause of all things, is worshipped and sought out by reason? We are confident therefore that true philosophy is true religion, and conversely true religion is true philosophy.'

Greek Influences
The Iconoclastic controversy of the seventh and eighth centuries had driven a number of Greek scholars into exile, and some of them fled to the West, bringing with them books which had not hitherto been available to Latin-speakers. Except for the ideas which Boethius had purveyed, little Greek philosophy later than that of Porphyry had yet made its way into the West.

In the second half of the eighth century and the beginning of the ninth, a few copies of Pseudo-Dionysius' works were sent about Europe by Popes and Emperors, but the most important of these was undoubtedly that which the Emperor Michael the Stammerer gave to Louis the Debonair at Compiègne in 827. The manuscript was deposited at the monastery of St. Denis (later to claim the special patronage of the Areopagite). It was translated by Abbot Hilduin (c.832–5). In 860, Charles the Bald commissioned a new version from John the Scot, who was in refuge at his Court from Ireland at the time, because of the threat of Viking invasions at home. Eriugena also translated a work of Maximus the Confessor and one of Gregory of Nyssa's books, but it was his versions of Pseudo-Dionysius which were to become popular and influential at least from the twelfth century.

FOR FURTHER READING

CHLGEMP, Part V.
Chadwick, H., *Boethius* (Oxford, 1981).
Daniélou, J., *Platonisme et théologie mystique* (2nd ed., Paris, 1953).
Gibson, M. T., (ed., *Boethius, his Life, Thought and Influence* (Oxford, 1981).
Marenbon, J., *Early Mediaeval Philosophy* (London, 1983).
Momigliano, A., ed., *The Conflict between Paganism and Christianity in the Fourth Century* (Oxford, 1963).

7

THE BEGINNING OF THE
MEDIAEVAL WORLD

1. THE REVIVAL OF LOGIC

It was a long time before Eriugena's ideas made their full impact,
and then it was chiefly for his rendering of Pseudo-Dionysius that
he was read. The preoccupations of the late Greek Christian philosophers were not those of the early mediaeval world. Of far greater
interest to the more philosophically-minded were the questions
which began to arise out of the study of logic. Just as a concern
with the origin and nature of things marks the thinking of the
early Christian philosophers, a preoccupation with logic marks the
centuries of the Middle Ages.

Aristotle's *Categories* sets out the first principles of logic. It
explains how to define the thing under discussion by a system of
classification of its substance (its essential nature) and its accidents
(those qualities it possesses which may change) such as its quality
(colour, value, shape), its quantity (size, number), its time, place,
state of activity or passivity, and so on.

Although Boethius made a translation of the *Categories* and wrote
a commentary upon it, there were at first few would-be logicians
who were prepared to work their way through his lengthy and
difficult text. Instead they preferred to use the *Categoriae Decem*,
an abbreviation of Aristotle's *Categories* with an accompanying
commentary, thought to be the work of Augustine.

The Categories and Theological Language
The interest in the *Categories* lay in the puzzle they posed about the
problem of talking about God. Clearly, we may speak of the divine
substance, but God cannot be said to be in any time or place, or to
have a size or a colour. The only category apart from that of substance which can perhaps be used of God is that of relation, when we
speak of his Fatherhood or Christ's Sonship. These scholars were

beginning to explore the subject which was to be of more consistent interest to mediaeval thinkers than any others: the nature and function of language and especially of theological language – most particularly the language of Scripture.

Universals

This brought them to the problem of universals. Until the early twelfth century the general consensus was with Augustine and the Platonists, that universals, or classes of things, had an existence in their own right. They were not merely labels, or convenient groups into which all animals (or all koala bears) could be placed for reference. They were related to the ideas or forms which began as notions in the mind of God and became patterns for his creation. An idea must be high in the order of reality in a universe where the abstract is more intelligible than the concrete, and closer to the ultimate divine reality.

Gerbert of Aurillac and Abbo of Fleury

It is with the work of the late tenth and early eleventh century that we enter this characteristically mediaeval world of Aristotelian logic and a Platonic theory of language. Two outstanding Benedictine scholars of the second half of the tenth century, Gerbert of Aurillac (c.940–1003) and Abbo of Fleury (c.945–1004) had in common an interest in both logic and mathematics which was rare for their time. Gerbert was educated at the monastic school of Aurillac, and then at the cathedral school of Ausona (Vich) in Spain, where he learned mathematics from Arabic scholars. He taught at the cathedral school at Reims and composed a textbook on geometry and a commentary on Boethius' *Arithmetica*, as well as writing on logic. Abbo studied at Paris and Reims in the cathedral schools, and in the monastic school at Fleury. Invited to England by Oswald Archbishop of York to assist him in his programme of restoring monastic life in England, Abbo spent a few years at Ramsay abbey, where he wrote a set of 'grammatical questions' for the monks he taught in the school there. He, too, concentrated upon improving and adding to the materials for the teaching of the seven liberal arts, particularly those which had been neglected. He wrote a monograph on two of Boethius' treatises (*On Categorical* and *On Hypothetical Syllogisms*), and a lengthy and erudite commentary on the *Calculus* of Victorius of Aquitaine. This draws on an impressively wide range of late-classical sources and shows him to have known something of the Platonism which was, for the moment, in obscurity among many of his contemporaries.

The mathematical elements in the teaching of both scholars were of less interest and importance for the time being than the stimulus they gave to more advanced work on logic. It was not until the twelfth century that the Platonic nature of the mathematical ideas to be found in Boethius' rendering of the Pythagorean Nicomachus of Gerasa on Arithmetic became generally apparent. In the eleventh century attention turned from the *Categoriae Decem* or summary of the *Categories* to the unabridged text itself, and the commentary of Boethius. Further possibilities of applying logic to the resolution of theological problems began to suggest themselves.

Berengar of Tours

Berengar of Tours (c.999–1088) studied at Chartres under Fulbert, who had been a pupil of Gerbert of Aurillac at Reims and at Chartres. He asked what kind of change might be brought about in the Eucharist by the consecration of the bread and wine. He concluded that it was contradictory to the principles of the *Categories* that the substance of the bread should be changed while the accidents remained the same, the bread continuing to look and smell and taste like bread when it had actually become the body of Christ. The response to Berengar brought about a clarification of the matter on the Church's part; it hardened into a doctrine of transubstantiation which had not been explictly stated before.

Lanfranc of Bec

The case against Berengar was taken up by Lanfranc of Bec (c.1005–89), later to be Archbishop of Canterbury, but already the most famous master in France. He had made the school at Bec a centre of attraction for ambitious young men, teaching logic and rhetoric there to an unusually high standard. He was, however, opposed to the abuse of these subjects by misapplying them to the solution of mysteries beyond their scope. He addressed himself to Berengar in the *Liber de Corpore et Sanguine Domini* as to one whose technical expertise has failed him. He believed that Berengar had made elementary mistakes in framing his arguments, preferred to avoid the use of formal syllogisms and such devices in favour of 'equipollent propositions', successive approximations which bring the argument by steps to its conclusion.

Lanfranc's most gifted and most famous pupil Anselm saw no such objection to the use of logic, but he in his turn encountered a contentious logician, Roscelin of Compiègne (d.c.1125), at one time another student at Reims. Shortly after Lanfranc's death, Roscelin put about a story that he and Anselm had both taught that there are three Gods, implying that Father, Son and Spirit are three distinct beings, or the Father and the Spirit were Incarnate with the Son. Anselm answered him in an open letter which he had to redraft several times, and which cost him more distress in the writing than any other work.

2. ANSELM OF CANTERBURY

Anselm of Canterbury, born in north Italy c.1033, was a natural philosopher and a speculative theologian of a calibre which had not been seen for many centuries. He is remarkable above all for his clarity of mind. With a limited range of sources to draw upon as a philosopher his philosophical principles are comparatively few. It may be that he owed his originality and uncluttered approach at least in part to the historical chance of being born at a time when the best education of the day equipped his mind so economically.

Augustinian Platonism
It is unlikely that Anselm had any knowledge of Plato's *Timaeus*. The first principles of his thought which are recognisably Platonic in origin came to him principally through his reading of Augustine. He made use of the simple rules of grammar and dialectic available to him in the textbooks he knew – Porphyry's *Isagoge*, the *Categories* and *Perihermeneias* of Aristotle, Boethius' commentaries and monographs, perhaps Apuleius' *Perihermeneias*. He drew from Augustinian assumptions about the nature of God and the Trinity, and creation, which Augustine himself owed in some measure to his readings in the philosophers, but which Anselm does not consciously identify as Platonist. He thought of himself not as philosopher or theologian, not as Aristotelian or Platonist, but as writing simply for reasonable men, about matters which God had designed to possess a 'beautiful reasonableness' for the faithful.

The Arts of Language
In his youth in Italy, and later at Bec under Lanfranc, Anselm mastered the elements of the art of the trivium, grammar, logic and a little rhetoric. After completing his education he became a monk, and spent ten years reading the Bible and the Fathers, especially Augustine. He had no pressing urge to write but he was a teacher by habit and inclination and used not only to read the Latin poets with his pupils but also to discuss with them the nature of God and the mystery of the Trinity. These Socratic gifts are evident in the

three 'treatises pertaining to the study of Holy Scripture' (the *De Veritate*, the *De Libertate Arbitrii*, the *De Casu Diaboli*) which he wrote in his forties and fifties, after many years of teaching and discussion of truth, freedom of choice and the nature of evil.

Pure Reasoning

The monks of Bec begged Anselm to write down what he had taught them, and it was for them that he composed his first book, the *Monologion*. He almost certainly intended its eighty chapters to make a complete statement of all that he had to say about the unity and Trinity of God and the divine nature. In it, he followed a method from which he was never to depart, though his use of it caused some controversy at first. He worked *sola ratione*, by reasoning alone, without citing authorities. Lanfranc, by then Archbishop of Canterbury, was sent a copy for his approval before Anselm allowed the treatise to be circulated outside Bec. He asked Anselm to support his arguments from authority. Anselm reassured him that he had said nothing which could not be found to agree with Scripture and the Fathers. He kept to his plan and made no major changes.

He saw no difficulty in a rational mind coming to a knowledge of the supreme Being in this way. Anselm had no developed doctrine of divine illumination; he found that if he contemplated the 'Inaccessible light' in which God dwells, the light was, if anything, baffling to the eyes of his mind. The process of discovery as Anselm experienced it took place in a mind open to God, but it was a rational, not a mystical process, conducted by a reason less in kind than that of its Creator, but of the same sort, and designed to perceive the reasonableness of his creation.

The Existence of God

The *Monologion* is not the most original of Anselm's works, but it is perhaps the treatise in which the Neoplatonic inheritance of assumptions and habits of thought is most apparent and closest to the surface of his mind. In it, Anselm is able to show, by leading the reader through his knowledge of all kinds of created 'goods', that there must be a single good, above all others. Anselm shows that the attributes of God, eternity, infinity, justice, immutability, and so on, are not accidents but all one in the substance of the supreme good. It is made apparent that this must be a good without a cause, and yet existing 'through' nothing and 'from' nothing. It exists through itself and through it all other things exist.

This supreme spirit is the Creator. It speaks both itself and its creation by means of one Word. It made everything else from nothing (John 1:3). Yet created things were not 'nothing' in respect to the thought of their maker, they existed in the divine mind from eternity.

The *Proslogion* was the only one of Anselm's works to be written because he himself felt impelled to attempt it. He says in the Preface that when he looked back on the *Monologion* he felt dissatisfied. Its arguments formed a chain (*concatenatio contextum argumentorum*), and he wanted to find a single argument which would alone show that God truly exists, that he is the Highest Good, and demonstrate whatever else we believe about the divine substance.

The argument, which came to Anselm with the suddenness of discovery, and after a long period of struggle, is famous as the ontological proof for the existence of God. Anselm believed that it proved more than God's mere existence because 'to be' was, for him, at its supreme exemplification, also to be good and true and beautiful, just and merciful and omnipotent, and he goes on to show in detail how his argument entails all this.

Anselm begins from what seems to him to be a first principle which no-one can deny. Everyone can grasp the notion of 'that than which nothing greater can be thought'. If he understands it, he must recognise that it exists, at least in his mind. Anselm proposes to show that it must exist not only in the understanding (*in intellectu*) but also in reality (*in re*). He argues that it is possible to conceive of something which exists both in the mind and in reality, and this is, indeed, essential for it to be that than which nothing greater can be thought because we have agreed that otherwise something greater can be thought. That than which nothing greater can be thought can be no other than God himself, and thus it seems that we have proved the existence of God.

This argument gave Anselm great joy when he hit upon it, and he was sure that it would please others equally. However, not everyone was uncritical of it. Gaunilo, a monk of Marmoutiers, put his finger at once on one weakness. He used Anselm's argument to prove the existence of an imaginary island, the most beautiful which could be thought. Anselm replied that his argument would work only in the special case of God, because God's existence was unique in its necessity. Thomas Aquinas pointed to another objection which, for him, so ruled out the argument as a proof for the existence of God that he does not include it among his 'five ways' of proving God's existence. He said that Anselm had misunderstood the deep grammar of his propositions, and was confusing the self-evident truth of the statement 'God exists', where the predicate is simply the same as the subject (i.e., God is his own existence), with a statement in which the listener understands the terms and their meaning. We do not, says Aquinas, know the essence of God directly, so we cannot know intuitively as a self-evident truth that God exists.

Anselm's argument rests on a number of Neoplatonic assumptions which he did not know to have been matters of controversy in their day, and which he assumes to be apparent to all educated men. He understood goodness and greatness and all such things as being susceptible of degree, so that it was natural to think of greatness in a hierarchical way, with Supreme Greatness God himself. It seemed natural to accept that all goods become one in God.

Above all, Anselm's conception of reality is Platonic. He believed that what is beyond sense-experience, in Boethius' two degrees, (mathematical truths which we know intellectually and theological truths which we know in an even higher intellectual way) are more real than what can be touched and seen – and the more real, the further they are away from the world of sense. At the ultimate level of reality stands God himself. To say that he exists in reality as well as in the mind requires a really very modest conceptual leap, if any at all, since his reality is intellectual in character. This is not a great leap such as would be needed if we were moving from the idea of an island to the real island. In mathematical truths, the idea and the reality are close together. In theological truths they are one.

Some Classical Problems

In his later works, Anselm sometimes touches on some of the classic problems of Greek philosophy: providence, for example, in the *De Concordia*, his last work, in which he tries to reconcile freedom of human will with divine foreknowledge, predestination and grace. He deals with the problem of evil in his treatise on the fall of Satan.

But under all his Platonism, Anselm was a logician. His conception of reason was indissolubly linked with the principles of Aristotle's elementary treatises on logic; reason was an instrument of a most practical and useful kind, in his experience, a God-given means of arriving at a clear understanding of the truths of faith. He was the last major thinker to find it so uncontroversial a tool for many centuries.

3. PETER ABELARD

If Anselm was largely an unconscious user of the work of early non-Christian philosophers, Peter Abelard was only too well aware that sometimes he was taking the part of the *philosophi*. He was Anselm's younger contemporary (1079–1142), but whereas Anselm taught in a small quiet group of friends in the monastic school at Bec, Abelard taught in a highly competitive environment, as master to ambitious young scholars. In many respects his mind was of a temper exactly opposed to that of Anselm. Quick to speak his mind on any subject, aggressive, assertive, a popular lecturer because he challenged contemporary masters and was exciting to listen to. Abelard was not, however, like Anselm, a teacher of Socratic gifts who could lead his pupils to think for themselves. All his life he was a centre of controversy. He travelled about the schools of northern France, ridiculing venerable masters such as William of Champeaux and Anselm of Laon, setting up his own school when no established school would have him. Twice, at Councils at Soissons in 1121 and at Sens in 1140, his teaching was publicly condemned.

The action which caused greatest offence was Abelard's sudden move from dialectic (in which he was undisputed master) to theology. Having heard Anselm of Laon lecture, he declared that he himself would lecture the very next day, on Ezekiel, traditionally a most difficult book. This appeared to his accusers more than an act of professional arrogance. Theology was too important to be treated so lightly. Bernard of Clairvaux, who led the attack at the Council of Sens, was scandalised by his presumption in setting himself up as a teacher of theology without having patiently studied under approved masters and given himself time to master the Scriptures thoroughly. He objected to the confidence with which Abelard approached the mysteries of the faith with the aid of dialectic. He was justified in accusing Abelard of overhastiness, but not perhaps in believing him to hold that there was nothing dialectic could not penetrate to.

Grammar and Logic

Dialectic for Abelard and his contemporaries was intimately associated with grammar. The two arts had markedly helped one another's development in the previous few years, because scholars began to perceive the existence of a good deal of common ground in their treatment of the nature and function of language. But most stimulating of all was the light the work threw upon the old problem of the differences between the rules obeyed by ordinary language and by the language of the Bible.

Problems of Language
In the *Theologia Christiana* Abelard finished in the last decade of
his life he points to the confusion which some readers experience
when they read the word *Spiritus*, which is both a proper name (of
the Holy Spirit) and a common name of many things. It is not
unusual for such a *nomen commune* to be 'transferred' so that it can
be used as the proper name of one thing. Abelard is touching on
what was to be a vexed question for future generations in his own
century. He implies that the Bible's usage is a transferred one, that
is, that it is borrowed from ordinary language. Other scholars would
prefer to make scriptural language the norm, and to regard all usages
of words for describing things in the created world as 'borrowed'.
The primacy of 'theological language' with its departures from ordinary grammatical rules, was thus established to an extent which
makes for extraordinarily inventive solutions, and for a preoccupation with such problems as whether to use a singular or a plural
verb when speaking of the Trinity.

More Classic Difficulties
Abelard was aware that he was discussing matters which had been
the subject of philosophical accounts in earlier centuries. Some at
least of those things which were said 'by the philosophers' about
the *anima mundi*, or soul of the world, can also, he claims, be
correctly understood of the Holy Spirit. The whole of Book II was
written 'Against the calumnies of the faithful on the use of the
testimonies of the philosophers'. Abelard is anxious to defend their
inclusion among the authorities. On the other hand he wrote in
Book III an *invectio* against those dialecticians who wish to understand God entirely in terms of human reason, and who think nothing
should be held by faith which cannot be supported by rational
argument. Abelard himself would like to think he takes a balanced
view.

The *Theologia Christiana* is not only the work in which he most
consciously confronts the difficulties of determining the relationship
between what Christian authors teach and what the philosophers
say (a concrete problem, and one much closer to twelfth century
hearts than the more abstract matter of the relationship between
theology and philosophy). It is also the work most closely concerned
with the classic problems of philosophy as they affect Christian
theology.

Abelard begins by looking at the highest good, and asking of
what it consists. He cites as his authorities, side by side: Augustine,
Scripture and Plato. 'According to Moses, the supreme good created

all good things,' he says, 'and even according to the assertion of Plato the Creator of all things is the Best' (*optimus*). In general, Abelard is delighted to discover a correspondence between the teaching of the *philosophi* and that of the Scriptures.

4. THEOLOGICAL LANGUAGE

The most read and most used textbook of theology throughout the later Middle Ages was written by Peter Lombard in the late 1140s or soon after. He studied at Bologna and Reims, and came to Paris to teach just before 1140. As an experienced master he saw a clear need for a handbook to the study of Scripture and the Fathers. He brought together in four books the opinions of the Fathers on the Trinity, creation, the problem of sin, the Incarnation and the virtues, the sacraments and the Last Things. The appeal of the collection lay in its convenience for reference purposes. But for our purposes the interest of the work lies in Peter Lombard's approach. He begins the whole survey by considering the way in which words are related to the things they stand for. He cites Augustine: 'All learning (*doctrina*), is about things or signs'. Peter Lombard discusses the 'things' man is intended to enjoy, beginning with the Holy Trinity, and he points out that the human mind is made in the image of the Trinity, so that the mind may progress in a 'trinitarian' way towards an understanding of God, the mind standing for the Father, knowledge for the Son, and love for the Holy Spirit. It may benefit from having, as it were, a built-in sign within it. He looks at the propriety of using language and the categories which are helpful in studying the created world or in talking about God. The whole amounts to an analysis of the liguistic problems which theology raises. It seemed to Peter Lombard the natural way to approach his subject, and his approach was remarkably durable in its appeal to the scholars of succeeding centuries.

The *Sentences* were not uncontroversial. They contained opinions – for example that insofar as he is a man, Christ is nothing – which recalled Abelard's teaching and led Walter of St. Victor to classify Peter Lombard with Abelard and others among the 'Labyrinths of Fancy'. There were even attempts to have the *Sentences* banned. But at the Fourth Lateran Council of 1215 the work was declared to be orthodox, and, indeed, in all but certain particulars, it is uniformly a safe book. It enshrined in a form which was to become a classic a number of the principles worked out in the first half of the twelfth century on the matter of theological language.

Transcending the Rules
The difficulty about theological, and more particularly Biblical language, was the emergence, by the end of the twelfth century, of two schools of thought. The first, represented by Peter the Chanter, Precentor of the Cathedral of Notre Dame in Paris (d.1197), took the view that the rules of grammar and dialectic could be used to explain away the difficulties. The other, one of whose more notable exponents was Alan of Lille, the *doctor universalis* who taught at Paris and in the South of France (d.1202), held that Scripture transcends all such rules, often turning them on their heads.

Peter the Chanter gave lectures on the ways in which Scripture uses words, which have survived in the form of a treatise *De Tropis Loquendi*. He made use of the latest work on fallacies. Since Aristotle's *Sophistici Elenchi* had recently become available in the schools, it had given a new zest to the old game of tracking down the Devil's fallacies. Peter is able to show that there are equivocal uses of words and phrases in Scripture which can be identified technically, and by this means reconciled, or at least made sense of, in terms of familiar rules of discourse.

Alan of Lille made perhaps the first of the new dictionaries of theological terms which were to become indispensable reference-books for preachers in the later Middle Ages. He collected examples of each term in the context in which it was used in the Bible, so as to show how many meanings each word has in Scripture. He prefaced the whole with a brief discussion of the way in which the Bible's language transcends ordinary rules, making one part of speech behave like another, accidents behave as substances, and so on. In a poem he wrote on the Incarnation and the seven Liberal Arts, he has a refrain: *Stupet omnis regula*. At the appearance of the Incarnate Word 'every rule is stupefied'; the *artes* are astounded. It is, he argues, to be expected that the Laws which govern human speech should be inadequate to explain the communications of the word of God to man.

5. THE BRANCHES OF PHILOSOPHY

These ideas took to their ultimate conclusion several notions which had been explored earlier in the century about the origin of the Liberal Arts. There existed side by side an explanation drawn from earlier encyclopaedias, especially those of Cassiodorus and Isidore, which explained who were the inventors or first exponents of the *artes;* and speculation, both fanciful and practical, about their origins. Hugh of St. Victor (d.1142) thought that men were measuring fields before there was such a science as geometry. Rupert of Deutz (c.1075–1129) described the Liberal Arts as giggling girls disciplined at last by the Holy Spirit and made to work hard in the service of God and man.

There was a fondness for drawing up schemes in which philosophy was divided into its branches. What was lacking perhaps was an awareness of the existence in earlier centuries of an altogether grander conception of philosophy as being concerned with great problems. It was theology which now increasingly became the subject which excited the mind with a sense of its vastness. The subjects which the twelfth century masters studied as 'branches' of philosophy were handled on the whole with pedestrian thoroughness and read with the nose close to the page. Each textbook was given its place in the scheme of philosophy in a short introduction which identified the author and said what the book was about and what purpose it was intended to serve and what was the profit to be had from studying it. The large speculative questions of the day arose out of the study of the Bible, rather than out of the study of the *artes*. The rules of the *artes*, chiefly those of dialectic, served to refine and clarify the problem and sometimes even to suggest its existence, but this chiefly at a technical and detailed level.

FOR FURTHER READING

Chenu, M. D., *Nature, Man and Society in the Twelfth Century* (tr. Chicago, 1968).
Henry, D. P., *The Logic of St. Anselm* (Oxford, 1967).
Hopkins, J., *A Companion to the Study of St. Anselm* (Minneapolis, 1973).
Jolivet, J., *Arts du langage et théologie chez Abélard* (Paris, 1969).
Marenbon, *Early Mediaeval Philosophy* (London, 1983).
Evans, G. R., *Old Arts and New Theology* (Oxford, 1980).

TWO TWELFTH CENTURY TABLES OF THE PARTS OF PHILOSOPHY

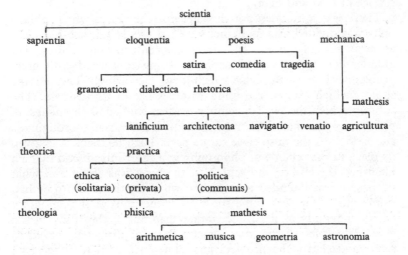

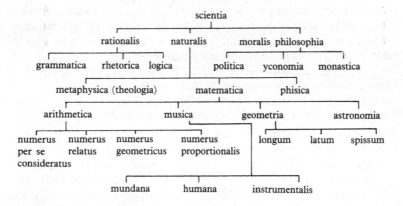

© *G. R. Evans*

8

THE ARRIVAL OF ARISTOTLE

1. ARABIC LEARNING

When Justinian closed the philosophical schools in Athens in 529, Christian scholars moved into Asia. Some of them had already settled at Edessa, where there had been a famous school since 363. There they were able to teach Aristotelian philosophy and Greek medicine until the school of Edessa, too, was closed in 489 (because the Emperor Zeno believed that they were teaching Nestorianism) and the masters went into Persia. After the Islamic conquest of Persia, the Califs there made use of their skills, and Aristotle, Euclid, Hippocrates and Galen, Ptolemy and other authors were translated into Arabic by the Syrian scholars' successors, in the late eighth and ninth centuries. Some writings which were not Aristotle's came to bear his name at this time, including the *Theologia Aristotelis*, which consisted of parts of Books IV, V and VI of Plotinus' *Enneads*, and the *Liber de Causis*, based on Proclus, both of which were to be important in the later Middle Ages.

Alkindi and the Agent Intellect

Arabic scholars did not rest content with merely translating. They wrote about and developed Greek ideas, selecting and juxtaposing and bringing into prominence points which because of their work were to make a mark on later mediaeval thought. In the ninth century Alkindi (d.873) wrote on a vast range of subjects – logic, metaphysics, natural science and politics. But perhaps his chief contribution to the work of mediaeval scholars was his attempt to follow up the implication of Aristotle's distinction between the intellect which is capable of understanding (the 'possible' intellect) and the creative intellect, the *intellectus agens* or Agent Intellect, which produces things which may be understood. The Agent Intellect seemed to Alkindi (as it had to Alexander of Aphrodisias, a second century Platonist and commentator on Aristotle) not part of the soul of the individual, but a separate, higher being. Alkindi indentified this Agent Intellect as the source of all Forms or Ideas in men's minds. If this view was correct, it made short work of the problem of universals. All general ideas and concepts understood by men are diffused into individual intellects from the Agent Intellect above. For Latin scholars this was a totally new view of the soul.

The Nature of Being and the Eternity of the Universe: Alfarabi

The old controversy over the eternity of the universe was as important to Moslems as to Christians; they, too, wanted to be able to show that a powerful Creator made it of his own free choice; that it was not simply a logical necessity that it should exist. Educated at Baghdad, Alfarabi (d.c.950) applied himself to this difficulty, on the basis of his knowledge of the logic of Porphyry and Aristotle.

He saw that a distinction might be made between essence and existence. He pointed out that it is possible to have an idea of what a thing is without the thing necessarily existing, so that essence and existence must be separate things. Essence is the higher mode of being of the two. The cause which brought the universe into being is in the first instance the source of the essences, and then of the specific existences of particular things which are not necessary at all to the essences. Thus a difference between universal and particular is made into something more than a convenience for labelling things. It is built into the very structure of the world, and the universal emerges as something which is independent of the existence of any specific example of itself.

Alfarabi developed the Aristotelian distinction between power and act in the intellect which had interested Alkindi. The ultimate Agent Intellect bestows forms on all the matter in the world, and knowledge on all the intellects. It is not in itself active in the sense of being busy with details. He made the trancendent Intelligence of the Neoplatonists a recognisable notion to mediaeval readers.

Avicenna and the Divisions of Philosophy

Avicenna (980–1037) perhaps the best-known of all the Arabs to the Latin West, divided philosophy in a manner highly congenial to his later mediaeval readers: into speculative and practical branches, concerned respectively with the search for truth and the living of a good life. The speculative he further subdivided into mutable and immutable. The first of these he took to be the subject of natural science dealing with particular existences. The second is concerned with essences, or the natures of things.

Avicenna and the Soul

The appeal of his writings is clear by, for example, a translation of Avicenna's book *On the Soul* into Latin sometime after 1150, by an unknown Jew, Avendeuth, who liked to call himself *philosophus*. He sent his translation to Archbishop John of Toledo, with a prologue explaining its purpose and summarising its contents. He points out that although men are composed of body and soul, they do not understand their souls as well as they do their bodies. This is natural enough: the body is obvious to sense-perception, but the soul can be grasped only by the intellect. Some men, 'given up to their senses' either believe the soul not to exist, or they think it no more than the mover of the body. How can a man love either himself or his God if he knows nothing of this better part of himself? Avicenna's book, the Prologue reassures us, contains everything Aristotle said about the soul, the senses, the understanding. The question of the nature of the soul and the modes of apprehension possible to it had all been covered by Augustine in the *Confessions* and elsewhere. But this was the new Aristotelian approach, which considered man scientifically in relation to the animal and vegetable kingdom as a whole, and allowed excursions into the science of optics and other areas. It was in such ways that Avicenna provided something mediaeval scholars now needed, a link between physics and metaphysics, human and supernatural sciences.

Avicenna stated a number of principles which were to become common currency in the later Middle Ages: the notion, for example, that the four elements, earth, water, air and fire, underlie the four 'humours', the phlegmatic, the melancholy, the volatile and the choleric, on which medicine was based.

Averroes: Faith and Reason

The most significant name of all, for later mediaeval controversy, is that of Averroes (1126–98). He studied at Cordoba and was expert in theology and philosophy, and also in law, medicine and mathematics. He commented upon Aristotle, but his most important original work lay in the attempt to work out a definitive position on the relation of philosophy and religion. This is what he came to stand for in mediaeval minds, and it was to pinpoint a controversy of very long standing indeed.

He wanted first to establish that philosophy was not dangerous so long as it was attempted only by minds capable of understanding it. Its proper domain is that of absolute truth. That can be reached only by demonstration. Lower down comes dialectical proof, which deals in probabilities, and lower still, matters of faith which have powers commensurate with the persuasive powers of oratory only. Above all, Averroes is a transmitter of Aristotle, but an Aristotle who is joined to Plato as the purveyor of a single unified system of thought. Aristotle's philosophy he held to be the only means of reaching absolute truth. Aristotle's teaching is the supreme truth, for his intellect was the greatest humanity has ever produced. Averroes called Aristotle a gift of Providence, a uniquely fine mind, bestowed on mankind so that whatever it was possible for men to know might be made accessible to them.

2. CONTACT WITH GREEK THOUGHT

The Translators

There were at least four places where Western scholars could find Greek learning. The First Crusade had opened up Syria as a pilgrim resort; enterprising scholars could settle there and learn Arabic and make their own translations. Stephen of Pisa worked in this way at Antioch in the second decade of the twelfth century, on medical texts. In Constantinople a number of Italians settled and learned Greek. When Anselm Bishop of Havelberg was sent as an ambassador to Constantinople in 1335 he engaged in a public disputation with the learned Nechites, Archbishop of Nicomedia, over the question which had divided the Greek and Latin Churches in 1054: whether the Holy Spirit proceeds from the Father and the Son, or only from the Father. He found three interpreters ready to hand, James of Venice, Burgundius of Pisa and Moses of Pergamum. They were all translators in their own right. Moses' work has not survived, but James of Venice translated the bulk of Aristotle's *Organon*, so that the new logic became accessible to Latin speakers. Burgundius of Pisa concentrated upon the Greek Fathers, translating 'word for word' (*de verbo ad verbum*) St Basil, St John Chrysostom and John Damascene. Of the two others, James's work was incomparably the more influential in his own century, because he was providing texts of logic which were eagerly sought for.

In Sicily and south Italy, the cosmopolitan culture of speakers of Latin, Greek, Hebrew and Arabic produced many capable of rendering Greek into Latin, including Adelard of Bath, the English scientist who early in the twelfth century translated Euclid.

The Spanish Connection

But it was in Spain above all that the translating took place. Averroes studied in Spain in the twelfth century, but for some time before that Spain had been a centre of Arabic and Jewish learning. The Jew Solomon Ibn Gabirol (Avicebron) (c.1020–58) made extensive use of dialectic in a treatise on the source of life, in which he proposed a fresh distinction between Creator and creature. He suggested that all substances except the divine are composed of matter and form. Maimonides (1135–1204) was another Cordoban, author of a book explaining Jewish theology in terms of a distinction between philosophical and rational knowledge, and the knowledge to be had through the Divine Law. Because of their contact with Arab scholars, the Jewish scholars in Spain were far more interested in philosophy than those of northern Europe. Gilbert Crispin, Abbot of Westminster from 1085, recorded a dialogue he had had with a Jew of Mainz in London about the year 1090; their dialogue shows no signs of Arabic influence, yet not long after it took place the converted Spanish Jew Petrus Alphonsus was helping to bring Arabic mathematics to England.

Christians had been slowly reconquering Spain from the Arabs until eventually, in 1085, Toledo fell into Christian hands again. The notion of going to Spain to learn from the Arabs about the thought of the ancient Greeks became an increasingly popular one. Adelard of Bath went there, as he had to Sicily and Syria and Hermann of Carinthia and Robert of Chester set out in search of mathematical and scientific works. They were encouraged by Peter the Venerable, Abbot of Cluny, to make the first translation of the Koran into Latin in the early 1140s. Peter wanted to understand better what the Moslems believed, the better to see how to convert them to Christianity.

Scholars working at Cordoba and Toledo especially began to attract the attention of northern European scholars who wanted to add to their resources. Dominicus Gundissalinus, author of an encyclopaedia in his own right, and John of Spain and Ben David among others, were asked by Bishop Raymond of Toledo (1126–51) to translate works of Aristotle and some of the Arab philosophers into Latin. Scholars from the north came to join them: Gerard of Cremona perhaps the most notable.

There was a gap between the reception of the New Logic and that of the principal philosophical works of Aristotle. Interest in the latter did not already exist and had to be prepared for by the gradual awakening of an enthusiasm for the mathematical subjects of the quadrivium and books on natural science. Aristotle offered something quite different from the treatment of Seneca or Pliny or Virgil's *Georgics*, something closer perhaps to the little-read *De Rerum Natura* of the Epicurean Lucretius. The translators had been getting on steadily with the work. Gerard of Cremona completed versions of the *Physics*, the *De Coelo et Mundo*, the *De Generatione* and the *Meteora*. By 1150 James of Venice had translated two of the most important works (for their later influence and philosophical significance) the *De Anima* and the *Metaphysics;* the third of these, the *Ethics*, did not arrive until the early thirteenth century when Robert Grosseteste made the first complete translation. The *Politics*, *Economics* and *Rhetoric* were translated from the Greek by 1250.

William of Moerbeke

In most cases, the older translations served the needs of such scholars as had taken Aristotle up, until in the second half of the century the Dominican William of Moerbeke (c.1215–86) set out to meet what was by now a demand for a more exact and scholarly rendering. He himself made the first translation of the *Poetics*, and was possibly also responsible for the first versions of other works.

Using the New Material: Alan of Lille

The new material began to have its effect upon old habits of thought even before it had been systematically taken into the syllabus of study and made a part of every scholar's training. Individual scholars quickly took up the new logic in the middle decades of the twelfth century, and some enterprising scholars even began to make use of the more difficult and challenging Greek works in original works of their own. Alan of Lille, one of the best-read men of the later twelfth century (d.1202) sought out every new work which came into France. He was a great absorber of other men's ideas. His particular taste was for obscure works such as the *hermetica*. From the *Asclepius* he derived one of the many Platonic motifs to appear in his writings, his picture of man poised half-way between angel and beast, able, by effort to become a god, and by self-indulgence to become a beast. He had also perhaps encountered the *Liber de Causis*, which had newly arrived in a Latin translation.

Axiomatic Theology

Whether from this, or from his reading of Boethius' *De Hebdoma-dibus*, from Euclid, or the *Posterior Analytics* of Aristotle, Alan hit upon the idea of constructing an entire system of theology beginning with a single axiom about the unity of God, and proceeding from it to the uttermost limits of the field covered by Christian doctrine. In calling his work the *Regulae Theologicae* he adopted a view of the scope of theology which was still relatively new. When Abelard composed his *Theologia Christiana*, he took 'theology' to cover those subjects which it had embraced for Boethius: the divine nature, the Trinity and the Creator's relations with the natural world. Alan not only extends it to include the doctrine of the Redemption, but also to cover the sacraments – the whole of systematic theology as Aquinas conceived it. He was abusing the possibilities of the demonstrative method in even making the attempt, and his 'axioms' look less and less like self-evident first principles as he proceeds. But he was not the only scholar of the day to try. Nicholas of Amiens was even more ambitious, attempting a complete demonstrative theology in which he uses Euclidean methods. He begins by listing his axioms, postulates and definitions, and then uses them systematically to arrive at established 'theorems' which he is able to employ in their turn at the next stage of the argument.

Revival of Old Problems
What was happening was a revival of interest in the philosophical methods and problems with which philosophers of early Christian times had been concerned. Greek and Latin thought, long divorced, were reuniting. It became clearer than it had been for many centuries, how much philosophy there was in Augustine. Above all, philosophy began to appear a grand and stimulating discipline again, and even a rival to theology. Algazel describes the dilemma in his *Metaphysics*, taking the view that theology is so difficult a science that natural science forms a necessary preliminary study. But he concedes that it has been usual 'among the philosophers, to put natural science first'.

3. THE UNIVERSITIES

The world of learning into which the new Aristotle came was an academic world. Out of the motley schools of the twelfth century were developing the first universities to resemble modern ones, with faculties and syllabuses and degrees. The leaders in the higher studies of law, medicine and theology were, for a time, Bologna, Salerno, Montpellier and Paris respectively. The Arts were taught everywhere, but at Paris, where the Arts and Theology were both taught to an unusually high standard, and later at Oxford, the juxtaposition of the new texts with the old manuals of grammar, logic, rhetoric and mathematics, and with the syllabus of theology, soon began to make apparent the incompatibilities of the two systems. It was impossible to avoid noticing the difficulties of reconciling what was taught out of the books of the philosophers with those aspects of Christian doctrine which dealt with the same or closely-related problems about the origin and nature of the soul, the creation of the world, and so on.

Pope Gregory IX saw the danger as early as 1228, and warned the masters of Paris not to teach a theology tainted by *philosophorum figmentes* or the 'ferment of worldly knowledge'. Some attempt in Paris was made to ban even private lectures on the writings of Aristotle and their commentaries. But some use of the material was unavoidable. At the new university of Toulouse in 1229 freedom to teach Aristotle was made an incentive to draw the best masters.

The Attempt at Synthesis

The most practical course of action for scholars anxious that the new philosophy should not disrupt the old orthodoxy appeared to be to make a synthesis, and attempt to reconcile the two, or at least to set out in order as much of the new learning as possible. This encouraged the production of massive works of comprehensive erudition made up in the *modus expositionis*, the 'expounding way' rather than in the *modus commentarii*, which involved detailed commentary on the text as it stood, rather than summary and explanation in brief. By summarising a scholar could include accounts of a vast range of texts. The masters responsible for much of this work were members of the two new Mendicant Orders, the Dominicans and Franciscans.

4. THE FRIARS

The founding of the orders of the friars in the early thirteenth century brought together again two traditions of learning which had been drifting apart. Although many masters in the schools spent periods of their lives in monasteries in the twelfth century (Peter Abelard) or retired to monastic life (Thierry of Chartres, Alan of Lille), the traditions of learning which were cultivated in monastic schools were different from those bred in the cut and thrust of the schools outside, where masters competed for students; the students themselves were often anxious to get themselves noticed so that they might find an opening in a career in the ecclesiastical civil service (John of Salisbury). Another Englishman, Stephen Langton, came into the mind of Innocent III, an old acquaintance at Paris, when he wanted a candidate to offer King John of England for the Archbishopric of Canterbury.

The Dominicans were designed from the first to be both a

religious Order and a body of learned men. They were primarily preachers, founded to convert the Cathar heretics in Spain and the south of France. It was important that as preachers they should be soundly grounded in theology so that they could meet any argument the heretics might put to them. They gave their considerable energies to setting up, in the very university towns and elsewhere, schools of theological instruction, not open to the world at large, but constituting (as many monastic schools of the twelfth century had not) an attractive alternative to the teaching of the conventional masters in the universities. They began to draw the most able young men away from them.

St. Francis had had a quite different vision of the mission of his friars, but not long after his death we find the Franciscan Order beginning to compete with the Dominicans in scholarship, trying to win the principal chairs at Oxford and Paris.

Perhaps the most important immediate result of this was the impetus it gave to the study of theology. Theology had always been something of a minority subject, with perhaps no more than a dozen or twenty masters in Paris in the late twelfth century. Now that the best minds of the day were engaged upon it, the question of what to do with Aristotle was pressing.

The Dominicans were given confusing instructions in their constitution of 1228. They were not to make a proper study of the books of philosophers or pagans, but they were allowed to look into them briefly. The attitude of most of their scholars was cautious and mistrustful. Nevertheless, they were, as a body, less inclined from the beginning than the Franciscans were to think Aristotle simply wrong.

5. ALBERT THE GREAT

In 1223 Albert the Great (1200–1280) became a Dominican at Padua where he had perhaps been a student of the *Artes* and possibly medicine. He taught in Dominican schools all over Germany, and then in Paris from c.1245. He was one of the promising young men Jordan of Saxony sought out in the universities after the death of St. Dominic, recruiting them into the Order so that Dominican preachers should be of the highest possible intellectual quality. Albert's most famous pupil at Paris was Thomas Aquinas, another recruit, this time from Naples.

Albert was recalled to Cologne in 1248, to organise the Dominican school there which was being turned into a *studium generale* or university-level institution. It was usual for Dominican friars to be trained to preach and teach in their own country because they knew the language and the local customs. Albert's time in Paris studying philosophy had, however, greatly enlarged his ideas.

Natural Science

From an early age Albert had shown an interest in natural science. He describes how he observed the effects of the earthquakes of 1222–3 in Lombardy. Now he began to study Aristotle and to find his work so valuable that he wanted to reconcile his teachings with those of the Church. He certainly did not want to see Aristotle censored and suppressed as some were already demanding. He says that members of his own Order encouraged him in this: 'Our intention in natural science is to satisfy, to the best of our ability, the brothers of our Order who have, for several years now, been asking us to put together for them a sort of book on physics, which would provide them with a complete natural science and make them well-equipped to understand the books of Aristotle'. Accordingly, Albert broadened the curriculum at Cologne, adding, for example, the study of Pseudo-Dionysius and Aristotle's *Ethics*, and much besides.

He made a gigantic effort to create a record of all learning, new and old. He was obliged, as his rival Roger Bacon sourly said, to make his own philosophy because he had never taken a degree in Arts. Faced with the difficulty that there were gaps in the Aristotelian corpus, and gaps, too, in what was available to him, he thought it important to give a complete account, and set about filling the gaps himself.

Supplementing Aristotle

Aristotle, Avicenna, Alfarabi, Gabirol, Augustine, are all found side by side in Albert's writings. He tried to be fairminded. He says, for example, judicially: 'If we consider the soul in itself we shall agree with Plato' (that is, that it is an independent substance); 'if we consider that it is a form giving life to the body, we shall agree with Aristotle.' The addition of non-Aristotelian material was necessary, he thought, even when he was giving an account of Aristotle's teaching. 'Our method will be to follow the sequence of Aristotle's thought, and to say in explanation and demonstration of it whatever may seem necessary . . . also we shall put in digressions, so as to clarify difficulties as they arise, or to add whatever may make the Philosopher's thought clearer to anyone.' Albert's concession to the authoritativeness of Aristotle's text is to 'say clearly' wherever he has departed from it or made additions to it.

6. ROGER BACON

Albert's rival and opponent Roger Bacon (c.1214–92) appears to have studied at both Oxford and Paris, where he was perhaps the first to give lectures on those books of Aristotle which had been banned. He became a Franciscan in the late 1150s (c.1157). Like Albert the Great he tried to catalogue the whole corpus of contemporary learning, but with the intention which was peculiarly his own, of encouraging the study of the sciences at first hand – that is, to avoid carrying even further the current mania for writing books about books. His first grand work, the *Opus Maius*, was sent to Pope Clement IV (1265–8), who had been an acquaintance of his at Paris. The *Opus Minus* was sent after it, and the *Opus Tertium*, both shorter, and intended to explain the first. In all three Bacon tried to encourage the reform of Christian learning.

Bacon had a great respect for Avicenna who seemed to him the 'leader and prince' (*dux et princeps philosophiae*) after Aristotle and a taste for experimental science, and for astrology and alchemy in particular. He was outspoken in their defence, and he brought himself under suspicion. He made enemies by criticising the great among contemporary theologians. After the death of Clement IV in 1268, Bacon had no protector and in the 1270s he was disciplined by his order and apparently restrained from writing. But the *Compendium Studii Theologiae* has all the marks of the old Roger Bacon.

Scholarly Standards: The New Criticism

Bacon had some insight into the historical complexion of the problem of reconciling philosophy and Christian truth. He examined the work of the past in the light of the circumstances in which it was composed – something which had been attempted by Peter Abelard in the *Sic et Non*, but which was unpopular with the orthodox ecclesiastical authorities because it made too much room for accusations of human error in the works of the Fathers. Bacon accused his own contemporaries of neglecting many things known to the ancients, for example the study of mathematics and languages, because they did not know their value. Some topics were neglected because the Fathers did not happen to discuss them, but Bacon pointed out that the Fathers lived in another time, when different things were important; moreover, they were not faultless; for example, Augustine used to criticise Jerome. These scholars of old were ignorant of foreign languages. Plato was translated, but not Aristotle, and the Fathers (here Bacon is referring to the Latin

Fathers) made use of Plato but not Aristotle as a result. Augustine himself translated the *Categories* (the *Categoriae Decem* was still attributed to Augustine), and Bacon praises both Augustine and Boethius for their translations, but he insists that the writings of the past lack something in being without the influence of the full works of Aristotle.

7. BONAVENTURE

One effect of this new consciousness of philosophy was to make the philosophical elements in Augustine more apparent. St. Bonaventure (1221–74), an Italian who became a Franciscan between 1238 and 1243 found Augustine so superior as a philosopher and Aristotle so full of doubtful matter that he wanted to see the study of Aristotle eliminated from the schools. Bonaventure's career as a lecturer at Paris from 1248–55 was interrupted by one of the periodic disputes in which the masters who were not members of either Order of Friars tried to restrain the Friars from their highly successful and competitive teaching, which was taking students from their classrooms and bread from their mouths. By 1257 Bonaventure was back, with his Order reestablished, and the degree of Doctor to his name. Early in 1257, however, he had been elected Minister General of his Order, and from then until 1273, when he was made Cardinal bishop of Albano, he took a leading part in events within the Order and outside it. In the last year of his life he was present at the Council of Lyons of 1274, and there he died.

The Reasonableness of Faith

Bonaventure was as confident as Anselm had been that the Christian faith could be made acceptable to all reasonable beings. He shared Augustine's picture of a divine illumination gradually making all things clear to the minds of the faithful. This can be seen at work in the mind's progressive mastery of the subject-matter of human knowledge.

The journey of understanding is most graphically described by Bonaventure in his *Journey of the Mind towards God*. He explains that the subject-matter of theology is that which a Christian must believe, in order to call himself a Christian. He may believe it by simple faith. Or he may ask questions about it. The task of theology is to make the 'credible' (*credibile*) into something 'intelligible' (*intelligibile*). This is not easy, or even possible, in every area of theology. The higher the mystery the larger the element of faith required and the more reason lingers as a mere follower. In the *Itinerarium Mentis ad Deum* we pursue the path of the mind towards the ultimate vision of God, beginning in the sensible world, with the perceptions of the senses, and proceeding to higher and more abstract understanding. 'This universe of things is a ladder whereby we may ascend to God, since among these things some are God's footprints, some temporal, some eternal, and hence, some outside of us, and some inside; it follows that we must begin with God's footprints, which are corporeal, temporal and outside us, and so enter on the Way that leads to God. We enter in within our own souls, which are images of the eternal God, spiritual and interior to us, and this is to enter into the truth of God. Finally we must reach out beyond and above ourselves to the region of the eternal and supereminently spiritual and look to the First Principle of all' (*It. Ment.*). There can be no going astray.

The Existence of God

For Bonaventure as for Anselm the very act of thinking implies the existence of God. He paraphrases Augustine and Anselm: 'Such is the truth of the Divine's Being that it cannot (with assent) be thought not to be'. (*Tanta est veritas divini esse, quod cum assensu non potest cogitari non esse*). 'It is the same thing to say that God exists as to say that God is God'. (*Si Deus est Deus, Deus est*). 'Being so certainly exists that it cannot be conceived as not existing . . . How could the human mind surmise that the particular things with which it comes in contact are defective and incomplete if it did not possess some knowledge of a Being who is utterly devoid of imperfection?'

FOR FURTHER READING

Cambridge History of Later Mediaeval Philosophy, ed. N. Kretzmann, A. Kenny, J. Pinborg, (Cambridge, 1982).

Bougerol, J. G., *Introduction to the Works of Bonaventure* (Paris, 1964).

Gilson, E., *The Philosophy of St. Bonaventure* (Paris, 1938).

Weisheipl, J. A., ed., *Albertus Magnus and the Sciences* (Toronto 1980).

9

THOMAS AQUINAS

The attempt to give a summary account of the new material so that it might conveniently be taught as in the works of Albert the Great and Roger Bacon, and the preference for leaving it largely out of account, typical of Bonaventure, were, in a sense, ways of avoiding the difficulties of a reconciliation between the Christian faith and ancient philosophy. It was Aquinas (c.1225–74) who confronted the problem directly, and with optimism.

He was an Italian, educated first at the abbey St. Benedict founded at Monte Cassino near Naples, and then at university in Naples. There he was attracted to the opportunities the Dominican Order offered him to combine his faith with scholarship. The Order made good use of him. He was sent to Paris, where he had Albert the Great as his master, and then he went with Albert to Cologne, to help run the new Dominican *studium generale* He returned to Paris and taught there, and was sent to various Dominican schools to set standards and to organise the syllabus. A year or two before his death, he returned at last to Naples, in 1272, where he was to set up a Dominican school.

The Authority of Revelation

His method of reconciling philosophy and theology was to regard philosophical progress as cumulative. The philosophical teaching of the pagans could then be reviewed in the light of the Christian revelation, so as to see how it had developed. This method was eminently sensible, given Aquinas' first assumption that, while in all other sciences argument from authority is weaker than argument from reason, in theology argument from authority is the strongest possible form of argument. The authority in question is not human but divine, and so it takes precedence over everything which can be established by human reason. It is necessary in theology to go about seeking the truth in a different way from that which is proper elsewhere: not by framing a definition or looking to what is self-evidently true to reason, but by considering the 'effects' God has, in the natural world as its Creator, or within the sinful soul by grace.

The Relationship of Theology and Philosophy

Although theology differs from philosophy first in requiring a quite distinct approach, it is not simply a separate subject. Aquinas's first question in the *Summa Theologica* is whether theology is anything more than a branch of philosophy. Boethius would seem to imply that it is not, in his *De Trinitate*, when he divides philosophy into physics, mathematics and theology. Aquinas is at some pains to establish not only that theology is more than that would indicate, but that it provides an essential complement and supplement to philosophy, without which man could not have been saved. If we define philosophy as knowledge which can be obtained by reason, as distinct from that which can be obtained by revelation, Aquinas would deny that such knowledge is enough. He believes that it is necessary for man's salvation that in addition there should be a knowledge revealed by God. God is himself beyond the direct and unaided reach of human reason (Isaiah 64.4). In order to know where to look, man must be given help. God must reveal himself, so as to show where he is to be found and what he is.

Thus Aquinas establishes the superior status of theology. It begins to appear, as he goes on, a comprehensive science, dealing with things which belong to different philosophical sciences, and considering each as it can be known in the divine light. Both speculative and practical branches of philosophy are included in theology. More, it is a powerful director of a science, treating even practical matters, such as human acts, in relation to the way in which its branches bring man to the perfect knowledge of God in which human happiness consists. So we come to the point where Aquinas can say that theology is nobler than all other sciences. Its superiority consists in two things: in having other sciences derive from it, and in the degree of certitude it establishes. Theology has as its subject-matter the divine being from whom all else derives, and so all other sciences may be said to derive from it. And it establishes a certitude which rests upon divine revelation, not upon mere human reason.

Analogy

One of Aquinas' most celebrated doctrines of philosophical theology is his theory of analogy. What he has to say about the subject is brief and his theory is incomplete because he did not work out his view on analogical predication. The task was completed for him in the sixteenth century by Thomas Cajetan in his treatise *On Analogical Names*.

Aquinas's own principal concern was with the difficulty of steering a way between two pitfalls. On the one hand, if we hold that nothing can be said of God at all because he is beyond the reach of human language, we fall into agnosticism; we cannot think or talk about God. On the other hand, if we take human language as being equally and indiscriminately applicable to God and to his creatures, we reduce him to the level of the limited beings normally called by these names.

It had been suggested by earlier thinkers (Anselm is especially clear on this) that when we use the word 'just' of God we speak of his substance, and at the same time of his mercy or goodness or truth, for all these attributes are one in God; they are not accidents which can change. When we speak of a just man we say something about a single quality of the man, an accident separable from his substance (he will not cease to be the same man if he ceases to be just). Aquinas proposes a device technically more sophisticated: that of an 'analogy of being'. His idea is that we arrive at a quasi-knowledge by comparing God with his creation. This kind of knowledge does not grasp the divine nature as it is in itself, but to some extent it illuminates it.

Two of the difficulties this theory raises are pinpointed by Aquinas himself. Suppose that in the case of things in the created world we compare A, B, C and D. If we know A, B and C, and we can say that A is to B as C is to D, then we can arrive at D. But if we make a comparison of A and B on the 'creation' side of the equation with a C and D on the divine side, we have not one but two unknown quantities, and so we cannot arrive at C or D. 'In all names which are said of many in an analogical sense, they must all be said with reference to one thing, and therefore this one thing must be placed in the definition of them all'. Or if we say that A is to B as B is to C the comparison will bring us to C only if B is identical in both cases. It will never be identical where A is human or creaturely and C divine. 'As smiling said of a field means only that the field in the beauty of its flowering is like to the beauty of the human smile according to the likeness of the *proportion*, so the name of "lion" said of God means only that God manifests his strength in his works, as a lion in his. Thus it is clear that as they are said of God, the signification of names can be defined only from what is said of creatures'.

There is a second unsatisfactory area if we consider causation as a common ground between the two things compared. An effect always resembles its cause, and an agent acts to produce its like. This applies, however, only when cause and effect belong to the same genus. This cannot be the case with God and his creation. God does not belong to a genus. Aquinas can find only 'existence' in common and even here there is a problem because the existences involved are different 'inasmuch as God exists in his own essence, and other things are beings by participation'.

There are other difficulties, too, implicit in Aquinas' thinking on the reconciliation of Pseudo-Dionysian principles of negative theology with the attempt to make any positive affirmation about God. In the proofs of God's existence, too, there is no mention of analogy. God is not spoken of as 'resembling' a first unmoved Mover, but *as* the first Unmoved Mover'.

Aquinas does not believe that man possesses as a gift of God a sense which, when it is developed by self-discipline and by the aid of grace, is capable of attaining the vision of God as he is. He holds that the human intellect cannot conceive of spiritual or immaterial things directly, but only by working from things which can be perceived by the senses, and which belong in the world of space and time.

The Existence of God

For this reason, Aquinas' five ways of proving the existence of God all begin from the evidence of the present in the created world, or ultimately rest upon such evidence. It is Aquinas' experience that God's existence is not self-evident to all men. That is one ground of his quarrel with Anselm's proof. It needs to be demonstrated because man has no intuitive direct perception of the divine being. He has to reason his way towards it, beginning with the evidence of his senses.

Thomas's point of departure in each case is the same. We can see that the sensible world must have a cause. And we can understand causation only if we postulate some First Cause which brings the chain of cause and effect to an end. We can see this most easily in the case of movement, because it is common enough to see something set in motion. The mover is separate from the thing moved. It must itself have a mover, and so on back to the first Mover of all. If there were no such mover it would be impossible to understand how the motion began in the first place. A similar sequence can be traced for causes and effects, for beings which are in process always of becoming, for the hierarchy of perfections in things which are intelligible only if they are understood in terms of an ultimate standard of perfection.

Faith and Reason

Until Aquinas began to take the problem of Aristotle in hand, the interpretations available to most Latin-speaking scholars were those of Arab thinkers. Averroes in particular made the study of Aristotle a matter of adopting a position on the question of the relationship between philosophy and theology. Averroes wanted to keep the two apart in a way Aquinas showed to be impossible, if the opening arguments of his *Summa Theologica* were to stand. Aquinas's commentaries began to make their impact, but not in time to prevent serious trouble from brewing. Siger of Brabant, a Master of Arts, at Paris, presented Aristotle from an Averroist point of view, and, in addition, he interpreted the idea of God as an efficient cause in such a way as to suggest that he was not a creative efficient cause, but merely a Prime Mover. In this and in other points he contradicts Christian orthodoxy and it was here that he raised the crucial point for the future of Aristotelian studies in the universities. If a philosophical conclusion contradicts Christian doctrine, is it possible for it to be true?

In order to curb this dangerous possibility the bishop of Paris, Stephen Tempier, issued a condemnation in 1270, of the propositions that the intellect of all men is one and numerically identical – a reference to the theory of the single Agent Intellect; that man cannot be truly said to understand; that human choice is not free but under necessity; that the heavenly bodies govern the events upon earth as the astrologers of old believed; that the world is eternal and had no beginning; that the soul is the 'form' of the man; that human acts are not under divine providence, and others, all reflecting old disputes.

It is not clear whether these views had all been professed by the same man or at the same time; more probably they seemed dangerous precisely because they were widely canvassed and no one individual was responsible for them. A set of questions addressed to Albert the Great in the same year, and answered by him in a treatise On Fifteen Problems, cover many of the same points. The significant thing about them is that all of them had been brought into prominence by the advent of the Aristotelian material. Albert the Great was not unduly perturbed. He suggests that if philosophers were rather better at philosophising, they might see these problems in a more sensible light. A competent theologian can make short work of them.

But the Papacy saw the danger as great enough to merit a condemnation in 1277 which attempted to scotch the notion that there could be a double standard of truth, one for the philosophers and one for the theologians, that is, that the same proposition could be simultaneously true from the point of view of faith and false from the point of view of reason. The condemnation merely expressed a widespread concern and exasperation about the mistaken habits of the philosophers; it says nothing new; its chief novelty is to take a defensive stand, to acknowledge an opposition between theology and philosophy, to see philosophy as the enemy.

It may also have achieved something else. 1277 emerged as a watershed; before that year thinkers assumed sometimes without much conscious choice, that the Greek view of things had force; after this date, Duns Scotus and Ockham tried to get away from the 'necessitarianism' of much Greek thinking, to a way of looking at God as a being who allows the world to flow out from his intelligible perfection as necessary consequences follow from a principle, but without himself being in any way compelled.

Boethius of Dacia

Boethius of Dacia, a Danish scholar teaching at the University of Paris in the 60s and 70s of the thirteenth century, is an example of the type of scholar who suffered in these circumstances. He had been an Averroist until the Condemnation of 1277, and then he seems to have entered the Dominican Order. He is the author of a large corpus, including the *Quaestiones* on Aristotle's *De Generatione et Corruptione*, a treatise on the *Eternity of the World*, and *De Summo Bono*, on the highest Good. He was interested, in short, in exactly the questions which were at issue in the Condemnation of 1277. The opening of the *De Aeternitate Mundi* sums up his dilemma well. He wants to bring faith and reason together, although he recognises them to be distinct things. Not to believe what cannot be demonstrated to the reason is heretical. To wish to believe without a reason being given is not 'philosophical'. Boethius wishes to bring about a *concordia* between faith and philosophy.

Duns Scotus

Duns Scotus was born in Scotland in 1266; he became a Franciscan as a young man and studied at Oxford and at Paris. In 1297, he returned to Oxford, teaching theology. In 1301 he returned to Paris to begin work on a doctorate in theology. Two years later, he was banished, along with many others who had supported the Papacy against the king of France, but the interruption was brief, and he was able to complete his doctorate in 1305 after which he was sent to Cologne to teach, dying there in 1307. He composed a treatise on the First Principle (*De Primo Principio*), some questions on the *Metaphysics* of Aristotle, some Quodlibetal Questions, and two commentaries on Peter Lombard's *Sentences*.

Scotus took Avicenna's side against Averroes, believing that the object of theology is God and that the object of philosophy is being. He took a pessimistic view of the powers of the human intellect. It cannot understand being as an abstraction, but must work by abstracting from the experience of the senses. The best a philospher can do is to go as high as he can up the ladder of abstraction.

Scotus' commentary on the *Sentences* is much concerned with the contemporary controversy between the philosophers and the theologians as to whether man in this life needs a *cognitio supernaturalis*. The philosophers concentrate upon the perfection of nature, and have nothing to do with supernatural perfection. The theologians know the defect of nature (because of the Fall of Adam) and the necessity for grace and supernatural perfections. The difference, then, lies between those who believe nature to be undamaged and a source of all the knowledge we need, and those who believe it to be profoundly corrupted by the presence of evil in the world, so that something more than the evidence it provides is needed by us.

FOR FURTHER READING

Chenu, M. D., *Towards Understanding St. Thomas* (tr. Chicago, 1964).
Gilson, E., *Jean Duns Scot* (Paris, 1952).
Patterson, R. L., *The Concept of God in the Philosophy of Aquinas* (London, 1933).
Weisheipl, J. A., *Friar Thomas d'Aquino* (Oxford, 1974).
Cambridge History of Later Mediaeval Philosophy.

10

THE MODERN WAY

In the second half of the fourteenth century scholars began to identify themselves as 'modernists', or as followers of the 'old way' (*via antiqua*). This was in part a distinction between 'Aristotelians' and 'Augustinians', and in some later mediaeval universities the student chose between two syllabuses. It is not easy to identify the beginnings of the new movement but certainly one of the founders of the *Via Moderna* was William of Ockham (c.1300–1349), an Englishman, who became a Franciscan, trained mainly at Oxford and a controversial figure, not only as a logician, but also as a writer of political treatises.

By now scholasticism was at its high point of technical precision. A number of Ockham's *Quodlibetal Questions* survive, records of formal debates at which the master settled such questions as whether it can be proved by natural reason that there is only one God and whether 'paternity' may be 'distinguished' from the Father. In some cases, the question is trivial; in others it is of the first importance; in others again it is a matter of a technical problem of the proper use of terms, as here.

Ockham was able to handle the technicalities of the schools with mastery but he was also capable of perceiving the large issues which sometimes underlay them.

Universals
Ockham made a radical new approach to the old question of the relationship between words and things, and in particular between general words and words for classes on the one hand, and for specific things on the other. Ockham's leading idea was that every positive thing which exists outside the soul is singular. A collective noun, or any sign which indicates a plurality, is still itself a singular.

Universals are signs which are not universal in their own being. Their 'universality' lies in their signification, not in themselves.

Ockham's account of universals takes almost to its extreme limit the 'nominalist' view which had appeared in earlier mediaeval centuries, among thinkers who regarded language merely as a set of conventional symbols devised by man to signify things.

Ockham takes issue with the problems raised by 'man' in, for example, 'man is an animal'. He wants to insist that nothing general or universal is meant by 'man' here, but that 'man' stands for each particular individual man in turn.

The Knower and the Known

Mediaeval thinkers had been in the habit of looking for an intermediary between the knower and what he knows. Such was the difference between the intellect which knows and the object of its knowledge that something seemed to be needed to act as a vehicle between them, some means by which the object could be turned into something the intellect could grasp. This was commonly thought of as a 'species'. Ockham saw no need to postulate the existence of species. He found no hint of them in his own experience. When something is red or shiny, he suggests, we simply see it to be red or shiny. We do not see a 'redness' or 'shininess' which we may regard as the species of red or shiny, and which enables us to identify the red or shiny in the particular case before us. Ockham regards the intellect and the object of its knowledge as capable of their own of bringing about a grasp in the intellect of the object before it. Certainly this is the case for objects which can be perceived by the senses, he argues, and 'abstract' knowledge can be seen to proceed from that.

Implications

If Ockham's principle is applied to the traditional problems of theology in its relations with philosophy, the picture looks bleak. Answers to large abstract questions will be negative, or at best uncertain. Metaphysics does not flourish where only the particular seems real. Ockham will not allow that universals are present even in the mind of God. Ideas he believes to be nothing but the specific things God can produce. He will have nothing to do with the chain of cause and effect which seemed to Aquinas so powerful a proof of the existence of God. Ockham restricts himself severely to the observation that, when a given thing is present, something we have fallen into the habit of calling its 'effect' habitually follows.

John Buridan

The *moderni* who followed Ockham's line of thought came to be known as *nominales* or *terministae* because of the view they took of the nature and function of language. Ockham's doctrine was censured in 1339 by the Parisian Faculty of Arts. It was not an easy position to grasp, and Adam Wodeham (d.1349), who had been a pupil of Ockham's at Oxford, wrote a preface for Ockham's logic in which he complained that many of his contemporaries were neglecting the study of logic and teaching errors out of ignorance, or unintelligible propositions, because they had not bothered to master the technical aspects of their art. There was no doubt some justice in this. But despite the rebarbative nature of Ockham's teaching he had a considerable body of followers among the most able of the next generation.

At Paris the leading spirit among the terminists was John Buridan. He was Rector of the University of Paris in 1328, and was still active more than thirty years later. He interested himself in both logic and metaphysics. As a logician he was a strict nominalist, but he tried to make sense of the difference Ockham had not succeeded in explaining away, between the way in which we think about concrete and particular things (this rabbit), and the way in which we think about a species (rabbit) or a genus. Buridan suggests that a universal can be grasped in two ways: as signifying singular things in a universal way (Ockham's position) or as signifying the universal 'way' or 'mode' in which our concept of rabbit takes hold of the rabbit in question.

2. JEAN GERSON

The clear-cut opposition between the *via antiqua* and the *via moderna* became blurred, with further work on both. As a scholar John Gerson (d.1429) was touched by these developments. Much of his work is a commentary upon them. He had been a pupil of Peter of Ailly, who adhered to the school of Ockham and Buridan, and in 1395 he succeeded him as Chancellor of the University of Paris. But he was not a full-blown nominalist at heart. It was rather that he regarded the realists as enemies of the truth. He disliked Plato more than he loved Aristotle. He saw the academic world as divided into two camps, and his own task as one of defending sound doctrine against heresy. This was something new. In patristic times the Church had had and needed apologists against the enemies of orthodoxy who called themselves Christians, and during the mediaeval centuries when the schools were becoming universities some individuals such as Peter Abelard and Gilbert of Poitiers had been brought to trial for their opinions; when the philosophical possibilities of Aristotle had gone to some men's heads in the thirteenth century, the Church had condemned certain propositions. But never before had the whole academic community appeared to be divided over a matter which split philosophers and theologians alike into parties, and which had to do with the very nature of language and of perception.

Gerson perceived the root of the difficulty early. In his *De Concordia Metaphysicae cum Logica*, he pointed out that much evil arose from the habit of conflating the spheres of logic and metaphysics. If logic was to deal with the nature of things and metaphysics with problems of language, the result was confusion. This was the way Ockham's logical revolution had been leading, and it had been followed by the realists, too, as they took up their opposing positions. Gerson had a further complaint, again dealing with a major problem of the century: that the study of philosophy encouraged a *Vain Curiosity in Matters of Faith*. He gave two 'lessons' on this theme, in 1402, in which he tells in an allegory of the besetting scholarly vices of the time: curiosity and the desire to be different, envy, contentiousness, disputatiousness, obstinacy, defence of error, a predilection for the literal, an unwillingness to give up one's own opinions, a dislike of simplicity and humility.

Gerson belongs with Bonaventure – whom he admired – in his suspicion of a philosophy got out of hand, and especially (for he is not opposed to all philisophy) the philosopy of the pagans, of Plato himself and the Moslems who had held such doctrines as that of a second Intelligence caused by the First.

The danger of bringing together philosophy and theology was the same in Gerson's day as it had always been – that there were natural points of contact and areas of common ground, which it was tempting to exploit and to try to expand.

3. NICHOLAS OF CUSA

If Jean Gerson wrote as a worried academic striving to heal the breach and bring the contemporaries to agreement on the importance of keeping philosophy under control, Nicholas of Cusa's (1401–64) approach was altogether more confident. He studied both law at Padua and theology at Cologne. He was never a professional schoolmaster, but an ecclesiastic, and so he had perhaps a certain detachment from the squabbles Gerson looked on with such distaste in the schools. He took exactly the opposite view from Gerson of how the conflict was to be resolved. Instead of trying to find yet another logical device for proving the case for or against mysticism, he turned to Plotinus.

Learned Ignorance

Plotinus represented simplicity, as against the vast complexity into which too much logic too finely chopped had brought contemporary scholarship. Nicholas was attracted by the idea of contemplating something which cannot be known because it cannot be measured against anything, which cannot be analysed, which is not simply larger than anything we know, but of another order, beyond magnitude. There can be no operation, intellectual or practical, which we can perform upon it, no addition or subtraction. We can have towards it at best a 'learned ignorance' (*docta ignorantia*), and Nicholas takes this as the theme of his *De Docta Ignorantia*. This infinite is without opposite or contrary (it is, as it were, both infinitely small and infinitely great). The infinite is a paradox expressed by Nicholas in an axiom to be found as early as the late twelfth century in the *Book of the Twenty-Four Philosophers* and in Alan of Lille's *Regulae Theologicae:* God is a sphere whose centre is everywhere and whose circumference is nowhere.

The advantage of this view was that it freed the mind from the old Aristotelian preoccupation with contraries. (In the commentaries on the *Categories* one of the questions asked about quantity, quality, relation and so on in turn, was whether examples of each may have contraries). The habit of looking everywhere for oppositions (in metaphysics) and contradiction (in logic) no doubt underlay in part the difficulty in which contemporary scholars found themselves.

Nicholas was a mystic. Here lay part of the attraction for him of the ideas of Plotinus and Hermes Trismegistus and Pseudo-Dionysius. Yet he wanted, not to arrive at a concept of God, as philosophers and theologians had striven to do since the earliest Christian times, but to reach a point beyond the forming of any idea of God. This was to go back to the notion that God is beyond and above Being. He 'is' not. There is therefore no commensurability between God and anything which exists, just as there is none between the infinite and the finite.

This incommensurability gives rise to apparent paradoxes, but it also shows the way in which they may be made to disappear. The very notion of *Docta Ignorantia* is paradoxical, and Nicholas opens his treatise with the challenge: 'How to know is not to know'. In studying the natural world, he explains, we arrive progressively at greater and greater certainty. If there are many stages in this process it is a laborious and difficult business to grasp the truth. If there are few, it is easy. This has to do with the closeness of that which we know already to that which we come to know, which Nicholas calls *proportio*. The most learned men are those who recognised how little they know, how far they are in *proportio* from understanding. Socrates thought he knew nothing and Solomon said that everything was difficult and inexplicable in words, and they were profoundly wise. The thing we should strive for is to know that we are ignorant (*desideramus scire nos ignorare*).

In order 'to know nothing to the full', it is necessary to examine the nature of the fullness with which we know it, that is, the nature of the maximum, continues Nicholas in paradoxical vein. Here we can see how close he is to Anselm, the unconscious Platonist. The great, according to Nicholas, is that than which nothing can be greater (*quo nihil maius esse potest*). Greatness is the same thing as unity, which is also entity (*coincidit itaque maximitati unitas, quae est et entitas*). It is, in other words, that point at which all good things become one in the divine. It is also incomprehensible, because it is the point at which things leave the realm of human understanding, where the greatest and the smallest become one in infinity. It is beyond our arriving at by steps of comparison. Analogy with anything in the natural world will not do it (*non potest igitur finitus intellectus rerum veritatem per similitudinem praecise attingere*).

Anselm and Cusa Compared

This was exactly what Anselm came to find unsatisfactory about his chain of arguments in the *Monologion*. There he asked his readers to work upwards in their minds by thinking of all the good things they had and arranging them in steps or stages, so that they could understand that the supreme Good was the point at which they all met. But he thought that would show only that the supreme Good existed, not what it was. To show what it was required the performance of the same exercise for each of the divine attributes, and then again to show that they were all one.

In the *Proslogion* he attempted to approach the supreme by way of the very idea that it is the *maximum*, it other words, to go directly to the top. To establish that would be to establish, at a stroke, all the other things we believe about the supreme nature. But in neither the *Monologion* nor the *Proslogion* does he claim that by these ladder-climbing methods man can reason from the natural world to a full understanding of God as he is. He would have agreed with Nicholas of Cusa that the 'quiddity' of things, which is the 'truth of their being' is unattainable to human understanding.

Nicholas' emphasis, however, is that of his age – on the impropriety of using words to name God ('he has no proper name') and on the notion that any affirmative statement made of God is based on an analogy with his creatures and is therefore invalid.

Meister Eckhardt

In certain respects Nicholas of Cusa's line of thought had been anticipated by Meister Eckhardt (1260–1329), a Dominican who had taught at Paris, but who was chiefly influential as a preacher and a mystic. He placed an emphasis, as Gerson did, upon the notion that God is beyond being. He believe him to be pure Intellection, so that we may say 'God knows', even though we cannot say 'God is'. Eckhardt, like Gerson, sought to make his listeners think of God as one, to emphasise the incomprehensible simplicity of God.

Eckhardt possessed a powerful cloquence, but it was Nicholas of Cusa who had the greater intellectual power. He achieved a more lucid statement of the change of emphasis he proposed. It was in essence a shift away from the complexities into which the study of Aristotle had led contemporary thought, and towards a revived Platonism. It came at a time when an interest in classical literature was reawakening, and when Plato's works were soon at last to appear in the West in the original.

4. SUMMING UP

The mediaeval thinkers had struggled against an impediment which hampered them at every turn. They had access to Greek thought only at second hand, principally through the Romans, Cicero and Marius Victorinus and Augustine and Boethius, and later through the work of Arabic scholars, but always in Latin. They never had free choice of the literature. Circumstances fed it to them book by book, and the habit of cautious conservation and respect for the authority of the text which was laid down on the collapse of the empire in the fifth century, encouraged them to read it with sometimes myopic thoroughness.

Another limitation – or, rather a guiding principle of their thought which laid certain restrictions on the direction it might take – was the overriding requirement of maintaining Christian orthodoxy. Every scholar in Christendom from the end of the Roman world had been educated within the system of schools provided by or answerable to the Church. Every philosopher was, to this extent at least, also a theologian. The study of even the most elementary principles of the *artes* raised theological questions. Peter Abelard's *Dialectica* is full of them.

The result was to foster a vast ingenuity, in small things first, but also in larger ones. It was this intellectual dexterity, this skill in discovering oppositions to be reconciled or used to play off one against the other, which was to go out of theology at the Reformation in favour of a concern with fundamentals.

The end of the Middle Ages is marked by great diversity in theological endeavour. A variety of methods and assumptions were current. In a sense, theological science had lost direction – at least, it had no single direction. Scholasticism had developed out of the lively and sensitive experimental work of the twelfth century, but in the end it had become something of a dead hand: a methodology which fettered thought by guiding it too rigidly.

But the fresh approach of the humanists to textual criticism began to throw new light on the study of the Bible. There was a move away from logic and back to the Fathers in some quarters. These things, while they did not entirely overlay the late mediaeval tradition, gave a new slant to old problems. New possibilities for theological science became apparent.

The sixteenth century is remarkable for two movements which substantially altered the habits of thought of all educated men: one of these, the Reformation, was in part a theological revolution, and the other, the Renaissance, was in part a philosophical and scientific revolution. The two are, at root, a single movement, an attempt to throw off what had come to seem the shackles of logical method and to strike out in new directions. The revolution in secular learning was stimulated by the arrival of many new books from the ancient world, both Greek and Latin, and was, to begin with, the work of one or two leading spirits. But in neither case was there a wholesale throwing away of the work of the past. Deeply embedded in the writings of Martin Luther and even in the poems of John Donne nearly a century later, are assumptions to be met in mediaeval writers from late Roman times onwards. The old training in the liberal arts went on, much modified, but still the basis of both philosophy and theology.

FOR FURTHER READING

Carré, M. H., *Realists and Nominalists* (Oxford, 1946).
Leff, G., *William of Ockham* (Manchester, 1975).
Cambridge History of Later Mediaeval Philosophy, especially part XI.

PART II

REFORMATION TO ENLIGHTENMENT

1
THE RENAISSANCE
BACKGROUND

In the present section of this work, we shall be considering the development of the science of theology from the first period of the Reformation to the end of the Enlightenment. This period witnessed the formulation of the critical questions which have tended to dominate modern theology. In the present chapter, we propose to outline some developments which took place during the later mediaeval period which are important to the development of the science of theology during the first phase of the Reformation.

1. THE MODERN AUGUSTINIAN SCHOOL

The late mediaeval period saw a number of developments of significance to the understanding of the science of theology at the time of the Reformation itself. The first section of this work drew attention to the rise of logico-critical attitudes in the later Middle Ages, due chiefly to the influence of the *via moderna*, originating from fourteenth century thinkers such as William of Ockham (c.1285–1347) or Jean Buridan (c.1300–58). This development was, however, paralleled by a rise in historico-critical studies, particularly concerned with establishing accurate texts of the works of Augustine. Although the two attitudes tended to be associated with different schools, the logico-critical attitude being associated with 'modern' theologians such as William of Ockham and Pierre d'Ailly, and the historico-critical attitude with more conservative theologians such as Thomas of Strasbourg, it now appears that a distinctive school of thought emerged during the late fourteenth century which combined both attitudes. The 'modern Augustinian school', as it had come to be known, combined a critical attitude to the received tradition with an emphasis upon establishing accurate texts of writers such as Augustine.

The origins of this 'modern Augustinian school' are generally regarded as lying in the revival of an academic Augustinianism at Oxford and Paris during the fourteenth century. The increasing isolation of Oxford as a centre of European theological activity through the Hundred Years' War and the ravages of the Black Death inevitably led to the Parisian 'modern Augustinian school' eclipsing its English counterpart. Furthermore, the Oxford theologian particularly associated with the revival of academic Augustinianism (Thomas Bradwardine) was not a member of any religious order, whereas the leading theologian of the Parisian school (Gregory of Rimini) was a member of the Order of the Hermits of St Augustine. The tendency of religious orders to propagate the theological opinions of their leading members, evident in the Dominicans' attitude to Thomas Aquinas and the Franciscans' to Bonaventure and Duns Scotus, meant that Gregory's opinions were developed and transmitted by his fellow-religious, such as Hugolino of Orvieto and Dionysius of Montina, where Bradwardine's were not.

The Transmission of the Augustinian Tradition
In the earlier mediaeval period, the works of Augustine and other patristic writers were frequently passed down in the form of 'florilegia', or collections of 'Sentences', of which the most famous is the *Four Books of the Sentences* of Peter Lombard. Although the quotations from Augustine's works were, on the whole, accurate, they tended to be cited out of context. In view of the considerable authority with which the Middle Ages invested the writings of Augustine, it was clearly a matter of some importance to establish the African bishop's opinions with accuracy. A theologian of the early Middle Ages who wished to do this, however, would have found himself impeded by several significant obstacles. For example, there was no reliable way in which these 'sentences' could be verified with reference to the original sources. Furthermore, as these 'sentences' tended to be cited out of context, there was no reliable way of establishing whether their context demanded a different interpretation from that which their source had placed upon them. Finally, a large number of pseudo-Augustinian works were in circulation in the Middle Ages, such as the 'semi-Pelagian' *Hypognosticon*. In several instances, theologians of the earlier mediaeval period thus found themselves unwittingly ascribing to Augustine opinions which were nothing less than Pelagian, thus greatly complicating the already difficult task of interpreting him. The only real solution to these difficulties lay in the field of source-critical studies.

The Significance of Gregory of Rimini
The invention of printing would do much to remedy this situation. This, however, lay in the future. A partial solution to this difficulty developed during the fourteenth century, and is particularly associated with the great Parisian theologian Gregory of Rimini (d. 1358), one of the greatest champions of Augustine in the fourteenth century. For the sixteenth century Spanish theologian Andreas de Vega, Gregory was *maximus et studiosissimus divi Augustini propugnator*. Gregory established his reputation at least partly through his source-critical studies on the texts of Augustine, so that his *Commentary on the Sentences* was read widely to learn the opinions of Augustine, as much as those of Gregory himself. An example of Gregory's source-critical attitude may be found in his discussion of the *Epistola ad Demetriadem*, widely regarded as an authentic work of Jerome. Gregory correctly concluded that the work must be regarded as originating from Pelagius, rather than Jerome: 'Neither this passage nor the letter from which it is taken is the work of Jerome: it comes rather from Pelagius'.

The historico-critical approach to theology, characterised by its emphasis upon accuracy of patristic citations and studies of their sources, received a major encouragement though two developments during the fifteenth century. The first of these was the rise of the humanist movement in the Italian Renaissance of the fourteenth and fifteenth centuries, with its characteristic emphasis upon the need to return to original sources. This programme was frequently stated in the form of the slogan *ad fontes*, although this phrase could bear a number of differing interpretations. The second was the invention of printing, which is unquestionably the most important technological development ever to have affected the science of theology. We shall consider these two developments separately.

2. THE SIGNIFICANCE OF THE ITALIAN RENAISSANCE

The Meaning of Humanism
The humanist movement is particularly associated with the Italian Renaissance and the revival in classical studies which it engendered. The use of the term 'humanism' to refer to the Renaissance movement known by that name is, in fact, an anachronism: the term does not appear to have been used in the fourteenth or fifteenth centuries, having been invented in the early nineteenth century by a German educationalist to refer to a programme of secondary education which laid emphasis upon the Latin and Greek classics.

As used today, the term has overtones of religious agnosticism or secularism, and it is important to appreciate that the Renaissance movement which is now known as 'humanism' did not possess such features. The Italian term *umanista*, dating from the period of the Renaissance itself, was used to refer to a university teacher of the humanities (such as grammar, rhetoric or poetry), in precisely the same way as the term *legista* was used to refer to a university teacher of jurisprudence. Recent studies have discredited the traditional view that humanism originated outside a university context, all the evidence indicating that humanism was an *academic* movement, based upon the universities of Renaissance Italy, with its leading figures usually holding chairs of rhetoric or grammar. In essence, the humanist movement was characterised by its love of written and spoken eloquence, and its concern to promote these by every available means. Of the means available, the most significant by far was the study of classical sources, such as the writings of Cicero, in order to learn the art of rhetoric from them.

An earlier generation of scholars tended to regard humanism as embodying the new philosophy of the Renaissance, in conscious opposition to the Aristotelian scholasticism of the earlier mediaeval period. It was once argued that the Renaissance was essentially an age of Platonism (whether based upon Plato himself, or the neo-Platonism of Plotinus or Augustine) in contrast to the Aristotelianism of the previous period. Although this analysis had the undoubted attraction of simplicity, it was simply not capable of explaining the stubborn persistence of Aristotelianism throughout the period of the Renaissance – a persistence illustrated in the writings of Cremononi, Pomponazzi and Zabarella. Furthermore, there are no compelling reasons for supposing that the humanist movement actually did have any philosophical concerns of particular significance. All the evidence available suggests that the Italian humanists of the *Quattrocento* were professional rhetoricians whose interests in classical writers were rhetorical, rather than philosophical. The significance of the persistence of Aristotelianism during the period will become clear when we consider the revival of Aristotelianism within Reformed Orthodoxy during the later sixteenth century.

Return to the Sources
Renaissance humanism was characterised by its fascination with the period of classical antiquity, possibly reflecting the Stoic idea of history as static, with the same ideas and standards pertaining throughout its course. The humanist movement laid great emphasis

upon the study of classical literature as a means of promoting written and spoken eloquence, and as such was obliged to study classical scholarship and philology in order to gain inspiration and instruction from the great acknowledged masters of the past. This principle, among others, underlies the humanist principle encapsulated in the slogan *ad fontes!* This familiar slogan, however, encapsulates not merely the principle of returning to the sources of antiquity: the means by which these sources should be approached is also specified. The classical texts of antiquity should be approached directly, bypassing the glosses and interpretations of later commentators. For example, the work of Lorenzo Valla (c.1406–57) on the Justinian *Pandects* inspired many lawyers to return to first principles and original texts in their teachings, where they had once learned Roman law through a filter of Accursian and Bartholian glosses. The removal of such 'filters' by a direct appeal to the original sources was a major element of the humanist programme of reform. The related idea that the Christian church could be reformed by returning *ad fontes*, to the bible and the fathers of the church, was but one aspect of the general humanist respect for the sources of antiquity: the bible should be approached directly, rather than through intervening 'filters' such as the glosses and commentaries of the mediaeval period.

Lorenzo Valla
Recent scholarship has established a link between Italian humanism and the revival of interest in the writings of Paul, which became particularly significant towards the end of the fifteenth century. Of especial importance in this context was the critical achievement of Lorenzo Valla in approaching the text of scripture with a new philological precision. As Valla himself declared: 'There are those who believe that theology is not subject to the rules of grammar. But I say that theology must observe the usage of the spoken, and particularly the written, language.' Thus Valla drew attention to defects in the Vulgate translation of scriptural passages of no small theological importance – for example, the improper use of *sacramentum* to translate the Greek *mysterion* in Ephesians 5:31–2, which implied that marriage was a sacrament in the strict sense of the term, or the mistranslation of the Greek participle in Luke 1:28. In this latter instance, the Vulgate translated the angel's greeting to Mary as, 'Hail, full of grace (*gratia plena*)', implying that Mary was essentially a vessel of grace: Valla correctly pointed out that the participle in question could not bear this interpretation, so that the angelic salutation should be translated as 'Hail, favoured one'. Valla's critical philological achievement appears to have stimulated

others, such as Marsilio Ficino and Pico della Mirandola, to dream
of establishing a new synthesis between the Christian faith and
classical antiquity, which would succeed where Aristotelian scholasticism had failed.

The Critical Method

The essential prerequisite for this programme was access to biblical
texts in their original languages, philological competence, and a new
mode of exegesis which would set the gospel message free from the
scholastic categories within which it had been imprisoned in the
Middle Ages. This programme would be initiated in the early
sixteenth century at various centres throughout Europe, but perhaps
most competently at the University of Alcalà in Spain. Antonio
Lebrixa, widely regarded as the most brilliant scholar of the team
which produced the famous Complutensian Polyglot, summarised
the new programme of approach to scripture as follows:

> Where we are faced with variant readings in the Latin manu-
> scripts, we must go back to the Greek manuscripts; where there
> are disagreements between the different Latin manuscripts, or
> between the Latin and Greek manuscripts, of the Old Testament,
> we must seek the truth in the original Hebrew source.

It will be clear, however, that this ambitious programme demanded
materials and methods which were not available in the *Quattrocento*,
or which were then in their infancy. Nevertheless, the fact remains
that the Italian humanism of the late Renaissance did much to
provide the northern European reformers with the tools which they
needed to accomplish their task.

The European Diffusion of Renaissance Humanism

Although there has been intense dispute among scholars as to the
origins of northern European humanism, the weight of evidence
suggests that, at every stage of its complex development, it was
inspired, influenced and informed by the humanism of the Italian
Renaissance. This is not to say that northern European humanism
was without indigenous roots, but simply to acknowledge the
remarkable influence which the Italian Renaissance had upon the
spirit of the age. How, then, were the new ideas and methods of
the Renaissance transmitted to northern Europe? Three main chan-
nels of transmission appear to have been established.

First, through northern Europeans who studied in Italy, before
returning home, bringing with them the new ideas of the

Renaissance. An excellent example of this phenomenon is provided in the person of John Colet, who brought the philological expertise which he acquired in Italy back to Oxford, whence it is known to have influenced others, such as Thomas Linacre and Erasmus.

Second, through the foreign correspondence of the Italian humanists. The characteristic humanist emphasis upon written eloquence naturally led to considerable interest in correspondence as an artform, a means of promoting the ideals of the movement abroad. The full extent of this foreign correspondence is, in fact, only now becoming apparent, as the vast task of cataloguing and analysing the remarkable number of such letters scattered in libraries throughout the length and breadth of Europe proceeds.

Third, through the dissemination of manuscripts and printed books. The humanist practice of dedicating manuscripts or books to wealthy northern European patrons not only ensured that they found their way into important libraries, but also that they were widely read by the patron's personal circle. The personal library of Frederick the Wise at Wittenberg is known to have contained a considerable number of such works. In due course, the Reformers themselves would dedicate their works to notable patrons, with similar motives to their Renaissance counterparts – thus Melanchthon dedicated an edition of his *Loci Communes* to Henry VIII in the (ultimately vain) hope that it would further the cause of the Lutheran Reformation in England.

3. THE SIGNIFICANCE OF PRINTING

The invention of printing is of incalculable significance to the development of the science of theology, and is of particular importance in relation to the course of the Reformation. For the Reformers, printing provided a means by which the new ideas of the Reformation could be made available to anyone capable of reading, and of sufficient means to afford books. As studies of the social class of those brought before heresy trials in the early phase of the Reformation make clear, the early Protestants tended to belong to the educated classes.

The Role of Booksellers

Perhaps too little attention has been paid in the past to the role of booksellers in the propagation of the Reformation: for example, there are excellent reasons for suggesting that it was Thomas Garrard the book agent, rather than Thomas Cromwell the politician, who did more to lay the intellectual foundations of the English Reformation, simply by his making available the tools of the new biblical learning to those who were well placed to use them. The significance of printing in relation to our study lies in the manner in which it made accurate texts of the bible and the fathers available to those who wished to make use of them.

Advantages for Scholarship

Let us suppose that two theologians, at Cambridge and Paris respectively, wished to resolve a disputed point by drawing upon the considerable authority of Gregory of Rimini. The manuscripts which they would be obliged to use would give very different readings at points, so that the unfortunate theologians would have found themselves unable to agree concerning what Gregory *said*, let alone what he *meant*. The advent of printing meant that books could be transported from one country to another where the original manuscripts could not. The editor of a work could thus take or send proof copies of the text to libraries containing manuscripts, and variant readings could be recorded in the margins for inclusion in the final edition. The loss of a printed book was a small matter, in that it could easily be replaced, whereas a manuscript was irreplacaeble. The advent of printing thus meant that standard editions could be produced and made generally available, thus greatly facilitating theological debate, and increasing the accuracy with which such sources could be cited. A theologian in Paris could thus be sure that his colleagues in Oxford and Bologna would have the same text before them as they disputed a particular point of interpretation. The production of printed editions of theological works thus became a matter of priority, and the contribution of humanist scholarship to this enterprise was of decisive importance.

Humanist Projects

One of the most significant of the early humanist editions was the eleven volumes of the *Opera omnia Augustini*, published in Basel by Johannes Amerbach, the product of intense editorial teamwork over the period 1490–1506. The reputation of Erasmus of Rotterdam was at least partly due to his massive editorial undertakings, particularly of patristic texts. His first edition of the works of Jerome (1516) was widely regarded as a wonder of the age, and was followed by editions of Cyprian (1520), Arnobius Junior (1522), Hilary (1523), Irenaeus (1526), Ambrose (1527) and Augustine (1528–9). It is, however, with another of his editorial undertakings that we are particularly concerned.

The First Printed Greek New Testament
Although Erasmus' editorial skills are frequently illustrated with reference to his production of the first printed Greek New Testament, its first edition is not a particularly good example of his editorial work. The stimulus for this work appears to date from 1505, when Erasmus discovered and published the *Adnotationes* of Lorenzo Valla. The first edition of the *Novum Instrumentum omne* appeared in 1516. It had been produced in haste, was based upon a mere four manuscripts, and included five verses which Erasmus had himself translated into Greek, not having access to the original. Furthermore, while the publication of the first Greek New Testament was of considerable importance, its significance should not be exaggerated. Had Erasmus not accomplished the task, the distinguished team of scholars at Alcalá in Spain would have done so shortly afterwards: the Greek text of the New Testament in the great Complutensian Polyglot was set up in type in 1514, although publication was delayed until 1520. In many respects, the Spanish edition was superior to that of Erasmus, who would make full use of its better readings for a subsequent (1527) edition of his own. More significant was the new Latin translation of the Greek text, which differed significantly from that of the Vulgate, printed alongside the original Greek, and accompanied by extensive notes justifying the alterations made. The resulting challenge to the authority of the Vulgate was of considerable significance, as we shall indicate below.

Challenge to the Vulgate
The increased textual accuracy which Erasmus was able to draw upon, when linked with his use of Valla's precise philological comments in the *Adnotationes*, permitted Erasmus to challenge both the *text* and the *translation* of the Vulgate. Certain of the disputed textual readings were of little theological importance (their relevance to the authority of the Vulgate aside) – for example, Erasmus challenged the longer ending to Mark's gospel, and the Matthean doxology to the Lord's Prayer. Others, however, had assumed considerable importance through their use as proof texts for important elements of catholic theology. For example, the Vulgate included the following verse as I John 5:7: 'For there are three that bear witness in heaven, the Father, the Word and the Spirit; and these three are one'. The verse had become an important element in the traditional defence of the doctrine of the Trinity and the divinity of Christ. Erasmus correctly challenged the inclusion of this verse on source-critical grounds, and by doing so, appeared to many

(such as Edward Lee, later archbishop of York) to have lapsed into some form of Arianism.

Challenge to Tradition

In many respects, however, the new Latin translation was of even greater importance, on account of the challenge which it posed to traditional catholic theology. For example, the Latin term *poenitentia* is ambiguous, and can be taken as referring to *either* the mental state of penitence or repentence, *or* to the sacrament of penance. The Vulgate text of Matthew 4:17 reads as follows: 'Do penance (*poenitentiam agite*), for the Kingdom of God is at hand'. Erasmus' translation was somewhat different: 'Be penitent (*poeniteat vos*), for the Kingdom of God is at hand'. In effect, Erasmus had obliterated the Vulgate's implied reference to the sacrament of penance, a trend which he confirmed by his later translation of the verse as 'Change your mind (*resipiscite*), for the Kingdom of God is at hand'. The challenge to the authority of the Vulgate was seen by many of Erasmus' contemporaries as a blow at the roots of catholic theology, even though Erasmus himself made no suggestion that the Vulgate should be abandoned in theological debate or in the liturgy. Nevertheless, Erasmus' critique of the Vulgate had been paralleled elsewhere (most notably in Jacques Lefevre d'Etaples' criticism of the Vulgate translation of Hebrews 2:7, which had attracted considerable attention), and the cumulative effect of this critique was to permit the Reformers to abandon the Vulgate translation of the bible on *scholarly* grounds, without being obliged to enlarge upon their theological misgivings concerning points of interpretation. Here, as in many other ways, the *scholarly* endeavours of the humanist assisted the *theological* concerns of the Reformers. However, as we shall demonstrate in the following chapter, superficial similarities between the humanists and the Reformers actually masked profound conceptual disagreements, which would only become fully apparent at a later date.

The Hebrew Text

Other humanists, such as Johannes Reuchlin, made available printed Hebrew texts of the Old Testament, as well as aids for their translation. Thus Reuchlin's *De rudimentis Hebraicis* (1506) became a powerful stimulus to the study of the Old Testament in its original language, and placed the scientific study of Hebrew on an entirely new basis. Luther is known to have purchased a copy of this work before he left Erfurt for Wittenberg in 1508, and the subsequent use to which he put it is an adequate testimony to its significance to our study. Similar remarks may be made concerning his edition of the Hebrew text of the seven penitential Psalms (1512), upon which Luther drew heavily, and his later *De accentibus et orthographia linguae Hebraica* (1518).

4. HUMANISM AND THE REFORMATION

Humanism Theologically Neutral

The humanist desire for reform within the church appears to have been essentially practical, directed primarily against the morals of the papacy, the low standards of clerical education, and the incomprehensibility of scholastic theology. Whereas Luther would criticise the theologians of the later Middle Ages for the doctrines which they taught, Erasmus reserved his criticism for the barbarous Latin in which they expressed them. There is thus every reason to suggest that the humanist movement was theologically neutral, in that its chief emphasis was upon the need to reform the *life* of the church through a return to the sources upon which it was ultimately based – the scriptures and the fathers. There was general agreement that the fountain stream of tradition was purest at its head, and that patristic scholarship was the means by which that purity might be tapped. In many respects, the humanist movement and the early Reformers were united in their common appeal to the fathers as witnesses to a form of scriptural exegesis and doctrine which avoided the distortions and accretions of the mediaeval period.

Authority of Augustine

In their early phases at least, both the Lutheran and Zwinglian Reformations may be regarded as a return, at least in principle, to the bible and Augustine as the sole legitimate sources of Christian theology. In May 1517, Luther wrote thus to John Lang:

> Our theology and St Augustine go forward, and, by the work of God, reign in our university. Aristotle is in continual decline, perhaps to future and permanent ruin. The lectures on the *Sentences* decline, and nobody can hope for an audience unless he puts forward this theology – i.e., the bible or St Augustine.

As studies of mediaeval theology rightly emphasise, the theology of the Middle Ages was largely based upon Augustinian foundations, although serious differences emerged in relation to the manner in which he was to be interpreted. The publication of the Amerbach edition of the works of Augustine thus marked an important milestone in the development of the science of theology, which gained added significance through its influence upon the course of the Reformation. The humanist movement, however, guaged the importance of writings in terms of their antiquity rather than their theological content, with the result that the patristic *corpus* as a whole was regarded as invested with the accumulated authority of antiquity, and no single writer within it as being pre-eminent. It will therefore be clear that a potential conflict existed between the Reformers and humanists over the status of Augustine within the patristic *corpus* as a whole. Erasmus, however, appears to have regarded Jerome as the most important patristic writer, and is known to have campaigned as early as 1515 to have him established as *the* theologian of the Christian church. In a letter of 21 May 1515, Erasmus wrote to Leo X arguing that Jerome was the only Latin theologian 'worthy of the title'. Similarly, Eramus' edition of the works of Arnobius Junior, several of which were highly critical of the Augustinian doctrine of grace, served to call into question the authority of the African bishop. Although this campaign was ultimately unsuccessful, it served to illustrate an area in which serious future disagreement between humanists and Reformers would develop during the first phase of the Reformation.

Humanist Foundations
As we begin to consider the development of the science of theology during the first phase of the Reformation, it is important to observe that the sources upon which that theology would be based were edited and published largely through the dedication and efforts of humanist scholars. Without humanism, there could never have been a Reformation, in that the sources and methods upon which the Reformation was initially based owed an incalculable amount to humanist scholarship. The full extent of that debt will become clearer when we consider, for example, the influence of rhetoric and humanist exegetical methods on the theology of John Calvin, and the subsequent influence of late Renaissance Aristotelianism upon later Reformed theology. Our attention now turns to the University of Wittenberg at the opening of the second decade of the sixteenth century, and its new lecturer in biblical studies: Martin Luther.

FOR FURTHER READING

Bouwsma, W. J., 'Renaissance and Reformation. An Essay in Their Affinities and Connections', in *Luther and the Dawn of the Modern Era. Papers for the Fourth International Congress for Luther Research*, ed. H. A. Oberman (Leiden, 1974), pp. 127–49.

Gray, H. H., 'Renaissance Humanism: The Pursuit of Eloquence', in *Renaissance Essays*, ed. Kristeller, P. O. and Wiener, P. P. (New York, 1968), pp. 199–216.

Kristeller, P. O., 'The European Diffusion of Italian Humanism', in *Renaissance Thought II. Papers on Humanism and the Arts* (New York, 1969), pp. 69–88.

idem., *Renaissance Thought and Its Sources* (New York, 1979).

Oberman, H. A., *Masters of the Reformation* (Cambridge, 1980), pp. 64–110.

2

THE THEOLOGICAL METHOD
OF THE REFORMERS

The intense scholarly activity surrounding the Reformation of the sixteenth century has made it increasingly difficult to define precisely what is meant by the term *Reformation* itself. This already difficult task is made impossible if we approach the Reformation with preconceived theological ideas about what was at stake in this great movement of the sixteenth century. There can be no doubt that the Reformation is an aspect of the Renaissance – in other words, that it drew heavily upon the textual and philological achievements of the Renaissance, and incorporated at least some of its critical and libertarian spirit. Nevertheless, it is also clear that the Reformation must be distinguished from the Renaissance in at least one vital aspect: it was fundamentally *theological* in character, concerned primarily with the critical evaluation of received doctrine in the light of the sources upon which they were ultimately based. In the first phase of the Reformation, these sources were essentially scripture and Augustine.

The growing recognition of the theological pluralism of the later Middle Ages is of particular relevance to evaluating the significance of the Reformation. As modern studies of the theology of the later mediaeval period have made clear, there was an astonishing degree of theological diversity during the period, including disagreement upon vital matters such as the doctrines of the church and justification, as well as more rarified matters such as the doctrine of predestination. In addition, the schism between Rome and Avignon in the fourteenth and fifteenth centuries made the important distinction between the private opinions of individual theologians and the public teaching of the church somewhat ambiguous, to say the least. Although the individual aspects of the Reformation were foreshadowed, to a greater or lesser extent, in the later Middle Ages, the Reformation differed from its late mediaeval precursors in at least one vital respect: it represented a concerted movement within a geographically limited region of Europe, resting upon an intellectual foundation which resulted from the application of an essentially coherent theological method, on the basis of which its teachings were propagated and sustained. It is therefore of importance to both the historian and theologian to ascertain the sources, methods and presuppositions upon which the theology of the Reformation was initially based, and which distinguished it from catholicism. In the present chapter, we are concerned with precisely this question, which we begin to answer with reference to Luther, Karlstadt, Zwingli and Bucer.

1. LUTHER AND WITTENBERG

The Reformation at Wittenberg
The Reformation is often portrayed as the rediscovery of the bible after centuries of neglect. It is more accurate to describe the Reformation as a return to the bible through the teachings of Augustine, and perhaps even more accurate to describe it as a triumph of Augustine's doctrine of grace over his doctrine of the church. The intellectual foundations for the Reformation may be regarded as having been laid at Wittenberg in the years 1516–19. Although Martin Luther was pre-eminent in establishing the general cast of the *vera theologia* which was forged at Wittenberg during those crucial years, it was essentially a corporate effort, involving the entire theology faculty under its dean, Andreas Bodenstein von Karlstadt.

The Influence of Augustine
Luther himself had begun to read the works of Augustine at an early stage in his career. Initially, he contented himself with the relatively accessible *de Civitate Dei* and *de Trinitate*, before obtaining his anti-Pelagian writings as they appeared in the eighth volume of the great Amerbach edition of 1506. Luther's early writings, even those from 1509, indicate his growing desire to base theology upon Augustine, rather than Aristotle and the scholastics. However, as we pointed out in the previous chapter, it was still not easy to obtain the works of Augustine in the second decade of the sixteenth century. This point may be illustrated with reference to an incident which took place in late September 1516, when Luther greatly offended Karlstadt by attributing to Augustine the opinion that man could not fulfil the law without grace, and simultaneously attacking the authenticity of the pseudo-Augustinian treatise *de vera et falsa*

poenitentia. Karlstadt was, however, unable to refute Luther on this point, not having access to an edition of the works of Augustine. He was unable to remedy this situation until January 1517, when he purchased an edition of Augustine's works at neighbouring Leipzig, probably at the great book fair held there annually. As a result of reading this edition, he was moved to defend publicly what he now knew to be the true theology of Augustine. Pre-empting Luther's more famous action of October of that year, he posted 151 theses on the door of the castle church, attacking scholastic theology in the name of Augustine himself, before going on that autumn to deliver a remarkable series of lectures on Augustine in which he openly stated the principles upon which the new theology which had gained the upper hand at Wittenberg was based:

> I congratulate you, fellow students, that the truth of sacred letters shines once more in our university! . . . Rejoice that you are able to hear, learn and understand the true bible from doctors of the church, and not from the schoolmen.

In this brief statement is summarised the methodological basis of the new theology of Wittenberg: scripture as interpreted through the fathers, and especially Augustine.

The Reforms in Theology
These principles were embodied in the reforms which Karlstadt introduced in the theological curriculum at Wittenberg in 1518, in which increased emphasis was placed upon biblical languages, with a simultaneous decrease in emphasis upon Aristotle and his interpreters. In outward appearance, there was much in common between these reforms and those advocated by the humanists: indeed, in 1519 Karlstadt would claim the support of 'the principal and most eminent of all theologians, our Erasmus' in the struggle for the reformation of the church. Underlying this, however, were real tensions between the Wittenberg Reformers and the humanists, which we shall consider in a later section.

2. ZWINGLI AND BUCER

The Reformation at Zurich
It is too easy for the student of the Reformation to overlook the fact that the Reformation was a heterogeneous movement, based upon a number of cities and a still greater number of theological person-

alities. There is every reason to suppose that Huldrych Zwingli initiated a reforming movement in Switzerland independently of Luther. Initially a humanist, Zwingli appears to have been won over to a form of *Christian* humanism through the influence of Erasmus. While still a pastor at Einsiedeln, he 'studied with unceasing vigour the Greek and Latin philosophers and theologians, day and night'. He made particular use of Erasmus' *Novum Instrumentum* of 1516, and gradually distanced himself from more secular forms of humanism. For Zwingli, such secular humanists wished 'to be followers of Catullus and Propertius, rather than of Paul and Christ'. After moving to Zurich to take up a cathedral appointment, Zwingli became seriously ill in September 1519. As he hovered between life and death, he appears to have become convinced of the total sovereignty of God, and of his own implication in God's purposes. We now find Zwingli's humanism finding its expression in a theology of the word of God which is far more radical than that of Luther – indeed, the *sola scriptura* principle is initially to be associated with the Zwinglian, rather than with the Lutheran, Reformation. As Zwingli himself expressed his conviction concerning the sovereignty of the Word of God: 'The Word of God will take its course as surely as the Rhine does'. The attraction of prominent humanists, such as Oecolampadius, into Zwingli's sphere of influence did much to establish the characteristic aims of the Zwinglian Reformation: a renewal of the life and doctrine of the church, based upon scripture and the fathers. Indeed, Oecolampadius was responsible for making theological scholarship the servant of the Reformation, editing and translating the fathers, and displaying competence in all three biblical languages in the course of his biblical lectures. In terms of their sources and their evident affinities with humanist aspirations, Zwingli's Reformation at Zurich parallels that of Luther at Wittenberg.

The Influence of Humanist Moralism on Martin Bucer.
Martin Bucer (1491–1551) entered the Dominican Order in 1506, and joined the evangelical faction as a consequence of his meeting with Luther at Heidelberg in 1518. Bucer is of particular interest to our study on account of his strongly humanist inclinations. In his early period, Bucer was influenced by the humanist school at Schlettstadt, and is known to have been engrossed with the study of Erasmus as a monk. This Erasmianism would persist throughout his career as a reformer. In part, his defection to the evangelical cause appears to have been on account of his conviction that Luther was merely stating openly what Erasmus had hinted at. Although

Bucer adopted the leading doctrines of the Reformation, such as justification *per solam fidem*, the rejection of the *liberum arbitrium*, the totality of sin and salvation solely through the cross of Christ, it is clear that he interpreted them in a fashion which owed more to Erasmus than to Luther. *Nam et sacra doctrina proprie moralis est:* the leading feature of Bucer's theology is generally recognised to be his emphasis upon ethics, which can be seen, for example, in his doctrine of *double* justification and emphasis upon the importance of good works. This emphasis is coupled with a distinctive understanding of the nature of theology which is of importance to our study.

For Bucer, the whole of scripture is law: *lex*. Bucer derives his understanding of the *lex spiritualis* through a philological analysis of the Hebrew term *torah*. As with Erasmus, the law is understood to be the *lex spiritualis* written on the heart of man, *doctrina et vitae institutio*, which teaches him *pie atque salubriter vivendum*. The strongly moralist approach which Bucer adopts to Christian theology is well illustrated by his discussion of the work of Christ. For Bucer, Christ is primarily understood as 1) a teacher of the law, 2) a moral example, and 3) the bestower of the Holy Spirit who enables man to keep the law. In each respect, Bucer faithfully reproduces the Erasmian doctrine of the *nova lex Christi*. This Erasmian emphasis is also evident in Bucer's doctrine of revelation, whether general (i.e. natural revelation) or special (i.e., biblical revelation).

Natural Theology

The concept of a natural divine revelation was well established during the first phase of the Reformation: although regarded with intense suspicion by Luther, it was enthusiastically upheld by Zwingli and others. For Zwingli and Bucer, the same basic truths may be found in ancient philosophy (particularly in Stoicism) as in the Christian religion: the superiority of the Christian revelation lies in its completeness and clarity. This natural revelation is, however, understood by Bucer to be primarily *ethical* in nature. Bucer emphasises the ethical nature of the Stoic religion as its chief virtue. A similar ethical emphasis is evident in Bucer's biblical exegesis. Bucer uses the concept of *tropological* exegesis to a remarkable extent, so that it effectively becomes the leading feature of his biblical exegesis. This is particularly significant in Bucer's Old Testament exegesis, where the historical sense of the text is subordinated to the spiritual. The concept of the tropological, or moral, sense of scripture was well established during the mediaeval period, referring to the essentially timeless application of a biblical text to matters of practical morality, so that Christian doctrine is basically *doctrina pietatis*. Bucer's exegetical antithesis between *externa* and *spiritualia* is effectively employed as a hermeneutical principle to discover the moral application of the text from its historical meaning.

3. CALVIN

The Influence of Humanist Rhetoric on Calvin

The Italian Renaissance witnessed a new interest in rhetoric, which is reflected in the fact that Aristotle's *Rhetorica* and *Poetica*, neglected during the mediaeval period, came to the forefront. Whereas the method of dialectic dominated mediaeval scholasticism, that of rhetoric gained the ascendency in the Renaissance. This new concern for rhetoric passed into early sixteenth century French humanism, where it assumed a much closer link with logic then it had in the Italian Renaissance: although the two disciplines were taught sequentially, they were inextricably linked. The young Calvin thus encountered a form of humanism somewhat different from that which Luther knew.

After his initial studies at the university of Paris, Calvin moved to Bourges to study law (1529–31). During his time there, Calvin developed the rhetorical techniques which he would later employ to such powerful effect in his sermons and homiletical literature, and which recent scholarship has suggested may have influenced the *substance*, as well as the *presentation* of his teachings. The latter is clearly influenced by the cultured and elegant fluency of Erasmus' Latin style, which Calvin would have encountered in the *Copia*, *Adagia* and *Colloquia*. More indirect appears to have been the influence of Guillaume Budé, particularly through his work on the Justinian *Pandects* (*Annotationes in quattuor et viginti Pandectarum libros* (1508)). This work of philology is of significance in a number of respects, particularly in that it by-passes the glosses of Bartholus and Accursius and proceeds directly to the orginal text – a technique which Budé would later apply to the New Testament, shortly before Calvin's arrival at Bourges. In many respects, Budé may be regarded as developing the earlier work of Lorenzo Valla, examining the semantic content and associations of words, and Calvin later applied similar methods in his Seneca commentary, as we shall note below. This commentary also shows considerable affinity at points with Budé's *L'Institution du Prince*.

Calvin's Classical Sources
The sources for Calvin's rhetoric appear to be the classical works of antiquity, such as Cicero's *de oratione* and *de inventione*, as well as Quintillian's *Institutio* and the *rhetorici minores* (Romanus Aquila, Rutilius Lupus and Julius Rufianus). Calvin regarded Seneca as second only to Cicero as a rhetorician, and, as judged from the Seneca commentary, Calvin absorbed much of the Stoic's rhetorical techniques. It is significant that the rhetorical structures, techniques and figures which Calvin notes most frequently in that commentary (particulary *accomodatio*, *amplificatio*, *praeteritio* and *prolepsis*) are those which dominate Calvin's own mature homiletical writings. Although he generally avoids the term 'rhetoric' on account of its pagan associations, it is clear that is is precisely this which he is referring to when he speaks of 'eloquence'.

The importance of rhetoric to the development of the science of theology in the Reformation relates to the proclamation of that theology from the pulpit. Rhetoric was concerned as much with the mastery of words for proclamation and instruction as with the more limited field of etymology and textual analysis. However, as we have indicated, a major question still debated within the learned literature is whether rhetoric was the tool or the master of Calvin's theology, which clearly raises the possibility that humanism may have exercised a greater influence over Calvin's theology than is usually considered to be the case.

Logic and Rhetoric
A further instance of the influence of humanist rhetoric upon Calvin's theology may be illustrated from the 1559 *Institutio*. It is an almost universal judgment that Calvin was a master of logic, and that this later edition of the *Institutio* brilliantly illustrates his application of logic to theology. The logic used, however, is not *syllogistic*, as might be expected, but a specific form of *rhetorical* logic based upon the *enthymeme*. There is a general tendency to assume that Calvin uses syllogisms, though in fact, it is difficult to discover a single instance of a pure syllogism in the 1559 *Institutio*. In its place, we find a highly effective form of rhetorical logic which substitutes the enthymeme for the syllogism. An enthymeme is usually regarded as a syllogism with one of its three elements (normally one of the premises) deliberately omitted, on the assumption that the reader or hearer will supply the missing element himself. An example of an enthymeme is the following: Premise: All men are mortal; Conclusion: Socrates is mortal. It is left to the

reader to work out that the stated premise is the major, and that the omitted minor premise is: 'Socrates is a man'.

The advantages of this device are twofold. First, it permits a highly effective rhetorical style, where the constant use of syllogisms would yield a more rigorous logic and an equally ponderous and unattractive style. The effectiveness of the *Institutio* of 1559 as a vehicle for transmitting Calvin's ideas is largely due to its highly polished style, and the apparent subordination of logic to rhetoric is but one aspect of this feature. Second, the omitted premise may actually be more contentious than might at first appear, perhaps containing terms which, although obvious in their everyday meaning, assume modified meanings when employed in a specifically theological context. By omitting this premise and permitting the reader to supply it, Calvin is able to avoid weakening his argument through being forced to draw attention to this point, and thus be side-tracked into discussions which are actually of relatively little importance in relation to the point he wishes to make. He may assume that his reader will supply the omitted premise with its terms defined very loosely, and thus proceed to draw the desired conclusion. Although this is clearly questionable in terms of logical rigour, it permits Calvin to develop a fluent exposition of his theology, and thus greatly contributed to the esteem in which the work was held.

Melanchthon

Calvin, of course, was not alone among the Reformers in making use of humanist rhetorical techniques. In his *Responsio ad Picum Mirandolum* (1558), Melanchthon stated the precise relationship between dialectic and rhetoric in exposition: a harmony of truth and expression is essential for both communication and inherent validity, in that the *style* of literature or oratory both *expresses and modifies* the meaning of the concepts employed. This important point serves to illustrate the fact that the use of rhetorical techniques can result in the modification of the theological concepts which they are used to develop.

4. EARLY TENSIONS BETWEEN HUMANISM AND THE
REFORMATION

On the basis of our discussion of Luther, Karlstadt, Zwingli, Bucer and Calvin, it will be clear that the first phase of the Reformation demonstrated strong affinities with the humanist movement. Despite these affinities with humanism, serious differences would emerge between the Reformers and humanists in the early phase of the Reformation concerning the *status* of the sources upon which both the Zwinglian and Lutheran Reformations were based, and the means by which these were to be used.

By 1519, the year of the Leipzig Disputation between Luther and Eck, there was a widespread conviction that Reformers and humanists alike were committed to a common cause. The pace of events in those crucial months obscured the fact that the alliance between the Reformation and humanism was seriously weakened through unresolved – and apparently unrecognised – tensions. Although these tensions would not surface for several years, they were there for those who cared to note them. The following methodological disagreements between humanists and Reformers may be noted.

Disagreement over the Status of Scripture

Although both humanist and Reformer agreed that it was invested with considerable authority, they could not agree on the *nature* and *implications* of that authority. Thus the humanist respected scripture on account of its antiquity, and the simplicity of its language and ideas; the Reformer respected scripture because through it he had access to the Word of God, upon which he held his theology to be based. Whereas the humanist thus endowed scripture with an authority comparable to that of other sources of antiquity, the Reformers held its authority to be such that it was necessarily unique. Although the *sola scriptura* principle is associated with Zwingli, rather than with Luther, it represents an excellent statement of the common understanding of the Reformers concerning the unique authority of scripture in matters of doctrine.

Disagreement over the Status of the Fathers

Both humanist and Reformer regarded the fathers as embodying a form of Christianity which was more authentic than that of the mediaeval period. Thus Philip Melanchthon felt able to state that the Lutheran Reformation was essentially a return to the teaching of Ambrose and Augustine. However, a serious difference emerged between humanist and Reformer concerning the status of Augustine within the patristic corpus. For the humanists, the authority of the fathers was based upon their corporate antiquity: no single father could be regarded as being pre-eminent. Erasmus' conviction that Jerome could be regarded as standing head and shoulders above the other fathers – which is at variance with the principle of antiquity –

reflects the importance which Erasmus attached to Jerome's biblical scholarship. The Reformers, however, regarded Augustine as the most eminent of the fathers on account of his *theology*, and tended to regard the Reformation as a return to the authentic teaching of the African saint, after centuries of scholastic distortion and confusion. Erasmus' edition of Arnobius Junior was therefore somewhat unwelcome, in that Arnobius had subjected Augustine to extensive criticism concerning his doctrine of justification – which the Reformers claimed as their own.

Disagreement over the Errors of Scholasticism

Both humanist and Reformer were highly critical of the scholastic theologians. However, their reasons for criticising these theologians were radically different. For Erasmus, for example, the scholastic theologians were guilty of employing unintelligible Latin and obscure terms – what was required was a more refined Latin style and a simpler vocabulary. For Luther, there was no difficulty about interpreting the scholastics – what was unacceptable was what they *said*, not *the way they said it!* In other words, Erasmus' elegant liberal humanism was offended by aspects of scholasticism quite different to those which so infuriated Luther.

Disagreement over the Role of Reason in Theology

One of the leading features of Luther's *theologia crucis* (theology of the cross) is its vehement rejection of the right of reason to have any say in matters theological. For Luther, it seemed that reason, Aristotle, the lawyers and the law were allies of Satan, threatening to destroy the gospel of grace. Luther's 'evangelical irrationalism' is ultimately an expression of his conviction that reason cannot comprehend the mystery of the justification of the sinner. The God of reason is ultimately a God who rewards man according to his works. Although Luther permits reason to have an important role in social and political matters, he refuses to permit it to have any significant role in theology. This highly critical attitude towards reason sets Luther apart from the humanists, who generally valued reason as man's highest faculty, the most appropriate means by which God might be found. Although some of the more humanist evangelicals, such as Melanchthon, attempted to restore reason to a more significant position in Lutheran dogmatics, the first phase of the Reformation in general witessed the role of reason in theology being carefully delimited.

5. CALVIN'S CRITIQUE OF HUMANISM

Several of the Reformers whose roots lay in humanism were obliged to make explicit the differences between the theology of the Reformation and humanism at several vital points. Of the early Reformers to have such humanist roots, John Calvin is generally regarded as the most important. We shall illustrate this point with reference to Calvin's implicit critique of his fellow-humanists in relation to two areas of importance: the doctrine of justification, and the doctrine of the knowledge of God.

The Doctrine of Justification

The doctrine of justification lay at the centre of the Reformation struggle in its early phase at Wittenberg. In early Reformed theology, however, a doctrine of justification had developed which was thoroughly humanist in its emphasis. Thus Zwingli, who is strongly humanist in much of his theology, makes man's justification conditional upon his moral regeneration, and Bucer subjected Luther's theology of justification to similar modification. In this, they were reflecting the humanist belief that justification was essentially the divine endorsement of man's moral regeneration. Calvin's theology of justification, which is stated at its clearest in the *Institutio* of 1559 manages to disengage the Reformed theology from humanism on this issue by a brilliant Christological exposition of the relationship between justification and sanctification, which effectively excludes the humanist concept of moral justification without in any way threatening the vital link between man's gratuitous justification and his subsequent obligation to perform good works.

The Doctrine of the Knowledge of God

The humanist movement placed great emphasis upon the corporate wisdom of classical antiquity. Part of this heritage was the doctrine of a natural knowledge of God, expressed most clearly in Cicero's *de natura deorum*. For Cicero, 'nature herself has imprinted a conception of the gods on the minds of all mankind', so that man has a 'prior notion' of God's existence and nature. Cicero's discussion of the knowledge of God effectively implied that Christianity was an instance of a widespread natural phenomenon – knowledge of God – which effectively called into question the uniqueness and finality of the Christian revelation in this respect. To many of the Reformers, the humanists appeared to be concerned to show how the classical philosophers were naturally able to arrive at the same insights which Christian theologians required revelation to discern.

Once more, Zwingli appeared to yield to humanism upon this respect, treating Socrates and other pious pagans of antiquity as Christians *avant la lettre*. Calvin's approach to this suggestion is of considerable significance.

As has been often noted, the first five chapters of the 1559 *Institutio* are devoted to a careful analysis of Cicero's doctrine of the knowledge of God, in which a clear division of opinion between Calvin and his classical source emerges, despite their evident similarities. First, Calvin concedes a natural knowledge of God, but insists that it merely prepares the way for *saving* knowledge, rather than defining that knowledge itself. Second, Cicero's emphasis upon the importance of natural knowledge of God is vitiated by the fragmentary and contradictory character of that knowledge; Calvin concedes such a natural knowledge of God, but argues that man is thus led to ask where a more certain and accurate knowledge of God can be obtained, and thence to examine the scriptures. In other words, man's natural knowledge of God serves aa a first step towards the definitive enounter in revelation.

Calvin's critique of Cicero presupposes that the reader is thoroughly familiar with classical Greek and Roman literature, and is clearly addressed to readers of humanist sympathies, intended to demonstrate the initial correlation between humanism and Christianity, and the ultimate superiority of the latter over the former. Calvin's use of Cicero in this respect is thus intended to challenge the inherent naturalism of certain humanist writers in this important matter.

6. THE SOURCES OF THEOLOGY: SCRIPTURE

In dealing with scripture as a source of theology, we are obliged to consider three inseparable questions. First, we must consider what is to be understood by 'Scripture' – i.e., the question of the canon of scripture. Second, we must consider the question of the nature and extent of the authority of scripture. Third, we must consider the question of how scripture, once its scope and the nature of its authority have been defined, is to be interpreted. We shall consider these questions individually.

The Canon of Scripture
By the end of the fifth century, the Latin-speaking church had effectively defined the canon of scriptures as that contained within the text of the Vulgate (although it may be pointed out that some

mediaeval versions of the Vulgate contained the spurious 'Epistle to the Laodiceans'.) The Epistle to the Hebrews was widely regarded as Pauline, although many preferred to refer to it as *eiusdem ad Hebraeos*. Although several theologians of the mediaeval period, such as Thomas Aquinas and Nicholas of Lyra, discussed whether Hebrews could be regarded as canonical, it was only to answer the question in the affirmative. The late mediaeval period witnessed renewed interest, arising out of the Hussite controversy, in the celebrated dictum of Augustine: 'For my own part, I would not believe the gospel, except as moved by the authority of the catholic church'. The dictum was used by many theologians of the late mediaeval period, such as Gabriel Biel, to demonstrate that without the authority of the church, Christians could not even trust the truths of scripture. As Biel puts it: 'The truth which the holy mother church defines or accepts as catholic is to be believed with the same veneration as if it were stated in Holy Scripture'. More signigicantly, it was also used to assert the authority of the church over scripture, in that it was the church who had determined the extent of the canon. With the rise of humanist biblical scholarship in the late Renaissance, however, a new critical approach to the canon came into being. Although humanist biblical scholars such as Erasmus and Cajetan did not actually question the canonical stuatus of Hebrews, some of the catholic epistles, and Revelation, they nevertheless raised doubts concerning their authorship.

The Lutheran Reformation witnessed a renewed attack on the accepted canon of scripture, partly on the basis of scholarly and textual considerations, but also on the basis of theological considerations. For example, in his *Preface to the New Testament* (1522), Luther argued that 'canonical' must be understood as 'apostolic', distinguishing two senses of this latter term. In addition to its traditional sense, 'apostolic' means that which has *apostolic nature* to it, even if it was not actually written by an apostle. Luther states this concept of apostolicity as follows in the *Preface to James and Jude:* 'The correct touchstone by which all books should be judged is whether or not they promote Christ. What does not teach Christ is not apostolic, even if Peter or Paul should teach it; conversely, what does teach Christ is apostolic, even if Judas, Annas, Pilate or Herod should teach it'. *Treibt es Christum oder nicht?* On the basis of this principle, Luther excluded four books from the New Testament, including the 'right strawy letter' itself. In his *Preface to the New Testament*, Luther comments thus: 'Thus the letter of James is a right strawy letter (*eyn rechte stroern Epistel*) in contrast to them, for it has nothing evangelical about it'. This confusion of *historical* and *theological* factors was, however, restricted to the Lutheran Reformation: no such distinction emerged within the Reformed church, although the period of the Enlightenment would witness a renewed critique of the canon of scripture, on very different gounds.

The Old Testament Canon

The Old Testament canon was, however, subjected to a more penetrating critique. The term 'Apocrypha' appears to have been introduced by Karlstadt in 1520, in his *de canonicis scripturis libellus*, and actually refers only to the pseudepigraphical works of the Old Testament which were taken up in the Greek and Latin bibles. Strictly speaking, the term should not be used to refer to other such writings from Syriac, Coptic and Ethiopic sources (and, more recently, from Qumran). The distinction between the Old Testament proper and the Apocrypha was of more than scholarly significance. For example, the catholic practice of praying for the dead was frequently justified on the basis of II Maccabees, and the standard defence of the doctrines of the invocation of the saints and purgatory also relied extensively upon apocryphal sources. Thus the English Reformer John Frith (c.1503–33) argued against the received doctrine of prayer for the dead on the basis of the non-canonical nature of the authorities cited in its support (such as II Maccabees 12:43–5). The Reformers' revision of the Old Testament canon was interpreted by their opponents as a form of theological chicanery. As Thomas More observed, Protestants appeared to base their theology upon 'scripture alone' – but only after having excluded from this category those works which happened to contradict Protestant teaching. Similarly, Luther's criticism of the canonical status of James was seen as an attempt to evade the scriptural foundations of the sacrament of extreme unction and the principle of justification by works.

The Canon and the Authority of the Church

The very existence of the canon of scripture thus provided the opponents of the Reformation with one of their most powerful weapons against the *sola scriptura* principle, in that the authority of scripture was seen to be a consequence of the authority of the church. Thus John Eck, Luther's opponent at the Leipzig Disputation of 1519, argued that 'scripture is not authentic without the authority of the church' – and as Luther had rejected this authority, he had at the very least involved himself in a serious contradiction. Although Melanchthon argued that the authority of the church in this matter related solely to distinguising authentic from inauthentic scripture, Augustine's *dictum* 'I should not believe the gospel except as moved by the authority of the catholic church' (*ego vero euangelio non crederem, nisi me catholicae ecclesiae commoveret auctoritate*) clearly referred to the *interpretation*, and not just to the *identification*, of canonical scripture. Zwingli responded to this frequently-cited Augustinian dictum by inquiring how Matthew's gospel, which was written to serve the needs of the church, could conceivably have been dependent upon the church for its authority: 'Is it not the greatest impiety to think that what sprang from the mouth of God (not man!) was not established unless human ignorance agreed to it?' The final Protestant answer to this dilemma came in the form of the principle of the 'internal testimony of the Holy Spirit', by which the canonical status of scripture could be discerned without reference to the authority of the church. This principle is probably stated most lucidly and persuasively by John Calvin, and became a standard feature of Protestant discussions of the status of scripture. Nevertheless, it seemed to many that this solution merely deferred the problem by one step, rather than resolving it: we shall return to this problem later in relation to the interpretation of scripture.

The Authority of Scripture

It was a commonplace in mediaeval thought to define theology in terms of the exposition of the scriptures: for Thomas Aquinas, *sacra doctrina* could be defined as *theologia quae in scriptura traditur*. William of Ockham asserted that 'holy scripture and the doctrine or assertion of the catholic church' had greater authority than the pope himself, in addition to stating that scripture was to be regarded as superior to any church father. Jean Gerson stated that the authority of scripture must be regarded as foremost among the articles of faith of the church. It would, however, be wrong to suggest that the *sola scriptura* principle can be detected during the mediaeval period, on account of the simultaneous assertion on the part of late mediaeval theologians that there existed a second channel of apostolic revelation in addition to scripture. By the early Middle Ages, the principle of *unwritten traditions* had become firmly incorporated into catholic theology. The argument by which Basil of Caesarea had deduced the divinity of the Holy Spirit (by appealing to extra-scriptural tradition) was extended far beyond its initial mediaeval application in the sphere of canon law, and came to be as used in support of the existence of an extrascriptural doctrinal tradition.

Scripture and Tradition

It is possible to discern two main understandings of the relation between scriptures and tradition during the later Middle Ages: 'tradition' was understood either as an *expansion* of scriptural teaching or as an *authoritative interpretation* of scripture. Whereas the Council of Trent would accord equal weight to scripture and tradition in matters of theology, the Reformers rejected the role of tradition altogether. As Zwingli stated this principle in his highly influential book, *The Clarity and Certainty or Power of the Word of God:* 'The foundation of our religion is the written word, the scriptures of God'. In essence, the *sola scriptura* principle amounted to the assertion that scripture *alone* was to be the normative criterion in theology. This view of the authority of scripture, of course, was ultimately based upon the belief that they were inspired by God himself, the 'records of the Holy Spirit' as Zwingli put it: 'God teaches through his Spirit, and through the letter that has been written by the inspiration of his Spirit and ordinance'.

Nevertheless, the opponents of the Reformation argued that this principle was based upon assumptions which appeared to be questionable, to say the least, involving confusion between two quite distinct propositions:

A. Nothing is to be believed which is contrary to Scripture.

B. Nothing is to be believed beyond Scripture itself.

In effect, mediaeval theology was based upon (A): scripture was the basis upon which the great 'cathedrals of the mind' (as Etienne Gilson has so aptly termed the great scholastic systems) were based. Similarly, many of the details of church order were not explicitly stated in scripture, although there was no particular reason for supposing that they were forbidden by it.

The Reformers appeared to wish to base their theology exclusively upon (B): theology was to restrict itself to what was explicitly stated within the pages of scripture itself. Thus Martin Bucer insisted that 'all doctrine must be derived from the divine scriptures, without anything being added or subtracted'. It is interesting to note that many scholars are of the opinion that Calvin attempted to organise the Genevan church exactly according to the Word of God, in effect trying to reconstitute the apostolic church, although Doumergue has insisted that Calvin established his church according to the *general principles*, and not according to the *detailed instructions*, of the New Testament. Furthermore, no external authority was to be recognised in the validation of the resulting theology, save scripture itself. As Bullinger stated this principle: 'Because it is the Word of God, the holy biblical scripture has adequate standing and credibility in itself and of itself'. The problem, as we shall see, is that the *sola scriptura* principle appeared to be unworkable in practice, even though its original intention was clearly understood. The difficulty rests in the question of how scripture is to be *interpreted*, which we shall now consider.

The Interpretation of Scripture

For the catholic, scripture was difficult to interpret, and required a reliable guide: this guide had been provided by God in the form of the church, whose interpretation of scripture in matters of doctrine was to be regarded as normative. For the early Reformers, particularly Luther and Zwingli, scripture was characterised by its *clarity*, which was such that the private individual could read and understand it. The later Reformers would draw heavily upon humanist exegetical techniques in establishing the precise meaning of scripture.

An excellent illustration of the influence of humanist exegetical methods upon Reformed biblical exegesis is provided by John Calvin's commentary upon Seneca's *de clementia* (1533). In this early work, dating from his humanist phase, we find Calvin using precisely the same methods for drawing out the meaning of a classical text as he would later employ in his biblical exegesis. Thus in establishing the meaning of phrases or words, Calvin begins by providing a philological explanation of the words in question, followed by an appeal to grammar and rhetoric. The final refinements of interpretation are provided by illustrating parallel uses of the terms or phrases from other sources of antiquity, as well as from additional writings of Seneca himself. Calvin, it may be emphasised, did not invent those methods – and their use in his early humanist period serves to emphasise the dependence of the Reformation upon humanist materials and methods in its first phase. Nevertheless, the basic presupposition, common to both Reformers and humanists, was that scripture was of sufficient clarity to permit its *direct* exegesis.

The divisions which resulted within Protestantism at such an early stage called this presupposition into question. An excellent example of this is provided by the eucharistic controversy between Luther and Zwingli, which culminated in 1528.

How was the gospel passage: 'This is my body' to be interpreted? For Luther, it was axiomatic that Christ did not use figurative language in his institution of the sacrament, whereas Zwingli argued that he used 'interpretative' language. In other words, Luther interpreted the crucial 'is' to mean nothing less that 'is literally identical to', whereas Zwingli regarded it as meaning 'signifies'. Luther appears to have been disgusted by Zwingli's exegesis: 'An unclear text is just as bad as no text at all! What kind of supper can it be, when there is no sure text or word of scripture?' Luther's doctrine of consubstantiation – which for Luther represented the clear meaning of scripture – was, in the eyes of Oecolampadius, nothing more than something which Luther had appended to scripture, and which was not to be taken seriously.

Radical Interpretation of Scripture

A more serious difficulty related to other reforming groups, which also based their theology upon scripture, and scripture alone, and yet achieved results which placed them far beyond the realms of orthodoxy. An excellent example is provided by Socinianism, which may be regarded as a forerunner of modern unitarianism. On the basis of the radical criticism of received doctrine in the light of Holy Scripture, the Socinians declined to believe in the Trinity and the deity of Christ, regarding these doctrines as unwarranted by scripture itself. The heterodoxy of the Radical Reformation illustrated the weakness of the *sola scriptura* principle, and was seized upon by Roman Catholic theologians as representing the inevitable outcome of a consistent application of the principle. The weakness of the principle was primarily due to the absence of any universal hermeneutical consensus within Protestantism: agreement upon the *source* of theology did not carry with it the necessary agreement upon how that source was to be interpreted. This difficulty was, however, partly overcome through an appeal to the fathers, as interpreters of scripture. We must therefore consider the authority which the Reformers ascribed to the fathers in general, and Augustine in particular.

7. THE SOURCES OF THEOLOGY: THE FATHERS

Patristic Study

At the heart of the Reformers' appeal to the fathers was the conviction that the mediaeval period had witnessed the corruption of the faith of the early church, and that the Reformation itself was primarily concerned with the restoration of the vitality, purity and simplicity of this primitive period. As we have already noted, the Reformation began under the influence of late Renaissance humanism, seeking to go back behind the synthesis of the fathers and scripture found in the *Sentences* of Peter Lombard, to the original sources themselves. A new age of patristic awareness opened up, with scholars (such as Erasmus, Oecolampadius, Lefevre and Beatus Rhenanus) and printers (such as Aldus, Amerbach, Cratander and Frobenius) collaborating to ensure that an adequate supply of patristic editions and translations was available for those who might wish to use them.

The rise of patristic studies is particularly associated with the second generation of Reformers, such as John Calvin, Philip Melanchthon, Wolfgang Musculus, Johannes Oecolampadius, and Urbanus Rhegius. Although secular humanists, such as Conrad Peutinger, valued the fathers largely because they exemplified a superior classical style, the Reformers had a serious theological purpose in studying them. We shall illustrate this with reference to Melanchthon.

As we noted above, the *sola scriptura* principle was inadequate as the sole methodological principle of Protestant theology, in that it permitted the private judgement of individuals to be given equal status to the corporate judgement of the community of faith. This point became particularly clear with the rise of the Radical Reformation (or Anabaptism) and Socinianism, which challenged traditional common teachings on matters such as the Trinity and the divinity of Christ. But how could such teachings be challenged, without compromising the *sola scriptura* principle? Melanchthon's solution to this difficulty, as he expounds it in his influential treatise *de ecclesia et autoritate Verbi Dei*, lay in an appeal to the patristic tradition.

Melanchthon's Appeal to the Fathers

Melanchthon's appeal to the fathers appears to reflect a general conviction, at Wittenberg and elsewhere, that the fathers' own theology was an authentically biblical theology. For Melanchthon, the fathers possess no independent authority of their own, but mirror that of scripture. Melanchthon argues that the teaching to be found in the primitive church was that which the fathers derived from scripture itself. To practise biblical theology necessarily means dealing with the fathers, since that was what they themselves were doing, and wished others to continue doing after them. Thus Melanchthon claimed that by promoting a theology based upon scripture alone, the Reformers were doing exactly what the fathers had done before them: where differences existed, they arose through the superior exegetical methods available at Wittenberg, and denied to the fathers. The priority of Augustine over other fathers was justified on the grounds that he was a reliable exegete, and the most eminent representative of a consciously biblical theology.

It will therefore be clear that the authority of the fathers was understood to reside in their reliability as biblical exegetes. This was not to say that they might not be challenged upon points of interpretation, in that the new philological precision of the Renaissance permitted them to be corrected upon points of detail. A convenient illustration of this is provided by the great Reformed theologian Wolfgang Musculus, who criticised Augustine's interpretation of the Latin verb *iustificare* ('to justify') as *iustum facere* ('to make righteous'). Conceding that this interpretation was perfectly possible on the basis of an analysis of the Latin word itself, Musculus points out that a consideration of its Hebraic origins leads to a more forensic understanding of the concept of justification. Although not questioning the authority of Augustine, nor the overall structure of his doctrine of justification (an essential element of Reformation theology), the new philological techniques of the Renaissance were used to correct him upon minor points, such as the proper interpretation of the term 'justification' itself.

The Patristic Witness to Scripture

Melanchthon and others held the patristic corpus to be endowed with a unique authority, in that it represented an authentically *biblical* theology which had been corrupted through scholasticism. Critics of this approach pointed out that the fathers were not unanimous in their opinions. Melanchthon replied by appealing to the idea of historical relativism: whereas in scripture an absolute distinction may be drawn between truth and error, this distinction became blurred in the process of exegesis. Thus Melanchthon argued that true patristic theology is a theology which reads the fathers *not as independent authorities, but as interpretations of scripture*, whose authenticity is to be judged on the basis of their scriptural foundations. The contradictions which exist within the patristic theology should serve to drive the modern theologian back to the source upon which that theology was based – *as the fathers themselves would have wished*. In other words, Melanchthon understands the appeal to the patristic testimony as a sophisticated refinement of the *sola scriptura* principle. The importance of this refinement will become clear when we consider the challenge posed to the theological method of the Reformers from their catholic and radical opponents.

Polemical Use of the Fathers

First, it served to blunt the charges of catholic opponents of the Reformation, who argued that the logical outcome of a consistent application of the *sola scriptura* principle was the destruction of the traditional foundations of the Christian faith. This charge had gained credibility through Socinian unitarianism, as noted above. In response, Melanchthon was able to argue that these traditional foundations were embodied in the patristic testimony, which the Reformers were not concerned to challenge, save on points of detail. The real point at issue with catholicism was the consequences of the degeneration of Christian doctrine during the mediaeval period, in which the authentic voice of the fathers had been stifled. Underlying the appeal to the fathers was the concept of the corruption of the authentic doctrine of the primitive church. This common presupposition of the Reformers was never defined with the precision which it appeared to demand, with the result that there was no general agreement upon when corruption set in. In practice, the last father to be regarded as reflecting the *primum et verum* appears to have been Bernard of Clairvaux, although the appeal to the fathers generally involved no patristic writer writing after the fifth century.

Second, and perhaps more significantly, the appeal to the fathers was a devastating weapon in the struggle against the radical wing of the Reformation, such as the Anabaptists and Socinians. Of particular importance was Melanchthon's use of Tertullian's principle that the *primum* was the *verum*. On the basis of the *Regel Tertulliani*, Melanchthon argued that, precisely because the radical theology was seriously at variance with that of the fathers, it could not be regarded as authentic. Thus Melanchthon appealed to the fathers to defend the practice of infant baptism against the Anabaptists. The theologians of the Radical Reformation were not slow in appreciating that the methodological programme of proceeding from the relative antiquity of the fathers to the absolute primacy of scripture itself, as the *primum et verum*, was potentially devastating when applied to their own interpretation of the *sola scriptura* principle. The radical Sebastian Frank wrote thus to Johannes Campanus in 1531:

> Foolish Ambrose, Augustine, Jerome, Gregory – of whom not even one knew the Lord, so help me God, nor was sent by God to teach. Rather, they were all apostles of Antichrist.

The Critical Approach to the Fathers
Melanchthon's appeal to the fathers was paralleled elsewhere during the first phase of the Reformation – for example, by Beatus Rhenus at Basel – and represented an important element of early Lutheran and Reformed theological method. By thus refining the *sola scriptura* principle, well-defined limits were placed upon the scope of the critique of the received doctrinal tradition, thus giving the magisterial Reformation a strong bias towards doctrinal conservatism.

Although Melanchthon's appeal to the fathers served an important purpose, its validity would soon be challanged. With the rise of post-Tridentine patristic scholarship within the Roman Catholic church, the existence of significant points of difference between the Reformers and the fathers, which could not be explained simply on the basis of improved exegetical methods, became increasingly clear. This led to the rise of a new literary genre within Lutheranism: the *critical dogmatic patrology*, such as Martin Chemnitz' *Oratio de Lectione patrum*. The most important example of this genre is due to the Orthodox Lutheran theologian Johann Gerhard.

Gerhard's *Patrologia sive de primitivae ecclesiae Christianae doctorum vita* discusses each father under four headings: his life, writings, positive statements (*elogia*) and 'mistakes' (*errata*). Thus Gerhard praises Irenaeus for defending basic apostolic teaching, and censures him for exaggerating the powers of human free will. Occasionally, a fifth category might be introduced – that of 'careless statements' (*incommode dicta*). Gregory of Nazianzus is thus accused of having caused others to lapse into superstition through some of his more obscure statements. In general, the purpose of the *Patrologia* was to indicate the areas of theology in which a given father may be relied upon, and those in which he must be treated with suspicion – and yet the very existence of this form of patrology served to demonstrate the extent of the divergence between the Reformers and fathers upon certain key matters.

8. THE SYSTEMATISATION OF THEOLOGY

One of the most difficult aspects of Luther scholarship relates to the fact that Luther was most emphatically not a systematic theologian. With the exception of his two Catechisms, Luther's theological writings are notable for the absence of any systematic interrelation of doctrine. Luther's writings over the period 1517–46 were almost invariably called forth by a concrete, specific historical occasion – he certainly did not have the leisure, and probably also lacked the talent, to produce a major work of systematic theology. It was this deficiency which the Augsburg Confession (1530) and its associated *Apologia* were intended to remedy. Nevertheless, it was essential that the new theology associated with the Lutheran and Reformed churches be set forth systematically, partly so that it could be taught and expounded more effectively, but also in order that it might be defended. It may be emphasised that the need to distinguish *Lutheran* from *Reformed* theology (and vice versa) came to be as important as distinguishing *Protestant* from *Roman Catholic* theology, as the rise of Confessionalism in the late sixteenth century demonstrates (see the following chapter).

In the present section, we propose to consider the literary forms in which the theology of the early Reformation was stated systematically, with a view to assessing the influence of the *structure* of scientific theology upon the *nature* of that theology itself.

A Scholastic Paradigm

In the mediaeval period, the most commonly encountered systematic presentation of theology was that of the *Commentary upon the Sentences*. It is quite probable that, the bible apart, no text has occupied so large a number of exegetes as Peter Lombard's collection of 'sentences': at least two hundred and fifty such commentaries are known. Every master of theology, from the thirteenth to well into the sixteenth centuries – including Martin Luther – began his career by commenting upon the Lombard's *Sentences*. But what literary *genre* would Protestant theologians use in the systematic exposition of the theology of the Reformation? Our attention is claimed by the 'Commonplaces' (*Loci Communes*) of Philip Melanchthon, and the *Institutio* of John Calvin, both of which exercised considerable influence upon the development of the science of theology in the sixteenth century.

'Common Places'

The origins of the term *loci communes* are due to humanist influence. Melanchthon, by his own admission, coined the term *loci theologici* by analogy with the *loci* (or *topoi*) of the classical rhetoricians – i.e., the 'places' or 'sources' from which proofs are deduced. From the time of Aristotle onwards, formal lists of such *loci* had been drawn up to facilitate the location of important proofs. Aristotle's *Topica* represented a collection of opinions which were to be considered as resting upon probable premises, thus leading only to probable conclusions. Cicero's *Loci*, however, were regarded as *sedes argumentorum*, the sources of knowledge, through which knowledge might be derived by the rhetorical tool of *inventio*. In this Ciceronian sense, the *loci* constituted part of the mediaeval *trivium*. In 1519, we find Melanchthon advising his students of logic to prepare lists of *loci communes* by subject, in order that they might become more skilled in disputation. In 1521, Melanchthon's *Loci communes rerum theologicarum seu hypotyposes theologicae* appeared, in which a systematic treatment of the main doctrines of the Christian faith, as established by the evangelical Reformers, was presented. Significantly, the Christological and Trinitarian dogmas were omitted, although they would be included in subsequent editions. Under each *locus*, Melanchthon gave a list of sources for the doctrine in question. Initially, Melanchthon used the term *hypotyposes* ('illustrations' or 'examples') in apposition to *loci*, indicating that he intended to provide his reader merely with material for his own subsequent doctrinal exposition (e.g., through *inventio*), rather than with a detailed exposition of doctrine as such.

Although his material was similar, in many respects, to the Lombard's *Sentences*, Melanchthon differed from the Lombard by drawing his examples almost in their entirety from the bible, rather than the fathers. The strongly Pauline cast of the work is evident when he discusses the *loci communissimi*, which relate to the doctrine of justification. Indeed, in their original form, the *Loci communes* appear to have been conceived as an introduction to the reading of scripture through a summary of the epistle to the Romans.

The *Loci communes* almost immediately achieved a normative status within Lutheran dogmatics, and the *genre* was widely accepted outside the Lutheran church. For our purposes, its significance relates to its *method* rather than its *contents*, in that Melanchthon was slow to give methodological justification to the arrangement of the collected *Loci*, and such justification, when it finally came, was somewhat unsatisfactory. As careful analysis of the sources of the *Loci communes* has demonstrated, Melanchthon appears to have done little more than take certain select topics from the Lombard's *Sentences*, and rewrite them in the light of the presuppositions and teachings of the early Lutheran Reformation. There is no underlying theological foundation for the arrangement of the material, despite the obvious interest in the *loci communissimi* relating to the doctrine of justification. The result of this weakness was that Lutheran dogmatics was slow in reaching inherent unity, as the principles upon which its dogmatics were constructed were not fully understood, nor did they command universal assent. The failure of early Lutheranism to approach, let alone match, the systematic exposition of theology associated with the Reformed church is partly due to the false start given to systematisation through Melanchthon.

Calvin's Institutes

In the case of Calvin's *Institutio* – which may be translated either as 'Institutes' or 'Institution' – a very different *genre* is encountered. The first edition of 1536 was modelled on Luther's Catechism of 1522, and was intended as nothing more than a primer. The need for systematic exposition of the Reformed faith led Calvin to expand it considerably, so that by 1559 the work had developed beyond recognition. However, Calvin succeeded where Melanchthon failed by altering the *structure* of the work to allow for its increased size. Rather than simply add material where appropriate to the 1536 edition, Calvin restructured the work completely, following a pattern very similar to that established by the Lombard's *Sentences*. The material is divided into four books, whose contents broadly parallel those of the Lombard's work. A discussion of the knowledge of God the creator (which includes an important analysis of the nature and limitations of natural theology) is followed by consideration of the knowledge of God the redeemer. The third book deals with the manner in which the *beneficia Christi* are applied (i.e., the doctrines of faith and salvation), and the fourth with the manner in which they are sustained (i.e., the doctrines of the church and sacraments).

Calvin's *Institutio* thus established the *structure*, as well as greatly influencing the *substance*, of the future systematic theology of the Reformed church, in that the framework which he established was found to meet the needs of the new era of confessional theology which was opening up in the late sixteenth and early seventeenth centuries. The rise of the scholastic method within Reformed Orthodoxy so soon after the publication of the 1559 *Institutio* may well reflect the highly systematised and structured theology bequeathed to his successors by Calvin. If any single work of Protestant dogmatics can be compared with Thomas Aquinas' *Summa theologiae*, that work is the 1559 edition of Calvin's *Institutio*.

Influence of Calvin's Institutes

The importance of the structure of the 1559 *Institutio* to the development of the science of theology in the period of Orthodoxy lies in its influence over international Reformed theology. Where the Reformed faith was propagated in late sixteenth century Europe, Calvin's *Institutio* was generally highly influential, and occasionally instrumental, in that propagation. Although his homiletical writings

particularly his biblical commentaries, were widely read and appreciated, they failed to exercise a comparable influence over European
religious thought. Although there has been renewed interest in
Calvin's homiletical writings in the last fifty years, the fact remains
that Calvin's ideas were propagated mainly through his dogmatic
writings, and specifically through the *Institutio*.

The French editions of the work are of particular importance in
this respect: from 1541 onwards, the French edition of the *Institutio*
became the basic manual of French Reformed theology, that of 1560
(based on the Latin edition of 1559) being particularly significant.
It is clear that the popular influence of the work was such that it
alone was responsible for the winning over of many French churches
to the Reformed faith. Those curious to learn the nature of the
Reformed faith naturally turned to the work for information: upon
being won over through it, they used it as a textbook, in order to
deepen their understanding of their adopted faith. Apart from
Calvin's own French translations, the work was translated into
numerous foreign languages. Thus no fewer than thirteen editions
of three different Dutch versions appeared between 1560 and 1650,
as well as numerous abridgements of the original. Of this latter
genre, particular attention should be paid to that of Guillaume
Delaune, which was particularly popular, while remaining faithful
to the original.

Of all the many influences which served to keep the theology of
Reformed Orthodoxy more or less in line with that of Calvin, the
Institutio was by far the most powerful. While never achieving a
status even approaching that of Holy Scripture, its influence over
Reformed theology appeared, at times, to be even greater, so that
scripture was effectively read through Calvin's spectacles. Nevertheless, significant differences between the two theologies would
emerge within decades of Calvin's death, as we shall document in
the following chapter. Our attention is now claimed, however, by
the problem of authority within the Reformation.

9. THE PROBLEM OF AUTHORITY IN THE REFORMATION

The new emphasis upon the role of scripture in theology associated
with the Reformation clearly raised the question of how an authoritative interpretation of scripture was to be recognised. We have
already noted the difficulties which the systematic application of the
sola scriptura principle raised for the Reformers, in that it appeared
to accord a similar status to long-standing traditional interpretations

of scripture (such as the Trinitarian and Christological dogmas, with which the magisterial Reformers had no quarrel) and radical reinterpretations of these along lines which the Reformers had to recognise as unorthodox. Melanchthon's appeal to the *testimonia patrum* was an important methodological qualification to the systematic application of the *sola scriptura* principle.

The question at issue, however, required careful consideration: what criteria could be applied to establish whether a given teaching was correct? In other words, where may one go in order to find authoritative theological statements? Within the Roman Catholic church, then as now, the answer was framed in terms of the *magisterium* – the teaching office of the church, whose function it was to safeguard the deposit of revealed truth committed to its charge. The Protestant failure to reach agreement on this vital question during the first phase of the Reformation is one of the most significant aspects of the history of the science of theology, and requires careful analysis.

Luther's Concept of Authority

For Luther, authority resided in the Word of God, which, up to about 1520, he tended to equate with scripture. However, during the 1520's, Luther became increasingly critical of the apostolic status of certain New Testament writings, as we noted earlier, with the result that he tended to define the 'Word of God' on the basis of his theological presuppositions. Thus he defined Romans as 'the true masterpiece of the New Testament, and the purest gospel of all', on the basis of his understanding of the significance of the *articulus iustificationis*. The intense difficulty which modern Luther scholarship has encountered in attempting to establish Luther's teaching on the *nature* and *location* of the Word of God must serve to illustrate the absence of any clear statement on the nature of religious authority within his writings, particularly those dating from his earlier period.

Zwingli

A similarly high estimation of the authority of the Word of God is encountered in the writings of Zwingli, particularly in the 1522 treatise *Von der Klarheit und Gewissheit oder Untrüglichkeit des Wortes Gottes*, in which scripture and the Word of God are frequently treated as if they were identical. Like Luther, Zwingli insisted that the church must be totally controlled and regulated by the Word of God; unlike him, Zwingli accepts scripture as a definite concrete body of writings, which cannot be modified on the basis of theological presuppositions. However, Zwingli appears reluctant to allow that disagreement might arise over the interpretation of scripture. 'The Word of God, as soon as it shines upon the understanding of man, illuminates it in such a way that he understands it, confesses it and becomes sure of it'. Indeed, Zwingli appears to exclude such difficulties or ambiguities as a matter of principle, on the grounds that it appears to subordinate the Word of God to human beings. In 1526, however, we find an apparent concession: 'If it is obscure in any place, it is to be expounded by the Word of God from another place'. The eucharistic controversy between Luther and Zwingli serves to illustrate the difficulties associated with this hermeneutical principle. Having established that the ultimate authority in matters theological is the Word of God, he is unable to provide a systematic description of how this principle, once conceded, is put into practice.

Calvin

In the case of Calvin, we find a similar appeal to the Word of God, which again appears to be treated as if it is identical with scripture. It may be noted that there is a suggestion that Calvin did not regard Revelation or II and III John as canonical, in that he did not write a commentary upon any of them. However, it is well known that Calvin did not write a commentary upon the Song of Solomon, yet, as his treatment of Castellio indicates unequivocally, he regarded this book as canonical.

In what does the authority of scripture reside? Calvin makes no general statements concerning the nature of the inspiration of scripture, although he states that the apostles were 'the certain and authentic secretaries of the Holy Spirit' (*les notaires jurez du Sainct Esprit – authentiques*, as he later translated the phrase into French). Similarly, he refers to the historical works of the Old Testament as having been written 'as dictated by the Holy Spirit' (*dictante Spiritu sancto*), thus giving ample support to the general view that Calvin operated with a mechanical and verbal theory of the inspiration of scripture. Nevertheless, it may be emphasised that Calvin did much to clarify *why* scripture is authoritative, and how that authority may be maintained independent of the authority of the church. Once more, however, the question of how scripture is to be interpreted comes to the fore, and Calvin's answer to this problem is of particular interest.

Calvin on Biblical Interpretation

Unlike Zwingli, Calvin explicitly acknowledges that there is a genuine problem associated with the proper interpretation of scripture. The believer requires a reliable guide, if he is to avoid the numerous pitfalls in relation to interpreting scripture. Calvin provided that reliable guide in the form of his *Institutio*. The preface to the French edition of 1541 is particularly illuminating in this respect, in that Calvin states that the *Institutio* 'could be like a key and an entrance to give access to all the children of God, in order that they might really understand Holy Scripture'.

Calvin's own theological works apart, this guidance was to be provided by the doctors of the church, within the structure of ministry developed by Calvin at Geneva. Of particular interest in this respect is the criterion stipulated by Calvin on the basis of which the doctors were to be selected by the other ministers and the Magistracy: 'No one may be elected who is not of sound doctrine and of holy life'. In effect, Calvin regarded the election of doctors and other ministers of the church as nothing more than an endorsement or ratification of the prior decision of the Holy Spirit. But, as will be clear, the guidance of the Holy Spirit, whether in ecclesiastical elections or in the interpretation of Scripture, is less easily discerned publicly than might be thought desirable, with significant consequences for the Protestant understanding of the nature and location of authority in matters of doctrine.

Authority: An Unresolved Problem

Indeed, the study of the science of theology over the period with which we are concerned suggests that the absence of consensus on the question of authority during its first phase constitutes the Achilles Heel of the Reformation. Of course, those who regard the Reformation as representing a liberation from the ecclesiastical tyranny of the mediaeval period may well feel that, far from representing a weakness, this absence constitutes the chief glory of the Reformation. For our purposes, it is important to note this point at this early stage, as it goes some considerable way towards explaining the subsequent development and diversification of Protestant theology in the following centuries. Our attention now turns to the consolidation of the theology of the first phase of the Reformation in the theological systems of its second phase – that of Orthodoxy.

FOR FURTHER READING

Pelikan, J. *The Christian Tradition. A History of the Development of Doctrine. 4. Reformation of Church and Dogma (1300–1700)* (Chicago and London, 1984).

McGrath, Alister E. *Luther's Theology of the Cross. Martin Luther's Theological Breakthrough* (Oxford, 1985) pp. 5–92.

Wendel, F. *Calvin. The Origins and Development of his Religious Thought* (London, 1974).

Fraenkel, P. *Testimonia Patrum. The Function of the Patristic Argument in the Theology of Philip Melanchthon* (Geneva, 1961).

Breen, Q. 'The Subordination of Philosophy to Rhetoric in Melanchthon', *Archiv für Reformationsgeschichte* 43 (1952) pp. 13–27.

idem., 'John Calvin and the Rhetorical Tradition', in *Church History* 26 (1957) pp. 3–21.

McGrath, A. E. 'Humanist Elements in the Early Reformed Doctrine of Justification', *Archiv für Reformationsgeschichte* 73 (1982) pp. 5–20.

Grislis, E. 'Calvin's Use of Cicero in the Institutes I:1–5 – A Case Study in Theological Method', *Archiv für Reformationsgeshichte* 62 (1971) pp. 5–37.

PROTESTANT ORTHODOXY

The seventeenth century witnessed the emergence of Protestant Orthodoxy, particularly within the Reformed camp, arising through the recognition of the authority of confessional statements such as that of Dort (1619) or Westminster (1647). Within this period, the various elements of post-Reformation Christianity had consolidated themselves, with the result that a state of permanent division within the Christian church became recognised as normal. Indeed, the significance of the Religious Peace of Augsburg (1555) lies partly in the fact that it explicitly recognises a religious pluralism. Within this pluralism, the various branches of post-Reformation Christianity sought to establish their distinct identities and legitimation, with great emphasis being placed upon *purity of doctrine*. It is this phenomenon of doctrinal emphasis, as widespread within Roman Catholicism as within Protestantism, which is characteristic of *Orthodoxy*.

In many ways, the period of Orthodoxy marks the opening of the modern period in theology. The seventeenth century witnessed the appearance of Descartes in theoretical philosophy, of Hobbes in practical philosophy, and Grotius in legal philosophy. The emergence of secular philosophy and legal theory, of state-centred rather than God-centred politics, and of mechanistic theories of causality did much to establish a society whose presuppositions were quite different from those of traditional theology. The secular settlement of the 'religious problem' by the Treaty of Westphalia (1648) appeared to suggest that religious freedom was essentially a matter of politics, rather than theology. Indeed, viewed from the standpoint of intellectual history, the development of the science of theology in the period of Orthodoxy frequently strikes the disinterested observer as irrelevant to the point of obscurantism, giving every indication of a dying, rather than flourishing, science. The protests of Pietism were well-founded, in that Orthodox theology appeared to become detached from personal faith.

It seems to be a general feature of the history of Christian thought, that a period of genuine creativity is immediately followed by one of petrification and scholasticism, as the insights of a pioneering thinker or group of thinkers are embodied in formulae or confessions. (The term *Confession* is particularly applied to Protestant professions of faith of the sixteenth and seventeenth centuries, such as the Augsburg Confession (1530)). For many critics of Orthodoxy, particularly within Pietist circles, Orthodoxy merely guarded the ashes of the Reformation, rather than tending its flame. The period of Orthodoxy between the first phase of the Reformation and the Enlightenment is characterised by its *confessionalism*, which effectively replaced the dynamism of the first phase of the Reformation with a static understanding of the nature of theology. It was this tendency which Alexander Schweizer (1808–88) criticised in his famous remark: 'Once the fathers confessed their faith – today most Christians just believe their confessions'. The rise of confessionalism is of importance in relation to the development of the science of theology, and we may begin the present chapter by considering precisely what is meant by the term.

1. THE RISE OF CONFESSIONALISM

A Hardening of Divisions
The controversies of the first phase of the Reformation, particularly those relating to sacramental theology, led to a well-defined division emerging between the *Lutheran* and *Reformed* wings of Protestantism. Broadly speaking, this division corresponded to those churches who looked to Luther, and those who looked to Calvin, for theological guidance. The rise of confessional theology, which is particularly associated with the period 1560–1618, served to harden the distinction between these two movements, by radically restricting the freedom of theologians to depart from, or modify, the doctrine of their tradition. This phenomenon is as characteristic of Roman Catholicism as of Protestantism during the period in question. The canons and decrees of the Council of Trent, the Synod of Dort, the Augsburg Confession and the Formula of Concord thus came to represent the standards of orthodoxy to which the theologians of the Roman Catholic, Reformed and Lutheran churches respectively were expected to conform.

In effect, the theologians of the churches of the Reformation inherited a tradition, defined in confessional documents of near-credal status, which originated in a polemical context. In other words, doctrines which had arisen on account of, or which assumed their specific form through, a response to a specific attack upon a tradition made during the first phase of the Reformation now stood as permanent features of that tradition, frequently when the original occasion for the attack was forgotten or shrouded in obscurity. Whereas the first phase of the Reformation saw a genuine exchange of views between representatives of the Lutheran and Reformed traditions upon matters such as the nature of the eucharistic presence, with a real possibility of agreement or compromise, the period of Orthodoxy saw only the permanent stalemate of controversy between two precisely-defined and well-established positions, with any possibility of agreement or compromise being precluded by the authority of the confessional documents and the traditions which they defined.

Confessionalism Defensive
The primacy of Orthodoxy (i.e., pure doctrine) during this period resulted from the desire to safeguard the insights of the first generation of Reformers, as expressed in the confessional documents of the Lutheran and Reformed churches, in the great classical dogmatic systems of the seventeenth centuries. On account of its very nature, confessional theology tended to emphasise differences between churches, rather than their common foundations. The inevitable result of this confessional approach to theology, which may be regarded as dominating Protestant theology up to the middle of the eighteenth century, was to reduce theology to the endorsement of confessional statements by a critical and selective appeal to authoritative sources, such as scripture, the fathers and reason. Furthermore, in terms of their theological method, Orthodox theologians tended to work with a scholastic methodology and set of presuppositions remarkably similar to those of the mediaeval period: the influence of Aristotelian logic and metaphysics upon Orthodoxy is of particular interest in this respect, and will be considered in some detail in the present chapter. In effect, the first generation of Reformers, such as Luther and Calvin may be regarded as marking the transition from one form of Aristotelian scholasticism (that of the Middle Ages) to another (that of Orthodoxy), although they themselves were neither Aristotelian nor scholastic in their outook.

Despite these critical introductory comments, the age of Orthodoxy witnessed significant theological developments, such as the definition of the relationship between faith and reason. The uniqueness of the period, however, lies in the doctrine of scripture which was developed by its theologians. The emphasis of the period on purity of doctrine, whether in intra-Protestant disputes or in controversy with Roman Catholic theologians, led to the question of the nature of the authority of scripture receiving priority. Although this question had been discussed in the first phase of the Reformation, it assumed a new urgency in the seventeenth century.

The Doctrine of Scripture
William Chillingworth (1602–44), the noted Caroline divine, gave what is probably the most epigrammatic statement of the *sola scriptura* principle in his celebrated maxim: 'The bible only is the religion of Protestants'. The need for Protestants to define the nature of the authority of scripture, although recognised as a corollary of the *sola scriptura* principle from the earliest period of the Reformation, assumed a new significance when the Council of Trent defined authority in terms of scripture and tradition.

A Doctrine of Inspiration
Whereas Luther had avoided a formal definition of the authority of scripture, his later followers felt the need to define the authority of scripture *objectively*, in terms of a doctrine of the *verbal inspiration of scripture*. This tendency can be seen in Matthias Flacius' *Clavis scripturae sacrae* (1567), where a distinctive concept of inspiration is developed. According to Flacius (1520–75), the very letters of the text of canonical scripture must be regarded as directly inspired by the Holy Spirit, down to the vowel points of the Hebrew text itself. This point was of particular importance, for it immediately established that scripture, as originally given, was inspired, and not any particular translation: the obvious target of Flacius' statements was the Council of Trent, which had recently stipulated that the Vulgate, rather than the original Hebrew and Greek texts, was authoritative. For Flacius, it is unthinkable that God should provide his church with an obscure or indistinctly recorded witness concerning him. The Holy Spirit is responsible for both the inspiration of scripture and its subsequent interpretation. For the Lutheran theologian Johannes Andreas Quenstedt (1617–88), scripture

> is the infallible truth, free from any error; in other words, in canonical sacred scripture there is no lie, no falsehood, not even the tiniest of errors (*nullus vel minimus error*) either in content or in word. Rather, each and every statement contained within it is

totally true, be it dogmatic or moral or historical, chronological, topographical or onomastic. It is neither possible nor permissible to attribute to the scribes of the Holy Spirit any ignorance, lack of thought or forgetfulness, or any lapse of memory, in recording Holy Scripture.

Of course, this assertion was not without its difficulties, as the Reformed theologian Polanus noted. The use of the Septuagint by some of the New Testament writers posed a particular difficulty, as it appeared to suggest that a *translation* of the original Hebrew text of the Old Testament was also infallible, at least in part.

A significant challenge to the doctrine of verbal inspiration was due to the Danish Pastor Hermann Rahtmann (1585–1628), who argued that the supernatural element associated with the inspiration of scripture only came into play when it was proclaimed – in other words, that scripture can only be regarded as inspired when it is proclaimed and causes faith, and not when it is not being used. This challenge was defeated by Jena theologians such as Georg Major and Johann Gerhard, but at the cost of asserting that scripture possesses an internal divine power, even when it is not being used. Nevertheless, Rahtmann's challenge foreshadowed others, which would eventually result in the Enlightenment critique of the Orthodox doctrine of scripture. It is therefore of interest to note that no confessional document of the Lutheran or Reformed church actually stated a doctrine of the verbal inspiration of scripture. Indeed, the very confessionalism which we noted in the previous section appears to have prevented any such doctrine being appended to the original confessional statements, out of respect for their authority. As a result, the later challenges to the Orthodox doctrine of scripture, and concessions made as a consequence, did not necessarily entail a weakening of the confessional basis of Orthodoxy.

2. THE RISE OF ARISTOTELIAN SCHOLASTICISM IN REFORMED ORTHODOXY

The first phase of the Reformation witnessed intense hostility towards the scholastic method, and particularly Aristotelian scholasticism. Nevertheless, within fifty years, the churches of the Reformation had reverted to precisely this form of scholasticism. How could this seemingly inconceivable *volte-face* have taken place? Before this question can be answered, the essential features of 'scholasticism' must first be defined.

What is Scholasticism?

A succinct definition of 'scholasticism' is: 'a method of theological and philosophical speculation that seeks the rational penetration and systematisation of revealed truth on the basis of philosophical concepts'. If any Reformer may be credited or castigated for preparing the way for the reintroduction of the scholastic method into Protestant theology, it is Philip Melanchthon, who insisted that philosophy be regarded as the *ancilla theologiae*, although it may be pointed out that Melanchthon's distinctive blend of Aristotelianism and Ciceronian Stoicism had less influence upon his theology than might be expected. The classic *locus* for scholastic philosophical theology was the *locus de Deo*, in which arguments for the existence of God assumed an important apologetic function (we shall be considering the significance of the re-emergence of such arguments in this *locus* within Reformed dogmatics in the present chapter). But the most attractive aspect of scholasticism was the possibility of constructing a scientific theology, resting upon well-defined presuppositions and methods, whose logical coherence would commend respect and attention. Just as the Protestants vied with their Roman Catholic opponents in the field of ecclesiastical architecture, a similar – if not greater – energy was expended on the construction of great 'cathedrals of the mind'.

The underlying motivation for the reintroduction of scholasticism appears to have been the desire to consolidate the gains of the first phase of the Reformation, by establishing the leading doctrines of Protestantism upon a secure scientific foundation. Calvin's formulations were found to be inadequate to meet the new polemical situation, and a more absolutist theology had to be developed in order to pose an effective challenge to the highly systematised theology of Roman Catholicism. Similar considerations underlie the subsequent rise of scholasticism within Lutheran Orthodoxy, although the need to challenge the by then equally highly systematised theology of Reformed Orthodoxy was undoubtedly an additional consideration. There was no scientific method available then other than that of Aristotle, and the failure of Ramus' challenge to Aristotelianism only served to increase his influence within Lutheran and Reformed Orthodoxy alike. It was therefore inevitable that the scholasticism (or, more accurately, neo-scholasticism) which was emerging within Orthodox theology would assume a strongly Aristotelian cast, particularly when the affinity between Reformed Orthodoxy and the late Italian Renaissance is considered.

The Revival of Aristotle

In a previous chapter, we drew attention to the persistence of Aristotelianism during the Italian Renaissance, and its revival in the northern Italian universities of the early sixteenth centuries. An earlier chapter drew attention to the rediscovery of Aristotle during the earlier mediaeval period, and its theological significance. Although Aristotle continued to be studied throughout the Middle Ages, the Renaissance marked an important alteration in the nature of mediaeval Aristotelianism. We have already noted the new interest in the *Rhetorica* and *Poetica*. The Renaissance also witnessed a greater appreciation of the *Posterior Analytics*, with a resulting emphasis upon the significance of logic. The resulting revival in Aristotelianism thus had a strongly logical character, and Renaissance Aristotelians who had theological interests – such as Pietro Pomponazzi (1464–1525) – tended to emphasise the necessity of involving logic in theology, while not challenging the supernatural basis of the Christian revelation.

Of greater importance, however, was the new understanding of the relation between logic and method which was being developed at Padua at the time.

Method

Giacomo Zabarella (1532–89) formulated the classic version of the teaching of the highly influential Paduan school on method as follows: *logic and method are identical*. Method is thus defined in terms of *syllogistic reasoning*. This limitation of method to a single specific discipline is of considerable importance, and many scholars recognise in Zabarella a figure of transition between the mediaeval and modern periods, in that he recognises the universalisation of method, and its identification with logic. Nevertheless, Zabarella limits method to *syllogistic* (i.e., Aristotelian) logic. This important principle, when applied to *theological* method, leads to the conclusion that *theological method is essentially the application of Aristotelian syllogistic logic*.

This understanding of the relation between logic and method is of considerable importance in relation to the development of Orthodoxy, as Aristotelian presuppositions and methods thence came to be incorporated into Protestant theology.

Beza and Scholasticism

Theodore Beza (1519–1605) is of particular significance in the introduction of Aristotelianism into Reformed theology, and was probably influenced in this respect by Peter Martyr Vermigli and Girolamo Zanchi. In the recently published correspondence of Beza may be found a letter in which the Reformer requests a work by Pomponazzi, in which the Italian Aristotelian demonstrated how reason and logic were essential to the science of theology. Beza himself subsequently appears to elevate reason in general, and Aristotelian logic in particular, to a status equal to that of faith in theological epistemology, and was thus regarded by an earlier generation of scholars as one of the first Protestant scholastics. This opinion has been confirmed by recent studies of Beza's theological method, and especially his doctrine of God.

The strongly rationalist character of Beza's thought is particularly well illustrated by his doctrine of predestination, which marks a significant modification of Calvin's teaching on the matter. Whereas Calvin's rather cautious statements on the doctrine are based upon scripture, and set in the context of his discussion of salvation, Beza's more confident statements are based upon an analysis of the concept of causality, and are set within the context of his doctrine of God. Calvin's Christocentrism is replaced by a rational system of final causation, which is particularly clearly stated in the *Tractationes theologicae* (1570–82).

Although the relocation of the doctrine of predestination may not appear to be of particular significance, a fundamental shift in emphasis has, in fact, taken place. For Calvin, the doctrine of predestination is but an aspect – and a very difficult aspect – of the doctrine of grace: it is most emphatically not a leading principle in his theological methodology. For Beza, the doctrine of predestination is a central doctrine, of decisive importance to his doctrine of God in particular and theology in general, which constitutes the logical basis for other doctrines. Reformed theology thus proceeded, not from the doctrine of *God* as such, but from the doctrine of the *divine decree of predestination*, in which the whole matter of salvation is regarded *sub specie aeternitatis*. Any doctrine which is a logical consequence of the doctrine of predestination must be accepted – and Beza employs *Aristotelian* logic in this respect, using argumentation which deduces one or more conclusions from a given principle.

Thus Beza unhesitatingly teaches the doctrines of *supralapsarianism* (i.e., that God predestined man to election or reprobation *before* the Fall of Adam, rather than after it) and of *limited atonement* (i.e., that Christ died only for the elect), the latter in particular marking a radical departure from Calvin's teaching on the matter. For Calvin, Christ died for all men, although his death is of no value unless its benefits are appropriated by faith; for Beza, Christ died only for the elect. Although it is possible to argue that both these doctrines are logically implied by Calvin's own teaching, the fact remains that Calvin chose not to teach them.

Inductive or Deductive?

Whereas the earlier theologians of the Reformed church, such as Calvin, had subsumed their discussion of matters such as predestination, election and reprobation under the general aegis of the *cognitio Dei redemptoris*, Orthodoxy tended to make the divine decrees themselves the proper starting point for theological speculation. Whereas Calvin made the redemption of man in Christ the starting point for his discussion of more rarified matters such as election and reprobation, Orthodoxy extrapolated from the basic *datum* of redemption to the divine decision to redeem, and thence to the divine decrees. These decrees themselves then became the logical starting point for a characteristically *synthetic and deductive* methodology, beginning with the divine decision to redeem, proceeding thus from the intratrinitarian decision to the *opus trinitatis ad extra* – i.e., the actualisation of that decision in time. Calvin's approach appears to be *analytic and inductive* – i.e., proceeding from the concrete event of redemption in Christ to an exploration of its implications (such as predestination and election) – and is thus able to remain profoundly Christocentric: Orthodoxy, by contrast, took its starting point in the intratrinitarian decision to redeem or damn – and thus assumed a strongly theocentric cast.

The fact that predestination is the central dogma of Reformed Orthodoxy thus reflects the theological method employed by the theologians of that school, and indicates how foolish it is to argue that Calvin must demonstrate a similar emphasis upon the dogma, in view of the subsequent development of the theology of the church which he influenced so strongly. This point may be illustrated from the comments on theological method due to Arminius (1560–1609), a noted critic of the Orthodox doctrine of predestination. In the second of his *Private Disputations*, 'On the method in which theology must be taught', he commented:

It has long been a maxim with those philosophers who are the masters of method and order, that the theoretical sciences ought to be delivered in a synthetic order, but the practical in an analytical order, on which account, and because theology is a practical science, it follows that it must be treated according to the analytical method.

If this procedure were followed, the theology of Calvin, rather than Beza, would result. We shall return to this point later, in relation to the Salmurian Academy and the Amyraldist controversy.

The fact that both Beza and Thomas Aquinas discuss predestination under the aegis of the doctrine of *God* rather than *salvation* may thus be taken as an indication of their common Aristotelian presuppositions and scholastic methodology, and in the case of Beza, certainly reflects the intrusion of Aristotelian metaphysics and logic into theology. Calvin's theology appears to have been carefully constructed to represent the scriptural teaching faithfully, with the result that certain doctrines are maintained in a state of permanent tension or delicate balance – the doctrine of predestination being an excellent example. Those who succeeded Calvin were not prepared to tolerate such tensions, which were difficult to accomodate within an internally consistent scientific theological system, with the result that the tensions within Calvin's theology were resolved simply by isolating certain elements at the expense of the additional qualifying doctrines which Calvin had placed alongside them. Thus Girolamo Zanchi (1516–90), Beza, Antoine de Chandieu (1534–91) and Lambert Daneau (1530–95) effectively destroyed the delicate balance of Calvin's theology through their desire for systematisation and internal consistency.

Dissident Voices

Beza's influence over the development of Reformed theology in the era after the death of Calvin was partly due to his position as professor of theology at the Genevan Academy, as a result of which he was able to exercise considerable influence over the theological programme of the Reformed church. It is significant that it was Beza who was responsible for the introduction of Aristotelian logic and moral philosophy at the Genevan Academy, and that his refusal to offer Peter Ramus (1515–72) a teaching post at the Academy is known to have been a consequence of Ramus' strongly anti-Aristotelian stance, as exemplified in his *Aristotelicae animadversiones* (1543). Although the introduction of Aristotelian logic followed as a matter of course at the Protestant Academies of Europe (especially the Dutch Academies at Leiden, Fraenker and Gronigen), thus giving Reformed Orthodoxy its strongly scholastic cast, there was one such Academy which declined to follow this general trend. The Protestant Academy at Saumur, a Protestant *place de sûreté* established by the Edict of Nantes in Catholic France, followed the logic of Ramus, rather than Aristotle, and declined to permit the application of Aristotelian logic in matters theological. Thus while Orthodoxy in general argued that it was legitimate to deduce such doctrines as limited atonement from the principle of divine election, the Salmurians rejected this, and by doing so, found themselves at variance with the common Reformed teaching on predestination.

In his *Praecognitorum philosophicorum* (published 1618), Bartholomaeus Keckermann (1571–1609) pointed out that Ramus was incapable of deducing the particular from a general knowledge of all things – e.g., the deduction of one's predestination from the general divine decrees by a synthetic and deductive methodology, as noted above. The Amyraldist heresy, which is specifically linked with the Salmurian Academy, arose on account of misgivings concerning the Orthodox Reformed doctrine of predestination, and it is significant that the Salmurian Academy did not share the logical foundations upon which Reformed Orthodoxy based its predestinarianism. With the exception of the Salmurian Academy, Aristotelian logic became the established tool of Reformed theology throughout Europe, and exercised considerable influence over both constructive and polemical theology. The strongly syllogistic character of Aristotelian logic is particularly well expressed in the polemical works of the Dutch Reformed theologian Sibrandus Lubbertus (1555–1625), especially those directed against Bellarmine and Vorstius.

Theistic Proofs

The influence of Aristotelianism upon Reformed Orthodoxy can also be illustrated from the arguments employed to demonstrate the existence of God, which bear a remarkable resemblance to those of Thomas Aquinas, based explicitly upon Aristotelian physics. Thus Franciscus Junius (1545–1602) appears to be dependent upon Aquinas to the very letter at points, particularly in his influential treatise *de vera theologia*. This dependence is even more marked in his disputation *de deo seu deum esse*, in which he gives an excellent précis of the 'five ways' (*quinque viae*) of Aquinas:

> Thence by the creation of the world there are five of these (arguments) which have been set forth for men: the nature of things, their guidedness, their motion, the nature of the efficient cause and its mode.

Underlying the five arguments for the existence of God is an Aristotelian understanding of the nature of causality (*causa efficiens, necessaria, formalis, movens, et finalis unica universi*). Similar remarks apply to the 1598 disputations of the Arminian Conrad Vorstius (1569–1622), as well as his later *Tractatus theologicus de deo*, which attracted wide attention on account of its rationalism and implicit Socinianism.

An important development in the evolution of Reformed Aristotelian scholasticism, too easily overlooked, is due to Zacharias Ursinus (1534–83). In his exposition of the Heidelberg Catechism (1584), the arguments for the existence of God are transferred from the doctrine of creation (where they had been placed by Melanchthon) to their traditional scholastic setting within the context of the doctrine of God. His use of syllogistic reasoning and the concept of efficient causality in the course of these arguments serves to set him further apart from Melanchthon, and his subsequent influence upon Reformed theology served to consolidate its developing Aristotelian scholasticism.

Apologetics

Underlying the incorporation of natural or rational proofs of aspects of Christian theology was a new concern for apologetics, a concern which received but scanty and inadequate attention in the writings of Luther and Calvin. The new interest in natural theology reflected a growing appreciation of the need to establish a rational foundation for Christian theology if it was to maintain its intellectual integrity and appeal. An extremely important development in this respect was the rejection by both Reformed and Lutheran theologians of the concept of *double truth* – i.e., the idea that a given proposition could be true *theologically* and yet false *philosophically*, or vice versa. God had to be the author of all truth, both philosophical and theological, and therefore truth had to be one. It was this conviction which lay at the heart of the Orthodox use of reason in theology, as exemplified by the use of the 'five ways' for demonstrating the existence of God. In view of the importance of the Orthodox discussion of the proper role of reason in theology, we shall return to this theme in a later section.

The influence of Aristotelianism upon Orthodoxy was not, however, restricted to the Reformed church: it assumed considerable significance within Lutheran Orthodoxy during the seventeenth century. The somewhat later development of this phenomenon within Lutheranism is partly due to the movement's weaker links with the Italian Renaissance, and partly to the peculiar method of doctrinal exposition employed by its theologians. We shall now consider the nature of Aristotelian influences on Lutheran Orthodoxy.

3. THE RISE OF ARISTOTELIANISM IN LUTHERAN ORTHODOXY

Philosophical Conflicts

The dominance of Aristotelianism in the German universities of the early seventeenth century has been well documented in a number of important studies. It was thus inevitable that the prevailing metaphysical presuppositions should find their way into Lutheran theology. Of particular importance in this respect was the Giessen Lutheran philosopher Christoph Scheibler, whose *Opus metaphysicum* (1617) was greatly admired by many, including the great Lutheran theologian Johann Gerhard (1582–1637). Gerhard's *Loci communes theologici* (1610–22) would become a standard work of Lutheran theology, and it is instructive to consider the full extent of the influence of Aristotle upon this important and influential theologian.

The re-entry of Aristotelianism into Lutheran dogmatics did not take place without considerable opposition. Thus the new interest in the humanities and Aristotelian philosophy which was evident at the university of Helmstädt from its foundation in 1576 appears to have led to the bitter controversy associated with Daniel Hoffmann (1540–1611). Hoffmann, the first professor of ethics and dialectics at Helmstädt, was outraged by the decree of 1597 forbidding the public teaching of the logic of Ramus. The theological significance of Ramus' logic was noted in the previous section. For Hoffmann, adherence to Ramus was equivalent to the rejection of the pagan philosophy of Aristotle, and he regarded the decree as an attack on the Christian faith itself. Developing insights derived from Luther himself, Hoffmann argued that reason in general, and Aristotelianism in particular, were naturally opposed to revelation, so that the truth of a doctrine was to be judged in terms of its irrationality. In effect, Hoffmann revived the doctrine of double truth, which had by then been generally abandoned – viz., that all that is true in philosophy is false in theology. The dispute was resolved through the expulsion of Hoffmann from the university, and the attempts of others to reintroduce the logic of Ramus to Helmstädt were defeated. By the second decade of the seventeenth century, Helmstädt displayed the Aristotelian features which were rapidly becoming charactertistic of Lutheran Orthodoxy: Aristotelian metaphysics and, to a lesser extent, logic were widely employed in the exposition and defence of doctrine.

Johann Gerhard
The rational and scientific character of theology is strongly defended by Gerhard in his *Methodus studii theologici* (1622). Although asserting the priority of theology over philosophy, Gerhard immediately concedes that the theologian is forced to employ logic in his definitions, methods and arguments. Inevitably, the logic used in this respect is that of Aristotle, the only alternative then available (that of Ramus) by then having been discredited, as within Reformed Orthodoxy. Furthermore, Gerhard finds himself obliged to interpret the biblical foundations of Lutheran theology *metaphysically*, which at times results in metaphysical 'demythologisation'. The Aristotelian understanding of causality is also employed, particularly in relation to the doctrine of justification. Thus in his *Loci Communes*, Gerhard identifies the various causes of justification as follows: *causa efficiens* = the grace of God; *causa meritoria* = the obedience and satisfaction of Christ; *causa formalis* = the remission of sin; *causa finalis* = declaration of righteousness on the part of God. Perhaps the most intriguing aspect of the influence of Aristotelianism upon Lutheran Orthodoxy, however, relates to Christology, and the concept of space underlying the notion of the incarnation.

The Concept of Space
What is understood by 'space'? The dominating concept within Greek thought is that of a *container* or *receptacle*, rather than a *relational*, notion of space. Thus for Aristotle, 'space' is the vessel into which, and out of which, things pass. It not only contains them, but exercises a certain force or causality in relation to them. Rejecting the idea of space being commensurate or isomorphous with its contents, Aristotle developed the notion that space is the limit or boundary of the container with its contents. This closed receptacle understanding of space was taken up by the theologians of Lutheran Orthodoxy in their controversy with Calvin's concept of the so-called *extra Calvinisticum*. The Lutheran theologians based their Christologies upon the axiom *finitum capax infiniti*, so that the incarnation had to be understood as the self-emptying of the infinite Christ into the finite receptacle of a human body. The intense difficulties which this interpretation occasioned were essentially a consequence of the metaphysical concept of space employed, rather than the theological principle which was at stake. This point aside, the strong influence of Aristotelian metaphysics upon Gerhard's Christology has often been noted, along with the inherent tensions associated with this development. Nevertheless, it is significant that Gerhard's Aristotelianism is more evident in his metaphysics than

in his method. The reason for this relates to the manner of doctrinal exposition of which Gerhard's *Loci* is the last great example.

Method in Doctrine

Perhaps the most serious obstacle to the development of Lutheran theology during the period of Orthodoxy was the method employed in doctrinal exposition. In the previous chapter, we noted Melanchthon's use of the *local method* of doctrinal exposition – i.e., the discussion of theology by *loci* or 'topics'. This method continued to be used within Lutheran Orthodoxy by theologians such as Johann Spangenberg in his *Margarita theologica* (1540), Niels Hemmingsen in his *Enchiridion theologica* (1557), as well as Gerhard himself in his *Loci*. By separating the various elements of Christian doctrine from one another, and considering them in isolation, the 'local method' prevented their mutual relationship from becoming apparent. As this mutual relationship was largely defined by the theological method employed in their deduction or exposition, the 'local method' greatly diminished the influence of Aristotelianism upon early Lutheran Orthodoxy. As we noted in the previous chapter, Reformed Orthodoxy was able to fully exploit the new understanding of the relationship between logic and method on account of the vastly superior method of doctrinal exposition bequeathed to his successors by Calvin.

This impediment to the development of systematic theology within Lutheranism was removed through the influence of Georg Calixtus (1586–1656), who took up the chair of theology at Helmstädt in 1614. Although Calixtus is particularly remembered for his syncretism, his significance for our purposes lies in his insistence that theology proceeds deductively from one supreme truth to the several doctrinal propositions which represent its component parts. This teleological method was expounded with some brilliance in his *Epitome theologiae* (1619), and was taken up with enthusiasm, even by those who opposed him on other matters. The new method was clearly capable of demonstrating the mutual relationship of doctrines where the 'local method' was not. Thus Abraham Calovius' *Systema locorum theologicorum* (1675–77), with its exploitation of both the so-called 'definitional' and 'causal' methods along Calixtine principles, is probably the best example of Lutheran scholasticism. Even here, however, the influence of Aristotle is considerably less than in Reformed scholasticism.

4. THE ROLE OF REASON IN THEOLOGY

We have already noted the importance which the theologians of Orthodoxy, both Reformed and Lutheran, attached to the use of reason in theology, and the apologetic significance of this. In the present section, we propose to examine the precise role which reason was allocated within the theology of this period.

Natural and Revealed

Within Orthodoxy in general, and Reformed Orthodoxy in particular, a distinction was drawn between *religio naturalis* and *religio revelata*. This distinction between natural and revealed religion goes back to Calvin's *Institutio*, and the theologians of Orthodoxy defined their relationship in terms essentially similar to Calvin's: *religio revelata* is the confirmation, consolidation and amplification of *religio naturalis*, while the latter mediates revelation's point of contact with man. This does not, however, mean that reason can derive Christian truth unaided.

Leonard Riissen states the limited role of reason in theology as follows, in his *Compendium theologiae Christianae* (1695):

Although reason is the instrument or the means by which we may be led to faith, it is not the principle on which dogmas of faith are proved, or the foundation upon which they rest, because:
1. The reason of unregenerate man is blind as regards law.
2. The mysteries of faith are above the sphere of reason, and man is unable to rise to them.
3. Faith is ultimately not to be resolved into reason, so that I ought to believe because I thus understand and grasp, but into the Word, because God thus speaks in Scripture.
4. Reason cannot be the norm of religion, either if it is corrupt (because it is not merely inferior to faith, but is actually opposed to it), or sound (because such reason is not found in corrupt man).

Reason Affirmed

Unlike Luther, who insisted that reason stood in opposition to faith, the theologians of Reformed Orthodoxy emphasised that the Christian faith was capable of working upon man directly through his reason. The great Swiss Reformed theologian Johann Heinrich Heidegger (1633–98) stated this principle thus: 'faith conquers reasoning, and leads every reason captive to obedience in Christ . . . faith does not destroy reason, but stimulates it; it does not coerce it, but directs it; it does not blind the mind, but illuminates it'. A similar understanding of the relation between faith and reason may be found in the Lutheran dogmatic works of the period, such as those of Gerhard.

It will therefore be clear that the theologians of Orthodoxy regarded reason as a natural ally in their service, rather than an enemy to be defied. Heidegger's comments on this relationship may be summarised as follows. The use of reason in theology is justified, for four reasons. First, the one true God may be demonstrated to be the author of revelation. Second, the logical harmony and rationality of revealed truths may be demonstrated. Third, the connection of the conclusions which results from each of these truths may thus be developed. Fourth, the entire scope of theology (e.g., natural theology and historical theology) may be brought into the dogmatic enterprise, rather than excluded from it. Heidegger also points out that reason may be used to judge revelation in certain respects – i.e., to establish whether it really *is* revelation, on the basis of whether it conforms to what is already known from the Word or from the inward illumination of the Holy Spirit. The third of Heidegger's points, however, merits further discussion.

The basic point which Heidegger wishes to make is that reason is able to establish the interrelationship of various revealed truths, and, through the process of syllogistic reasoning, proceed from premises to conclusions. The use of Aristotelian logic in this connection has already been noted, and requires no further discussion. But what of the status of the premises and the conclusions reached on their basis? Is there not a clear distinction between the original premises, which rest solely upon revelation, and the conclusions drawn from them, which rest upon a combination of revelation and reason?

The Scope of Logic

This important point was fully appreciated by the Reformed theologians of the period, who drew a distinction between 'simple articles' (*articuli simplices*) and 'mixed articles' (*articuli mixti*). The former (such as the doctrines of the Trinity and the means of salvation) were known purely from revelation, and the latter were recognised as being rational deductions from the former. The role of reason was therefore significantly different in the case of each type of article, as Johann Heinrich Alsted (1588–1638) pointed out in his *Theologia scholastica didactica* (1618): 'Since theological questions are of two types, simple and mixed . . . no one of sound mind could fail to see that philosophy can be applied to proof only in the latter category, and merely to statement and explanation in the former'. A similar distinction is made by Lutheran theologians of the period, such as Quenstedt, although with slight variations in the terms used, and with clear misgivings concerning the definition and use of *recta ratio* in theology. Thus *articuli puri* are those known only through the Word of God, whereas the *articuli mixti* are those known partially through reason. Similarly, a greater degree of caution can be detected in works of Lutheran dogmatics concerning the role of reason in ascertaining the *articuli mixti:* these articles are those which may be known through reason's own resources, although they require confirmation through revelation in the Word of God. It is this consideration which results in Lutheran dogmaticians tending to regard faith as a higher kind of certainty than knowledge arrived at by reason through its own inferences.

The use of syllogistic logic in theology was, however, by no means restricted to Protestant Orthodoxy, and its use and limitations may be illustrated from the catholic Spanish universities of the early seventeenth century. The question at issue was essentially the same as that discussed by Heidegger and Alsted – the relation between revealed and natural premises, and conclusions resulting from syllogisms involving them. For example, consider the following syllogism: It is revealed that God was in Christ; it is revealed that Christ was man. Therefore there are two natures, human and divine, within Christ. In view of the revealed status of both the premises, the conclusion is as certain as the premises.

But what if the major premise is revealed, and the minor unrevealed?: All men are born in original sin; historical investigation demonstrates that Cicero was a man. What conclusion follows from this syllogism? Is it revealed that Cicero was born in original sin? If this conclusion is accepted, it follows that the conclusion of the syllogism is more certain than one of its premises. Roderiguez de Arriaga, who had profound misgivings concerning the theological use of syllogistic logic, thus pointed out that it was more certain that Cicero was born in original sin than that he existed in the first place.

A more serious difficulty is encountered when the major premise is unrevealed and the minor revealed: All men smile. Christ was man. Does it therefore follow that Christ smiled? The orthodox answer to this difficulty was that, while Christ's capacity to smile is revealed to us, the historical possibility that he *did* smile is not revealed to us because the universal premise upon which it is based depends on an induction.

It will therefore be clear that the application of syllogistic logic to theological premises was not without its difficulties and limitations.

5. PURITANISM AND PIETISM

Puritanism Defined

Puritanism, in the strict sense of the term, was essentially the English manifestation of Reformed theology which laid great stress upon both the experimental basis of Christianity (foreshadowing Pietism in this respect) and upon the divine sovereignty in election, as expressed in the *decretum absolutum*. The Puritans may be regarded as those members of the Church of England between the years 1564 and 1640 who, though critical of its theology, liturgy and church polity, nevertheless remained within it. Terms such as 'Brownist', 'Separatist', 'Barrowist' or 'Anabaptist' were used to describe those who, though criticising the Church of England for similar reasons, did so from outside its bounds. The recent attempt on the part of Marxist historians to establish that Puritanism, when stripped of its religious trappings, may be reduced to certain political and social attitudes which were of significance in relation to the Civil War must be regarded as inadequate. The historical evidence available suggests that the term 'Puritan' was regularly used in the period 1570–1640 to refer to those members of the Church of England, whether lay or ordained, whose attitudes towards that church ranged from tolerance to outright rejection, and who were primarily concerned to presbyterianise it from within.

The Theological Basis of Puritanism

The theological basis of Puritanism is unquestionably that of Reformed Orthodoxy. This becomes clear when the works of William Perkins (1558–1602) and William Ames (1576–1633) are examined: the influence of Theodore Beza is everywhere evident, apparently derived from the *Summa Totius Theologiae*, and the Aristotelian scholasticism which underlies Beza's theological method can be shown to have passed into Perkins'. The strongly predestinarian cast to Perkins' theology arises for precisely the same reasons we noted earlier in the case of Beza and Zanchi. Indeed, Perkins' famous 'chart of salvation', contained in his *Armilla Aurea* (1590) is based directly upon a similar scheme drawn up by Beza. This chart, which resembles an early map of the London Underground system, allowed those who found difficulty in reading to follow out the course of their election upon well-established Bezan paths. Perkins did much to promote the Bezan doctrines of election and limited atonement in the period before the Synod of Dort, and effectively established both as leading features of Puritan theology and spirituality. The later work of John Owen (1618–83), *The Death of Death in the Death of Christ*, represents what is probably the clearest statement of these Puritan doctrines, along with an excellent exposition of its logical foundations.

The Legacy of Puritanism

The most significant developments relating to Puritan theological method would take place in America. It must be recalled that the early American Puritans were refugees from an intolerant England. An old theology was planted in the New World, where it developed in a significantly different direction (e.g., the New England Theology). The legacy of Puritanism is chiefly to be sought in the New World, where its influence upon the piety and culture of a new nation, with no indigenous theology to oppose or even influence it, was incalculable. No student of American history can ignore the Puritans, who shaped a nation in the image of their God. Unfortunately, these later developments lie beyond the scope of this study. However, one major aspect of later Puritan spirituality – the emphasis upon an evangelical piety dominated by an emotional searching for spiritual communion with God – would play an important part in the movement known as Pietism, which initially developed within German Lutheranism, and subsequently exercised considerable influence upon English-speaking theology through men such as John Wesley (1703–91) and Cotton Mather (1663–1728). The importance of Pietism to our study lies in the fundamental questions which it raised concerning who was competent to practise the science of theology: it is to this question which we now turn.

The Essence of Pietism

At its best, the movement generally known as pietism may be regarded as a reaction on the part of a living faith against the empty formulae of Orthodoxy. The term 'Pietism' is particularly applied to the movement within Lutheranism which originated with P. J. Spener (1635–1705), through his founding of the *collegia pietatis* and the publication of his *Pia desideria* (1675). The dominance of Aristotelian scholasticism within Lutheran Orthodoxy had by then reached such a stage that biblical scholarship and exegesis were largely overlooked. In 1686, A. H. Franke and P. Anton had joined a *collegium philobiblicum* at Leipzig in order to gain what they could not obtain at the city university – a serious study of biblical exegesis.

The success of this *collegium*, which was paralleled elsewhere at the time, was to cause a radical decline in attendance at the faculty lectures on Aristotelian metaphysics, leading to the eventual suppression of the *collegium* by the theological faculty.

In essence, Pietist criticism of Orthodox theology was directed against its form, rather than its substance, in that the manner in which it was treated and the method in which it was studied were regarded as unacceptable. For Spener and the Pietists, the teaching church must be regenerate, and possess a living faith (*lebendiger Glaube* – the origin, incidentally, of John Wesley's 'lively faith'). True theology presupposes faith and regeneration, since theology is essentially a practical science (*habitus practicus*). In other words, all theological knowledge presupposes faith on the part of the knower. The Pietist emphasis upon the necessity for personal renewal, which originated from pastoral considerations, is clearly stated by Spener in his *Pia desideria*: 'It is by no means enough to have knowledge of the Christian faith, for Christianity consists rather of practice'. Scientific knowledge on the part of theological teachers is no substitute for personal peity. For the Pietists, the surest way of effecting this transformation of university teachers of theology was the intense study of scripture, which was to be read with a view to promoting piety, rather than as an academic exercise. As has often been emphasised, neither Spener himself, nor Pietism in general, contemplated any real change in the doctrinal content of theology – the point at issue was primarily the application of faith to life. However, the rise of Pietism served to highlight questions relating to the science of theology which were emerging in the aftermath of the Reformation.

Stress on Experience
While not initially disagreeing with the Orthodox doctrine of scripture, the Pietists laid emphasis upon a living faith and an inner experience of the realities to which scripture bears witness. The mere acknowledgement of the authority of scripture, or a knowledge of its contents, need lead no further than a dead, historical faith – for Pietism, it was essential that the truth of the scriptural assertions be experienced personally, as the saving power of grace is recognised and experienced. We have already noted the emphasis which Orthodoxy placed upon the need for pure doctrine: Pietism regarded the question of the *content* of faith as being of significantly lower priority than the question of whether or not the individual could really be said to have faith in the first place. To state this in more formal terms: both Orthodoxy and Piety were concerned with the nature of faith; for Orthodoxy, however, this concern was primarily with

fides quae creditur (i.e., the objective content of belief), whereas for Pietism *fides qua creditur* (i.e., the faith by which one believes) was of decisive importance.

This approach to theology was regarded with distaste by many of the theologians of Lutheran Orthodoxy. Conrad Dilfeld argued that Spener's demand that theologians should seek the enlightenment of the Holy Spirit and regeneration was quite superfluous, if not offensive: had not everyone been regenerated in baptism, and received the gift of the Holy Spirit once for all? And while conceding that the absence of such regeneration might prove an obstacle to an individual's salvation, Dilfeld argued that it hardly posed an obstacle to his becoming an academic theologian. Spener, he argued, appeared to confuse *theology* and *prophecy*. Nevertheless, the rise of Pietism posed one of the most difficult questions relating to the science of theology at the time – namely, who was competent to practise it? In the mediaeval and early Reformation periods, the implicit assumption had been that all men were believers by virtue of their baptism, and hence that anyone who displayed the necessary intellectual equipment was capable of pursuing the science of theology. By the middle of the seventeenth century, however, this presupposition could no longer be allowed to pass unchallenged, so that the question posed by Pietism was, in fact, inevitable. Was theology essentially an academic discipline, similar to the secular sciences, capable of being practised by anyone – or did it require a personal commitment to its content?

Illumination of the Spirit

The real point at issue in the controversy concerning *theologia irregenitorum* was the nature of the operation of the Holy Spirit: whereas Orthodoxy taught that real spiritual illumination may, and indeed *must*, take place before regeneration, for the simple reason that it is only from and through such illumination that regeneration may take place, Pietism insisted that regeneration must precede all true knowledge, including theology. The theological foundation for this later Orthodox teaching, which Pietists found so detestable, lay in a significant modification of the doctrine of the *testimonium spiritus sancti*. In earlier Lutheranism, this had been understood as the internal operation of the Holy Spirit within the individual through which scripture was illuminated and faith thus generated. For later Orthodox theologians, such as David Hollaz (1648–1713), the 'testimony' in question has become entirely objective, referring to the pure doctrine contained within scripture. Before saving faith was possible, a prior assurance of the truth of Christian doctrine was required, in that the individual must have a correct appreciation of the nature of the Christian faith before he can appropriate it to himself. Whereas in earlier Lutheran theology, the internal testimony of the Holy Spirit was understood to relate to the assurance of justification or adoption of the individual (i.e., an assurance concerning *fides qua creditur*), Quenstedt and Hollaz laid emphasis upon the testimony of the Holy Spirit relating to an assurance that the *doctrines* of Holy Scripture are true (i.e., an assurance concerning *fides quae creditur*). Thus the illumination of the Holy Spirit is understood to operate *before* conversion – i.e., while the individual is still unregenerate. According to Hollaz, if this were not the case, conversion would be an impossibility. Given that theology is concerned with the doctrine of the church, as revealed in Holy Scripture, it therefore follows necessarily that theology can be undertaken by anyone, whether regenerate or unregenerate. It must be pointed out, however, that the Orthodox case had been greatly weakened through the moral theology of Georg Calixtus, as expounded in his *Epitome theologiae moralis* (1634). Calixtus, intending to give Christian ethics an independent position with regard to the philosophical ethics then in the ascendancy, had insisted that the subject of Christian ethics was not mankind in general, but believers – i.e., the regenerate.

Challenge to Pietism
The dangers of the Pietist approach to theology were recognised and stated by the great theologian of Lutheran Orthodoxy, Valentin Ernst Löscher (1673–1749), particularly in his celebrated *Vollständiger Timotheus Verinus* (1718–22). Löscher emphasised the dangers of subordinating the objective content of faith to a religiosity which is subjective and psychological. The Pietist insistence that only the regenerate can be true theologians undermined the objective content of faith, which could be apprehended without a 'living faith'. Furthermore, Pietist theologians frequently insisted that the only effective preaching was that of the regenerate. For Löscher, this amounted to denying the independence of the Word of God and the power inherent in the objective content of the Christian faith. Nevertheless, it must in fairness be pointed out that Lutheran Orthodoxy had tended to make the efficacy of the Word of God dependent upon the office of the preacher, and that Pietism had merely drawn attention to the problem posed by unregenerate preachers. Whereas Orthodoxy had indeed upheld pure doctrine, it had done so by holding to the formalised and historicised truth of scripture: Pietism, in marked contrast, tended to judge the truth of

theological statements in terms of their subjective effectiveness, and particularly their promotion of piety.

6. CATHOLICISM AND CARTESIANISM

Although there had been sporadic criticism of both the Lutheran and Reformed theologies on the part of Roman Catholic theologians from the third decade of the sixteenth century onwards, the most significant, penetrating and sustained critique was mounted in the final decades of the century.

Richard Simon's Biblical Criticism

Thus Richard Simon (1638–1712), recognising that the bible was the 'religion of Protestants' (to use Chillingworth's phrase), attempted to demonstrate that scripture was far from self-authenticating, and required the authorisation and interpretation of the church. In his *Histoire critique du Vieux Testament* (1678), Simon demonstrated, on the basis of its literary styles and duplicate narratives, that the Pentateuch was not written by Moses, but was compiled during the time of Ezra. In many respects, Simon anticipated the nineteenth century German critics. This approach, however, was regarded as damaging to Roman Catholic as well as Protestant, and was not taken up with any enthusiasm by the apologists of the Catholic Reformation. For Jacques Bénigne Bossuet (1627–1704), Bishop of Meaux, it was more profitable to dwell upon the inconsistencies of Protestants than those of Moses.

Bossuet

In 1688, Bossuet's *Histoire des variations des églises protestantes* appeared, and rapidly established itself as one of the most formidable weapons in the arsenal of the Catholic Reformation. For Bossuet, the Christian religion came from its divine author perfect and complete: the true church had maintained immutably the deposit of truth which had been given to it at its foundation. The criterion of doctrinal orthodoxy was to be sought in historical inquiry, in that such an inquiry would demonstrate the continuity and stability of the corpus of catholic doctrine from the earliest of times to the present day. The new interest displayed by Roman Catholic theologians in the patristic writers reflected the growing realisation that the fathers were not, after all, Protestants – a realisation confirmed by the publication of the eight folio volumes of

Marguérin de la Bigne's *Bibliotheca Patrum* (1575), and developed by the Jansenists Antoine Arnauld and Pierre Nicole.

Claiming the Fathers

The new confidence among Roman Catholics in the patristic provenance of catholic dogma was felt in the Protestant camp. It is significant that the most important work of Protestant patristic scholarship in the seventeenth century was Jean Daillé's *Traité de l'employ des saints pères* (1631), written in response to Cardinal du Perron's appeal to the fathers on behalf of catholic dogma. In this work, Daillé drew attention to the inconsistency of the patristic testimony – and thereby undermined the Protestant as much as the Roman Catholic appeal to the fathers. It is not impossible that Daillé's patristic scepticism paved the way for the somewhat eccentric thesis of the Jesuit Jean Hardouin, who startled his fellow Jesuits in 1709 with the assertion that all the ecclesiastical writers of antiquity, with the exception of the Latin versions of Holy Scripture, were crude mediaeval forgeries.

Uniformitarianism

Related to the new confidence in the patristic provenance of catholic dogma, a new element became significant in the Roman Catholic critique of orthodoxy. For Bossuet, Protestants have varied in the faith which they profess from the unchanging deposit of faith of the church – and by doing so, have forfeited their claim to orthodoxy. As Bossuet stated this principle:

> The church's doctrine is always the same . . . The gospel is never different from what it was before. Hence, if at any time someone says that the faith includes something which yesterday was not said to be of the faith, it is always *heterodoxy*, which is any doctrine different from *orthodoxy*. There is no difficulty about recognising false doctrine: there is no argument about it: it is recognised at once, whenever it appears, merely because it is new.

Since Protestantism represented an innovation, it was heterodox for that very reason. It will be clear that Bossuet's views on doctrinal stability would require revision when the concept of doctrinal development became generally accepted. However, Bossuet's axiom (that variation in doctrine is always a sign of error) had enormous popular appeal, as may be seen from the response of Edward Gibbon and others to its confident assertions. The *Histoire des variations* also did much to convince many, particularly Anglicans, of the futility of constructing dogmatic systems, and thus did much to promote anti-dogmatism in eighteenth century Anglican Latitudinarian circles.

A Universal Method?

In an earlier section, we drew attention to the significance of the new methodological insights of the late Italian Renaissance, especially those associated with the Paduan school, for the development of Reformed theological method. The fundamental question which attracted increasing attention during the later sixteenth century related to the universalisation of method: was there a single method, capable of being employed in every intellectual discipline, or was there a variety of such methods, each appropriate for different areas of investigation? The early seventeenth century saw a growing conviction that there existed a single universal method which was capable of being applied to every intellectual discipline from mathematics to theology. The growing appreciation of this point in relation to political science may be illustrated from the writings of the great Dutch Arminian theologian and jurist Hugo Grotius (1583–1645), particularly his *de jure belli ac pacis* (1625).

Grotius

In this work, Grotius applied the method of mathematics to political science, thus challenging the previously prevailing opinion that there were specific methods appropriate to each intellectual discipline. Grotius, however, must be regarded as a figure of transition from the older view (that there are individual methods for specific disciplines) and the Cartesian view (that there exists a universal method, capable of application in any discipline) for two reasons. First, Grotius did not regard the method of mathematics as a particular application of a general method. Impressed by the achievements of mathematicians, he merely attempted to apply their methods in an unrelated discipline. For Descartes, the method of mathematics was but one application of the general method. Second, Grotius employs other methods in addition to that of mathematics, and restricts the area of political science in which the method of mathematics may be applied. Although he appears to consider that the method of mathematics is capable of being applied in any discipline, its area of application within that discipline is restricted. This reductionist approach may be compared with Descartes' holistic approach, by which the universal method may be applied to any discipline in its totality.

Descartes

The significance of Descartes to the development of the science of theology in the seventeenth and eighteenth centuries lies in his postulation and exposition of a *universal method*, which is capable of being applied to any discipline. In the highly significant *Discours de la méthode* (1637), Descartes postulates a universal method (*méthode*), capable of being employed in any discipline, whether metaphysics or medicine. The precise manner in which this universal or general method is to be used in a given discipline (*moyen* or *façon*) is established through the systematic application of the general method. In other words, the general methodology is capable of being applied in specific manners of procedure within specific sciences, and of defining those procedures in the first instance.

In view of the emphasis of contemporary Reformed Orthodoxy upon syllogistic logic in theological method it is important to appreciate that Descartes' attempt to provide an 'unshakable foundation of truth' (*inconcussum fundamentum veritatis*) is not based upon a syllogism. In formulating his principle of 'universal doubt', Descartes intended to establish an 'Archimedean point of certainty' by demonstrating that doubt brings about its own extinction by establishing an indubitable reality. *Ego cogito, ergo sum.* Through doubting, the existence of a doubting being is indubitably established. The presence of the *ergo* does not, however, imply that this conclusion is a syllogism. If it were, the major premise would have to be: 'Whatever thinks, exists', and the minor premise 'I think', in order for the conclusion: 'Therefore I exist' to be legitimately deduced. However, the major premise is actually nothing more than a formal generalisation of the content of the proposition *cogito sum*. Descartes uses the term *ergo* merely to indicate the analytical unity of being and thinking. *Prima cognitio, me esse rem cognitantem.*

Reception of Cartesianism

The influence of Descartes upon the theology of the period was considerable. His principle of 'universal doubt' was regarded with suspicion by Reformed theologians such as Voetius, who understood him to say that it was only by doubting the Christian faith, or God himself, that true theology could be attained. Descartes' notion of *Deus deceptor* was regarded with horror, its purely methodological function being misunderstood. Similarly, Descartes' emphasis upon the human mind as the sole indubitable reality was of considerable significance in assisting the rise of subjectivism. Descartes' insistence upon a universal method in every discipline inevitably meant that theology was itself subject to the general method, and could not lay claim to exemption from critical analysis on account of its subject matter. This principle would be used extensively during the Age of Reason, particularly in the *Aufklärung*, and its enunciation by Descartes may be regarded as the programmatic statement of the rationalist and naturalist theology of the Enlightenment.

The full significance of Descartes' ideas was not appreciated by his contemporaries. Although they were aware of the fact that a major new element had been introduced into the world of ideas within which they would be obliged to operate, they appear to have misconstrued the nature of that element. Contemporary attacks upon Descartes tended to concentrate upon his alleged atheism, and his seemingly blasphemous attempts to forge a theological method out of doubt. In his *Novitatum Cartesianarum gangraena* (1677), Peter van Mastricht argued that every area of Christian doctrine was the weaker for the influence of Cartesian philosophy. However, the full significance of the principle of the universalisation of method does not appear to have been appreciated. Similarly, the potential significance of the knowing self as the centre of thought does not appear to have been noted at the time, although Christoph Wittig's *Consensus veritatis* (1682) does seem to hint at the possible consequences of subjectivism in theology. The full consequences of the universalisation of method would, however, become fully apparent in the *Aufklärung*, and we shall return to this theme in a following chapter.

FOR FURTHER READING

Heppe, H. *Reformed Dogmatics set out and illustrated from the Sources*, revised and edited by E. Bizer (London, 1950).

Pelikan, J. 'Natural Theology in David Hollaz', *Concordia Theological Monthly* 18 (1947) pp. 253–63.

Platt, J. *Reformed Thought and Scholasticism. The Arguments for the Existence of God in Dutch Theology 1575–1650* (Leiden, 1982).

Preus, R. D. *The Inspiration of Scripture. A Study of the Theology of the Seventeenth Century Lutheran Dogmaticians* (Mankato, Minn., 1955).

idem., *The Theology of Post-Reformation Lutheranism. A Study of Theological Prolegomena* (St Louis, 1970).

The reader who has German should consult the following:

Althaus, P. *Die Prinzipien des deutschen reformierten Dogmatik im Zeitalter des aristotelischen Scholastik* (Darmstadt, 1967²).

Baur, J. *Die Vernunft zwischen Ontologie und Evangelium. Eine Untersuchung zur Theologie Johann Andreas Quenstedts* (Gütersloh, 1962).

Bizer, E. 'Die reformierte Orthodoxie und der Cartesianismus', *Zeitschrift für Theologie und Kirche* 55 (1958) pp. 306–72.

Petersen, P. *Geschichte der aristotelischen Philosophie im protestantischen Deutschland* (Leipzig, 1921).

Schröder, R. *Johann Gerhards lutherische Christologie und die aristotelische Metaphysik* (Tübingen, 1983).

Weber, H. E. *Reformation, Orthodoxie und Rationalismus* (2 vols in 3: Gütersloh, 1937–51).

4

ANGLICANISM

In the previous three chapters, we have been concerned primarily with theological developments which took place on the Continent of Europe. Our attention now turns to the important developments which were taking place in England over the period 1550–1800. In the earlier part of this period, the newly-emerging Anglican church began to develop its own characteristic theology which cannot be regarded as Lutheran or Reformed, despite its evident affinity at points with these Continental religious movements. The Anglicans of the late sixteenth century were prepared to acknowledge the great continental Reformers as their teachers rather than their masters, and developed a considerable degree of independence from the two main Protestant theological traditions by then established in western Europe. Although earlier theologians of the English Reformation, such as Robert Barnes, attempted to align the theology of the movement with its continental counterparts, the English Reformation pursued a course which, for political rather than theological reasons, was essentially independent. The Elizabethan Settlement of 1559 served to confirm the political and theological independence of Anglicanism – largely for reasons of political expediency – without giving it a firm theological basis of its own. The tensions within the Anglican church in the period immediately following the Settlement, particularly those arising from the activities of Puritans greatly hindered the establishment of a characteristically Anglican theology. The first steps were, however, being taken towards indicating the direction in which Anglican theology would develop, without defining its final form, by Richard Hooker (c.1554–1600).

1. RICHARD HOOKER

The first five books of Hooker's *Laws of Ecclesiastical Polity* (1594–7) represent an important *apologia* for the Elizabethan Settlement, particularly its episcopal system, occasioned by the criticisms of its Roman Catholic and Puritan opponents. In the course of his defence of the Settlement, however, Hooker outlines a theological method quite distinct from those of his Roman Catholic or Protestant opponents, and the subsequent fame of the *Ecclesiastical Polity* is largely due to this.

Limitations of Scripture

We have already noted the nature of the *sola scriptura* principle, and the difficulties attending its systematic application, particularly that of establishing its authoritative interpretation. For Hooker, the chief defect of the appeal to scripture as the sole source of authority, particularly in matters of church polity, relates to the manner in which individual interpretations of scripture come to have authoritative status. It is clear that Hooker has Calvin's Geneva in mind when he asserts that scripture does not lay down any specific arrangements for ecclesiastical polity. Hooker concedes that there are many matters, such as the doctrine of the Trinity, which are 'in scripture to be found nowhere by express literal mention, only deduced out of scripture', but refuses to concede that the precise rules of church order are either directly revealed in, or may be deduced from, scripture. This in no way detracts from 'the sufficiency of scripture unto the end for which it was instituted' – but Hooker insists that this 'end' is the manner in which salvation is effected, and not the more pragmatic matter of ecclesiastical polity. It is only through a mistaken 'desire to enlarge the necessary use of the word of God' to hold that 'scripture ought to be the only rule of all our actions'. In other words, Hooker argues that the laws of ecclesiastical polity may be deduced on the basis of extrascriptural principles, providing that the resulting laws do not contradict scripture.

Natural Law

For Hooker, it is incorrect to maintain that 'only one law, the scripture, must be the rule to direct us in all things', in that God has actually ordered the universe in such a way that he established a series of laws, 'some natural, some rational, some politic, some finally ecclesiastical'. Hooker therefore appeals to the principle, associated with Thomas Aquinas, that the whole created order exhibits a definite ordering, which Hooker identifies with 'that order which God before all ages hath set down with himself, for himself to do all things by', or the order 'which he himself hath set down as expedient to be kept by all his creatures, according to the several

conditions wherewith he hath endued them'. The 'law' in question
is not understood as a divine command, but as a pattern of characteristic behaviour, which Hooker considers to be 'investigible by
reason, without the help of revelation'. The laws which guide the
motion of the planets and the laws which govern man's moral actions
are examples of the general ordering of creation, which reason may
discover. In other words, Hooker argues that there are rational
principles guiding the ordering of the universe, and that these principles may be discerned by the application of unaided reason.

In arguing for such a whole series of laws which find their *fons
et origo* in God, Hooker places himself within the tradition of natural
law, expounded with particular clarity by Thomas Aquinas. Thomas
is associated with the position known as *Intellectualism*, by which
the divine will is understood to act in accordance with reason, and
all law is traceable to an ultimate law, identical with the divine will,
and thus rational. This position may be contrasted with *Voluntarism*,
associated with William of Ockham, by which the divine will itself
is made the arbiter of law and morality. For the intellectualist, God
acts according to established laws; for the voluntarist, he establishes
laws by his acts. The divine will may therefore be ascertained by
intelligent reflection upon the created order, in effect yielding *two*
sources for divine law: scripture and nature:

> It sufficeth therefore that nature and scripture do serve in such
> sort that they both jointly and not severally either of them be so
> complete that unto everlasting felicity we need not the knowledge
> of anything more than these two may easily furnish our minds
> with on all sides.

This two-fold division of knowledge of the will of God broadly
corresponds to natural law and revealed law (which Hooker terms
'divine law'). The final stage in Hooker's argument for the justification of a system of laws of ecclesiastical polity not directly based
upon scripture is the appeal to the grounding of such laws in *natural*,
rather than *revealed* law, in much the same way as other 'human
laws' (to use Hooker's phrase).

It will be clear that Hooker's approach to the *sola scriptura* principle represents a decisive modification of its early Lutheran or
Reformed exposition, although it will be observed that this modification is introduced with a view to establishing the laws governing
man's conduct, rather than matters of doctrine. To those who
argued that scripture established a precise set of rules to cover every

contingency of human existence, down to taking up a straw, Hooker replied that this represented

> only a desire to enlarge the necessary use of the word of God; which desire hath begotten an error enlarging it further than (as we are persuaded) soundness of truth will bear. For whereas God hath left sundry kinds of laws unto men, and by all those laws the actions of men are in some sort directed; they hold that one only law, the scripture, must be the rule to direct in all things, even so far as to the 'taking up of a rush or straw'.

Limitations of Reason

Hooker is, of course, aware of the limitations of reason: 'nature is no sufficient teacher what we should do that we may attain unto life everlasting'. Yet these limitations of reason are limited to the sphere of doctrine – a sphere in which there is no comparable limitation on the part of scripture. Where scripture is silent and reason steps in is in the sphere of human law, of which the laws of ecclesiastical polity are part.

Hooker and the theologians of Reformed Orthodoxy have similar understandings of the role of reason in theology, as may be seen, for example, in their pronouncedly Thomist appeal to nature. However, where Reformed Orthodoxy appealed to nature in order to provide a point of contact for divine revelation, Hooker appealed in order to provide a means of interpreting and supplementing that revelation – i.e., through the concept of a hierarchy of natural laws. Similarly, both acknowledged that reason had a positive role to play in theology. However, Hooker declined to follow Reformed Orthodoxy in developing a scholasticism based upon systematic deduction and synthesis.

Limitations of Tradition

Hooker's theological method is therefore based upon the appeal to scripture and reason, within the context of the hierarchy of divinely-established laws which govern creation. Nothing which cannot be shown to be based upon these sources can be regarded as necessary to salvation – and Hooker therefore excludes tradition as a source of 'supernatural necessary' truth. Taken together, nature and scripture are 'so complete' that they provide man with everything he requires to know in order to be saved. In effect, Hooker's arguments against tradition as a third source of truth are based upon his conviction that whatever scripture and reason 'jointly and not severally' attest is true, and therefore that whatever they do not attest is *not* true. If tradition merely restates what can be established through scripture and reason, it is redundant; if it states anything which is 'neither in scripture, nor can otherwise sufficiently by any reason be proved to be of God', it has forfeited its claim to truth. Tradition is therefore at best unnecessary, and at worst untrue. However, Hooker is prepared to allow a positive role to tradition in the justification of the existing order and rites of the Church of England: here he explicitly acknowledges the importance of the 'judgement of antiquity' and the 'long continued practice of the whole church'. In matters of doctrine, however, Hooker appears reluctant to allow tradition a comparable role.

In establishing that reason had a definite and theologically substantiated role to play in theology in general, and biblical interpretation in particular, Hooker did much to lay the foundations for the Caroline divinity of the seventeenth century, when a theological method which many Anglican scholars regard as characteristic of Anglican theology became established. We now turn to consider the sources and methods of the Caroline Divines.

2. THE CAROLINE DIVINITY: SOURCES AND METHODS

Continuity and Discontinuity
The seventeenth century was of momentous significance in the life of the English church, witnessing a series of events which threatened to alter the English nation and its newly-established church beyond recognition. The Civil War (1642–6), the execution of William Laud (1645), the rise of Oliver Cromwell, the execution of Charles I (1649), the restoration of the monarchy (1660) and the Revolution of 1688 bear witness to the political turbulence of the period, while the foundation of the Royal Society (which received its charter from Charles II on 15 July 1662), and the publication of Isaac Newton's *Principia Mathematica* (1687) and John Locke's *Essay concerning Human Understanding* (1690) testify to the perhaps more significant revolution taking place within the world of ideas. Despite these revolutionary developments, there was a substantial continuity of institutions and beliefs. The survival of the monarchy and episcopal system was paralleled by a survival of the world of thought within which its bishops lived and worked.

There is a remarkable degree of continuity between the theology of the Anglican divines at the beginning and the end of the seventeenth century, as may be ascertained by comparing the teaching of Launcelot Andrewes (1555–1626) and John Tillotson (1630–94).

One of the relatively few areas of discontinuity observed relates to the doctrine of justification, where it is clear that a decisive shift of opinion takes place during the century, probably on account of an understandable reaction against the Puritanism of the period of the Commonwealth.

It is with these Anglican theologians of the seventeenth century – collectively known as the 'Caroline Divines', although not strictly confined to those who were active solely during the reigns of Charles I (1625–49) or Charles II (1660–85) – that we are concerned in the present section.

Scripture and Reason
The Caroline Divines developed a theological method which rested upon an appeal to three sources: scripture, reason and tradition. Launcelot Andrewes (1555–1626), Bishop of Winchester, stated the sources of Anglican theology as follows: 'one canon . . . two testaments, three creeds, four general councils, five centuries and the series of fathers in that period . . . determine the boundary of our faith'.

In the previous chapter, we noted Hooker's appeal to scripture and reason, and the important distinction between Hooker's understanding of their relationship and that of Reformed Orthodoxy. The joint appeal to scripture and reason was taken up with enthusiasm by Anglican divines in the early seventeenth century. Thus the same William Chillingworth who, in his *Religion of Protestants a Safe Way to Salvation* (1637), declared that 'the bible only is the religion of Protestants' also acknowledged the crucial role of reason in its interpretation, 'reason being a public and certain thing, and exposed to all men's trial and examination'. For Chillingworth, reason was 'the only principle, beside Scripture, which is common to all Christians'. Similarly, Robert Sanderson (1587–1663), Bishop of Lincoln, explicitly acknowledged this relation between scripture and reason in his *Pax ecclesiae* (published 1678): 'Scripture we acknowledge to be a perfect rule . . . yet not as excluding the use of reason, but supposing it'. The influence of Thomas Aquinas is as evident in the case of Sanderson as it is in that of Hooker, particularly in relation to the concept of natural law. Furthermore, like Hooker, Sanderson had grave misgivings concerning what he regarded as the unacceptable use of reason in theology, which he exemplified in the use of Aristotelian logic to deduce a theology from the divine decree of election, which we have already noted to be characteristic of Reformed Orthodoxy, as well as English Puritanism. As Sanderson himself put it, reason must 'learn to know

her distance' in theology. Similarly, Chillingworth, while empha-
sising the 'compleat and total' nature of scripture, simultaneously
regarded it as being 'imperfect and partial', its omissions being
supplied by the use of 'right reason, grounded on divine revelation
and common notions written by God on the hearts of all men'.
The priority of scripture over reason is made particularly clear
by Jeremy Taylor (1613–67), Bishop of Down and Dromore. In his
Doctor dubitantium (1660), Taylor considers at length the procedure
which must be adopted if reason and revelation appear to disagree.
If reason can persuade us that the belief in question is not actually
a revelation, then the difficulty is averted – but if the belief *is*
accepted as revelation, 'we must force our reason to comply with
this'. In common with Hooker and the emerging Anglican tradition,
Taylor insists that reason has a decisive role to play in theology –
however, this is not *unaided* reason, but reason 'not guided only by
natural arguments, but by divine revelation and all other good
means'.

The Appeal to Antiquity

The third element of Anglican theological method during the seventeenth century, in addition to scripture and reason, was the testimony of the patristic writers. The appeal to antiquity was of
particular importance in Caroline anti-Puritan polemical works,
especially in relation to matters of church government and practice,
both disciplinary and liturgical – for example, the justification of
the episcopal system of church government. In many respects, the
Anglican theologians of the late sixteenth and seventeenth centuries
adopted an attitude similar to that of Philip Melanchthon towards
the patristic writers. Thus John Jewel (1522–71), Bishop of Salis
bury, argued that the newly-established Anglican church had 'come,
as near as we possibly could, to the church of the apostles and of
the old catholic bishops and fathers'. Similarly, Andrewes insisted
that 'there is no principal dogma in which we do not agree with the
fathers, and they with us'.

The practice of appealing to antiquity did not, however, represent
any compromise of the primacy of scripture in early Anglican theological method. As in the case of Melanchthon, the Caroline Divines
appealed to the fathers because they were interpreters of scripture
during a period when, according to Archbishop Laud, 'the Church
was at its best'. The presupposition of the appeal was that the
nearness of the fathers to the scriptures in time guaranteed the
accuracy and authenticity of their interpretation of scripture.
Tradition, therefore, was not regarded as an *independent* element of

the Caroline theological method but, as in the case of reason, as a means of establishing the proper interpretation of scripture. Sanderson's attitude to tradition is significant. Conceding that an appeal to tradition (i.e., the 'known constant judgement and practice of the universal church') is appropriate when the meaning of scripture is obscure, he insisted that we should not 'pin our belief upon their sleeves, so as to receive for an undoubted truth whatsoever they hold, and to reject as a gross error whatsoever they disallow, without further examination'. But on what basis, it may reasonably be asked, should this 'further examination' be based? Inevitably, the examination is conducted upon the basis of reason and scripture, the latter tending to be recognised as more important. John Hales (1584–1656), a member of the Tew Circle, argued that the only possible ground of faith was the plain and generally accepted sense of scripture, rather than 'depth of knowledge, nor knowledge of antiquity, or sharpness of wit, nor authority of councils'. Tradition must have its value established by determining whether it is in accordance with the principles embodied in revelation, and whether it can be justified by right reason. Thus Jeremy Taylor commented that the fathers and councils, while providing useful corroboration to conclusions established on other grounds, have no authority in themselves, and concludes that 'we are acquitted by the testimony of the primitive fathers from any other necessity of believing than of such articles as are recorded in scripture'.

The Tew Circle

The generally low esteem in which Taylor and his contemporaries held the fathers appears to be largely due to Jean Daillé (1594–1670), whose *Traité de l'employ des saints pères* (1632) fully documented the contradictory opinions of the fathers. The later work of John Pearson (1613–86), Bishop of Chester, would do much to blunt the force of Daillé's critique of the fathers, particularly his denial of the authenticity of the Ignatian epistles. This development, however, took place too late to have a significant effect upon Caroline theological method. The profound influence upon Caroline theology of Daillé's negative evaluation of the patristic testimony was partly due to the Tew Circle, which was centred upon Lord Falkland's residence at Great Tew, near Oxford. The circle, founded in 1532, included such men as William Chillingworth, Sidney Godolphin, Henry Hammond, Edward Hyde (later Earl of Claredon) and Gilbert Sheldon (later Archbishop of Canterbury), and appeared to embody much of the spirit of Renaissance humanism. Daillé's critique of the coherence of the patristic testimony is clearly reflected

in Edward Hyde's *Of the reverence due to antiquity* (1670), to name
but one instance.

Nevertheless, the Tew Circle had misgivings concerning the
presuppositions of the appeal to antiquity which were essentially
independent of Daillé's critique: whereas Laud and Andrewes
regarded the reliability of an interpretation of scripture to be directly
related to its antiquity, and Tew Circle regarded the antiquity of a
given interpretation of scripture to be of minor significance. Thus
Hyde's *Of the reverence due to antiquity* emphasises the inferior
learning of the fathers, as well as noting Daillé's demonstration of
the incoherence of the patristic testimony. While not challenging
the historical significance of antiquity, Hyde declined to assign it
the same theological significance as Andrewes. Similarly, Lucius
Cary (later Lord Falkland), the leader of the Tew Circle, refused
to allow the patristic testimony anything other than a supplementary
role in theological method, the primary sources being scripture and
reason.

The Caroline Synthesis
It is clear that the emerging Anglican practice of appealing to scripture, reason and tradition in no way implies that the three elements
are to be regarded as possessing equal status. In particular, tradition
– as embodied in the patristic testimony – was regarded as a useful
means of supplementing what was known through scripture and
reason, but as having no theological role in its own right. The
Caroline Divines respected antiquity, but declined to be bound to
it, feeling at liberty to criticise it in the light of the superior learning
made available through the Renaissance achievements in the fields
of philology and textual studies. However, the Caroline synthesis of
the three elements was relatively short-lived. New challenges to the
theological method which the Carolines established were evident
even as Charles II returned to England from exile. The earliest such
challenge came from the Cambridge Platonists, to whom we now
turn.

3. THE RISE OF RATIONALISM

The Caroline Divines had not envisaged scripture, reason and
tradition as having equal status within their theological method: the
primacy of scripture was not called into question by the recognition
of the two additional elements. The primacy of scripture was challenged increasingly towards the end of the seventeenth century,

with increasing emphasis being placed upon the role of reason in theology.

The Cambridge Platonists

This tendency within Anglican theology was probably due ultimately to the influence of Cartesianism, although it may be more immediately traced to the Cambridge Platonists, who flourished between 1633 and 1688. Benjamin Whichcote (1609–83), reacting against the pessimistic Puritan estimate of fallen man's abilities, emphasised the need for reason to be fully involved in theology: 'nothing without reason is to be proposed; nothing against reason is to be believed'. For Whichcote, 'reason' is not understood merely as man's rational capacities, but also the illumination of the human soul whereby it is caught up in the divine reason. It is this illuminationist concept which underlies Whichcote's references to reason as 'the candle of the Lord' or 'the candle of God's lighting within men'. It will be clear that this concept of reason is quite distinct from that which characterised the empiricism which was beginning to characterise English thought at the time, or the Aristotelian syllogistic logic which characterised Reformed Orthodoxy and Puritanism alike. This point is emphasised by Whichcote's pupil John Smith (1618–52): for Smith, truth 'is not so much enshrined as entombed' in theological systems; it is 'but a thin airy knowledge . . . which is ushered in by syllogisms'.

A similar appeal to reason, understood in this peculiar sense, may be found in the writings of Henry More (1614–87). It is significant that More appeals to the Christian Platonist Clement of Alexandria in support of his contention that the human intellect was the image of the divine Logos, and to Plotinus in support of the notion of 'divine sagacity', which More regarded as a 'divinely indued' higher principle, 'more noble than reason itself'. Following Whichcote, a distinction is drawn between reason as 'firmness of ratiocination' and as 'the light of understanding'. We have already noted how the earlier Cambridge Platonists accepted as axiomatic that 'the spirit in man is the candle of the Lord', and More follows this philosophy of immanence in developing a theology which is essentially a mysticism based upon a foundation of reason. The contrast between More's Platonism and the new empiricism which was developing at the time is highlighted by More's vigorous defence of innate ideas and notions.

Reason or Reasonableness?
The development of the emphasis upon reason within seventeenth century Anglicanism was chiefly due to two factors. First, there was a widespread reaction against the pessimistic Puritan estimate of fallen man's intellectual capacities, and doctrines such as double predestination which were regarded as resulting from it. Second, the successes of the 'new philosophy' (i.e., natural science) suggested that the secrets of nature were now available to unaided reason. The new interest in natural theology led to emphasis being placed upon the divine *wisdom* displayed in creation, rather than the divine *sovereignty* displayed in election. The emphasis placed by the Cambridge Platonists upon reason and toleration were taken up by the Latitudinarians, a group of divines who regarded matters of doctrine, church government and liturgy as being of relatively minor importance. For the Latitudinarians, religion had the capacity to commend itself to men by its inherent reasonableness. In many ways, they possessed prophetic insight: the 'new philosophy' was rapidly gaining ground, and unless religion was able to establish itself on the same grounds as science, there was every danger that it would be permanently excluded from serious consideration. However, the Latitudinarians' concept of 'reason' was quite distinct from that of the Cambridge Platonists, the former tending to regard reason as a purely natural human faculty and having no time for the vitalism, mysticism or what might loosely be called immanentist ways of thinking of the latter. Reason was conceived in impersonal and mathematical terms, a faculty carrying with it its own authentication and legitimation. It was for this reason that the suspicion arose that the Latitudinarians effectively equated revealed and natural religion, with religion being regarded as chiefly concerned with the acquisition of practical virtues such as charity, justice and sincerity.

Subversion of Antiquity
The first significant casualty of the new confidence in reason was the appeal to the primitive church. The early Christians were increasingly regarded by the Latitudinarians as rather primitive and superstitious, and their opinions therefore carried little weight. In 1748 Conyers Middleton published one of the most important contributions of the Latitudinarians to the new spirit of free inquiry and rationalism which was beginning to dawn. *A free inquiry into the miraculous powers which are supposed to have subsisted in the Christian church from the earliest age* was not, and was not intended to be, an attempt to discredit the concept of the supernatural: what

Middleton was concerned to discredit was the authority of the primitive church by demonstrating the absence of miraculous events during the period. The accounts of miracles in the period of the primitive church – such as Theodoret's account of Simon Stylites on his pillar – are sufficiently absurd to persuade Middleton that the fathers were superstitious, prejudiced and ignorant to the point that they would forge evidence of miracles, or lie concerning events in order to keep up the appearance of miraculous divine intervention. For Middleton, it comes as no surprise to learn that the fathers believed in relics, celibacy, fasting and prayers for the dead: in every case, the same ignorant and prejudiced superstition may be seen. The eighteenth century knew better – and if Roman Catholics could find suport for their beliefs and practices in the patristic testimony, then so much the worse for Roman Catholicism.

Natural Theology revived
If the new confidence in reason led to the weakening in the appeal to the fathers, it witnessed a new interest and confidence in natural theology, reflecting the Latitudinarian desire to establish contact and common ground between theological method and the 'new philosophy'. John Wilkins (1614–72), Bishop of Chester, was particularly influential in forging such contacts through his role in founding the Royal Society, whose first secretary he became. The development of a scientific theological method was, however, greatly hindered through the absence of a coherent universal method, capable of being applied to theology and science alike. The development of such a universal method is largely due to the English philosopher John Locke (1632–1704), whose *Essay concerning human understanding* was published in 1690. It is to an analysis of Locke's theological method which we now turn.

4. THE THEOLOGICAL METHOD OF JOHN LOCKE

The publication of Locke's *Essay* in 1690 marked a watershed in English thought, both religious and secular. Its insistence upon the necessity of the universalisation of method in all intellectual disciplines had profound consequences for Anglican theological method in the eighteenth century, and may be regarded as giving epistemological justification to the intensification of interest in natural theology on the part of Anglican theologians. If God's existence, nature, character and purposes could be established on the basis of empirical reflection upon the natural order, theology would be able to establish itself as a serious intellectual discipline in the eyes of the 'new philosophers'.

Locke's Empiricism
The basic outlines of Locke's epistemology are readily ascertained, and may be stated as follows: all knowledge derives from experience. Knowledge in the strict and proper sense of the term (i.e., demonstrative knowledge, characterised by universality and certainty) can only be found in the form of universal truths stated in propositional form – and such knowledge must begin from experience, as the abstract ideas which are linked in the mind as knowledge are the result of the 'abstraction' of the 'materials' which are given to the mind in experience. Experience is complex, and must be resolved if the coexisting abstract ideas which form the material of demonstrative knowledge are to be isolated, identified and correlated. The mind must therefore actively 'decompose' the received complex of ideas into simple components, associate or combine them with one another, and thus correlate them in propositional form. 'Abstraction' is effectively a process of selective attention, in which particular attention is paid to one feature in the received complex of experience, whilst ignoring whatever other features may be associated with the object of experience. Thus the mind actively pays selective attention to the common feature of chalk, snow and milk, and associates the word 'whiteness' with this common feature. In this way, the mind can build up a repertoire of simple ideas, such as colours, and by associating such simple ideas, may derive complex ideas from them.

'The true method of advancing knowledge, is by considering our abstract ideas'. Locke's empiricism is evident in his assertion that abstract ideas arise only through experience – an assertion which is closely linked with the denial of the existence of innate ideas, notions or principles. In this respect, Locke departs from the Cambridge Platonists. The theological significance of this principle lies in the fact that the existence of an innate idea of *God* is denied: 'though the knowledge of a God be the most natural discovery of human reason, yet the idea of him is not innate'. How, then, can God's nature and existence be determined *empirically* – i.e., through the analysis of experience alone?

The Existence of God
Locke sought to express the evidence for the existence of God in terms of a demonstration which would have the same status as mathematical certainty. For Locke, the proposition that 'there is an

eternal, most powerful, and most knowing Being; which whether anyone please to call *God* it matters not', can be known with a far greater certainty than any other proposition concerning the external world. His argument for the existence of 'a God' may be summarised as follows. First, the premise that *something* exists is established as an empirical proposition, on the basis of man's self-awareness of his own existence. 'To shew, therefore, that we are capable of knowing, i.e., being certain that there is a God . . . I think we need go no farther than our selves, and that undoubted knowledge we have of our own existence'. Our knowledge of our own existence thus establishes that *something* exists, and allows Locke to pass on to his second premise: that everything which exists derives its existence and its character from another being. Given the premise that a thinking being (i.e., man) exists, Locke argues that it necessarily follows that there must be an eternal first cause to explain his existence. Locke thus argues for the existence of a 'cognitative' being, which he identifies as God. In effect, Locke's argument for the existence of God is little more than the standard argument from design. Although his argument begins from premises which can be known from observation and experience (e.g., that living things exist), it is invalid without the introduction of additional premises which are not based upon experience – and which thus cannot be regarded as 'empirical'. We shall return to this point shortly.

Having established the existence of 'a God', Locke turns to consider the nature of this 'Being'. Locke's essential premise for the deduction of the character of God is the following: 'It is evident, that what had its being and beginning from another, must also have all that which is in and belongs to its being from another too. All the powers it has must be owing to and received from the same source'. In other words, Locke argues that if A is the cause of B, any characteristic of A is necessarily also characteristic of B. This presupposition, which is essential to Locke's deduction of the moral character of God, is neither analytic nor self-evident, and *a priori* rather than *a posteriori* – in other words, it is not derived from experience, on the basis of an empiricist method. As Hume would later point out, the concept of causality employed far exceeds that of the mere conjunction or linking of events which form the basis data of sense experience. Locke, however, uses this premise in his allegedly 'empiricist' deduction of the character of God.

It is important to note that Locke has avoided applying moral epithets (e.g., 'good') to this Being at this stage. Locke's teleological principle – which is not *a posteriori* in character – is used by him to support his fundamental contention that God is essentially all that man recognises as good, extended to infinity. Locke regards 'God' as a complex idea, not resulting directly from experience, nor from abstraction itself, but from the mental association of various simple ideas resulting from the analysis and subsequent 'composition' of experience.

The idea of God is *constructed by man*, on the basis of his analysis of the received complex of experience, and is not *given directly to him* in that experience. In effect, 'God' is a complex idea, made up of simple ideas linked to the idea of 'infinity': 'there is no idea we attribute to God, bating infinity, which is not also a part of our complex ideas of other Spirits'. 'God' is therefore constructed and conceived in terms of 'qualities and powers, which it is better to have than to be without'. In other words, God is all that is desirable, writ large.

Difficulties in Locke's Method

It is at this point that Locke's theological method begins to exhibit its inherent circularity. We have already noted his general *a priori* teleological principle, that an effect must derive its being or perfection from its cause, and its non-empirical character. This premise can only lead to results most embarrassing for Locke, as the 'deity' thence comes to be the cause or source of all the qualities of the universe – and must therefore possess all these qualities itself. Locke's argument therefore proves the existence of an *evil* God with as great a conviction and logical rigour as it proves that of a *good* God.

A more serious difficulty is that the deduction of 'all those other attributes which we ought to ascribe to this eternal being' is, in fact, made to depend upon an *a priori* moral judgement of the individual. The egocentricity of Locke's account of experience (frequently cited as its major deficiency) thus passes into his theology, in that the deduction of the moral character of God is made to depend upon an *a priori* moral judgement on the part of the individual. The complex idea of 'God' is constructed by selecting from the available array of simple ideas those which it appears most appropriate to the individual to enlarge to infinity. In effect, morality appears to take precedence over theology, in that at least some of the 'qualities and powers, which it is better to have than to be without', are fixed on moral grounds. However arbitrary this might at first appear, Locke claims that morality is capable of demonstration: '*Moral knowledge is as capable of real certainty, as mathematicks*'.

If moral knowledge *is* capable of demonstration, as Locke here claims, it will follow that the moral ideas resulting, when linked with that of 'infinity', will lead to a concept of 'God' which is essentially independent of the individual's moral judgement. However, Locke appears to be inconsistent at this crucial point, in that he frequently appears to make ethics dependent upon the *known will of God*.

It is clear that Locke held that true morality is only possible if it were known precisely what God had commanded as axioms of a deductive ethics, and from which a demonstrative science of ethics could be constructed.

The difficulties posed by Locke's ambiguous statements concerning the correlation between ethics and theology were seized upon by Thomas Burnet, one of his earliest critics:

> You allow, I think, *moral good and evil* to be such antecedently to all human laws: but you suppose them to be such (if I understand you right) by the divine law. To know your mind farther, give me leave to ask, What is the reason or ground of that divine law? Whether the arbitrary will of God, the good of men, or the intrinsic nature of the things themselves.

Locke's discussion of the moral character of God in the *Essay* involves the appeal to a correlation between ethics and theology – and yet no such correlation has been established during the course of the *Essay* itself.

Inductive or Deductive
The fundamental presupposition underlying Locke's method is that it is possible to argue from human goodness, happiness, etc., considered as intrinsic to man himself, to the ultimate source of these qualities – i.e., God himself. If human understandings of good, etc., are understood to depend upon and ultimately refer to divine goodness, the notion of innate moral principles has apparently made its re-entry into a domain from which it has been excluded on *a priori* grounds. In other words, God's nature has been *presupposed* where it was meant to be *deduced*. Locke's statements on the matter are subject to a regrettable circularity. Nevertheless, it is clear that Locke has established a direct link between the moral judgement of man and the ethical character of God, as well as grounding his discussion empirically, thus permitting a universal method to be used in theology and in natural philosophy.

Although Locke was undoubtedly attracted to the idea of a deductive system of ethics based upon self-evident axioms, he never appears to have developed such a system, although there is manuscript evidence to suggest that he was serious in his intentions. Locke appears to have been deeply impressed by the Newtonian demonstration of the power of empiricism in relation to the natural sciences, and thus to have been persuaded that the evident existence of *natural* laws suggested the existence of a natural *law* – i.e., that the mechanistic regularity of nature implied a similar established ordering on the moral plane. This idea, however, does not appear to have been developed by Locke to any significant extent.

The Scope of Revelation
Locke's religious ideas were further developed in *The reasonableness of Christianity as delivered in the Scriptures* (1696), in which he was led to supplement his rationalism with revelation, on account of the patent insufficiency of reason. Locke appeals to divine revelation in order that man's rational and empirical knowledge of God may be developed in a more orthodox manner. For Locke, 'revelation is natural reason enlarged by a new set of discoveries communicated by God immediately, which reason vouchsafes the truth of, by the testimony and proofs it gives, that they come from God'. According to Locke, revelation is experienced through the reading of scripture, which he understands to consist of a series of discourses of logically related propositions containing determined ideas composed of simple ideas which may be obtained through common experience. In effect, Locke adopts a propositional approach to revelation, presupposing that scripture is made up of discrete, epistemically atomic units, which can be identified and correlated by the process of resolution. The writers of scripture may thus be said to have conformed their expressions to the ideas 'which they had received from revelation'. As such, the scriptural writers were devoid of 'partiality', presenting a 'clear, plain, disinterested preaching of the gospel'. Locke explicitly states that the writers of scripture were infallible, free from error, partiality and secular interests. As such, it might seem that he has laid a sound foundation for the supplementation of a *natural moral* knowledge of God with one based on scripture. However, a closer examination reveals that this is far from being the case.

The difficulty which arises may be stated thus: if revelation is essential to establish theological truth, how may it be accomodated within the context of Locke's empiricism? Locke treats scripture as if it were capable of being resolved into discrete, simple units, which can be shown to be coherent with one another. However, this hermeneutical presupposition stands alongside Locke's assertion that all ancient writings – *with the unique exception of the scriptures* –

and interpretations of such ancient writings are fallible and prone to error, on account of natural difficulties and obscurities associated with words: 'Though every thing said in the text be infallibly true, yet the reader may be, yea cannot chuse but be very fallible in the understanding of it.'

In so far as theology requires interpretation of scripture, proceeding upon agreed hermeneutical principles, it must be conceded that *present* revelation, in so far as it is mediated through, and represents an interpretation of, scripture, is also fallible and prone to error. The empirical status of revelation is therefore questionable.

Locke's Influence

As with Newton's *Principia Mathematica*, which we shall consider in the following section, the full impact of Locke's writings on method was not felt until the following century. William Lyons' *Infallibility of Human Judgment*, which appeared anonymously in 1713, is an excellent example of a theological work which implements Locke's epistemology consistently. In many respects, Locke's writings on method may be regarded as the philosophical equivalent of Newton's writings on physics, and both were destined to exercise considerable influence over the 'Age of Reason', particularly through Deism. Before considering Deism, however, we must consider the nature and theological impact of the 'new philosophy' of the second half of the seventeenth century.

5. THE NEW PHILOSOPHY AND ANGLICAN THEOLOGICAL METHOD

The seventeenth century saw the results of the 'new' (i.e., natural) philosophy studied with intense interest by men with no formal scientific training. Copernicus' explanation of the irregularities in planetary movements in terms of orbital, axial and precessional motion; the increasing appreciation of the heliocentricity of the solar system; Galileo's planetary observations using the newly-invented telescope – all were eagerly studied by an intelligent public. Milton's references to the new astronomy in *Paradise Lost* (1667) suppose that his reader is familiar with at least the general nature of its findings. Although Ralph Cudworth (1617–88) and Robert Boyle (1627–91) did much to advance natural philosophy and religious appreciation of its significance, our attention is claimed by the genius of Isaac Newton (1642–1727).

Newton

In 1669, at the age of 26, Newton succeeded Isaac Barrow to the Lucasian Chair of mathematics at Cambridge. By then, he had already begun work on his theory of planetary motion which was finally published in his *Principia Mathematica* (1687). This remarkable work, written in about eighteen months, employed the novel methods of differential and integral calculus (which Newton called the 'method of fluxions') to deduce the laws of motion and of universal gravitation. Indeed, the methods were so novel that Newton had to recast them in terms of classical Euclidian geometry in order that his readers could follow his arguments. The Newtonian universe was a universe of law, in which the planets moved, following their courses on the basis of a natural force which could be empirically discerned and treated mathematically to yield a supremely mechanical universe. Newton's 'rules of reasoning in natural philosophy', expounded and justified at length in the *Principia*, were a means for proceeding from the familar terrestial world, which was open to experimentation and analysis, to the unknown celestial world. It was this aspect of his work which caught the imagination of his theologically-minded contemporaries, such as Richard Bentley (1662–1742).

Apologetic Value of Newtonianism

It must be remembered that the intensely mathematical nature of Newton's *Principia* rendered it totally unintelligible to all save a few; these few thus provided the means by which Newton's ideas could be interpreted to a wider public. John Ray's *Three physico theological discourses* (1690) popularised the appeal to the Newtonian physics to demonstrate the existence and character of God from the natural order. One of the most significant such interpretations was due to Bentley, who in 1692 delivered a series of eight lectures in which he expounded the theological significance of Newton's work. The regularity of the universe, as established by Newton, is interpreted as evidence of design. The new interpretation of the phenomena of nature is thus seen as confirming the essential truths of the Christian religion. Thus his final three lectures were entitled 'A confutation of Atheism from the origin and frame of the world'. According to Bentley, Isaac Newton, 'that excellent and divine theorist' had demonstrated beyond reasonable doubt that God 'doth inform and actuate the dead matter and support the frame of the world'. Since 'transverse and violent motion can be only ascribed to the right hand of the most high God', it follows that this God is responsible for the movement of all the heavenly bodies. Bentley's interpretation of Newton appears to have broadly corresponded with the latter's intentions. In a letter written to Bentley as he was preparing his lectures, Newton described his central purpose in the *Principia*:

> When I wrote my treatise about our system, I had an eye on such principles as might work with considering men for the belief of a Deity; and nothing can rejoice me more than to find it useful for that purpose.

Although Newton wrote several works of a more theological nature (such as his studies on the prophet Daniel and the book of Revelation), his *Principia* is his most significant theological work, despite its uncompromisingly mathematical tone. When the work appeared in its second edition (1713), Roger Cotes declared in his preface that the 'distinguished work' which lay before the reader would be found to be the 'safest protection' against attacks on religious truth, in that it demonstrated the existence of 'the great Maker' whose wisdom was eloquently demonstrated in the 'most wise and excellent contrivances of things'. Newton himself added a 'general scholium' in which he indicated that his 'proofs of God', made on the basis of his physics, were as important as the laws of physics themselves.

The Significance of Newtonianism
The concept of a universe which was regulated on the basis of divinely-established laws had enormous apologetic potentialities, as Anglican theologians of the eighteenth century were quick to observe. The remarkable rise in interest in natural theology which can be observed within Anglican theological circles at the time was largely due to the Newtonian triumph in the field of celestial mechanics. Just as the Psalmist held that the 'heavens declared the glory of God', the Newtonian physics was widely held to declare the divine wisdom. Even François Voltaire (1694–1778) conceded that the Newtonian physics necessarily demonstrated the existence of a 'superior being who has created everything and arranged everything freely'. William Derham (1657–1735) used the argument from design to great effect in his *Physico-Theology* (1713) and *Astro-Theology* (1714), arguing that the order and regularities of the universe were characteristic of the creator himself.

The new natural theology must, however, be distinguished from that of the mediaeval period in several important respects. Whereas mediaeval natural theology tended to be based upon a Ptolemaic cosmology and the Aristotelian scheme of causality, the new natural theology was based upon the world of observable, contingent phenomena, which was regarded as being open to empirical and rational inquiry. The concept of final causality was abandoned in favour of the mathematical description of motion, which in itself was regarded as evidence of its divine origin and guidance. However, both forms of natural theology fell victim to Hume's critique of the nature and validity of causal connection, which he held to rest upon a confusion of relations of matters of fact and the relation of ideas. Furthermore, the mechanistic conception of the universe permitted post-Newtonian physics to dispense with the idea of God as *prima causa* without undue difficulty. Laplace later replied to Napoleon, on being asked why God was not mentioned in his *Mécanique céleste:* 'Je n'avais besoin de cette hypothèse-là'. More recently, of course, the Einsteinian critique of Newtonian physics has necessitated a further, and perhaps more drastic, revision of the appeal to nature for theological purposes. Nevertheless, the dawn of the eighteenth century saw the new confidence in the divine ordering of creation finding its theological expression in a system which posed a powerful challenge to traditional Anglican theology. It is to a consideration of this system – Deism – that we now turn.

6. THE RISE OF DEISM

Rational Religion

The term 'Deism' is used to refer specifically to the 'Enlightenment philosophy of religion' – the belief that there exists a natural religion prior to and taking precedence over all religions of revelation, which declares to man the objective conditions conducive to his happiness, and in whose observance lies his salvation. The basic Deist presupposition is stated with particular clarity by Tindal, who holds that natural religion consists in 'the belief of the existence of a God, and the sense and practice of those duties which result from the knowledge, we, by our reason, have of him and his perfections'. Earlier, Charles Blount (1654–93) stated that religion originally consisted in a purely rational form of worship, such as that presented by the ancient philosophers, and that it was subsequently perverted into a variety of cultic religions. The only demands made of man by true religion are rational, whereas those made of him by the 'perverted religions' include sacrifice and expiatory gifts which arise purely from the self-interest of their priests.

Proponents of Deism
The origins of Deism are generally held to lie with Lord Herbert of Cherbury (1583–1648), although the movement received powerful impetus through the works of John Locke, especially *The Reasonableness of Christianity* (1695). This work was followed by John Toland's *Christianity not mysterious* (1696), which emphasised the adequacy of the natural revelation of God, and called into question the need for any supernatural revelation in addition. For Locke; revelation was essentially a means for confirming truths which could be ascertained through reason: although Locke regarded this as safeguarding the reasonableness of Christianity, others regarded it as rendering supernatural revelation unnecessary. This latter position was defended with some force in Matthew Tindal's *Christianity as old as the creation* (1730), with its revealing subtitle, *The gospel a republication of the religion of nature*. Tindal, in fact, adopted a rather moderate approach to supernatural revelation, merely holding it to be superfluous: other Deists, such as Anthony Collins, held it to be perverse when viewed in the light of natural reason and morality. Collins defined 'Free-thinking' as follows:

By Free-Thinking then I mean, the use of the understanding in endeavouring to find out the meaning of any proposition whatsoever, in considering the nature of the evidence for or against it, and in judging of it according to the seeming force of weakness of the evidence.

The light of nature permitted man to find a religion worthy of his rational faculties, untrammelled by the sacerdotalism of Roman Catholicism or the perversities of Protestantism, and such a religion was provided by the original religion of nature itself.

Rationality and Morality
The presupposition underlying Deism was that man was a rational creature, *animal rationale*. This presupposition was challenged by the satirist Jonathan Swift (1667–1745), Dean of Dublin. In a letter to Alexander Pope, dated 29 September 1725, Swift argued that man was merely capable of reason, rather than rational – i.e., *animal rationis capax* rather than *animal rationale*. For Swift, man is capable of a modest degree of reason only when he has experienced the renewal of his existence through divine forgiveness. For Pope, this made Swift a misanthrope, a charge which Swift was quick to refute: 'I do not hate mankind, it is *vous autres* who hate them because

you would have them reasonable animals, and are angry for being disappointed'.

We have already noted the effective challenge posed to the appeal to the patristic testimony as an element in Anglican theological method during the early eighteenth century, with the result that eighteenth century Anglican theology was effectively based solely upon scripture and reason. In its later phase, Deism developed a highly effective rational critique of scripture, which reduced the basis of Anglican theology to reason alone. This tendency is evident in Collins' early work, particularly his *Essay concerning the use of reason* (1707), in which he explicitly states his intention to prove the necessity of the use of reason to 'distinguish falsehood from truth in matters of revelation'. The strongly moralist cast of later Deism results in religion being defined in essentially moral terms: thus Tindal states 'that the religion of nature consists in observing those things, which our reason, by considering the nature of God and man, and the relation we stand in to him and one another, demonstrates to be our duty'. Thus scripture is to be believed when it affirms human duties which are consonant with reason, or makes statements about God which are consonant with his character as the supremely moral being. However, the revelation recorded in scripture is not totally reliable. On the basis of a brief survey of biblical personalities from Abraham to Paul, Tindal argues that they were far from infallible, so that their statements are to be regarded with scepticism. For Tindal, recipients of revelation merit trust only if they were of unimpeachable moral integrity. Furthermore, the statements which scripture makes concerning God must be evaluated in terms of what reason declares to be appropriate for such a supreme moral being. Tindal thus criticises biblical passages which speak of God swearing or becoming angry, and especially those which speak of him deceiving people, or breaking his promises. All scriptural statements must be evaluated in terms of their congruence with rational morality: one must 'admit all for divine scripture that tends to the honour of God and the good of man; and nothing which does not'. Having got 'clear ideas of the moral character of the Divine Being', one must accept that 'no doctrines can come from him that do not have these characters stamp'd on them'.

Tindal's intention appears to have been to demonstrate that supernatural revelation, when properly identified and understood, is consonant with reason. Nevertheless, the difficulties he experienced in demonstrating this only served to strengthen the conviction of many, that revealed religion is superfluous, being merely a more obscure republication of natural religion.

Rationalist Criticism
In the case of Thomas Chubb's *True gospel of Jesus Christ asserted* (1738), we find rational presuppositions and criteria being employed to reduce still further those portions of scripture which may be regarded as authentic divine revelation. The proclamation of Jesus himself, as recorded in the four gospels, must be distinguished from the theological statements made concerning him elsewhere in the New Testament, particularly in the epistles. The doctrine of the Atonement is identified as such a theological statement which is particularly offensive to reason and morality. Even in the gospels, however, may be found statements attributed to Jesus which are contradictory, or which are quite unworthy of him. The criterion which Chubb employs in this respect is significant: he states 'that not only credibility, but also a conformity to our natural notices of things, and to the eternal rule of right and wrong in the subject, ought to be the boundaries of our faith and practice'. Furthermore, Christ's proclamation cannot be permitted to include his passion, death, resurrection or ascension, but is restricted to his teaching. As if to exclude any possibility that Christ made theological statements concerning himself, Chubb argues that 'Christ preached his own life if I may so speak, and lived his own doctrine', thus identifying his moral way of life as the most important aspect of his existence. Christ's way of life corresponded exactly to the law of nature, and its continuing significance is that of a moral example and model.

It will be clear that later Deism was only prepared to recognise supernatural revelation if it conformed to reason and natural morality. As such, it could not contradict nor even extend natural revelation, having no independent existence in its own right. Furthermore, as the difficulties encountered by Tindal demonstrated, supernatural revelation was difficult to interpret where natural revelation was clear. Although Deism initially regarded scripture as confirmed by reason, the later Deists subjected scripture to such a devastating critique on the basis of their rationalist presuppositions and methods that it became regarded as at best superfluous, and at worst open to the superstitious interpretations of the clergy which had done so much to further their own interests and hinder the republication of the religion of nature.

Dissolution of the Caroline Synthesis
As noted earlier, the Caroline divinity was based upon three sources: scripture, reason and tradition (in that order of priority). By the middle of the eighteenth century, scripture and tradition had either been rejected totally, or declared to be superfluous through the

omnicompetence of reason. It will therefore be clear that Anglican theological method underwent a decisive alteration over this period, with far-reaching consequences. The 'Age of Reason' thus saw two of the three elements of Caroline divinity (scripture and tradition) virtually excluded from consideration, and forced orthodox Anglicanism to take its stand upon reason alone. The very slight degree of success which it enjoyed by doing so may be judged from the fact that Collins' *Discourse of Free-thinking* (1713) was so successful that the term 'free-thinker' practically became synonymous with 'atheist'.

Butler's apologetic Strategy

The most significant attempt to meet Deism upon its own ground was due to Joseph Butler (1692–1752), who responded to Tindal at some length. In his *Analogy of Religion, natural and revealed* (1736), Butler conceded that 'natural religion is the foundation and principal part of Christianity'. Conceding the difficulties in interpreting Scripture to which the Deists had drawn attention, Butler observed that the 'book of nature' was equally full of ambiguities, obscurities and contradictions. The Deists had rejected certain aspects of Christianity because they regarded them as contrary to reason and beyond understanding. According to the Deists, the religion of nature afforded a knowledge which is clear and free from all ambiguities, thus permitting them to discard the ambiguities and uncertainties of revealed religion. However, as Butler emphasised, the all too obvious existence of the cruel, the random and the irrational in nature must call the Deist appeal to nature and the rationalism of natural religion into question. Nature is not a realm in which light and reason are supreme. As John Stuart Mill would later remark, 'nearly all the things for which men are hanged or imprisoned are nature's everyday performances'. For Tindal, 'God's will is so clearly manifested in the Book of Nature that he who runs can read it'. For Butler, nature is permeated by regions of mystery and obscurity, not to mention areas of total darkness. Given that such difficulties are encountered in interpreting nature, Butler argues that similar difficulties may be expected and permitted in interpreting supernatural revelation. Butler had little difficulty in exposing the shallow optimism and naiveté of this approach to nature – an exposure which was perhaps the chief achievement of the *Analogy*.

Butler developed this point further, by pointing out that the facts of nature, while failing to provide grounds for establishing the *certain* truth of natural religion, nevertheless provide a basis for establishing the *probable* truth of revealed religion. Just as nature can be known through experience, despite its ambiguity and uncertainty, so revealed religion can be known with as least as great a degree of reliability, given its comparable obscurity and ambiguity. Butler's emphasis upon probability, rather than demonstration, as the guide of life permitted him to conclude by defending the claims of revealed religion. Of particular interest, however, is Butler's response to Tindal's complaint against the scandal of particularity.

The Scandal of Particularity

In his *Christianity as old as creation*, Tindal drew attention to what he regarded as a major scandal arising from the doctrine of special revelation. If God is just and loving, he must have given an equal chance of salvation to every man. Why, then, were so many generations permitted to be born and die in ignorance of the true revelation of God? Why did God send his Messiah so late in the course of human history? Christianity, according to Tindal, must be as old as creation if God is to avoid the charge of injustice or capriciousness. For Tindal, 'the Gospel was the republication of the law of nature, and its precepts declarative of that original religion, which is as old as creation'. Revelation, therefore, must be coextensive with natural religion, and be implanted within the nature of every man. As it is God's will that 'all men should come to a knowledge of the truth', it follows that God must have given the means by which all men could, at every period in human history, attain this truth. The notion of a subsequent special revelation in history is at worst scandalous, and at best superfluous.

Growth of Moral Insight

Tindal's objections were best met by proposing progression in the supernatural revelation of God to mankind. Thus Butler develops what approaches, but does not actually constitute, a doctrine of progressive revelation. Butler insists that revelation is given and unchanging – but the *interpretation* of that revelation may develop during the course of history. Using recent developments in physics as an 'analogy of religion', Butler argues that in both the natural and supernatural spheres, men may discover more and more through the continual application of the intellectual equipment with which they have been endowed by God:

> Nor is it at all incredible that a book, which has been so long in the possession of mankind, should contain many truths as yet undiscovered. For all the same phenomena, and the same faculties of investigation, from which such great discoveries in natural

knowledge have been made in the present and last age, were equally in the possession of mankind several thousand years before. And possibly it might be intended that events, as they come to pass, shall open and ascertain the meaning of the several parts of scripture.

In effect, Butler challenged the Deist interpretation of supernatural revelation as a body of knowledge given at a moment in history, and which was previously unknown, by proposing a gradual divine disclosure from the creation onwards, commensurate with the capacities of those to whom it was directed. Although many of Tindal's opponents wished to limit the period of progressive revelation to the period of the Old Testament, Butler appears to allow that such progression is evident in the New Testament period, and may even continue today. In addition, Butler points out that the 'book of nature' is read somewhat differently in the eighteenth century than in the pre-Newtonian period, so that development in *natural* religion must also be conceded. Natural philosophy and theology alike progress with the passing of time. Although Butler is far removed from Lessing or the Enlightenment theory that Christianity itself merely represents one phase in man's religious development, it is clear that the foundations for precisely such a theory were being laid in England during the eighteenth century.

Our attention now turns to the development of the ideas of English Deism by the theologians of the Enlightenment – one of the few known instances in history where English ideas have exercised a decisive influence over German theology.

FOR FURTHER READING

McAdoo, H. R. *The Spirit of Anglicanism. A Survey of Anglican Theological Method in the Seventeenth Century* (London, 1965).
Mossner, E. C. *Bishop Butler and the Age of Reason* (New York, 1936).
Stephen, L. *A History of English Thought in the Eighteenth Century* (2 vols: London, 1876) Vol. 2, pp. 74–277.
Mackie, J. L. *Problems from Locke* (Oxford, 1976).

5

THE ENLIGHTENMENT

The Renaissance philosopher Hermann Cardanus prophesied that a profound change would come about in the Christian religion in the year 1800: *Necesse est anno Christi millesimo octingentesimo magnam mutationem futuram esse in Christi lege*. This prophecy exercised a profound influence over some of the later theologians of the German Enlightenment, such as Gotthold Ephraim Lessing (1729–81), as the year 1800 approached. The growing strength of rationalism within the Christian church in England, France and Germany seemed to support the prophecy, and point to a new religious era, characterised by the sovereignty of reason. The spirit of the Enlightenment is perhaps most graphically illustrated by Christian Wolff's *Vernünfftige Gedanken von Gott, der Welt und der Seele des Menschen, auch allen Dingen überhaupt* (1720). The title of the work indicates the universal scope of Wolff's 'rational thoughts', as well as their foundation. More significant, however, is the frontispiece to the work, which depicts the smiling sun of reason breaking through the dark clouds of superstition and ignorance, bringing enlightenment to a grateful world. The widespread belief in the omnicompetence of reason reached its zenith in the eighteenth century Enghlightenment, as the 'superstitions' of Christianity were exposed to the full power of rational criticism.

1. RELIGION AND REASON

Although the Enlightenment is usually regarded as characterised by a highly critical and sceptical attitude towards religion, it must be emphasised that this represents a dangerous simplification. While this judgement is certainly valid in the case of the French Enlightenment, it is far from clear that it can be applied to the movement as a whole, as, for example, it occurred in England or Germany.

Hostility of the Philosophers

The French Encyclopaedists indicted religion as an obstacle to intellectual progress and a just social order. Thus Baron d'Holbach (1723–89) argued in his *Politique naturelle* that religion merely encouraged man to fear invisible tyrants, thus making them prone to servility towards earthly tyrants, such as those of the *ancien régime*. Holbach's anti-religious programme included the translation of numerous works of English Deism into French. Similar strongly anti-religious attitudes can be instanced from the polemical writings of Denis Diderot (1713–84) and Jean le Rond d'Alembert (1717–83). Thus Diderot, in his *Traité de la tolérance*, argued that even English Deism had compromised itself upon crucial issues, permitting religion to survive where it ought to have been eradicated totally. The French Revolution of 1789 is correctly regarded as exhibiting a comparably hostile attitude towards religion, perhaps best exemplified by the events of 10 November 1793. Mme. Maillard was enthroned as the Goddess of Reason in Notre Dame de Paris, a suitable 'temple of philosophy' having been constructed for the occasion. Curiously, God having thus been abolished, he was reinstated the following May, when the French people learned that they believed in the existence of a 'Supreme Being', whose worthy worship constituted the fulfilment of man's duties.

Enlightened Religion

In contrast, the Enlightenment in England and Germany was characterised by its tendency not so much to reject religious belief, but merely to alter the form which it took. It is significant in this respect that there was no French equivalent to Pietism or Methodism, both of which served to relate religion to life, thus ensuring its continued relevance, even in the lowest social classes. As has frequently been emphasised, for example, the theologians of the German Enlightenment (usually referred to as the *Aufklärung*) were not concerned with the dissolution of religion, but with establishing its proper transcendental justification and foundation. As in France, the influence of English Deism upon the course of the *Aufklärung* was considerable. Thus Tindal's *Christianity as old as the creation* was translated into German in 1741, and extensive reviews of the English Deistic controversy were published. Of these reviews, the most significant is probably Baumgarten's *Nachrichten von einer Hallischen Bibliothek*, which first began to appear in 1748.

In many respects, the spirit of the Enlightenment of the eighteenth century may be detected in English Deism, whose presuppositions and methods we considered in the previous chapter. In its naturalism, moralism and rationalism, the Enlightenment, reflected a general trend within eighteenth century Europe. The naturalism of the movement reflected the new awareness on the part of its members of the successes of natural philosophy, and most significantly of the achievements of Newtonian physics. The moralism of the movement reflected the widespread conviction that Christianity was a matter of practice, rather than belief. In this respect, the *Aufklärung* is generally regarded as having developed insights of Pietism, reflecting in this the surprising degree of continuity between the two movements in Germany. It is significant that the emancipation of ethics from theology dates from this period. The rationalism of the movement, which is generally regarded as its leading feature, reflected the new confidence in the power and autonomy of human reason. We begin our analysis of the development of the science of theology during the Enlightenment by considering its rationalism and moralism – i.e., its concepts of pure and practical reason.

Mere Reason
Reason has always been an essential element of theological method. In the early phase of the Reformation, the rhetorical procedure of *inventio* was applied to theological *loci;* in Reformed Orthodoxy, this was replaced by Aristotelian syllogistic logic; the Cambridge Platonists appealed to an immanent divine principle within man. By the end of the seventeenth century, however, a new approach to reason began to develop. The Aristotelianism of the seventeenth century was abandoned, and the concept of reason associated with later Deism – i.e., reason as man's purely natural and autonomous faculty of ratiocination – became established as normative for the period of the Enlightenment.

The development of the rationalism of the Enlightenment took place in a number of stages. First, it was argued that the beliefs of Christianity were capable of being defended rationally. Reason was an ally in Christian apologetics, and Christian truth ought to be demonstrated to be consonant with reason, or at least in harmony with other intellectual disciplines. Second, it was argued that, as Christianity was consonant with reason, it merely reproduced what could be known through reason, and was therefore essentially redundant. Although not in any way questioning the authenticity of the Christian revelation, its allegedly rational character was exploited by its opponents to demonstrate the superfluity of its content. Third, it was argued that the entire body of the Christian revelation should be examined in the light of reason, with a view to eliminating those aspects of the Christian religion which could not be reconciled with reason. Every Christian doctrine must undergo trial before the court of reason. This approach led to the rejection of such doctrines as original sin as contrary to reason and morality.

The Authority of Reason

Nevertheless, this entire process appears to have taken place without a fundamental examination of precisely what was to be understood by the 'reason' allocated so magisterial a role in matters theological. There appears to have been a general and unquestioned assumption that man's higher consciousness is a constant quantity. In other words, reason was assumed to be a constant, unvarying and universally distributed conglomerate of moral and spiritual convictions, essentially independent of the historical and cultural situation of the rational individual. In part, the significance of David Hume (1711–76) and Immanuel Kant (1724–1804) was to call such presuppositions into question, and raise doubts concerning the role of pure reason in any intellectual discipline, theology included. Although the period of the Enlightenment witnessed a new confidence in reason, the same period saw the foundations of that confidence being eroded from within the movement of the Enlightenment itself.

Critique of Reason: Hume

According to Hume, all the contents of the human mind are derived from experience. These contents take the form of perceptions of two types: impressions (i.e., the immediate data of experience, such as sensations), and ideas (i.e., faded copies or images of impressions employed in reasoning). Hume is thus committed to a phenomenalist account of human knowledge (i.e., one that is limited to appearances). This important restriction upon the scope and nature of human experience is clearly laden with epistemological consequences of some significance for theology.

Hume's critique of the concept of causality is of considerable significance in relation to the Deistic interpretation of the 'new philosophy', and particularly of the concept of causality implicit within Newtonian mechanics. For Hume, causality is nothing more that the generalisation of an empirical experience based upon the spatial contiguity and temporal priority of two events: 'cause' and 'effect'. Hume's critique of the concept of causality becomes particularly significant when he draws attention to the difficulties associated with the notion of God as cause. A causal relationship can only be thought possible where a constant conjunction is observed. God cannot be observed, so that the observer is denied the means by which he can properly proceed from effect to cause. Conceding the natural tendency on the part of man to think of God as the cause of the order of the universe, Hume insisted that there was actually no cogent reason for doing so. A further significant application of these principles relates to Hume's demonstration of the evidential impossibility of miracles, which further strengthened the Deist case. Hume wished to establish as axiomatic the principle that 'no human testimony can have such a force as to prove a miracle, and make it a just foundation for any such system of religion' – a principle in keeping with the rational spirit of Deism. Applying considerations such as these with a rigour far surpassing that of the Deists, Hume effectively argues for a world-view in which God is excluded on the basis of methodological presuppositions.

In his *Enquiry concerning Human Understanding*, Hume draws his conclusion:

> When we run over libraries, persuaded of these principles, what havoc must we make? If we take in hand any volume; of divinity or school metaphysics, for instance; let us ask, Does it contain any abstract reasoning concerning quantity or number? No. Does it contain any experimental reasoning concerning matter of fact or existence? No. Commit it then to the flames: for it can contain nothing but sophistry and illusion.

Hume thus effectively regarded the world as a closed system, from which God was excluded. Although this conclusion was not totally unacceptable to the Deists, Hume's demonstration that rationalism could only lead to scepticism effectively destroyed the naive rationalism of the earlier part of the century. Applied consistently, Hume's method leads to the disintegration, rather than the establishment, of knowledge. By reducing all cognition to perception, and excluding any purely intellectual faculty for recording and analysing such perceptions, Hume effectively makes real knowledge an impossibility. Where rationalism had established itself, at least in its own eyes, as the victor over superstition, it now found itself defeated by scepticism. The significance of this defeat for English Deism was considerable, even allowing for other factors which were contributing to the weakening of its force, and the decline of the movement followed as a matter of course.

Critique of Reason: Kant

Hume's ideas would be developed, as had those of English Deism, in Germany. Thus in his *Prolegomena* (1783), Immanuel Kant ascribed to Hume his awakening from his dogmatic slumbers, although it is highly probable that this is merely a rhetorical comment designed to present his *Critique* as a reply to Hume's *Enquiry*. It is certainly ridiculous to suppose that it was through reading Hume that Kant was able to resolve his difficulties concerning the synthetic *a priori*, particularly when the influence of the noted anti-Wolffian philosopher Christian August Crusius (1715–75) upon Kant's development is considered. The significance of Crusius to Kant's development lies in his failure to answer the question of whether there is any genuine correspondence between the way the world is and the way the individual thinks it is. Crusius had fallen back upon Descartes' appeal to *Deus deceptor*, arguing that God, who does not deceive, guarantees the truth of that which we cannot think to be false, and the falsehood of that which we cannot think to be true. However, as Arnauld and others had pointed out with some force, the Cartesian appeal to a non-deceiving God was circular, for whatever arguments one uses to establish the existence of such a God must ultimately rest upon the acceptance of certain principles as self-evidently correct – the conclusion, in fact, which requires demonstration.

Kant's own solution to the problem with which Crusius had wrestled may be summarised in the phrase *transcendental idealism*. Acknowledging two sources of knowledge – intuition (immediate perception, given through the senses) and understanding (intuitions of the forms of space and time, and categories of the understanding) – he restricted knowledge to phenomena (i.e., the appearance or *Bild*), rather than noumena (i.e., the thing as it is in itself, the *Ding-an-sich*), while insisting upon *a priori* grounds that the world of noumena actually existed. By demonstrating that human knowledge is restricted to phenomena, rather than things in themselves, Kant effectively showed that such knowledge is objectively valid for phenomena alone.

Critical Philosophy

The philosophy of the *Aufklärung* prior to 1781 may be characterised as *pre-critical* – i.e., characterised by the Wolffian assumption, expressed in the 'Principle of Sufficient Reason', that human knowledge was possible and valid. The arrival of Kant's critical philosophy, particularly the publication of his *Critique of Pure Reason* (1781), challenged this presupposition. For Kant, man must submit himself to a searching examination of his own capacities, and thence be guided by the results of this self-criticism. The critique of reason is reason arriving at an understanding of itself. Although the consequences of this new critical understanding of the limits of pure reason would not significantly affect the course of the science of theology during the period with which we are concerned, Kant may be regarded as defining the problems which others (such as A. B. Ritschl) would be forced to deal with in the following century.

Important though these critical insights were, they would ultimately have little influence upon the theology of the *Aufklärung*. Indeed, it is possible to argue that the new directions taken in German theology in the early nineteenth century owed more to Romanticism than to Kantianism. We shall return to Kant later in the present chapter. For our purposes here, it is adequate to note that the rationalism of the Enlightenment was at its peak during the period 1720–81, and that this rationalism would be subjected to significant modification through the development of Kant's critical philosophy. Once rationally investigated, reason was demonstrated not to be omnicompetent, but to have limits within which it could be relied upon, in theology as in other disciplines. Our attention now turns to the remarkable influence which the political philosophy of Thomas Hobbes appears to have had upon the *Aufklärung*, particularly in relation to the concept of God.

2. THE SECULARISATION OF GOD

The Secular State

In many ways, the true precursor of the Enlightenment was the new understanding of the nature and function of the State which began to emerge in northern Europe during the seventeenth century. Hugo Grotius had demonstrated that the mediaeval distinction between *lex naturae* and *lex divina* was unnecessary, and argued that the law of nature, natural morality, national and international law alike could all be founded and justified on a purely rational basis, without the necessity of divine revelation. These ideas were developed at some length by Baron Samuel Pufendorf (1632–94), the first German professor of national and international law, in his *De jure naturae et gentium* (1672), provoking bitter opposition from the Orthodox theologians of Jena and Leipzig.

In England, Thomas Hobbes had represented the State as the means towards the end of the welfare of the individual, and this understanding of the *persona civilis* had been extended to include God as the moral governor of the universe, working towards the end of the welfare of his world. Hobbes had extended this understanding of the relation between the State and the individual to include a rationale for punishment of individuals by the State. Given that the State exists as a means towards the end of the welfare of the individual, the function of punishment within this context is to deter the individual from contravening the civil law – which amounts to an action contrary to his own interests, although he may not realise this – or to reform him, should this deterrence fail. The impact of Hobbes' theory of the State, and the related matter of the function of punishment within that context, upon German theology was delayed through the influence of Leibniz' *Théodicée* (1710).

In this work, Leibniz propounded the view that the *civitas Dei*, the moral world, is an end in itself, rather than the means to some other end, in contrast to Hobbes' eudaemonism. Nevertheless, Hobbes' understanding of the nature and function of the State became the common possession of European culture. The full theological significance of this understanding was, however, only fully developed in Germany. That the *Aufklärung* developed in a theological manner to an extent quite absent from its English counterpart is generally considered to reflect the different political situations in the two countries. In England, the movement of free inquiry had assumed a political nature which was impossible for its German equivalent, so that the movement was obliged to assert itself in the field of literature and the humanities. Thus the common ideas which found political expression in England could only find cultural and religious expression in Germany. The *Aufklärung* is particularly notable for its transference of this political understanding of the nature and function of the secular State to a religious context (i.e., God), so that God was effectively 'modelled' on the newly-emerging understandings of the State.

Transposition to the Individual

The explicit transference of Hobbes' understanding of punishment from the civil realm to the relation between God and man is initially associated with Johann Konrad Dippel (1673–1734). According to Dippel, God's intention must be regarded as the well-being of the individual. The effects of sin relate solely to man, in that his well-being is threatened by its existence. There is thus no need for God to punish sin, for sin carries with it its own natural punishment.

It is of interest to note that the most penetrating criticism of Dippel's doctrine of reconciliation by his contemporaries was due to the Wolffian I. G. Canz. Unlike Dippel, who regarded the divine government of mankind as the means towards the end of man's well-being, Canz retained the Leibnizian concept of the *civitas Dei* as an end in itself. The establishment of moral order among mankind is thus regarded as an end in itself rather than a means to a higher end, such as the well-being of man. As such, Canz is able to follow Leibniz in allowing a retributive justice of God, in addition to the purely natural punishment recognised by Dippel.

Implications for Doctrine
The consequences of this understanding of the nature of God for Dippel's understanding of the Atonement are considerable. First, he departs from the Orthodox scheme of reconciliation in that he declines to allow a divine wrath which can be said to be directed against sinners, which the death of Christ can be said to appease or satisfy. Furthermore, as sin is accompanied by its own natural punishments, it is clear that there is no real sense in which Dippel can allow Christ to have taken away man's punishment for sin. Although Dippel understands Christ's passion and death as a model for man's conquest of sin, he insists that it is merely set before man as an example, and has no soteriological significance unless it is successfully imitated. Christ's death cannot be said to remit the divine punishment of man's sins precisely because sin has its own *natural*, rather than *supernatural or divine* punishment. Dippel's transference of the function of the State to God thus leads to a serious challenge to the framework of the Orthodox doctrine of reconciliation. This challenge was intensified through the development of the historico-critical approach to Christian doctrine and the new critical approach to Scripture, both characteristic of the *Aufklärung*, with the eventual result that the framework of a leading doctrine of the Christian faith was totally destroyed. As we shall demonstrate in a later section, Kant was responsible for a partial rehabilitation of the Orthodox doctrine of reconciliation through his analysis of the presuppositions of morality. Kant claims our attention in the present section, however, for his modification of the moralism of the earlier *Aufklärer*.

Kantian Moralism
Although sharing many of the presuppositions of the moralism of the *Aufklärung*, it is interesting to note how Kant diverges from them. For Kant, as for the *Aufklärung* in general, the fundamental content of the gospel message must be regarded as moral. Indeed, the cornerstone of Kant's theology in general is often stated to be the priority of the apprehension of moral obligation over everything else. This thesis is developed in his important essays of 1793, collected together under the title *Die Religion innerhalb der Grenzen der blossen Vernunft*. 'All that man believes himself to be capable of

doing to please God, apart from a moral way of life, is mere religious delusion (*Religionswahn*) and pseudo-worship (*Afterdienst*) of God'. In this, Kant may be regarded as reflecting the characteristic moralism of the *Aufklärung*, although it must be emphasised that he diverges from it at points of importance. For example, the *Aufklärung* tended to adopt an essentially utilitarian approach to moral obligation: God makes no demands of man, save those which are in man's own interest. For Kant, the emphasis falls upon the concept of moral obligation (*das Sollen*) as an end in itself. For Kant, to base morality upon the known commands of God is to make ethics heteronomous: rather, he argues, ethics must be regarded as being based upon the self-imposed categorical imperative of the autonomous human will. The term 'categorical' (*unbedingte*) might be better translated as 'unconditional'. For the *Aufklärer*, moral imperatives were conditional – i.e., 'Do good, because it is in your own interest to do so'. For Kant, the moral imperative is unconditional – i.e., he recognises only the obligation to do good, irrespective of its consequences for the moral agent. Man's sense of moral obligation must be regarded as prior to the correlation of virtue and happiness. Furthermore, Kant insists that the apprehension of *das Sollen* is quite independent of 'another being above man' (i.e., God), although he concedes that, through an act of faith, *das Sollen* may be correlated with the idea of God as a 'moral legislator apart from man'.

Kant's critique of the heteronomy of ethics is significant, and requires further attention. For Kant, 'heteronomy' is the assumption that the will of a rational creature is subject to moral laws or principles, rather than the result of its own rational decisions. In the *Critique of Pure Reason*, he listed six types of moral theory which teach that the determinant of the human will is either an empirical state of affairs or an idea of reason, rather than its own moral legislation. Thus Kant cites the empirical theory of Michel de Montaine as an example of the former inadequate type (in that the principles of morality are held to be determined by education), and the theories of Wolff (who held morality to be based upon the idea of inner perfection) and Crusius (who held it to be based upon the will of God) as examples of the latter. For Kant, the failure on the part of these moralists to recognise the heteronomous character of their ethical systems constituted the root of the unsatisfactory state in which he found the theory of morals.

Although these insights date from the closing years of the German Enlightenment, and thus exercised little influence upon its development, the challenge posed to Dippel and others by Kant's insistence upon the autonomy of ethics and the categorical character of moral obligation is clear. Just as Kant had criticised the rationalism (i.e., the concept of pure reason) of his contemporaries, so he also modified their moralism (i.e., their concept of practical reason).

3. THE CRITICAL APPROACH TO SCRIPTURE AND DOGMA

The *Aufklärung* is characterised by its new critical appraisal of the sources of Christian theology, particularly the status of scripture and the concept of divine revelation. Indeed, it is somewhat ironic that reason itself would only be subjected to a similar critical appraisal towards the end of the Enlightenment period.

Revelation under Fire
The most significant casualty of the critical spirit of the *Aufklärung* was the concept of supernatural divine revelation. The antithesis between a natural and revealed knowledge of God had been established within the primitive church, and extensively discussed subsequently, such as during the Reformation period. The new element introduced into the discussion by the theologians of the *Aufklärung* was not so much the distinction between a natural and supernatural knowledge of God as the total rejection of the latter.

The distinction between a natural and supernatural knowledge of God relates to the sources, the mediation and the appropriation of the objective content of the Christian faith itself. Broadly speaking, the antithesis between the two may be stated as follows. *Naturalism* is the conviction that the basic elements of the Christian faith, when correctly understood, are immediately accessible to unaided human reason, whereas *supernaturalism* holds that at least some elements of the Christian faith are not accessible to human reason, and require to be disclosed by other means. The *Aufklärung* is characterised, in keeping with its naturalist presuppositions, by its rejection of the concept of supernatural divine revelation, particularly as expressed in the Orthodox doctrine of the inspiration of Scripture.

Reimarus and Lessing
This development within the *Aufklärung* is particularly associated with the publication of the *Wolfenbüttel Fragments* by Lessing over the period 1777–8. Lessing, then librarian at Wolfenbüttel, published the first fragment of the work in 1777, entitling it *Von Duldung der Deisten. Fragment eines Ungenannten.* Although Lessing attempted to mislead his readers into thinking the fragments were

originally written by Johann Lorenz Schmidt, it eventually emerged
that the true author was the Wolffian Hermann Samuel Reimarus
(1694–1768). Lessing had been given permission to publish the
fragments posthumously by Reimarus' family, on the condition that
their author should not be identified: the unequivocal identification
of the author dates from 1827, when the Hamburg city library (to
which the fragments were entrusted by Reimarus' son) published
details of the work.

Although the fragments initially aroused little interest, the publication of the second series of extracts by Lessing in 1778 excited
considerable interest through the author's assertion of the impossibility of a revelation which could be relied upon by all men. Reimarus regarded it as unthinkable that God reserved knowledge of
himself for the numerically small Israelite nation, or for a Christian
church which comprised but a small part of the human race. The
idea of supernatural revelation was to be abandoned in favour of a
more securely based and ethically acceptable natural religion. In
many respects, Reimarus did little more than propagate views
already widespread within English Deism.

For Lessing, the significance of the fragments lay in their representing a historian's attack upon the historical possibility and reality
of revelation. Revelation cannot be historically proven, in that no
historical event can be demonstrated, in the strictest of senses.
Furthermore, the appeal to revelation in the accidents of history
appeared to be ridiculous: 'When will they cease to want to hang
nothing less than the whole of eternity on a spider's web?'

The significance of Lessing's comments may be appreciated when
Johann August Ernesti's important essay of 1773 on the necessary
connection between historical and dogmatic theology is considered.
For Ernesti, dogmatic theology was necessarily based upon historical
theology, in that it was the task of theology to establish the correct
interpretation of the facts of revelation recorded in scripture. All
depended upon *vera intelligentia verborum et historiarum*, in that it
was through these that divine revelation was mediated. Lessing's
challenge to the theory that necessary truths could be conveyed
through the accidents of history clearly called the presuppositions
of this approach into question.

Kant: Reason and Revelation

In general, however, the theologians of the *Aufklärung* adopted an
attitude towards divine revelation similar to that of later Deism: the
concept was not denied, but was restricted to a corroboration of
what was already known through reason. In addition to making

revelation superfluous, this also ensured the rational and natural character of the Christian religion. Once more, however, it is necessary to note Kant's modification of this position. Kant is certainly a rationalist, although, as we have noted, he is much more aware of the limitations of pure reason than many of those who went before him. For Kant, there is a fundamental weakness in human nature which makes divine revelation necessary. As Kant puts this in his important treatise of 1793 on the limits of religion within reason alone, the religion of pure reason 'can never be relied upon to the extent it certainly deserves, namely to the extent of the foundation of a church upon it alone'.

Positive Religion

It is in the context of the naturalism-supernaturalism debate that the term 'positive religion' came to be applied by the *Aufklärer* to Christianity. The term was intended to convey the distinction between a pure religion of reason, and such a religion 'complemented' by revelation. The term was generally used by those theologians of the *Aufklärung* who were critical of the radical rationalism associated with the movement. The term is usually regarded as having been introduced by Ernesti in 1773, and was extensively employed by his pupils, such as Samuel Friedrich Nathanael Morus (1736–92), in his *Epitome theologiae christianae* (1789), and Christoph Freidrich von Ammon (1766–1850), in his essay of 1793, *Ist das Christenthum eine positive Religion?* Ernesti drew an important comparison between positive religion and positive lawgiving: although man's natural instincts are good, they require supplementation by a *cultum arbitrium*. It may be noted that the content of his putative revelation is understood to be primarily moral – i.e., a revelation of the decrees of the divine will. Many of the *Aufklärer* who used the term 'positive religion' did so in order to reject its application to Christianity. Thus Ammon argued that it was inconceivable that two sources of positive truth (i.e., reason and revelation) could exist, while Johann Gottlieb Fichte (1762–1814) argued (e.g., in his *Versuch einer Kritik aller Offenbarung* (1792)) that it was morally impossible for a revelation to give man positive instruction. A significant modification of the term appears to have taken place in the older Tübingen school (i.e., the circle based upon Gottlob Christian Storr (1746–1805)), who appear to have used the term 'positive' to refer to the *doctrines*, rather than the *moral precepts* of Christianity, and it is possible that this concept of positivity may have influenced the young Hegel's famous essay on the subject of 1795.

Biblical Criticism

The new critical approach to Scripture dates from the second half of the eighteenth century, and may be regarded as having been initiated by Ernesti's *Anweisung für den Ausleger des Neuen Testaments* (1761), in which an exegesis of the New Testament was undertaken without regard to its dogmatic consequences. In 1771 the first of the four parts of Johann Salomo Semler's *Abhandlung von der freien Untersuchung des Kanons* was published. Semler's critical biblical investigations were primarily concerned with the transmission and nature of the biblical text, and led him to the conclusion that the New Testament canon had undergone a historical development, growing by degrees, and therefore cannot be regarded as 'inspired' or 'authoritative'. Semler pointed out that the closing of the New Testament canon was only recognised by ecclesiastical authorities, and that 'thoughtful readers' may keep an open mind on the nature and extent of the New Testament canon. The criterion advocated for the canonicity of a work is the 'inner conviction through truths which are found in these Holy Scriptures – but not in all parts and individual books'. Semler thus identified the strict historical investigation of the origins of the individual New Testament texts, as well as the New Testament as a corpus, as a theological task of priority. For Semler, it may be emphasised, the canon was no longer a *theological*, but merely a *historical*, concept. The earliest clear statements of the *historico-critical approach* to both scripture and dogma, so characteristic of the later *Aufklärung*, may be found in this work of Semler.

Semler later extended his historico-critical approach to the Old Testament, treating it as the book of a religion other than Christianity (i.e., the dogmatic assumption of the essential coherence, unity and progression of the two Testaments was rejected). Judaism and Christianity are regarded as two distinct and independent religions, each of which produced its own religious books, requiring different exegetical techniques. It is therefore of interest to note that the motivation for the study of the Old Testament in its own right originated from eighteenth century rationalism. For Semler, the books of the Old Testament have no inherent connection with the Christian religion, neither can they be regarded as defining, even partially, its basis or content. The national particularism and external character of the Jewish religion had, according to Semler, later been replaced by the universality and internal character of the Christian religion – but the latter still retained vestiges of the Jewish religion, which it was the task of critical theology to eliminate. We shall indicate below how the sacrificial interpretation of the death of Christ was regarded as one such vestige of Judaism, and illustrate the consequences of its elimination in a later section. In 1779, Johann Gottfried Eichhorn published his historical introduction to the first three chapters of the book of Genesis, a work which was subsequently republished and expanded by Johann Philipp Gabler in 1790–93. Gabler drew particular attention to the consequences of the new scientific approach to the chapters in question for the Christian doctrines of creation and the Fall, and established the principle that dogma 'must depend upon exegesis, and not conversely, exegesis upon dogma'. For Gabler, exegesis meant historico-critical analysis of the texts. He felt able to draw a contrast between the strictly scientific procedure of biblical theology and the cultural dependence of dogmatic theology. The results established by biblical theology have a permanent validity, precisely because they arise through the meticulous comparison and analysis of texts, representing a purely historico-critical investigation. Similar critical attention came to be paid to the New Testament (e.g., in Johann David Michaelis' *Einleitung in die göttlichen Schriften des neuen Bundes* (1788)), with the result that biblical studies tended to become historico-critical, rather than dogmatic. A similar attitude may be detected in Gabler's celebrated inaugural lecture at Altdorf in 1787, *Oratio de iusto discrimine theologiae biblicae et dogmaticae*. It was but a small step from this position to that associated with Karl August Gottlieb Keil (1754–1818) – that historico-critical studies constitute not merely the basis, but also the substance, of dogmatic theology.

In his *Versuch eines fruchtbaren Auszuges der Kirchengeschichte des Neuen Testaments* (1773–78), Semler argued for the following historico-critical principles to be rigorously employed: a constant return to the original historical sources; the interpretation of the history of the primitive church on purely naturalist principles; the use of psychology to assist in the understanding of historical development; and finally, the recognition that development has taken place in the history of the church itself. Implicit in this final principle was the thesis that doctrinal formulations were historically contingent, and therefore subject to historical criticism with a view to theological re-evaluation. It is this thesis which would be developed with particular precision by Lessing, and is partly encapsulated in his famous dictum: 'Accidental truths of history can never become the proof of necessary truths of reason'. The dogmatic formulations of the primitive church were thus regarded as a response to a specific cultural situation which no longer pertains. It was the task of historico-critical studies to determine the dogmatic formulations most appropriate to the present-day situation.

The Historicity of Dogma

It is for this reason that the great 'histories of dogma' came into being, in order that the cultural influences which exercised such an influence upon the formulation of Christian doctrine in its formative period might be identified and eliminated through the historico-critical method (which, as we have emphasised, was regarded as independent of any cultural situation). The very term 'history of dogma' itself, introduced during the Enlightenment period, is significant, suggesting that the supposedly absolute 'dogma' of the church was nothing of the sort, and that the doctrinal pronouncements of the church were actually matters of historical contingency. The rise of historical thinking at the time challenged the uncritical mediaeval and Orthodox acceptance of dogma without allowance for its historical contingency. As Friedrich Loofs (1858–1928), the great historian of dogma pointed out, 'The history of dogma is a child of the age of the German *Aufklärung'*. Thus from its beginning, the history of dogma has actually been written by its critics, as a tool for its elimination. This tendency may be illustrated from an important work which appeared towards the end of our period, W. Münscher's *Handbuch der christlichen Dogmengeschichte* (1797). Münschter argued that dogmas underwent alteration and development, often for purely arbitrary reasons. The importance of this new critical approach to the origins of Christian doctrine may be illustrated from the important work of Georg Steinbart, *System der reinen Philosophie oder Glückseligkeitslehre des Christenthums* (1778).

For Steinbart, the foundations of the Orthodox doctrine of man's reconciliation to God through the death of Christ rested upon foundations which the new spirit of historical inquiry made untenable. Augustine's doctrines of original sin and of the total corruption of man through the Fall were merely aspects of his early Manichaeanism which he inadvertently incorporated into his Christian theology. The correct Christian teaching on this matter was that of the Greek fathers and Pelagius. The concept of the imputation of Adam's sin to his posterity is dismissed upon similar grounds. Steinbart also develops Semler's historical insights into the New Testament when he argues that much of the material in the New Testament relating to the interpretation of the death of Christ is merely an accomodation to the Jews, and not an essential part of the Christian gospel. 'The doctrine of the sacrificial death of Jesus is the bridge for all those who stand where the Jews were in the time of the apostles: our thinking Christians, however, are already on this side of the water'. In other words, the sacrificial language of the New Testament is merely a cultural accomodation to the Jews, enabling them to leave their Judaism behind and enter into the church, and has no permanent significance for the Christian church.

Steinbart illustrates the manner in which the new historico-critical approach found its dogmatic application in a radical criticism of received doctrine. His critique of original sin is of particular interest, as linked with other developments of the period, it contributed to the total disintegration of the Orthodox doctrine of reconciliation through Christ to which we shall return in a later section. In the following section, we wish to draw attention to an important difference between the methods of the Enlightenment in Germany and France, which we shall illustrate with reference to the critique of the doctrine of original sin.

The French Enlightenment Critique of the Doctrine of Original Sin

Whereas the theologians of the *Aufklärung* criticised the doctrine of original sin on the basis of a critical analysis of its origins, and the cultural factors which contributed to its original formulation, the philosophers of the French Enlightenment criticised it on account of its apparent anthropological pessimism. While there is clearly some danger in every generalisation, it may reasonably be argued that the German Enlightenment criticised traditional Christian theology on the basis of new historical insights and methods, while the French Enlightenment criticised it upon the basis of the unacceptable consequences of Christian theology for man's socio-political situation.

If the philosophers of the French enlightenment had one goal in common, that goal was the eradication of the concept of original sin. Voltaire (1694–1778) and Jean-Jacques Rousseau (1712–78), though divided on other matters, were united in their common critique of this central doctrine of Augustinian anthropology. The significance of the concept of original sin lies in its ramifications for the intellectual and moral capacities of mankind. Even in its weaker forms, the doctrine implied that man's natural faculties and abilities were compromised and partly incapacitated. Such a doctrine was totally at variance with the French intellectual and moral optimism of the eighteenth century.

Pascal

The philosophical implications of original sin had been analysed by the seventeenth century *savant* Blaise Pascal (1623–62), and received wide attention in his posthumously-published *Pensées* (1670). For Pascal, original sin effects the absolute impotence of reason, which is totally incapable of arriving at any kind of certainty by its own efforts, and is thus obliged to surrender itself to faith if it is to arrive at any form of truth. The only way in which man may comprehend the mystery of his own nature is through the recognition of the mystery of the Fall, which discloses the key to man's inherent self-contradictions. Man's existence is torn between his incessant strivings to reach beyond himself and his perpetual lapses beneath himself, so that his consciousness places before him a goal which he simply cannot reach. The irreducible dualism of human nature can only, according to Pascal, be understood in the light of the Fall – a mystery which is only apprehended by faith, and not by rational inquiry.

The essential point which Pascal emphasised was that there appeared to be a necessary, rather than accidental, objective, rather than subjective, limit upon human knowledge. If man was, and remained 'self-transcendent', a rational account of his nature was excluded from the outset. This brilliant philosophical analysis of the implications of original sin set the scene for critique of the doctrine within the French Enlightenment.

Voltaire and Rousseau

Voltaire's *Remarques sur les Pensées de M. Pascal* attempt to ridicule, rather than analyse, Pascal's insights into human nature. What for Pascal represented the problematical contradictions of human nature became for Voltaire the delightful variety of human existence, a demonstration of the strength and adaptability of human nature rather than a symptom of its inherent tensions. Nevertheless, Pascal's radical questioning concerning the origins of human evil had raised difficulties which Voltaire could not avoid. The obvious method of avoiding the problem was to resort to Leibniz' optimism – an optimism which Voltaire had himself discredited in his much-read *Candide*. Where Pascal appealed to the mystery of original sin in his attempt to account for the origin of human evil, Voltaire found himself forced to concede that a real difficulty accompanied his own anthropology in this respect. Moral evil must be regarded as an inevitable feature of human nature. If it were not for human weakness, life would be monotonous, in that the greatest impulses of human life and existence arise from human appetites and passions. This view was stated with particular clarity in *Le monde comme il va* (1746), in which Voltaire effectively argued that weaknesses, faults and serious moral shortcomings were an inevitable aspect of human nature, but that they were outweighed by human social and cultural achievements.

It is significant that Voltaire was not followed by Rousseau in this conclusion: for Rousseau, man's social and cultural achievements are purely superficial when compared with his inner poverty. His social relationships are ultimately based upon sheer egotism and vanity, and his aspirations purely illusionary.

The common feature of the French Enlightenment's critique of the doctrine of original sin was the acknowledgement of the reality of human sin, and the simultaneous denial of the traditional Christian explanation of its origin and consequences. Man's tendency towards evil is merely a consequence of his ignorance or social conditioning, which education and social development may ultimately hope to overcome. The working out of these convictions may be seen in the political philosophy of the period, and to a limited (but highly dramatic) extent in the Revolution itself. Nevertheless, the French Enlightenment's critique of original sin was generally characterised by its reluctance to enter into a debate on the theological level, the divorce between theology and philosophy having developed to such an extent that philosophy conducted its religious criticism entirely on its own terms. Thus Voltaire's criticism of Pascal is notable for its failure to deal with the central religious conviction which underlies his philosophy of human existence, and his marked preference for concentrating upon more superficial matters.

The Destruction of the Orthodox Doctrine of Reconciliation
The total disintegration of the Orthodox doctrine of reconciliation arose – notably in the work of Steinbart – in the following manner. First, the Augustinian doctrine of original sin was denied, with a corresponding emphasis being placed upon man's natural moral capacities. Man is therefore not by nature alienated from God, although he may impose such an alienation upon himself by acts of sin. These acts of sin are, however, conceived dysteleologically – i.e., they are regarded as working against man's own interests, defined in terms of his perfection and happiness. This leads to the second important consideration: the essence of sin is understood to lie in the harm which it does to man himself. God is only indirectly implicated, in so far as he is a means by which man's proper end is achieved. Sin is most emphatically not understood as an offence against God, for which an appropriate satisfaction or penalty is required. If Christ's death on the cross is therefore to have any significance for man, this significance must be located in the *effect which it has upon man himself*. This important conclusion finds its most appropriate expression in an ethical or exemplarist theory of the Atonement, characteristic of the theologians of the later *Aufklärung*. Christ's death serves as an example and inspiration to man,

motivating and encouraging him to emulate the outstanding moral character of Christ. If Christ can be said to redeem man in any sense, it is in the sense of redeeming him from *unacceptable or false concepts of God*. Thus Steinbart declares that Christ has redeemed man from the *idea* of God as a tyrant, and from the *idea* of Satan. The notion of redemption as intellectual liberation is characteristic of the *Aufklärung*.

It will therefore be clear that the *Aufklärung* brought about a significant alteration of the understanding of the 'essence of Christianity' through its presuppositions and methods. Whereas for an earlier generation of German theologians, the essence of Christianity lay in the redemption of sinful man through Christ's death on the cross, for the *Aufklärer* it lay in the possibility of moral perfection through the imitation of the example of Christ. The new methods (e.g., the new approach to history) and presuppositions (e.g., the secular concept of God) combined to eliminate the traditional understanding of the nature of the Christian faith itself.

4. CONSEQUENCES FOR CHRISTOLOGY

Naturalistic Assumptions
We have already noted the naturalist, moralist and rationalist character of the theological presuppositions of the *Aufklärung*, and their influence upon the Aufklärung understanding of the work of Christ. To summarise this understanding once more:

1. Christ is understood as having been a *teacher* in his lifetime, and a supreme *example* of self-giving in his death. A purely exemplarist theory of the Atonement makes its appearance for the first time in the Enlightenment. (Peter Abelard, who is often represented as having taught such a theory of the Atonement, presents a much more traditional account of the work of Christ than is usually appreciated. The mistaken characterisation of Abelard's theory of the Atonement as purely exemplarist appears to have arisen through the inaccurate historico-theological investigations of the theologians of the *Aufklärung* and later liberal Protestantism).

2. Christ is understood as the morally perfect man, embodying the fully realised potential of every man in himself. In other words, Christ possesses to a greater degree that which every man has latent within him. Christ's function is thus to enable man to realise his full human potential through informing him that it is within his reach, and inspiring him to attain it.

These accounts of Christ's significance are notable for their studied evasion of any *supernatural* elements in relation to the work of Christ, whether in relation to Christ's person, or the mode by which his influence is transmitted to individual believers. This may be contrasted with the Christology of Orthodoxy, which insisted that the significance of Christ should be interpreted in transcendent and supernatural terms. It is significant that the term 'supernaturalism' is encountered for the first time during the period of the *Aufklärung* (in *Sokratischen Unterhaltungen über das Älteste und Neueste aus der christlichen Welt* (1789)). It is therefore clear that the Christology of the *Aufklärung* is fundamentally Ebionite, and that it assumes this character through the presuppositions which underlay the theology of the *Aufklärung*.

Kant: Morals and Reductionism
In a letter of 28 April 1775, Kant outlines an approach to the teaching of Jesus which parallels the 'Quest for the Historical Jesus' then gaining momentum, and which we shall discuss in a later section.

I distinguish the *teaching* of Christ from the *account* which we have concerning the teaching of Christ, and in order to get at the former, I try above all to extract the *moral* teaching from all precepts of the New Testament. The former is surely the fundamental, and the latter an ancillary, doctrine of the gospel.

Kant insisted, however, that the *idea* of moral perfection is prior to the recognition of such perfection in Christ. 'Even the saint of the gospel must first be compared with our idea of moral perfection, before he can be recognised as such. . . . From where do we derive the idea that God represents the highest good? Only from the idea, which reason *a priori* derives of moral perfection'. In other words, the idea of moral perfection does not require to be historically realised in the person of Christ, or anyone else, if it is to function as a moral stimulus and example. Furthermore, while there is no reason whatsoever why the historical realisation of this principle should not take place, Kant emphasises that its ultimate source is reason itself. Kant refers to this principle as an 'archetype residing within our reason', which is prior to the recognition of such perfection in Christ. Christ is thus the historical realisation of the archetype of moral perfection – but an archetype which exists independent of, and prior to, Christ. In other words, had Christ never existed, human morality would not be significantly disadvantaged as a result. Kant's insistence upon the autonomy of ethics thus leads to an endorsement of the later Enlightenment tendency to see Christ as republishing natural morality, rather than establishing an alternative, or even a supplementary, morality.

The Quest for the Historical Jesus

The origins of the 'Quest' are usually regarded as lying in one of the Wolfenbüttel Fragments published by Lessing, *Von dem Zwecke Jesu und seiner Jünger*. Before Reimarus, no historical conception of the life of Jesus appears to have been attempted, although it is possible to argue that the ground was prepared for such an attempt through Johann Jakob Hess' *Geschichte der drei letzten Lebensjahre Jesu* (1768). The fundamental principle which would govern the 'Quest' was stated by Reimarus thus: 'We are justified in drawing an absolute distinction between the teaching of the apostles in their writings, and what Jesus himself proclaimed and taught in his own lifetime'. We have already noted the use of this principle in later English Deism (e.g., with Chubb). A correct historical understanding of the teaching of Jesus – which Reimarus limits to 'Repent, and believe the gospel' – can only be attained by leaving behind the dogmatic presuppositions of Christianity. When this is done, it becomes clear that Christ did not intend to found a new religion, but merely to clarify and intensify the moral demands of the old (i.e., Judaism). The 'Resurrection' and so on are mere inventions, which obscure the moral urgency of Jesus' preaching. Reimarus laid particular emphasis upon the eschatological expectations of Jesus, and argued that their non-fulfilment constituted a major difficulty. Similar ideas were developed, although less powerfully, in Franz Volkmar Reinhard's *Versuch über den Plan, welchen der Stifter der christlichen Religion zum Besten der Menschheit entwarf* (1781). As the movement gathered pace, the early tendency to combine naturalism and supernaturalism (evident in Hess' *Geschichte*) gave way to a more thorough-going rationalism and naturalism, particularly well exemplified in Karl Heinrich Venturini's *Natürliche Geschichte des grossen Propheten von Nazareth* (1800).

Tendentious Use of Critical Method

The difficulty which was faced by the *Aufklärer* was that the New Testament appeared to portray Christ in terms which went far beyond their naturalism and moralism. The 'Quest for the Historical Jesus' is an excellent illustration of how the theologians of the *Aufklärung* were able to reconstruct the New Testament picture of Christ in a manner consistent with their naturalist, moralist and rationalist *presuppositions* by the application of the new historico-

critical *methods* which were then being developed. The supernatural
elements in the New Testament portrait of Christ were represented
as arising through misunderstandings or cultural conditioning, and
were thus eliminated, to be replaced with more acceptable natural
elements. Thus Christ was not raised from the dead – he was merely
rescued from premature burial. The essential assumption was that
an essentially simple (i.e., natural, moral and rational) religious
message, based upon the teachings of the founder of Christianity,
had become distorted and obscured through the intrusion of a
number of unjustifiable and arbitrary (i.e., supernatural and transcendent) hypotheses, which it was the task of modern theology to
identify and eliminate through the application of the critical
historical method, and thus permit the authentic teaching of Jesus
to enter into the modern (i.e., eighteenth century) period. The
elimination of these elements could be carried out at every level, as
the new science of the 'history of dogma' was demonstrating, but
was best done at their source – i.e., the New Testament itself. The
period of the German Enlightenment thus witnessed the origins of
a quest which would assume increasing importance and a new
character in the following century. It is interesting to note that it
becomes increasingly inaccurate to speak of the 'Christology' of the
Aufklärung from 1790 onwards, the term 'Jesuology' being more
appropriate.

Summing Up

In the present chapters, we have documented the remarkable
changes in presuppositions and methods which have characterised
the science of theology over the period 1500–1800. The Reformation
witnessed a new attitude to the three traditional sources of theology
(scripture, tradition and reason), with the former being regarded as
absolute in its authority, although the role of the patristic testimony
and reason in its exposition were acknowledged. It is interesting to
note how the role of reason in the first phase of the Reformation is
essentially that of *inventio* in rhetoric. Over the period in question,
however, the rise of confidence in reason, through the remarkable
scientific developments which the period witnessed, inevitably
meant that scripture and tradition were subjected to increasingly
critical analysis, culminating in the period of the Enlightenment.
The rigorous application of the historico-critical method, with its
naturalist, moralist and rationalist presuppositions, appeared to spell
the end of traditional Christian theology, and Orthodoxy appeared
unable to defend itself in the face of this relentless critical challenge.
Scripture and tradition alike – the grounds on which Orthodoxy

was best prepared to defend itself – were now regarded as historically contingent and culturally conditioned, and thus as unsuitable foundations for the necessary truths of reason. How could a religion which, at least in its traditional forms, made transcendent and supernatural claims survive in so rationalist an intellectual climate? As the year 1800 approached, and with the memory of the French revolution so deeply embedded in the European consciousness, it seemed that Cardanus' prophecy was being fulfilled, and a new age of the religion of pure reason was about to dawn. However, although the influence of the Enlightenment would continue to be felt even down to the present day, this influence lay more in the critical questions which the movement raised than in the answers which it gave. The European cultural situation, particularly in Germany, underwent a radical change, and Christian theology along with it. The *Aufklärung* was abandoned, rather than refuted, as a new interest in the human spirit gained momentum.

FOR FURTHER READING

Becker, C. L. *The Heavenly City of the Eighteenth Century Philosophers* (New Haven, 1932).

Cassirer, E. *The Philosophy of the Enlightenment* (Princeton, 1951).

Cragg, G. R. *Reason and Authority in the Eighteenth Century* (Cambridge, 1964).

idem., *The Church and the Age of Reason 1648–1789* (London, 1976).

Flew, A. *Hume's Philosophy of Belief* (London, 1961).

Frei, H. *The Eclipse of Biblical Narrative. A Study in Eighteenth and Nineteenth Century Hermeneutics* (New Haven/London, 1974).

Gay, P. *The Party of Humanity. Studies in the French Enlightenment* (New York/London, 1964).

McGrath, A. E. 'The Moral Theory of the Atonement. An Historical and Theological Critique', *Scottish Journal of Theology* 38 (1985) pp. 205–20.

Schweitzer, A. *The Quest of the Historical Jesus. A Critical Study of its Progress from Reimarus to Wrede* (London, 1954).

Hornig, G. *Die Anfänge der historisch-kritischen Theologie. Johann Salomo Semlers Schriftverständnis und seine Stellung zu Luther* (Göttingen, 1967).

Schollmeier, J. *Johann Joachim Spalding. Ein Beitrag zur Theologie der Aufklärung* (Gütersloh, 1967).

McGrath, A. E. *The Making of Modern German Christology* (Oxford, 1986) pp. 9–31.

PART III

NINETEENTH AND TWENTIETH CENTURY THEOLOGY

NINETEENTH AND TWENTIETH CENTURY THEOLOGY

1

THE TRANSITION TO
MODERN THEOLOGY

1. THE LEGACY OF THE ENLIGHTENMENT

The eighteenth century was dominated by a movement commonly
known as the Enlightenment. This movement was characterised by
an emphasis upon autonomous human reason. It saw the beginnings
of modern science – particularly in the work of Newton. This
yielded a rather mechanical view of the physical universe as a closed
system governed by its own laws. It saw the emancipation of moral
theory from theological and ecclesiastical control. It also saw the
complete emancipation of philosophy from theological dominance.
Within theology it strongly questioned all appeals to authority,
whether of the Bible or the church. It was highly critical of any
kind of special revelation. It was sceptical in its attitude to stories
of miracle.

The Limitations of Enlightenment
On the whole this was not an atheistical scepticism. However, the
God in whom the educated classes found it possible to believe was
very remote from the world and the everyday concerns of humanity.
They found it credible that in the beginning God created the world.
But having created the world he did not meddle in its affairs. He
ordered physical creation according to the laws of mechanics. To
spiritual creation he gave the powers of reason and the moral law.
It was widely believed that any further interference would be an
assault upon the uniformity of nature and the rational autonomy of
man.

However, there is more to human existence than reason and moral
will. A reaction against the astringent rationalism of the Enlightenment movement was therefore inevitable. This came in what is
commonly known as the Romantic Movement. It began in the
latter decades of the eighteenth century. It dominated much of the

nineteenth. It affected every aspect of European culture. In particular it brought profound changes in theology.

The Rediscovery of 'Spirit'

Just as 'reason' was the key word for the Enlightenment, so 'spirit' was the key word for the Romantic Movement.

It is not easy to say what was meant by 'spirit'. The main centre of the Romantic Movement was Germany. The German word *Geist* has a much broader and richer meaning than the English word 'spirit'. It refers to the whole man in every aspect of his humanity. It is essentially a unifying concept.

In this respect it captures something of the role played by the concept of spirit in the New Testament. It is through the agency of the spirit that estranged man is reunited with himself, with his neighbour, with nature and with God. It is through the agency of the spirit of God that God and man were united in the womb of Mary. It is through the descent of the spirit of God upon Jesus at his baptism that this union is first publicly disclosed. It is in the communion of the spirit that the church is united to God as the body of Christ.

For the Greeks, spirit was something quite different. It was associated with only the intellectual aspect of man. This Greek bias still tends to linger in the English use of the word. St Paul, under Judaeochristian influence, applied it to the whole man whose integrity has been restored in Christ.

It is therefore entirely appropriate that the theologians of the early nineteenth century, who were reacting against the narrow rationalism of the Enlightenment, should make spirit the key concept of their interpretation of religion and christianity. Enlightenment rationalism separated the natural from the supernatural. The new theology sought to reunite them.

It must be acknowledged, however, that the writers of the Romantic Movement, in their recovery of the concept of spirit, did not derive it entirely from the New Testament. It acquired some pagan and pantheistic overtones as well. This was to lead to some severe complications when the revitalised concept of spirit was taken up into christian theology.

Protestant Orthodoxy

Throughout the eighteenth century the substantial conservative majority within the church had put up a stout resistance to Enlightenment rationalism. This led to an exaggerated emphasis on authority – either of the Bible or of the church – within both protestant and Roman Catholic Orthodoxy. An equally exaggerated emphasis was placed on the intervention of the supernatural in the natural world. Miracle, special providence and divine predestination became crucial issues. The management of the world down to the minutest detail of apparently chance events was ascribed to God. The discontinuity of revelation with human reason was stressed as never before.

On the face of it, this hardening of conservative ecclesiastical orthodoxy was in direct opposition to the main tendency of the Enlightenment. In a deeper sense, however, both the Enlightenment and the contrasting ecclesiastical orthodoxy were opposite sides of the same coin. Both emphasised the transcendence of God over the world in such a way as to make him spiritually irrelevant. The one banished him into a transcendent, metaphysical eternity and reduced him to the stature of a god for intellectuals and philosophers only. The other emphasised his externality to the universe by turning him into a *deus ex machina* – an omnipotent being, external to his creation, but secretly governing all that comes to pass. The action of God in the world was what he did *to* and *for* men rather that *in* and *with* them.

It was the special problem and the task of nineteenth century theology to bring God back into the heart and the life of man.

A New Dawn

There were other respects in which times were ripe for theological upheaval. The French Revolution brought the eighteenth century to a close. Both politically and culturally it shook the whole of Europe to its foundations. It was not a socialist revolution. It was not about property, but about privilege, status and authority. In rejecting privilege it made every man his own master. In rejecting authority it challenged the sacral basis of both church and state. At the same time it generated among the romantics hopes and visions of a brave new world. England was facing the beginnings of an industrial revolution. The American colonies had broken free. If 'liberty, equality, fraternity' were the key words of the French Revolution, 'emancipation' was the key word of its American counterpart.

This new world of opportunity had its price in the loss of old certainties, old securities, old unities. The nineteenth century has often been thought of as an age of conservatism and security. It was in fact an age of revolution and turmoil. It was also an age of social and cultural disintegration. The Holy Roman Empire broke up into autonomous nation states. National consciousness began to play a new and exaggerated role in the spiritual consciousness of the people. It displaced the concept of European christendom.

The elements of human culture became increasingly isolated from one another – science from ethics, commerce from community, facts from their meaning and religion from life. But the fight back in the name of the unity of nature and spirit began with the transition from the eighteenth to the nineteenth century. Theology had a vital role to play in the search for this new unity.

Two men, Friedrich D. E. Schleiermacher (1768–1834) and George W. F. Hegel (1770–1831) are usually credited with being the founders of this new type of theology. They were the theological giants of the period. But the continuity of their thought with that of their immediate predecessors should not be ignored. They did not arrive like a bolt from the blue. They are more easily understood in context.

2. ROMANTICISM

Storm and Stress
It is a pity that the word 'romantic' has now come to be associated with sentimentality. Nothing could be further from the original import and intention of the Romantic Movement. It was realistic rather than sentimental. In its early manifestation, in what is called the 'Storm and Stress' (*Sturm und Drang*) movement, it insisted that it is not only ideas but also passion, force and action that shape events. The creative shaping of reality comes as much from imagination as from thought. It asserted the ascendancy of free spirit over the Newtonian mechanics of nature. It sought a unitary vision of reality over against the analytic divisions of critical rationalism.

In a refreshing, sometimes brilliant, sometimes fantastic way theology became part of the stock in trade of poets, playwrights, novelists, essayists, historians and even politicians. In former times the sole handmaiden of theology had been the stately muse of philosophy. Now she found herself surrounded by a whole bevy of new handmaidens – some of them, perhaps more distracting than attentive.

Goethe
Johann Wolfgang von Goethe (1749–1832) was the greatest of the Romantic poets. His status can be compared only with that of Shakespeare. He was not a Christian; but he did recognise a divine principle underlying man and nature. He rejected the god of

traditional Judaeo-Christian orthodoxy. In that tradition he found God represented as external to the world. 'What sort of God would it be,' he asked, 'who only pushed from without?' His somewhat cavalier religious stance is summed up in the frequently quoted passage, 'In the study of nature we are pantheists. When we write poetry we are polytheists. Morally we are monotheists'. He believed in the indwelling of divine spirit in all creation and all life. In this he was typical of the whole Romantic Movement. Creation he saw as a continuous process of creativity. It is particularly manifest in the creativity of man.

Herder

Goethe stood in a class by himself. But he was surrounded by a galaxy of distinguished writers of similar spirit. They all exercised some influence on the development of the new theology. Johann Gottfried von Herder (1744–1803) was, next to Goethe, the main influence in bringing the 'Storm and Stress' movement into being. He had two great antipathies which he contributed to the Romantic Movement – a distaste for arid rationalism and a revulsion from authoritarian, ecclesiastical tradition. More positively, he emphasised access to truth through intuitive sensibility. He stressed the importance of the individual and the idiosyncratic. Therefore he respected tradition as representing the individuality of peoples and nations. But he insisted that such tradition must be interpreted in accordance with the knowledge and insights of modernity. Every age has its own special revelation and discloses a facet of the divine spirit. The harmony of the whole is the self-disclosure of God. In this Herder expressed a typical Romantic attitude to religion.

The Old Testament, he suggested, is to be interpreted as the folk poetry of the Israelite people. It should be set alongside the traditions of other peoples.

It was also typical that he treated the image of God in man as our best clue to the nature of divine spirit. The myth of the Fall he regarded as no more than ancient superstition. Further, while the eighteenth century had tended to confine the image of God to the rational and moral aspects of human nature, Herder opened it up to include every aspect of our emotional and aesthetic life. 'Religion', he said, 'is the highest humanity, the final blossoming of the human soul.'

Novalis

Another powerful influence on Romanticism was Friedrich von Hardenberg (1772–1801), better known by his pseudonym, Novalis.

He was the most romantic of all the romantics. He initiated a tendency to idealise the Middle Ages and to see in them a flowering of the youth of Europe.

The new, romantic spirit manifested itself in every aspect of life and culture. In music, the formal elegance of Mozart and Haydn gave way to the striving, aspiring spirit of Beethoven. In architecture the preciousness of baroque gave way to the more expansive spirit of neo-gothic and neo-classical styles. In painting and sculpture there was a reaction against the restraints of academic art, which found only the great and prestigious worthy of representation. The new realism in art sought significance in the every-day.

3. ROMANTICISM AND RELIGION

Behind all this there was a conviction that divine spirit is pervasively present within the world and especially within the life of man. The artist and creative writer are the priests and prophets of this divine spirit, who is the source of their inspiration. Religion was still regarded as the highest pinnacle of human culture; but it was felt that it needed to be liberated from ecclesiastical bondage on the one hand and rationalist reduction on the other.

Kant's Contribution to Theology

Oddly enough, it was Immanuel Kant (1724–1804), that pillar of the Rationalist Enlightenment, who opened the door upon the way forward for the new theology of the Romantic Movement.

1. Kant, in the *Critique of Pure Reason* (1781), had shown that science is possible because man, through the forms and categories of his mind, actually shapes the world of his experience so that it makes scientific sense. This gives subjective spirit (*Geist*) primacy over the objective world of nature and matter.

2. In the *Critique of Practical Reason* (1788) he had shown that the real self is the free self. In the exercise of free moral decision we are involved with reality as it truly is, not just as it appears to the understanding. This, again, gave a primacy to free spirit over against the world of Newtonian physics.

3. In the *Critique of Judgment* (1790) he deals with those judgments in which we ascribe beauty, sublimity and purpose to the world. Although he could find no logical basis for the unequivocal objectivity of such judgments, he did acknowledge that we are obliged to treat them as if they had an objective ground in reality.

This opened the way for a new approach to the self-disclosure of God as objective spirit in the world.

It was, after all, Kant who said, '*Two things fill the mind with ever new and increasing admiration and awe . . . the starry heavens above and the moral law within.*' This is an anticipation of the Romantic spirit.

Fichte

Johann Gottlieb Fichte (1762–1814) carried the Kantian emphasis on the creative and legislative powers of human reason still further. For him subjective spirit is supreme. We make and project our own world; but we do so only within the constraints of the moral order in which alone true objectivity is to be found. He virtually identified God with the moral order.

Schelling

Wilhelm Joseph von Schelling (1775–1814) completed the bridge between Kant and the nineteenth century. He rejected Fichte's emphasis on subjective spirit as the ultimate reality. After all, he pointed out, we do experience the world of nature as something given. Nature has a life of its own of which we are only part. Nature is objective spirit. It is a living system moving from the inorganic to the organic, from the organic to consciousness and from consciousness to moral and aesthetic awareness.

This notion that the objective world, as well as subjective experience should be interpreted as a manifestation of spirit became the most fundamental and formative conviction of the new philosophy and the new theology.

FOR FURTHER READING

(These are mostly general works many of which will have a bearing also on other chapters.)

Barth, Karl, *Protestant Theology in the Nineteenth Century*, London, 1972.

Cunliffe-Jones, Herbert, (ed.), *A History of Christian Doctrine*, Edinburgh, 1978. (pp. 461 ff).

Heron, A. I. C., *A Century of Protestant Theology*, London, 1980.

Mackintosh, H. R., *Types of Modern Theology. Schleiermacher to Barth*, London, 1937.

Nicholls, W., *Systematic and Philosophical Theology*, Harmondsworth, 1971 (*Pelican Guide to Modern Theology*, vol. 3).

Reardon, Bernard M. G., *Religious Thought in the Nineteenth Century Illustrated from Writers of the Period*, Cambridge, 1966.

Tillich, P., *Perspectives on Nineteenth and Twentieth Century Protestant Theology*, London, 1967.

Vidler, A. R., *The Church in an Age of Revolution, 1789 to the Present Day*, Harmondsworth, 1961 (*Pelican History of the Church*, vol. 5). Revised ed. 1971.

Welch, C., *Protestant Thought in the Nineteenth Century, Vol. I, 1799–1870*, New Haven, Conn., 1972.

2

SCHLEIERMACHER

The situation we have just described called for a fresh start in systematic theology. The nineteenth century responded to this with a profusion of theological novelty.

F. D. E. Schleiermacher is usually given the title of father of modern theology – though Hegel deserves to share that honour equally with him. He was a leading figure in the movement which rediscovered 'spirit' as the key concept for the interpretation of the human condition. He shared and developed the new vision of man as more than an aggregate of intellect, will and passion associated with a body. Man is a living, personal whole. It is in this wholeness of his person that he is spirit.

1. INTERPRETING RELIGION

Religion is Irreducible
Schleiermacher based his interpretation of religion on this understanding of man. Religion, he maintained, is the very heart of man's experience as living spirit. In its essence, therefore, religion is not a matter of believing a special sort of metaphysical philosophy. This he maintained against the rationalist deists. Neither is it a matter of assenting to a code of doctrinal propositions. This he maintained against the prevailing orthodoxies of his time. Nor is it reducible to morality. This he maintained against the Kantians.

Religion, he insisted, is not reducible to any elements other than itself. He was himself a man of deep and intense religious experience. He was brought up in a pietistic, Moravian household. He moved beyond that particular ethos though he always acknowledged his debt to it. He became a minister of the Reformed church. After entering academic life he continued to preach every Sunday.

Religion as 'Feeling'

If religion is not reducible to anything other than itself, what is it? Schleiermacher had to find a word. Unfortunately he chose the word 'feeling'. This has led to endless misunderstanding. The traditional psychology divided man's capacities into three distinct 'faculties' – thought, feeling and will. On this basis it would seem fairly clear that if, as Schleiermacher maintained, religion is not a matter of thought (philosophical or dogmatic) or of will (ethics), then its essence must lie in the third faculty, feeling. 'Feeling' in this context could readily be understood as mere emotion. Schleiermacher left himself wide open to this interpretation.

He was so understood by his illustrious colleague in Berlin, Hegel. It was mainly for this reason that Hegel rejected Schleiermacher's theology as worthless. Hegel insisted, with good reason, that you cannot make truth claims for a mere emotion. Yet the teachers and prophets of religion do make truth claims.

The trouble was that Schleiermacher's own psychological insight had moved far beyond the old faculty psychology in a way which anticipated modern psychology. The new concepts and terminology had not yet been developed, however. He was trapped in the language of the old psychology while endeavouring to say something that went far beyond it.

What he meant by 'feeling' as the basic mode of religious experience was not mere emotion but immediate consciousness – the most fundamental form of human consciousness at a level prior to that at which it is diversified into intellect, emotion and will.

The 'Speeches on Religion'

It must be admitted, however, that this was not altogether clear in the early publication which brought him instant fame, *On Religion, Speeches to its Cultured Despisers*. The first edition of this epoch-making little book was published anonymously in 1799. It was re-issued in a heavily revised edition in 1806 under his own name. Religion, he there tells us, is neither a special kind of knowing nor a special kind of morals. Religion is in essence piety and piety is something more than 'an instinct craving for a mess of metaphysical and ethical crumbs'. It is a felt relation to the infinite, an intuition of the infinite, 'a sense and taste for the Infinite'. In the *Speeches* he uses a wide variety of other terms apparently synonymously – the All, the Universe, God. Because of this he was not unreasonably suspected of pantheism. Because of his use of the word 'feeling' he was also suspected of subjectivism. He was also suspected of relativism because, in the *Speeches*, every religion is treated as having its own validity as an expression of religious feeling.

Significance of the 'Speeches'
But before we consider these criticisms, let us look at the more positive achievements of the *Speeches*.

1. He offered a solution to the problem of the relation of faith to science and philosophy by making it independent of both.

2. He offered a solution to the problem of the transcendent God 'out there' (whether of Deism or Orthodoxy). He did this by denying any genuine religious significance to talk about God which was not directly related to an immediate, felt relation to the divine.

3. He offered a new solution to the question of the relation between the sacred and the secular. He affirmed that every aspect of experience is pervaded by this felt relation to the divine. Everything finite is experienced in the context of a felt relation to the infinite. If everything thus participates in the realm of the sacred, there is no distinct realm of the secular. Equally, if there is no distinct realm of the secular, there can be no distinct realm of the sacred. This was the beginning of the movement towards modern christian secularity.

4. He moved the conceptual framework of theology from a cosmological to an anthropological basis. Instead of looking for a divine cause and controller of the universe, theology began to look for a theological interpretation of human experience.

For better or worse, these four trends remained characteristic of modern theology.

'The Christian Faith'
In the great work of his maturity, *The Christian Faith*, he gave some precision to what, in the *Speeches*, he had expressed with rhetorical abandon. Even there, however, it is not always easy to discern precisely what he meant. He identified the religious feeling as 'the feeling of absolute dependence'. It is temptingly easy to interpret this in purely psychological terms. This would be a mistake. He was feeling after what would today be called an existential interpretation of religious experience and commitment. However, the vocabulary and concepts of existentialist philosophy had not yet been developed.

It is helpful in attempting to interpret *The Christian Faith* to have some regard to his less theological work on 'Ethics', 'Dialectics' and 'Hermeneutics', contained in his published lectures.

The 'Borrowed Propositions'

He begins *The Christian Faith* saying that he has to borrow some propositions from ethics. These consist in the recognition that human beings exist not as isolated individuals but in community and in relation. 'Ethics' is for him a very broad concept. It concerns every aspect of free, human activity. He rejects the Kantian divorce of the moral self (the real self according to Kant) from the empirical self of experience. Ethics is for Schleiermacher the science of what today would be called human ecology. Its characteristic theme is love rather than law. Its central, normative concept is the highest good rather than duty.

The self as free agent cannot be conceived as pure subject as in Kant. We discover ourselves in our response to others and to our environment. We disclose ourselves to others in the expressiveness of that reponse.

This means that not only our knowledge but our whole existence has a dialectical structure. It consists in a relation between a given situation and our free response to it. This is worked out in his lectures on 'Dialectic'.

In order to act freely in relation to our social and natural environment we must form some understanding of our situation. The process of understanding is analysed in his lectures on 'Hermeneutics' – a discipline which Schleiermacher virtually invented. He approached it first with reference to the problems involved in interpreting a text. (Schleiermacher was an industrious translator. He translated the works of Plato.) He showed that it is not enough to understand the grammar and vocabulary of a text. In order to interpret you have to understand the author and his situation. This means that hermeneutics involves not only the understanding of life situations. It involves the way in which we come to recognise, understand, respect and love one another. This applies even to our understanding of our natural environment.

Interpreting Religious Experience

The common factor which is the basis of our shared understanding of ourselves and our world is the sheer 'givenness' of our existence. (Schleiermacher does not use that word. He uses the very Germanic term *Irgendwiegewordensein* – literally, 'somehow or other having come to be'.) Concomitant with this immediate awareness of the sheer happens-to-be-so character of our finite existence there is an immediate awareness of a relationship to the infinite and eternal. These two factors are the web and the woof of our feeling of absolute dependence.

This felt relation is not itself a specific emotion. It can come to expression in the whole range of our emotions.

Being related as a constituent factor to a given moment of consciousness . . . it thereby becomes a particular religious emotion, and being in another moment related to a different datum it becomes a different religious emotion, yet so that the essential element, namely the feeling of absolute dependence, is the same in both.

That Schleiermacher's treatment of the feeling of absolute dependence is not to be interpreted as an exercise in the psychology of religious emotion but rather as an anticipation of modern existentialist theology is made conclusively clear when in the same passage he goes on to say,

This is not consciousness of ourselves as individuals of a particular description but simply as individual, finite existence in general.

We are dealing with a structural factor in individual consciousness, not with a specific emotion.

2. INTERPRETING CHRISTIAN DOCTRINE

God
The feeling of absolute dependence is more than the consciousness of our own contingency. It has a positive content. It is the feeling of being in relation with that on which our existence ultimately depends.

As regards the identification of absolute dependence with 'relation to God' . . . this is to be understood in the sense that the *whence* of our receptive and active existence, as implied in this self-consciousness, is to be designated by the word 'god' and that this is for us the really original signification of the word.

Therefore, our talk about God, though it is the expression of something more appropriately described as feeling than idea, does refer to a reality beyond ourselves. It is more than the expression of our self-understanding. However, we cannot know God directly as we know objects in the world. We can know God only within the felt relationship of absolute dependence.

This means that when we say 'I believe in God' we are not formulating a theory about the existence of an absolute, personal being. We cannot know anything about God as he is in himself. None the less, it is a proper and appropriate expression of pious feeling that we should speak of him as person and as Father.

Creation

The doctrine that God is the creator of the world is the basic expression of this felt relation to the 'whence' of our existence and our world. It is not a theory about a first event at the beginning of time. On this interpretation Schleiermacher thought to eliminate all possibility of conflict between theology and science.

Attributes of the creator God such as his omnipotence, omniscience and eternity are not to be interpreted as affirmations of a metaphysical philosophy. They also express immediate awareness. 'The religious consciousness becomes . . . actual only as consciousness of his *eternal power*.' He thus thought to eliminate all possibility of conflict with philosophical ontology.

Revelation

This was a very sharp point of controversy between rationalists of the Enlightenment and conservative churchmen. The rationalists saw revelation as an offence against the autonomy of reason. This tension was inevitable so long as revelation was understood as divinely inspired verbal communication.

For Schleiermacher revelation is a spiritual reality prior to its verbal expression. God makes himself known to mankind through our feeling of absolute dependence. The sacred literature, doctrine and cult of any religion are secondary to this. Revelation is a universal phenomenon. The religions of the world all have their element of revealed truth, since all are expressions of the basic form of religious consciousness. In *The Christian Faith* Schleiermacher makes it clearer than he did in the *Speeches* that this does not mean that it is a matter of indifference which religion one professes. There are degrees of perfection and imperfection in religious consciousness. One religion may express a purer form of piety than another. In Jesus Christ a perfect and flawless religious consciousness is disclosed to us. Therefore Christianity may truthfully claim to represent final revelation.

In this way Schleiermacher thought he could eliminate the conflict between revelation and reason.

Miracle

This was another bone of contention with the philosophically enlightened. Since Newton, there had been increasingly widespread consciousness of the symmetry of the laws of nature. Therefore the very idea of miracle as an event running counter to these laws was not only incredible; it was an affront to the wonderful symmetry of God's creation.

Schleiermacher rejected the notion of miracle as an event running counter to a law of nature. Any event is a miracle in so far as it heightens our consciousness of the relation of all creation to the Eternal, the Infinite, the Divine. To the truly pious the whole of nature is a miracle. The miracle stories of the New Testament are therefore to be treated as symbols rather than factual reporting.

Sin and Grace

The distinctively christian form of the feeling of absolute dependence has a double aspect. We are aware of our utter dependence first of all in our resistance to it. In all of us there is an urge to be independent and autonomous. This is what the doctrine of original sin is about. The story of the Fall of Adam and Eve is not a biography of the first man and the first woman. It is a symbolic account of a universal element in human experience.

But over and above this anxious effort to establish our own existence for ourselves we also have a trustful and blessed experience of being sustained and cherished in our existence. This is what the doctrine of grace is about.

The heightened awareness of these two fundamental elements of human existence and of the triumph of grace over sin in Christianity derives wholly and directly from Jesus Christ.

Christ and the Church

For Schleiermacher Christ and the church are inseparable. One main difference between Schleiermacher's stand and that of simple pietism was his recognition that religious experience is never private to the individual. Jesus is known as the Christ only through religious consciousness as it is shared in the christian community. Jesus is recognised as the initiator of this consciousness. The New Testament should be seen as an account of the genesis of this shared, spiritual relationship.

Jesus is the revelation of God in that he initiates a new and wholesome form of human self-consciousness. We recognise in him a perfect God-consciousness. He initiates us into his own perfect, felt relation to God. He thus becomes himself the presence of God to us.

We also recognise in him the perfection of humanity. The perfection of divine immanence in him and the perfection of his humanity are one and the same. This is the sense in which the credal affirmation that he is truly God and truly man is credible and true.

The primary datum is something felt in Christian religious consciousness. It is a shared consciousness within the body of the church. Doctrines of the person of Christ are secondary to that. To treat them as primary is to betray the real substance of the christian tradition.

It is a mistake, therefore, to treat the fundamental Christological affirmations such as those of Nicaea and Chalcedon as descriptions of metaphysical elements compounded in the make-up of Jesus of Nazareth.

On these grounds he rejects the two-nature Christology as thoroughly pagan. The union of God and man in Jesus Christ is a religious communion. So intimate is this union, however, that there is 'a veritable existence of God in him'. This is how we should interpret such titles as Son of God.

This is the first appearance of what has since come to be known as Christology 'from below'. That is to say, it is a Christology which begins from the humanity of Jesus rather than the divine *Logos* or eternal Son.

This approach assumes, however, that well-substantiated knowledge of the life and personality of Jesus is historically available. Schleiermacher had no serious doubts about this. The acute problems of historical criticism did not arise till the next generation.

Its vulnerability on this issue is seen by some as the weakest point in Schleiermacher's whole theological architectonic. On the other hand he did in some measure anticipate a solution to the negative results of historical criticism of the Gospels in suggesting that it was the total impact of the person of Christ upon the faith of the church rather than specific knowledge of the facts of his life and sayings that constitutes the substance of the faith. 'Christian doctrines are accounts of the Christian religious affections set forth in speech'.

Subjectivity and Objectivity

In taking this view of doctrine he did not leave himself as wide open to the charge of subjectivism and relativism as is commonly supposed. He acknowledged objective controls.

Firstly, doctrines must be scripturally true, for the Scriptures express the consciousness of the original community gathered about

Jesus. This does not mean that they should merely repeat New Testament expressions. They must faithfully interpret them for the times.

Secondly, although doctrine is not as such a factual or scientific statement, it must none the less be compatible with the known facts. In this sense it must be scientifically true.

Thirdly, it must be ecclesiastically true in that it does not express the merely individual consciousness of single persons, but the shared religious consciousness of the whole Christian community.

Despite these controls, however, the question of the relation between truth claims and expressions of pious feeling remains the major obscurity of Schleiermacher's theological system.

Of his greatness, however, there can be no doubt. It has been justly said of him that he did not so much establish a school as initiate a new era.

FOR FURTHER READING

Brandt, R. B., *The Philosophy of Schleiermacher*, Westport, Conn., 1941, repr. 1971.

Niebuhr, R. R., *Schleiermacher on Christ and Religion*, London, 1965.

Funk, Robert, (ed.) *Schleiermacher as Contemporary*, New York, 1970.

Dawson, J. F., *Friedrich Schleiermacher: The Evolution of a Nationalist*, Austin, Tex., 1966.

3

THE HEGELIAN POWERHOUSE

1. THE PROVENANCE OF HEGELIAN THEOLOGY

Much of Hegel's writing is so splendidly obscure that it is difficult to find two people who agree as to precisely what he meant. Interpretations range from Idealist to Existentialist, from Fascist to Marxist. Yet his development of the dialectic method has been so influential in a variety of guises that he remains to this day a power to be reckoned with. That is what the title of this chapter is intended to suggest.

Schleiermacher and Hegel
Schleiermacher and Hegel saw one another as in total disagreement. As colleagues in the University of Berlin, they held one another in total disregard. In fact they had more in common than they realised.

Their Similarities
1. Each in his own way sought to re-establish recognition of the inwardness and intimacy of God in man.

2. Both were deeply influenced by the Romantic Movement. Both wanted to accommodate this movement without losing the intellectual rigour of the Enlightenment.

3. Each in his own way was passionately concerned to release Christianity from authoritarian support and to make it credible to free-thinking, modern man.

4. Both sought these ends on the basis of a profoundly perceptive and original analysis of human self-consciousness. In each case this was intended to show a) that there is an essential relationship between the human and the divine spirit and b) that christianity is the best expression and the fullest realization of this relationship.

5. In their novel interpretations each endeavoured to preserve the main features of traditional dogma.

6. Both affirmed the fundamental unity of the spirit of man against the Kantian dismemberment of the conscious self into totally discrete functions.

The fundamental difference between them, however, was that Schleiermacher attempted to do this on the basis of an expanded notion of 'feeling'. Hegel extended the notion of 'reason' to make it coextensive with every aspect of spirit.

Early Theological Writings

Hegel's early writings were overtly theological. The importance of his early, unpublished theological writings was not appreciated until they were brought to public attention by Wilhelm Dilthey in 1905. It is now clear that much of his later philosophy arose directly out of these early theological concerns.

He wrote for his own use and frequently revised a critical life of Jesus. It was never published.

The philosophers of the Enlightenment – particularly as represented by Lessing – were particularly vexed by the question, How can the eternal and universal truths of religion be contained and expressed in a particular historical event? Hegel tackled this problem head on by claiming that Jesus not only taught the truth but in his historic person *was* and *is* the truth.

The human spirit is fully realised only in spiritual unity with the divine. In Jesus Christ such a unity is manifest. This is the sense in which Jesus is divine as well as human. Stories such as those of the virgin birth and other miracles are to be understood as symbols of this truth. They are not reports of actual events.

Jesus is a particular spirit. God is universal spirit. The form and substance of their unity is love. Love is more than an emotional relationship. It is the profoundest kind of knowing. It transcends the distinction between knower and known. This was the first time since St Augustine that love had been raised to the level of an ontological principle.

This pointed the way for the young Hegel's solution to the other major problem which troubled the philosophers of the Enlightenment with regard to the Christian religion – that of the relation of autonomous reason to authority.

Reason and Authority

Hegel treats the Judaism of Jesus' day as the ultimate instance of authoritarian religion. In Judaism, according to Hegel, God is wholly external to his creation, ruling it from without. His laws are the commands of naked authority. The religion of Jesus, on the other hand, is one of sheer inwardness. The spirit of God is so identified in love with the inner workings of his human spirit that divine authority is wholly at one with the inner authority of conscience and reason. Thus the conflict between the 'givenness' of revealed religion and the free autonomy of the rational, moral self is overcome.

The conflict thus overcome extends beyond religion. The objective, factual character of the world sets definite limits to our freedom and autonomy. The universal name for this limitation of free selfhood is 'fate' or 'destiny'. The truly free person is the one who learns so to love the destiny that God has given him that he also freely chooses it. This was perfectly realised in Jesus Christ – especially when he freely chose to go to the cross.

The task of spirit is to come to terms with its world and its fate. It is not to do this in passive subjection, however. The destiny of spirit is to do this in a way which emulates the victory of spirit over world and fate in Jesus Christ.

Spirit in the World

Hegel works this out in his first major publication – *The Phenomenology of Spirit*. Here he tackles the problem of how rational spirit exists in a world of brute fact, free spirit in a world of apparently fateful necessity, feeling spirit in a world of apparently natural indifference. The accepted Kantian view was that there is an absolute contrast between the free self and the world of objective fact. Not so, says Hegel.

What he in effect asks of the reader in the early chapters of *The Phenomenology of Spirit* is to conduct a fairly simple mental experiment. Try to think of pure consciousness existing apart from any relationship to an object. You will find that you cannot. A consciousness which is not a consciousness *of something* is inconceivable. Therefore subjective spirit and objective fact (the free self and the hard resistance of the world) do not exist in absolute contrast and opposition. They are interdependent.

Now turn to the other pole of the relation. Try to think of a pure object apart from its relation to a thinking subject. This is even more obviously impossible. As soon as you try to think of it, you *are* relating it to a thinking subject. As a thing in itself it is quite literally unthinkable.

Nature and mind exist in polar relationship. Both are manifestations of spirit. Mind is the subjective pole. Nature is the objective pole. Within this polar relationship the task of spirit is to realise its unity and fulfilment.

If you cannot relate positively to your world you cannot feel at home in it. This is the condition which Hegel called 'alienation'. He calls this the 'unhappy diremption of spirit into self and not-self'. But reason, as the active principle of spirit, has within itself the capacity to overcome this unhappy conflict. Reason is here understood as the total, active expression of spirit. In knowledge reason overcomes the opposition between the subjective self and the objective world. In getting to know and understand the world we begin to form a personal and spiritual relation with it.

In imagination and art reason embraces the world in a deeper kind of communion. In action reason becomes dynamic. We transform the world in accordance with the needs and aspirations of subjective spirit. Thus in thought and science, feeling and imagination, will and action, spirit comes to recognise its other self in its object. Subjectivity and objectivity enrich and enhance one another.

Spiritual Religion

Religion is the endeavour of spirit to sum up all these various activities of reason and to bring them to a unified fulfilment.

Religion, to perform this function, must be folk religion. It must be totally integrated with the spirit of the society and culture of which it is a function. Otherwise it becomes an instrument of false objectification and alienation. Therefore the images and doctrines in which religion is expressed must change and develop with the changing times and circumstances in which it lives. To fix the images and dogmas of a given period in an authoritarian way is worse than sterilising religion. It positively demonises it.

This is why the teaching of Jesus represents the perfection of religion. He totally rejected the external, authoritarian God of the Jews. He insisted on inwardness and spontaneity. He recognised that this could not be achieved in arbitrary, subjective caprice. He saw that true inwardness and spontaneity could be realised only in the recognition of the ultimate identity of subjective and objective spirit. The inner principle of this recognition is love. We learn to act towards the neighbour (objective spirit) as towards ourselves (subjective spirit). We learn to 'consider the lilies of the field'. Our relation to the whole realm of nature is like our relation to our neighbour. It is only in finding the objective counterpart of our own subjective spirit in the world that we can be truly ourselves. Hegel ties this up with the cosmic imagery of eschatology. In the end the whole of creation will be manifested as spirit. He thus, for the first time, united the ethics and the eschatology of Jesus in a way that was to transform both.

He thought that the church had betrayed this insight of Jesus into the reciprocity of the inner and the outer expressions of spirit. In its protestant as well as its catholic form it had transformed christian truth into the very kind of extraneous, authoritarian structure against which it was directed. It thereby identified itself with the sort of structure which crucified Jesus because it could not tolerate him. His radical freedom was too much for it.

Absolute Spirit

In his re-interpretation of Christian doctrine Hegel finds his main clue to understanding God as infinite and absolute spirit in his analysis of finite spirit.

If we try to think of God as absolute, infinite spirit apart from his relation to the world, we find ourselves faced with the unthinkable. God becomes an unthinkable, unimaginable blank. This corresponds with the unthinkableness of pure consciousness unrelated to an object. Therefore God, as absolute, subjective spirit must be thought of as going forth from himself into objective spirit. This is the meaning of the doctrine of creation.

Just as at the level of finite spirit, this sets up an 'unhappy diremption of spirit into self and not-self'. This is alienation of the world in its separateness from and opposition to God as subjective spirit. This is the meaning of the doctrine of the Fall. (The story of Adam and Eve is a symbolic myth.)

Absolute reason, however, as the active principle of infinite, absolute spirit, goes out of itself in recognition of its objective pole. The Word, Reason or *Logos* of God goes forth from him in creation. ('In the beginning was the Word . . . By him all things were made . . .) However, God overcomes the estrangement of his word in the objective, created world by identifying with it in the person of his incarnate *Logos* in Jesus Christ. This is the meaning and truth of the doctrine of the Incarnation.

The doctrine of the Incarnation, suffering, death and Resurrection of Jesus Christ encapsulates the meaning of the whole history of creation.

Philosophy of History

In his philosophy of history Hegel tried to show that it is by a kind of self-giving that subjective spirit finally attains victorious unity with objective spirit. For example, in the humiliation and alienation of slavery, the masters eventually become dependent on the slaves. This enables the slaves to create a new and less alienating form of society. With remarkable ingenuity Hegel manages to place a spiritual interpretation upon every aspect of social, cultural and political history. The law and authoritative structures of the state are the objective expression of spirit. The whole of political history is a dialectical movement of spirit in which it seeks a reconciliation of subjective and objective spirit. The ultimate destiny of the state is that its objective structures should become a perfect expression of the subjective spirit of the people. It is this social and political aspect of Hegel that has recently attracted most attention. He has been interpreted by some as harbouring communist implications, by others as harbouring fascist implications. However, if we will allow Hegel to speak for himself it is clear that we cannot stop short at a socio-political interpretation. The key to his true meaning and intention is theological.

The cross and resurrection of Jesus is the ultimate and absolute reconciliation of subjective and objective spirit. The alienation of the world is wholly overcome in him. This is the meaning and the truth of the doctrine of atonement.

The historic process in which finite spirit overcomes alienation implies an ultimate identity of subjective and objective spirit in a communion of love. In Christian tradition this is promised as a final consummation when 'the glory of God shall cover the earth as the waters cover the sea'. This is the meaning and the truth of the doctrine of the last things.

The communion of subjective and objective spirit is the life of God in the Holy Spirit. The Holy Spirit is the reconciling activity of God in universal history. In God as Absolute Spirit this is an eternal process. It is not bounded by the successiveness of time. There is in God an eternal communion of subjective and objective spirit and the Holy Spirit is their uniting principle. This is represented in the doctrine that God is three persons in one essence – the Father, who is the source and is pure subjective spirit, the Son in whom the divine spirit goes forth into objectivity and the Holy Spirit in whom there is a perfect communion and unity of both. This is the meaning and the truth of the doctrine of the Trinity.

From Theology to Philosophy

Hegel went a stage further. Religion, he said, could only *represent* the truth. Philosophy, once it had learned to interpret the dialectic of spirit, could *state* the truth. In his own philosophy Hegel appeared to claim to make the transition from religious representation to conceptual expression of the truth of God.

He has often been interpreted as claiming thereby that his own philosophy supplanted religion and theology. This interpretation can be contested, however – especially in view of the importance he attached to folk religion. It is also all too often forgotten that his whole philosophical system developed directly from his early efforts to make credible sense of the Christian faith.

2. THE LEFTWING HEGELIANS

Right and Left Hegelianism
It was David Friedrich Strauss (1808–1874) who classified the Hegelian disciples into right and left wing groups.

Hegel had eliminated from the gospel those supernatural elements which the rationalists found incredible. But at the same time he treated the whole created order as an expression of spirit. Thus the conflict between the natural and the supernatural was transcended and resolved in the dialectic of subjective and objective spirit.

The right wing Hegelians gave the primacy to subjective spirit. This gave strong support to traditional belief in God as absolute spirit. The leftwing Hegelians gave the primacy to what Hegel had called objective spirit – i.e., to matter rather than mind, to facts rather than concepts, to causal relations rather than the interplay of ideas, to objects rather than consciousness. This reintroduced the conflict between spirit and nature. This conflict was further intensified by the growth of scientific positivism and the technical control of nature. The cosmic scope of the Hegelian dialectic was destroyed. Nature was no longer seen as the objective projection of the divine mind. It became simply the realm of brute fact.

Hegel may have conceived the incarnation of the Word of God in Jesus Christ in a way different from tradition; but at least for him the Christ retained the lineaments of divinity as a figure of cosmic significance. For Hegel's leftwing successors the significance of the Christ was restricted to the sphere of the human and the historical.

D. F. Strauss
Strauss caused a great furore by the explicit scepticism of his *Life of Jesus* in 1835. This was a major landmark in the history of theology. It brought into the open critical, historical questions about the factual reliability of the Bible which had remained dormant for the most part since the publication by G. E. Lessing of the *Wolfen-büttel Fragments* in 1874–8.

We shall return later to the historical question. In some ways too much has been made of Strauss's denial of the historical actuality of the narratives of the supernatural in the life of Jesus. After all, both Schleiermacher and Hegel had already implied as much. More important was the fact that Strauss did not regard the tales of the supernatural as merely false or fictional inventions. He interpreted them as myths. Myths he regarded as vehicles of truth. The myths of the New Testament are not mere superstitious fictions. They are its most significant element. Their proper subject, however, is not Jesus as a historic individual. Their subject is the whole human race. 'It is,' he says, 'Humanity that dies, rises and ascends into Heaven . . . By the kindling within him of the idea of Humanity, the individual man participates in the divinely human life of the species'.

Feuerbach
This notion was systematically developed by Ludwig Feuerbach (1804–72) in a way that had fateful consequences. His main works of theological interest are, *The Essence of Christianity* (1841), *The Essence of Religion* and *Principles of the Philosophy of the Future* (1843).

The Essence of Christianity begins with the observation that man is distinguished from animals by his ability to abstract from his individual existence and think in terms of species and essences. What religion expresses is this consciousness which man has of his own species and essence. The way in which Feuerbach identifies the idea of the species and essence is important.

In the concept of the species man is aware of his own essence, not as finite, limited and imperfect, but as perfect, complete and infinite. But at first he sees this, his essential nature, as something outside himself. 'Religion is the childlike condition of humanity; but . . . in childhood man is an object to himself under the form of another man.' Therefore, 'the divine being is nothing else than the human being, or, rather the human purified, freed from the limits of the individual man, made objective'. So, '*Homo homini deus est*' – man is the god of man.

This is the beginning of the modern projectionist theory of religion which was later to be taken up by Sigmund Freud, among others.

For Feuerbach this projectionist theory did not mean that religion is simply illusion. It is seen by him as a necessary stage in the progress of humanity towards maturity. Christianity is seen in this respect as both the worst and the best of all religions. In the doctrine of the incarnation it arrived at a realization of the true identity of

God and man. However, it also represents the ultimate in man's estrangement from himself. This is expressed in the doctrine of total depravity. 'That God may be all man must be nothing.' The ultimate in human self-estrangement centres on the fact that the Christ had to sacrifice his real humanity to the divinity revealed in him. However, this is also the door through which he returns to perfect unity with the Father. The Christian believer participates in this. But so long as this remains at the level of traditional religion, it happens only in imagination. For example, the monk renounces the actual love of real women in favour of the image of perfect womanly love in heaven. The final step must be the return from heavenly images to earthly reality. With the recognition of the identity of God and man the worship of a transcendent being must be replaced by reverential attitudes to humanity. 'What yesterday was still religion is no longer such today . . . What today is atheism tomorrow will be religion.'

This aspect of Feuerbach played a significant part in the recent 'secular christianity' movement.

Feuerbach developed the concept of the distinctiveness of the 'I-Thou' relation as he found it in Hegel. He perceived even more clearly than Hegel that we do not have our humanity within ourselves as isolated, self-contained individuals. Humanity is a relational property. We receive our humanity from each other. 'Only through his fellow man does man become clear to himself and self-conscious; but only when I am clear to myself does the world become clear to me.' His sensitive treatment of this aspect of human spirituality and its sanctification in religion commands respect as much as his atheism causes shock.

Feuerbach, unfortunately, has been claimed as the father of many brands of atheism very different in spiritual quality from his own. He is better known as a stepping stone to Karl Marx than he is in and for himself. This is less than his just deserts.

Marx

Karl Marx (1818–83) can scarcely be classed as a theologian. However, no history of theology can ignore him. Firstly, his interpretation of the dialectical progress of history towards socialism was derived directly from Hegel's interpretation of Christian eschatology. Secondly, Marxism is the most powerful ideological rival to Christianity in the modern world. Thirdly, recent studies of Marx – especially the younger Marx – have shown him to have more spiritual insight than his political and economic interpreters give him credit for. Finally, in modern 'political theology' Marxism has been admitted into the forum of theological debate as a possibly valid interpretation of Christian eschatology.

Marx accepted Feuerbach's emphasis on the material and concrete as a proper correction of Hegel's philosophy of spirit and idea. He wanted to go further, however. Feuerbach, he thought, had finally failed to extricate the problem of human alienation from the realm of ideas. Reconciliation, in Feuerbach, was based upon a *reinterpretation* of Christianity and the human situation. Alienation is to be overcome, in Marx's view, not by interpreting the world but by changing it. It is man's objective, economic and social circumstances which give rise to alienation. It is these that must be changed to overcome alienation. Religion is merely a distraction from this revolutionary task.

3. SOCIAL SCIENCE AND REDUCTIONISM

At much the same time as these left-wing developments of the Hegelian dialectic were reducing the meaning and reference of religion to the human plane, a quite undialectical reductionism was developing in France. It was positivist in method and approach. Positivism treats experimental and observational science as the model of all knowledge. It considers only the objective pole in knowledge. In this sense it is undialectical.

Comte and Positivism
On this basis Auguste Comte (1798–1857) adopted a sociological approach to questions of religion and morality. Indeed, it was he who first coined the term 'sociology'. His interpretation of religion rested on the doctrine that the intellectual and cultural development of mankind has passed through three main stages – the theological, the metaphysical and the scientific. This idea of the three stages of man was derived largely from Saint-Simon (1760–1825). It does not seem to have occurred to Comte that this notion itself has a thoroughly mythological ring to it. It is a modern myth which has been remarkably persistent. It has lurked in the undergrowth of the jungle of religious anthropology ever since.

Comte did not regard what he took to be the beginning of the scientific age in our own times as the end of religion. On the contrary, religion, in its final, scientific phase, was to be understood sociologically and to become the religion of humanity. He refers to humanity in its totality as 'The Great Being'. In his *System of Positive Polity* (1830–42) he envisages the ideal society as a kind of religious utopia in which the collective 'Great Being' would be the object of worship. Its priests would be sociologists, educators and administrators. All matters of morals and cultural formation would be in their hands. The whole vision is terrifyingly suggestive of George Orwell's *Nineteen Eighty-four!*

Durkheim and Sociology of Religion

Emile Durkheim (1858–1917) has a better claim to be the true founder of modern sociology. In his *Elementary Forms of the Religious Life* he explored the hypothesis that the meaning of religion can be reduced to its social significance. By studying so-called primitive peoples he hoped to find the simple essence of religion. He based his work largely on the field reports of Spencer and Gillen on the Australian Aborigines. They identified the Aboriginal religion as 'totemism'. Its essential feature, Durkheim found, was associated with the fact that peoples living in the most primitive, food-gathering type of culture ordinarily foraged in isolated family groups. Only on special occasions did they come together to celebrate their common ancestry and cohesion. Such occasions gave rise, it was alleged, to a feeling of dependence on the whole group – a feeling akin to Schleiermacher's 'feeling of absolute dependence'. The crowd effect reduplicated this emotion. In this way the sense of the sacred was generated. Parallels with revivalist meetings spring to mind – as indeed they were meant to do.

The totem is the sacred emblem of the group, more holy than the group itself. Celebrating the totem in a quasi-sacramental ritual not only expressed, but was believed to invigorate the common life of the totemic group.

Durkheim's empirical study of religion drew attention to the correlation between theological ideas and the society in which they are generated in a manner such that this could no longer be ignored.

Frazer and Anthropology

There were, however, major difficulties. The first is that Durkheim's work was based upon an anthropological science which was still in its infancy. The towering influence of Sir James G. Frazer (1854–1941) is all too evident. The latter part of the nineteenth century and the beginning of the twentieth was the great age of the armchair anthropologists. Sir James Frazer was their doyen. His erudition is beyond question. He was inclined, however, to read his theories of totemism and magic into whatever evidence came to hand. All the great armchair anthropologists were inclined to do this, basing their theories of religion on an indiscriminate use of the highly interpreted reports of a wide variety of indifferently qualified workers in the field. Their findings lent support to various reductionist theories of religion – e.g. the astonishingly unscientific attempt of Sigmund Freud (1856–1939) to reduce the significance of religion to some of its more obscure psychological concomitants. His *Totem and Taboo* (1919) is based on an even more uncritical use of Frazer than that of Durkheim.

From the standpoint of Judaeo-Christian theology, the pervasive difficulty with all such theories which attempt to reduce the significance of religion to the inter-human and the intra-mundane is their failure to account for the prophetic element in religion. It may readily be granted that religion usually does, in one of its aspects, undergird the social structure of the community with which it is associated. But it may also, in certain circumstances, occasion revolt against it. The recognition of a transcendent God whose significance cannot be exhausted in terms of the intra-mundane is essential to this function. Theology had to wait for Karl Barth before it was effectively reminded of this.

FOR FURTHER READING

Findlay, J. N., *Hegel: A Re-examination*, London, 1958.

Fackenheim, E. L., *The Religious Dimension in Hegel's Thought*, Bloomington, Indiana, 1967.

Caird, Edward, *Hegel*, Edinburgh, 1833.

Caird, E., *The Social Philosophy and Religion of Comte*, Glasgow, 1893.

Harris, H., *David Friedrich Strauss and his Theology*, Cambridge, 1973.

Kamenka, E., *The Philosophy of Ludwig Feuerbach*, New York, 1967.

Simon, W. M., *European Positivism in the Nineteenth Century*, Ithaca, New York, 1963.

Toews, J. E., *Hegelianism*, Cambridge, 1980.

Willey, B., *Nineteenth Century Studies*, London 1949.

CONSERVATION AND INNOVATION IN GERMANY

1. MEDIATING THEOLOGY

After every high there comes a low. None of the next generation of theologians attained the level of creativity and ingenuity of Schleiermacher or Hegel. Their followers were unable to sustain either the rigour or the subtlety of their dialectic. They either emphasised the radical, critical element so as to lose contact with the theological roots of the faith, or they clung to the conservative elements and abandoned critical rigour.

Conservative Confessionalism

Within the churches there still persisted a strong element of old-fashioned supernaturalism. Many responded to the new theologies by becoming more deeply entrenched behind the defences of biblical fundamentalism and the authority of the confessions. The intellectual leader of this school was Ernst W. Hengstenberg (1802–69). He and his associates were not at all interested in any kind of mediation between the new theologies and ecclesiastical tradition.

Many, however, felt the pressures of modernity and the need for some theological adjustment, though they were not ready to accept the apparently outrageous novelty of either Schleiermacher or Hegel. This gave rise to the Mediating School which sought some middle way between modernity and tradition.

What is Revelation?

One of the major issues was the doctrine of revelation. Ever since the Enlightenment the idea of a body of information supernaturally communicated and believed in obedience to divine command had been incompatible with the new spirit of rational autonomy. Hegel had solved the problem by making divine revelation identical with the whole process of reason. Schleiermacher had identified revelation with the feeling of absolute dependence. Both solutions, by making revelation a universal factor in human consciousness, seemed to eliminate the notion of special revelation.

Marheineke

Philipp Marheineke (1780–1846) was one of the first to make the suggestion that if we think of special revelation, not as a body of privileged information in propositional form, but as an event or series of events in which God discloses himself, then there is no embarrassment over the relation of revelation and reason. This understanding of revelation has prevailed in many quarters and continues to be a powerful influence on contemporary theology. It does not identify the Scriptures directly with revelation but treats them as witnessing to the revealing and saving events.

But there was also a question as to whether such events belonged to the continuum of nature and history or were to be seen as supernatural interventions.

Marheineke wanted to have it both ways. He could agree with Schleiermacher that the divine presence in Jesus Christ is manifested in his perfect God-consciousness or feeling of absolute dependence. He could agree with Hegel that the Incarnation represents the union of finite and infinite, of universal and particular, which is the ultimate destiny of spirit. However, he wanted *also* to say that the Incarnation is a supernatural event in which the heavenly enters into the earthly from beyond, in which God acts from without upon his creation. It is difficult to see how the two ways of interpreting the revealing and saving events of the gospel can be made compatible. They rest upon completely different and incompatible conceptions of the relation between nature and supernature, between the creaturely and the divine. In any case it is difficult to see how the decision to interpret some of the narratives about the supernatural on an inner-worldly basis and others on an other-worldly basis could be anything but arbitrary.

Dorner

Another of the mediating theologians, Isaak Dorner (1809–84), adopted a much bolder approach to the notion of revelation as event and the idea of the acts of God in history and nature. He saw miracle as the key concept in this connexion. Taking up an idea that had been first mooted by Schleiermacher, he suggested that miracle is not to be thought of as an extraneous intrusion of the supernatural into the natural. Divine power is a sustaining, pervasive force in all nature. We acknowledge this in the sense of wonder which we feel when we contemplate the created order. We feel this in varying degrees at special times and places when nature seems to open up and disclose this spiritual power. The biblical miracle stories are to be understood as arising out of special instances of this. They anticipate that final and perfect unity with God which is the ultimate destiny of all creation.

The incarnation is the supreme example of miracle in this sense. It is the human personality of Jesus which is the vehicle of the divine presence in him. In this, Dorner was much influenced by the new psychology which regarded human personality as an organic unity of its parts rather than centred on a metaphysical soul. Every personality, he said, is permeated by the divine in some limited measure. Jesus was a man whose whole being was totally permeated by the divine. This is how the doctrine of the incarnation is to be understood.

This implies, however, that the divine presence in Jesus grew to its fulness and perfection in him with the growth of his personality. Dorner accepted this implication. The incarnation of the *logos* of God in Jesus Christ is not complete until the resurrection.

The Principle of Process
This suggests that there is an element of process and development in God himself. This seemed to contradict the traditional doctrine of the eternal changelessness of God. Dorner was prepared to accept this implication also. Increasing reluctance to place too rigid an interpretation on the doctrine of divine immutability was to remain a feature of modern theology right up to the present day.

Dorner insisted that there must be an element of process in God. Admittedly, in his moral perfections God must be changeless. Otherwise there would be imperfection in him. But he is also the living God. As the God of love he enters into relation with his creation. Therefore God's eternity must contain some real relationship to time.

Here we see the beginning of something which has increasingly drawn the interest of modern man. Nowadays it is called 'Process Theology'.

Rothe
This theology of process, as a feature of the more venturesome among the mediating theologians in the immediately post-Hegelian period, was most prominent in Richard Rothe (1799–1876). He was a very devout man as well as an acute scholar. Though he derived much from Hegel and Schleiermacher, he distinguished his

approach to theology sharply from both. In particular he separated theology totally from both philosophy and the new psychology of religion. Both of these begin from the self. Theology begins from the objective idea of God.

However, God is not imprisoned within his own objective transcendence nor excluded thereby from his creation. The experience of living in relation to something absolute is universal in humanity – though not all recognise this for what it is. As the ground of the ethical man's aspiration and the pious man's devotion, God must be personal. He is the absolute person. However, a person can be a person only in relation. To be an ethical person in the fullest sense of the word is to love.

To be a partner of God's love the *whole* of creation, and not just man, must be spiritually significant and directed towards the ethical values of love. You cannot create moral value as you would fashion a doll, however. God may provide the conditions for the emergence of moral value and provide the inspiration towards it. But by its very nature it is something which can emerge only in and with the will and action of free, spiritual beings. Therefore God created a natural, material order to provide the conditions for the emergence of free, ethical spirit. All life, from its lowest to its highest forms betokens this emergence of spirit. Man is an integral part of nature and the highest stage in this process. (It is remarkable that this was thought out some time before Darwin published his *Origin of Species.*)

Rothe goes on to treat the events of biblical history as the emergence of spirit in man. Jesus is the perfection and the anticipatory fulfilment of this process. His life, action and destiny have the power finally to liberate the spirit of man from the chains of material nature.

He not only anticipates some aspects of modern process theologies in this way. He also went on in his studies of early church history to suggest that the original Christian community was not a church. Its concerns were not restricted to the religious aspect of people's lives. It was a total, caring community. In this sense Christianity should be seen as transcending religion (as that term is normally understood). Its ultimate expression should be in the secular world in a caring community.

Thus we find the 'secular christianity' of the nineteen-sixties remarkably anticipated in the eighteen-forties. The roots of our modernity go deeper than we think!

2. THE ERLANGEN SCHOOL

The Primacy of Experience

For most churchmen of those days even those moderate attempts to mediate between the new style of theology initiated by Schleiermacher and Hegel and the formulae of orthodoxy were too radical. Among the more conservatively orthodox, however, Schleiermacher's emphasis on religious experience was influential even among people who totally rejected his system. There was at the beginning of the nineteenth century in Europe a movement of the spirit which came to be known as the Awakening. It stressed the *experience* of justification by faith rather than the formal doctrine. This corresponded to the revivalist movements in Britain and America. It was, however, significantly different. In Anglo-Saxon revivalism attention was directed away from the doctrinal formulae of the Confessions. Emphasis centred on the personal 'testimonies' in which people recounted their conversion experience. In Germany such religious experience was seen more as a confirmation of the doctrinal Confessions and as informing the sense in which they were to be understood. This put new life into the protestant confessions – especially the Augsburg Confession (1530) of Lutheranism. It mitigated their external authoritarian character and rediscovered the inward confirmation of their truth in the experience of justification by faith.

Friedrich A. G. Tholuck (1799–1877), who wrote in this spirit, was a very influential figure, especially through some of his more illustrious pupils. He became Professor of Theology at Halle and taught, among others, Albrecht Ritschl and Martin Kähler. In England he had some influence on the Oxford Movement through his friendship with Edward Pusey.

The Erlangen School

The main centre of this new style of confessional theology, however, was Erlangen. The spirit of the Erlangen school is best summed up in its most distinguished representative, Gottfried Thomasius (1802–75). He said,

> We have been loyal to the confession of our church and have honestly supported it against the many ways in which it is challenged; but it is not the case that for us the Confession was ever something binding restrictively upon us. It is, rather, something which emerges from within. We affirm it because it expresses

what we already believe. We affirm it because it chimes in with what the Bible says to us.

However, this combination of the evidence of religious experience with the authority of the Confessions raised some acute problems. It relied heavily on an analogy with the human, religious experience of Jesus Christ. But, if one followed the creeds and confessions as traditionally understood, this raised the question: How could Jesus be the subject of genuinely human experience when his personality was overwhelmed and dominated by the omnipotent, omniscient, impassible Person of the eternal Son of God?

Kenosis

For a solution to this problem they turned to Philippians 2:5–11. This states that the eternal Son of God 'emptied himself' to become incarnate in Jesus. He emptied himself of all the divine attributes which are incompatible with human finitude. This became known as the Kenotic christology (from the Greek *ekenōsen* – 'he emptied'). It enjoyed quite a vogue at the time in Germany and later in Britain. It is now virtually dead. However, the fact that it arose at all is significant. It pointed up the extreme difficulty of combining a theology based on human experience with a confessional tradition centred on an unambiguously objective conception of the supernatural acts of God. This was the crucial problem of the mediating theologies. It has persisted into our present debates.

3. RITSCHL

It was Albrecht Ritschl (1822–89) who brought European theology to its next phase. He emphasised the prophetic aspect of the Judaeo-Christian tradition.

In the second half of the nineteenth century radical changes were taking place in Europe. The economy was becoming industrialised and the people urbanised. The dream of imperial unity in Europe had finally faded with the dying ambitions of Napoleonic France. The autonomy of nation states increased. Society was increasingly seen as something to be managed rather than a natural growth.

Ritschl's Reputation

Ritschl was the prophet of this new age. His early scholarship was in the fields of New Testament and ecclesiastical history. This influenced his approach to systematic theology. He moved theology from a philosophical and speculative base to a biblical and historical foundation.

The most important of his writings was *The Christian Doctrine of Justification and Reconcilation*, published in three volumes between 1870 and 1874. The first volume was historical, the second biblical and the third systematic. It is the third volume which changed the face of Christian theology for a generation or more. It appeared in English in 1902.

Ritschl's dominance in theology during the latter part of the nineteenth century was virtually complete. Thereafter he plunged into an obscurity almost as dramatic as his former emininence. His dominant influence in Germany was one of the casualties of the First World War. It perished with the disillusionment which then overwhelmed continental Europe.

Between the wars he continued to exercise a considerable influence in Britain and America. But after the Second World War even the English-speaking democracies lost confidence in the liberal ideals in which they were nurtured. Ritschl became the butt of everyone's contempt. However, a revival of interest in Ritschl has recently begun and given a more balanced and positive appreciation of his work.

Ritschl's Dominant Principle

Ritschl's main intention, like that of Schleiermacher before him, was to get back to the religious heart of theology. It seemed to him, however, that Schleiermacher's emphasis on feeling and states of consciousness had degenerated into sentimental pietism. Hegelian Idealism, he thought, had turned theology into speculative metaphysics. Against both Ritschl argued that the heart of religion is neither in feeling nor intellect, but in the committed will. It is essentially value judgment.

Because of this stance he has often been stereotyped as a Neo-Kantian. Certainly, like almost everyone else in his day, he was influenced by Kant. But he took creative liberties with the Kantian system. The same is true of his use of the philosophy of his eminent colleague in Göttingen – Hermann Lotze. His theology was not captive to either system.

It is a mistake to impose on Ritschl a degree of philosophical systematisation which is simply not there. One must allow him a certain degree of judicious inconsistency. He quite explicitly disavows any intention to be a philosopher. His poorest publication is *Theologie und Metaphysik* (1881), a pamphlet in which he attempted to set out the philosophical structure of his theology.

This was a mistake of his old age. For the most part, so long as he could work out a theology which yielded a coherent *way of life*, he was prepared to leave problems of formal consistency to those that way inclined.

Spirit Over Nature

The essence of all religion, in Ritschl's view, is the tension between spirit and nature. This reflects the failure of Schleiermacher's and Hegel's attempts to found religion on the union and interpenetration of spirit and nature. A major cause of this failure was the astoundingly successful marriage of mathematical and experimental science in the intervening period. The physical world showed promise of becoming entirely calculable. Physical materialism and determinism were rapidly gaining ground. Ludwig Büchner's *Force and Matter* was causing a great stir at the time. Darwin's *Origin of Species* appeared in 1859. It seemed to extend the promise that all that had formerly been called spirit could be adequately interpreted in purely natural and material terms.

While others responded to this situation by defending the god of the gaps in scientific knowledge, Ritschl proposed a much more radical solution. There are two ways, he said, in which we relate to reality. In one we establish facts in the context of science and knowledge. In the other we make evaluations in the context of free decision. Religion and theology pertain to the latter system. The two systems impinge on one another, since they relate to a common reality. However, the propositions of one system cannot be derived directly from those of the other. Nature and spirit, therefore, are not two substances, but two sets of relations in which reality manifests itself.

Value judgment and freedom of decision go together. There is no point in one without the other. Thus it is as a free, deliberating agent that man is spirit. It is the destiny of spirit to establish its freedom from and dominion over nature. Blessedness is the wholeness and integrity which a man enjoys in freedom from and dominion over nature. With nature Ritschl includes not only the physical world, but also the objective structures of society.

Sin is a weak, spiritless subjection of our freedom to the 'elements of this world'. Nature, when it is allowed to inhibit and distort human freedom, is thought of in a sense analogous to that in which St Paul speaks of 'this world'.

Freedom is not arbitrary wilfulness. It is determination of the will by our true self-end. The notion of self-end is one which he takes from Kantian ethical idealism. It is simply the idea of an over-arching purpose in one's life.

It is this freedom that makes man a person. God is absolute spirit, therefore he is absolute person. However, this knowledge of God as a personal being is not arrived at by speculative inquiry. It is not a metaphysical theory. It is given directly through the revelation of God in Jesus Christ. We understand and express the revelation of God by analogy with human personality and spirituality. We know him only as he relates to us in revelation and salvation.

Ritschl never doubted that Christianity is the perfect religion and the final revelation of God. The work of Christ consisted in establishing and exhibiting the absolute freedom of spirit in relation to nature. He exhibits the freedom of spirit not as a triumphalistic dominion over nature, but as moral victory.

The death of Jesus has traditionally been interpreted as sacrifice. However, the sense in which it is sacrifice has been seriously misunderstood. It is not sacrifice in the negative sense of self-sacrifice. It is rather costly self-fulfilment. It is not a punishment from God vicariously borne on our behalf. It is a resounding victory over sin achieved in perfect and loving obedience to the fatherly will of God. Jesus' special vocation was to do just that.

Vocation

The notion of vocation plays a very important role in Ritschl's theology. It was, of course, a concept already deeply and prominently imbedded in the Lutheran tradition. It had a special significance for Ritschl. He accepted the Kantian account of the universality of the moral law. However, he was far more interested in the way in which it was to be applied in concrete situations. No individual can fulfil every duty. He can only do what his special circumstances demand of him. This is his vocation.

Jesus' vocation was unique. He was called to exhibit the very essence of what it means to have a vocation under God. His whole life is consistently devoted to this. He is consistently the faithful child of God. This is the gound of his unique integrity. The meaning of his death cannot be understood except in the light of his whole life of loving dedication.

This very bold reaction against traditional forensic or objective interpretations of the atoning death of Christ was not a private idiosyncrasy of Ritschl's. It was a powerful expression of a movement of thought and spirit running through the whole of Christendom. Shortly we shall note Anglo-Saxon expression in relation to Calvinism. Here it appears as a revolt within confessional

Lutheranism. Its double thrust is firstly, that the atoning death of Jesus must be seen to make moral sense and secondly, that it must be interpreted in the light of the moral quality of his whole life.

Living as the faithful child of God, Jesus acknowledges the self-end of God as his own self-end. This constitutes a moral and spiritual identity with God. Therefore in the spiritual quality of his sonship he reveals God as loving Father.

The 'Pro-Nobis' Principle

In our response of faith we enter into and share the faithful sonship of Jesus. This, rather than believing correct doctrine is what faith is really about. It is a general principle of Ritschl's epistemology that we do not know things as they are in themselves, but only as they impinge upon us. We know God only in his action upon us. In this Ritschl was following Luther rather than Kant or Lotze. In Christ we know God as he is for us (*pro nobis*) rather than as he is in himself (*a se*).

On the same principle, the person of Christ cannot be known and understood apart from his saving work. In taking this view, Ritschl saw himself in line with Melanchthon's principle, 'to know Christ is to know his benefits'.

Realised Eschatology

Along with the loving fatherhood of God and the moral sonship of Jesus Christ, the kingdom of God is the third key concept in the theology of Ritschl. He restored to the kingdom of God a prominence in the theological scheme of things which it had not enjoyed since the compilation of the Synoptic Gospels.

He acknowledged that there are three ways in which the biblical teaching about the kingdom of God may be interpreted. Each finds some support in the biblical tradition. The first interprets the apocalyptic elements literally. It awaits the coming of the kingdom as a cataclysmic divine intervention. The second interprets the talk of the kingdom as symbolic of a heavenly realm which is not of this world. The third interprets the kingdom as a progressively growing realm of moral and cultural achievement within historic time. Ritschl rejected the first as primitive, fantastic and no longer credible. The second he rejected as the outcome of Greek metaphysical distortion. The moral teaching of Jesus makes it plain that the third interpretation is correct. With Ritschl worldly Christianity had arrived and had come to stay.

Under Ritschl's influence the doctrine of the kingdom of God became the basis of Christian spirituality and Christian action for the next fifty years and more. He proposed to resolve the age-old controversy between the Augustinian and the Pelagian trends in theology by setting both in balanced relationship to one another. His favourite simile for the kingdom of God was that it is like an ellipse with two foci. One is the religious, the other is the ethical. In the relïgious relation God is active and we are passive. We are the recipients of his forgiveness and his love mediated through the life and passion of Jesus Christ. The faith in which we receive this, however, is inseparable from our active and committed response. We identify with the self-end of God. God, in his love, adopts the blessedness of the human race as his self-end. Therefore the active role of the Christian is in serving this end.

He is highly critical of pietism for its quietist attitudes and Roman Catholic spirituality for its alleged idealisation of monastic retreat from the world. The Christian sphere of action is, according to Ritschl, very definitely in the world.

The Autonomy of Faith
Despite his historical approach, Ritschl did not place faith at the mercy of scientific, critical research. He was as averse to the identification of the content of faith with bare historical fact as he was to its identification with bare metaphysical fact. Despite his basing theology firmly on the life and teaching of Jesus, he refused consistently to attempt any critical, historical reconstruction of Jesus' life. He refused on the grounds that such an attempt would, in the very presuppositions of its methods, surrender the conviction 'that Jesus belonged to a higher order than all other men'. That critical, historical scholarship might assist this judgment, he never doubted. That such research might one day undermine the whole basis of Christian theology seems scarcely to have occurred to him. This was to be the Achilles heel of subsequent Ritschlian theology.

FOR FURTHER READING

Barth, K., *Protestant Theology in the 19th Century*, Part II (pp. 342 ff), London, 1972.

Pfleiderer, O., *The Development of Theology in Germany since Kant*, London, 1890.

Welch, C., *God and Incarnation in Mid-Nineteenth Century German Theology: Thomasius, Dorner, Biedermann*, New York, 1965.

Mueller, D. L., *An Introduction to the Theology of Albrecht Ritschl*, Philadelphia, 1969.

Hefner, Philip, *Faith and the Vitalities of History: A Theological Study Based on the Work of Albrecht Ritschl*, New York, 1966.
Garvie, A. E., *The Ritschlian Theology*, Edinburgh, 1899.
Richmond, J., *Ritschl: A Reappraisal*, London, 1978.

5

ROMANTICISM AND IDEALISM IN THE ENGLISH-SPEAKING SCENE

At the beginning of the nineteenth century the industrial revolution was much further advanced in Britain than in any other country in Europe. Great changes in society were afoot. It was an age of quiet, though none the less painful, revolution.

In these circumstances, theology tended to have a strong practical interest. This has remained typical of Anglo-Saxon theology generally. It was concerned to promote the spiritual health of both the individual and the nation. This was in large measure due to the influence of the Awakening and the Romantic Movement.

1. COLERIDGE

Coleridge (1772–1834) was in many ways the intellectual leader of the Romantic Movement in Britain. J. S. Mill recognised only two great intellectual landmarks in his time – Coleridge and Bentham. These two represented the options of romantic idealism on the one hand and positivist utilitarianism on the other. Either you saw beyond the world to a more comprehensive reality which claimed our reverence or you saw it merely as a given set of circumstances to be observed with detachment by science and managed to our advantage by industry.

Coleridge and Carlyle were among the few English-speaking scholars who were at that time familiar with developments in German philosophy after Kant. Coleridge knew something of Schleiermacher and Hegel; but the main influence on his conceptual formation was Schelling.

Reason and Imagination

Coleridge upheld the autonomy of reason against all authoritarian assaults. But he inderstood 'reason' (like most romantic idealists) in a very extended sense. Imagination, with its capacity to see life whole was a major organ of reason. It was for him more important than the mere ability to argue and deliberate. He was thus, after the manner of Schelling, able to unite Rationalist, Idealist and Romantic elements and to unite the artistic and the theological concepts of inspiration.

In the first place he introduced a new and more spiritual understanding of authority. This was authority without authoritarianism. The theory of verbal inspiration of the Bible, then almost universally held, was rejected. He pointed out that the almost exclusive emphasis of late protestant orthodoxy on the verbal inspiration of the Scriptures gave them merely extraneous authority. It tended to stifle the internal operation of the Holy Spirit.

The Inspiration of Scripture

He thus opened the door to a freer and more lively understanding of inspiration at a time when this was badly needed. He went further. In allowing his understanding of inspiration to be guided by his literary and poetic insight, he opened the way for a more critical reading of the Bible. The Bible, without loss of its intrinsic authority, can be read and criticised like any other book. It is not homogenous in spiritual quality. We may distinguish within it a development from the primitive to the spiritually refined. Read as a whole, however, in a free, enquiring spirit and in the light of the highest sentiments it inspires in us, it will commend itself as indeed inspired by God.

This opened the door for the introduction of the so-called 'higher' criticism into Britain. This application of critical method to the Scriptures was already well-established in Germany. It gave rise to considerable ecclesiastical concern when it broke upon the English scene, even in the mildest possible way, with the publication of *Essays and Reviews* by some Oxford scholars in 1860.

Subjectivity

The second thing which Coleridge did to bring about a more internal and spiritually lively understanding of the faith was to give the *coup de grace* to the already moribund natural theology based on the mechanical 'evidences' of an intelligent creator in the complexities and practical adjustments of the natural order – William Paley's notorious watchmaker God. In place of this natural theology Coleridge suggested a theology of nature. The intimations of God in nature are of a more subtle kind than those of mechanics.

He moved towards an apologetic which was more anthropological than cosmological. To show human need for Christianity is a better commendation of it than talk about first and final causes in the universe.

Insight and Authority

Finally, Coleridge gave a new meaning to the authority of the church. This was parallel to his treatment of the authority of the Bible. We must, he argued, depart from the formal, institutional view of the authority of the church. This is unspiritual. If we approach the church and its teachings in a spirit of free yet humble inquiry, we shall be so captivated by the intellectual coherence, the moral sublimity and the spiritual wholesomeness of it all that we shall, without any sacrifice of reason, spontaneously recognise her intrinsic authority.

In this regard Coleridge's thought had a considerable influence not only on Newman and the Oxford Movement, but also on Thomas Arnold (1795–1842) and his son Matthew (1822–88) as well as F. D. Maurice.

2. MAURICE

F. D. Maurice (1805–72) was the son of a Unitarian minister, but eventually became an Anglican and was ordained in 1834. It was his teaching on Christian social ethics that aroused most interest in his day; but since then his more fundamental theology has received the attention it deserves.

The Heart of Maurice's Theology

He saw the social unity of mankind as a function of the Fatherhood of God. The dignity and the brotherhood of man is also a function of the God-manhood of Jesus Christ. These two propositions are the centre of Maurice's theology.

He wrote very voluminously – far too voluminously, in fact. The most important and rewarding of his publications is *The Kingdom of Christ*.

God, the ultimate reality and source of all creation, has within himself a social structure. God is a being in whom persons in relation form an essential unity. This is the basis of creaturely society. The Father, Son and Holy Spirit, in the distinction of their persons and the unity of their essence are the exemplar and the ground of all community. With this the doctrine of the Trinity came into its own again in a way which was scarcely known in Western Christianity – though it had been an important aspect of trinitarian doctrine in the Eastern church from earliest times.

Man is made in the image of God. This means that in essence he is in the image of Jesus Christ. The first Adam is only the raw material. His essence is his destiny in Jesus Christ. Man does not have his humanity as a private possession. His true humanity is his being in the image of God. This he has by sharing in the form and essence of Jesus Christ. To participate in Jesus Christ is also to participate in the spiritual fellowship of all humanity. One cannot acknowledge Jesus as the Christ without by the same token acknowledging all humanity as brothers and sisters.

Sin is self-centredness. It is the attempt to amount to something in ourselves. It is the attempt to find the meaning of our lives apart from our relation to others. This is the same as the attempt to live without acknowledgment of the Fatherhood of God.

However, fallen man does not cease to be what he truly and essentially is – the child of God in the image of God. Rather he becomes blind to what he really is and lives a lie. In redemption the Christ does not perform an operation upon us whereby a part of our human essence, lost to us through sin, is restored to us. Rather, he opens our eyes to our true selves.

The atonement does not consist in the virtues of Christ being arbitrarily imputed to selected sinners. The atoning work of Christ discloses the truth about man – that in spite of sin he is still the child of God. In Christ 'we find how humanity has been a holy thing, though each man felt himself to be unholy'. It follows from this that the sacraments of the church are not an added supernatural gift but rather a disclosure of the real human situation.

The Social Dimension

Maurice was unique, in his time, in the way he earthed his theology in its social implications. He saw the family as the unit in which we learn the basic truth of what the gospel discloses. It is an order of society ordained by God. In it we first learn respect and love for others. The history of Israel exhibits the nation as the larger unit of social cohesion ordained by God. In Christ, however, we are members of a universal community. This is represented by the church. 'The church is human society in its normal state.'

Maurice attempted to combine this extremely open view of the church and its ethical role in society with a firmly episcopal conception of its structure. However, he was also very ecumenical in spirit. To absolutise any system or point of doctrine was, in his view, not merely an error; it was a sin. Though his insights were brilliant, Maurice was not a systematic theologian. He hated systems and schools of thought. He saw them as divisive.

Christianity was in his view something to be lived out rather than thought out. With his convictions about the social meaning of the gospel this led him into the beginnings of the Christian Socialist Movement. In the distressing social conditions of the time this was a timely initiative. Maurice was associated in this movement with Charles Kingsley and John M. Ludlow. He was widely regarded as its leader. One should not be tempted to see in this the beginnings of what today is known as political theology. Contemporary political theology is dominated by the concept of class struggle. Maurice and his associates had little notion of this. They sought to restore the natural *harmony* of the orders of society.

It was as much for his association with Christian socialism as for his allegedly unorthodox views on atonement, election and reprobation that he was asked to vacate his chair of theology in Kings College, London, in 1853. He was eventually appointed to a chair of moral philosophy in Cambridge.

3. NEWMAN AND THE OXFORD MOVEMENT

Tractarianism

The Tractarian or Oxford Movement was another impulse towards renewal in the church. It later came to be thought of as a movement towards Rome, high churchmanship and anglo-catholicism. It did develop these tendencies, but that was not its initial impetus or intention. Initially it was an aspect of that pervasive spiritual Awakening to which reference has already been made. It was never an organised movement but a loosely cohesive group, centred in the University of Oxford. Their common concern was to deepen the spiritual life of the Anglican communion. To this end they sought to unite evangelical zeal with the whole substance of christian doctrine rather than the narrow theological base of revivalism. They resisted the individualism of the evangelicals with an emphasis on the corporate being of the church and advocated a fuller use of the sacraments as objective means of grace.

Newman

John Henry Newman (1801–90) was their greatest theologian, though he eventually left them to be ordained in the Roman Catholic

Church. Romantic influence on the Oxford movement was limited and restrained. Newman was not so deeply influenced by Coleridge as Maurice; but he did share Coleridge's mistrust of external 'evidences' for the truth of Christianity. He sought confirmation of Christian doctrine in its intrinsic credibility.

Religious Assent

Although his famous *Essay in Aid of a Grammar of Assent* was not published till 1870 – long after his conversion to Rome – it nevertheless represents a line of thought which was central to his early theological development. Faith, for him, was more than mere intellectual assent. It is an act of the whole person. It is a decision for a way of life. Such decisions are seldom made on the basis of proof, but on the basis of sufficient assurance. Such assurance is possible because there is in the intellect an authority similar to that of conscience for the will. He says,

> It is on no probability that we are constantly receiving the information and dictates of sense and memory. . . . These are certain truths, and from them each of us forms his own judgments and directs his own course.

He goes on to claim that, in a comparable way, the truths of revealed religion may be known with assurance. There is a peace of mind which comes with proper obedience to the truth analogous to the ease of conscience which comes with obedience to moral demand.

The logical correlate of such certitude is an infallible teaching authority. He could not accept the protestant view that the Bible alone constitutes such an authority. The Bible needs an interpreter.

Development

He also held that a spiritual truth must unfold in time and develop its own history. It cannot remain fixed in the biblical forms and expressions of a now remote past. Doctrine must develop in order to remain the same. This argument was set out in his *Essay on the Development of Doctrine* (1845). This is a work of historic importance. It initiates in the English-speaking world the recognition that doctrine must be interpreted in relation to its historic setting. At a time when modern, critical history was about to bring its full weight to bear on all forms of christian tradition this was a liberating principle. It was also a dangerous principle, however. It opened the way to historical relativism. The Roman Catholic authorities were distinctly uneasy about this aspect of their distinguished convert's teaching.

4. CALVINISM UNDER ATTACK IN SCOTLAND AND AMERICA

Degenerate Calvinism
In all this it was mainly Calvinism – or rather the desiccated and distorted form which it had by then assumed – which was under attack. Even the Anglican communion, though it had never been wholly Calvinist, was extensively under Calvinist influence until the nineteenth century. Those elements of Calvinism which the eighteenth century had unduly stressed and which the nineteenth century found unspiritual and morally offensive were the elements most prominently retained in the Thirty-nine Articles of Religion – original sin, total depravity, election, predestination and an aridly forensic view of the atonement. It was, for example, for his somewhat free interpretation of election and atonement that F. D. Maurice was officially requested to vacate his chair. Even Methodism, despite its emphasis on the subjective aspect of atonement, retained substantial Calvinist elements.

In Scotland, where a sadly degenerate Calvinism remained supreme, the confrontation was all the more severe. Two things upon which Calvin had insisted tended to be forgotten. The first is that all insight into the nature of God is associated with a corresponding insight into the human condition. The second is Calvin's sensitive appreciation that when language is used to express the mysteries of God it is to be interpreted in a manner appropriate to its context.

Bereft of these graces, the Calvinist emphasis on the transcendence of God placed him in an external relation to the world. His grace and providence become manipulative, election and predestination a lottery and atonement a legal transaction. Such unspiritual misrepresentation of Calvin was caricatured by Robert Burns in the first stanza of 'Holy Willie's Prayer',

> O Thou, who in the heavens does dwell,
> Who, as it pleases best Thysel,
> Sends ane to heaven, an' ten to hell,
>   A' for thy glory!

John McLeod Campbell (1800–72)

McLeod Campbell was the most distinguished of the protesting voices within Scottish theology. He had much in common with F. D. Maurice. Both were concerned to deliver Christianity from a God whose relations to his creatures were external and manipulative.

Both were influenced by a remarkable layman, Thomas Erskine of Linlathen (1788–1870). His *Remarks on the Internal Evidences for the Truth of Revealed Religion* was published in 1820, five years before Coleridge's *Aids to Reflection*. He argued that if any revealed truth is to be appropriated into the soul, it must be both reasonable to the mind and illuminating to the conscience. In *The Unconditional Freedom of the Gospel* (1828) he stressed that atonement is first and foremost about pardon. God's love is universal. Therefore there must be some sense in which his offer of pardon is universal. We are not on trial.

John McLeod Campbell was a close friend of Thomas Erskine. He took up and developed his interpretation of the atonement. The atonement, in his telling phrase, 'must be understood by its own light'.

Like Erskine, he treats the fatherhood of God as basic. As righteous father he must abhor sin. As loving father he forgives sin. The moral reconciliation of the just wrath and the loving pardon of God cannot be brought about by a pseudo-forensic transaction in which Christ bears the wrathful punishment for our sins and his righteousness is imputed to us. If the outcome is to be forgiveness, then what is called for is not satisfaction but a perfect repentance. Man, the sinner, is incapable of such perfect repentance. Therefore God's own eternal Son comes in the flesh to offer a perfect repentance on behalf of mankind. As we acknowledge this in faith, we are retrospectively released from the burden of sin and guilt. Prospectively we are initiated thereby into a new life of infinite moral and spiritual potential.

On this view, the suffering of Christ is not penal. It is the pain with which the truly righteous one experiences and bears the evil of the world. It is the pain of encountering sin as God sees it. In this way the death of Christ is interpreted in the light of his life.

One may well ask whether the notion of vicarious penitence makes any more sense than that of vicarious punishment. But it does at least transpose the discussion out of the categories of abstract justice into those of personal relationship.

From this time onwards the pressure to interpret all doctrine in the light of its significance for personal existence becomes more and more insistent.

The American Scene

About the same time the Reformed tradition was beginning to be treated with even more venturesome freedom in the United States of America. There too Calvinism had been the main doctrinal influence – not only for presbyterians, but also for congregationalists and even for baptists.

The people of America were beginning to develop a new way of life and with it a new theology. In the eighteenth century Jonathan Edwards had already exercised a powerful transforming influence upon Calvinism. In reconciling it with rationalism and Newtonian science he had changed its ethos. He integrated into it the revivalist emphasis on emotion and personal decision. This weakened the doctrine of predestination. This effect was intensified by the manipulative evangelical techniques employed to bring people to decision as, for example, by Charles G. Finney (1792–1875). This opened the door to a spirit of optimistic activism which has been characteristic of America ever since.

In many other respects America provided the occasion for significant new developments in theology. As America emerged from the War of Independence it became not only a new nation but a new movement of the human spirit. This movement of the spirit was parallel to, but different from, both the French revolution and the Romantic movement in Europe. The spirit of rationalism persisted longer in America than in Europe. Rationalism of the French type played a key role in the ideological struggle against the privileges of the British king and empire. However, on American soil it became a rationalism with its own element of indigenous romantic spirit. It was sympathetic to religion though intolerant of dogma. It was practical and pragmatic rather than theoretical. In its concern for life, liberty and the pursuit of happiness it incorporated the whole spirit of man, not just his intellect. Thus there never was the same opposition between Rationalism and Romanticism in America as there was in Europe.

Charles Hodge

America produced some of the best attempts to restore Calvinism to its former glory. For example, Charles Hodge (1797–1878) made the best attempt of the century to restore Calvinism to something like what John Calvin had originally intended. He established for Calvinism an honoured place in the Princeton theology which it has retained to this day.

Nathaniel Taylor
The main creative trend in American theology, however, was towards a more radical revision of the Reformed stance. Nathaniel W. Taylor (1786–1858) was one such innovator. He argued,

1. that the goodness of God must make sense in terms of human moral understanding;
2. that sin implies responsibility in the sinner and that responsibility implies an element of freedom of choice;
3. that the revelation of God must be rationally intelligible and credible.

Taylor made tortuous efforts to accommodate these principles to traditional Calvinism. However, in so doing he had to qualify the doctrines of total depravity and predestination and election almost out of existence.

Channing and Unitarian Theology
The growing body of Unitarians in America were even less inhibited and took these trends much further. The basic concerns of the Unitarians were the moral goodness of God, the freedom, responsibility and perfectibility of man and the compatibility of revelation with the judgments of rational common sense. Their denial of a metaphysical Trinity was consequent upon and incidental to these issues.

William Ellery Channing (1780–1842) was their most distinguished theologian in this early period. He insisted that Scripture was to be interpreted like any other text. Against trinitarian doctrine he emphasised the unity of God as correlative with the unity and coherence of truth and value. He insisted upon the human integrity of Christ's person as a centre of ethical decision. He stressed the moral supremacy of God as against his sheer omnipotence. He upheld moral freedom against the current understanding of the Augustinian doctrine of grace.

Bushnell and Congregationalism
Among the congregationalists Horace Bushnell (1802–1876) was a significant figure. He was ahead of his time in developing a philosophy of religious language which anticipated some aspects of twentieth century linguistic philosophy. He observed that the normal reference of language is objective. To describe subjectivity – thought and spirit – language has to be used indirectly and in a variety of symbolic modes. Theology, he suggested, has been too inclined to treat religious language as though it were purely objective. Many theological misunderstandings arise from this.

Specifically, in the case of the atonement, a crude and literal interpretation of traditional doctrines is spiritually vacuous and morally offensive. Original sin is not to be understood literally as inherited guilt. That is moral nonsense. The truth which that doctrine expresses is that the inescapable influences of a corrupt society begin at the moment of birth. The saving work of Jesus Christ consists in his bringing divinely inspired innocence into this fallen situation. His life and sacrifice are efficacious for salvation because they are perfectly expressive of the boundless love and costly forgiveness of God. However, the images of traditional dogma are still to be respected because they have shown themselves capable of sustaining the life and spirit of the people.

In all of these developments the rigid structure of late Calvinist orthodoxy was severely threatened. Heresy trials were common and their outcome seldom edifying. On the whole, Lutheran confessionalism – especially in the movement typified by the Erlangen School – proved itself more flexible, even if less consistent, in accommodating the new spirit.

FOR FURTHER READING

Barth, Robert J., *Coleridge and Christian Doctrine*, Cambridge, Mass., 1969.
Boulger, James D., *Coleridge as Religious Thinker*, New Haven, Conn., 1961.
Bouyer, L., Newman: *His Life and Spirituality*, London, 1958.
Chadwick Owen, *The Mind of the Oxford Movement*, London, 1960.
Christiansen, T. B., *The Divine Order, a Study in F. D. Maurice's Theology*, Leiden, 1973.
Hudson, W. S., *American Protestantism*, Chicago, 1960.
Niebuhr, H. R., *The Kingdom of God in America*, New York, 1937.
——*Theology in America: The Major Protestant Voices from Puritanism to Neo-Orthodoxy*, New York, 1967.

6

HISTORY AND HISTORICISM

The Enlightenment movement in the eighteenth century is often credited with initiating modern, critical history. Certainly, it did produce some stirrings in that direction. But on the whole that movement was more interested in universal principles than particular facts. History as an empirical science was mainly the invention of the nineteenth century. Only then did the systematically critical use of sources begin. Leopold von Ranke's *History of the Latin and Teutonic Nations* was a landmark in this respect.

1. BIBLICAL CRITICISM

The Old Testament
When the new methods of historical science were first applied to the biblical tradition, their initial impact was on the Old Testament – especially the so-called books of Moses, the first five books. There had been some anticipations of this in the eighteenth century; but it was with W. M. L. de Wette's *Contributions to the Introduction of the Old Testament* (1806–7) that it became a genuinely critico-historical exercise. It was not until its presentation by Julius Wellhausen (1844–1918) that what became known as the Four Document Hypothesis became established beyond all reasonable doubt. This showed that the Pentateuch is a compilation in which four documentary sources of dates varying between 750 and 450 BC have been interwoven. There followed further refinements of this hypothesis, but they need not concern us. The main outlines of Wellhausen's conclusions have stood the test of time. Other books of the Old Testament were soon subject to similar treatment.

The New Testament
The same scholarly techniques were soon applied to the New Testament. By far the most sensitive area in New Testament criticism

was the life and teaching of Jesus. This had immediate consequences for systematic theology. It could not have come at a more disturbing time. Traditional theology had been content, along with St Paul, to place its main emphasis on the birth, death and resurrection of Jesus. From Schleiermacher to Ritschl, however, theology had come to rely more and more upon an interpretation of the human personality, life-style and teaching of Jesus. This increased the reliance of theology upon trustworthy knowledge of the historical Jesus at the very time when that was about to come under attack.

Consequences of Criticism

Thus, with the application of the methods of modern critical history to the gospel tradition both the traditional and the modern theological camps lost out initially. The traditionalists suffered because the major supernatural elements in the tradition, such as virgin birth, miracles, resurrection and ascension, were among the first casualties to fall to the new weapon. It is noteworthy that this was as much for methodological reasons as on grounds of inadequate evidence. The historian does not include the possibility of the intervention of an incalculable supernatural agency in his purview. Otherwise his whole system of critical, historical judgment would fall to the ground. He calculates his probabilities on the basis of known possibilities.

The retreat of the modernists to the natural and humanly historical elements in the tradition fared little better in the long run. Historical research into the life of Jesus turned out to be an undertaking that raised more questions than it could answer.

Lives of Jesus

Lives of Jesus had been written aplenty before the advent of scientific history. Some were pietistic harmonies of the Gospels. Others were ideologically motivated projections of the writer's own philosophy. Even when the Romantics and the Hegelians reaffirmed the importance of a historical perspective, they did not do so in the spirit of objective, empirical enquiry. Schleiermacher used his lectures on the life of Jesus to illustrate his own theology. Albert Schweitzer rightly says of these lectures, which were published posthumously, that their value 'lies in the field of dogmatics, not history'. Hegel too, though he talks a lot about history, uses it to illustrate rather than test his philosophy.

Hegel's left-wing disciple, David Strauss, introduced a new phase in the historical criticism of the gospel. His radical elimination of the supernatural in his *Life of Jesus* caused a great furore. But more

important than his conclusions was his method. Firstly, he subjected
not only the events of biblical narratives to historical criticism.
Under the influence of his great teacher F. C. Baur (1792–1860), he
established the view that the traditions themselves must be treated
historically. Tradition must be interpreted in the light of its genesis
and development. Secondly, he gave a new and more positive
meaning to the concept of myth as a hermeneutic key to the New
Testament.

The Category of Myth

Formerly, in so far as the element of myth had been recognised in
the New Testament, it was regarded as mere superstition and falsehood. Strauss saw it as a vehicle of truth. Strauss maintained that
it is the mythological element which is the religious substance of
the gospel. Myths are ideas or universal truths expressed in narrative
form. He thus gave to the concept of myth a prominence which it
never had before, and which it has never since lost, in New Testament interpretation.

According to Strauss, the universal truth embodied in Jesus Christ
and expressed in the myths of his birth, his supernatural powers,
his resurrection and his ascension is the essential unity of God and
man. This stance shows strong Hegelian influence.

However, in the growing positivist spirit of late nineteenth and
early twentieth century scholarship, interest in the 'hard facts'
behind the gospel narratives again became dominant for a time.
With this the quest for the historical Jesus became truly historical
in what, for better or worse, has become the currently accepted
sense of the term.

Source Criticism

The main instrument of this quest was initially the critical examination and comparison of the four Gospels. That St John's Gospel
was mainly theological interpretation rather than history was widely
acknowledged from the outset. The main evidence, therefore, had
to be sought in the first three Gospels.

The first major step was the elaboration of the 'Markan hypothesis'. On the basis of a comparative study of parallel passages in the
first three gospels it was established beyond reasonable doubt that
Mark's was the earliest Gospel and that Matthew and Luke had
copied from him. Secondly, by the same technique it was established
that there must have been another source, consisting mainly of the
sayings of Jesus, shared by Matthew and Luke, but not used by
Mark. This source is no longer extant. It came to be known as 'Q'

(from the German *Quelle* = source). On the whole, the Markan hypothesis has stood the test of time. So, too, to an only slightly lesser extent, has the 'Q' hypothesis.

For a time these discoveries raised high hopes that the 'hard facts' of the life and teaching of Jesus could be recovered through the study of these earliest documents. It soon became clear, however, that even St Mark's Gospel was thoroughly theological in motive and intention. It was not straight history or biography. It was theology written in narrative form. The meaning and content of 'Q' became increasingly a matter of debate.

Two decisive blows were dealt to the high hopes raised by the Markan hypothesis by Wilhelm Wrede (1859–1906) and Johannes Weiss (1863–1914). Wrede argued powerfully that the only satisfactory explanation of the many contradictions and anomalies in the Markan account is that Messianic status was attributed to Jesus only after his death in the light of resurrection faith. Weiss showed that in the lifetime of Jesus Judaism consistently conceived of the kingdom of God as a sudden, cataclysmic, divine intervention. Jesus, he argues, quite clearly stood in this tradition and accepted it. It was only after the kingdom of God had failed to appear during his lifetime or immediately after his death that a different teaching came to be ascribed to him.

Schweitzer
Albert Schweitzer, in his justly famous *The Quest of the Historical Jesus* reviewed the entire development of this line of research from Reimarus to Wrede. He found himself in inescapable agreement with the view that Jesus expected the advent of the kingdom of God within his own lifetime and, in the end had to face shattering disappointment.

However, Schweitzer did not regard Jesus as a mere deluded enthusiast. He speaks movingly of this man who, in the perfect consistency of his moral commitment to the kingdom of God, threw himself on the wheel of life to make it turn. He was crushed beneath the wheel; but his spirit still lives among us. Schweitzer concludes, 'The abiding and eternal Jesus is absolutely independent of historical knowledge and can only be understood by contact with his spirit which is still at work in the world'.

This conclusion cannot stand, however. It is astonishing to the point of incredibility that the conclusion that history is irrelevant should be reached on the basis of a historical inquiry. The pressures of history cannot be so easily evaded. Schweitzer's concept of the moral quality of the spirit of Jesus immediately and mystically present to us is, in fact, conditioned by his historical judgment as to what actually took place and what manner of man Jesus actually was. His conclusions in this regard are debatable.

The Method of Gospel-criticism

It is the method he employs that is of greatest interest for our present purpose. The method was not his invention, but he brings it to focus. Firstly he tries to go behind the text of the Gospels to the oral tradition which they represent. Secondly, he forms a judgment as to the probable genesis and development of this oral tradition. Thirdly he forms a judgment as to what manner of man could have given rise to such a remarkable tradition. In all this, historical judgment is so interwoven with moral, spiritual and theological insight that they can no longer be separated.

It was this inextricable involvement of spiritual and theological judgment with historical judgment which was explicitly recognised by Martin Kähler in his influential *The so-called historical Jesus and the historic, biblical Christ.*

Because of this intertwining of the historical and the theological from this point onwards, it is not possible to pursue the question of the historical Jesus as a separate issue any further at this point. We shall return to it later when it again becomes critical in connection with the theology of Rudolf Bultmann.

Anglo-Saxon Biblical Criticism

From the standpoint of conservative biblicism, the most notorious and damning feature of liberal theology was its ready acceptance of biblical criticism. What strikes one in retrospect, however, is not the sceptical radicality but the sober caution and moderation of Anglo-Saxon Liberal biblical criticism as compared with its continental counterpart. Biblical criticism had made its public debut with characteristic restraint in Britain in *Essays and Reviews* (1860), by a group of Oxford scholars. The moderation of that volume scarcely justified the furore of protest which it aroused in the churches.

As we have seen, the scholarly brilliance and erudition of German biblical criticism was beyond question. Its weakness, however, has always been that it is apt to be bemused by its own latest discovery. Thus at any given time the whole interpretation of scriptural tradition is apt to be left hanging by a single monofilament of the latest critical insight. In the latter half of the nineteenth century the dominant novelty was the rediscovery of the apocalyptic context of the teaching of Jesus. We have already seen this typically represented in Wrede and Schweitzer. Such a total apocalyptic emphasis seemed to void the message of moral significance. Schweitzer had virtually to invent a moral significance for Christianity in his ethic of 'respect for life'.

Liberal theology required a more balanced diet for its survival. It relied heavily on a historical Jesus who could be seen not only as a man of his own day but also as an exemplar for humanity of every age. It centred upon a vision of the Kingdom of God, perhaps as not *of* this world, but certainly as growing *in* the world. This called for a more cautious and broadly based use of biblical criticism. Typical of this balance and moderation was C. H. Dodd who said,

> We seem to be confronted with two diverse strains in the teaching of Jesus, one of which seems to contemplate the indefinite continuance of human life under historical conditions, while the other appears to suggest a speedy end to these conditions. A drastic criticism might eliminate one strain or the other, but both are deeply embedded in the earliest forms of the tradition known to us. It would be better to admit that we do not possess the key to their reconciliation than to do such violence to our documents.

Dodd's concept of 'realised eschatology' was a significant attempt to resolve this dilemma and played an important part in the development of the Liberal emphasis on the Kingdom of God.

This critical moderation was not the outcome of compromise or lack of scholarly rigour. It arose from the sound hermeneutical principle that the Gospels must be interpreted with moral and spiritual insight as well as historico-critical objectivity. This admittedly carries the risk that we read our own moral prejudices into the Gospel. But this is a risk which cannot be avoided. It certainly cannot be evaded by recourse to learned insensitivity.

This balanced caution in the use of the latest devices of biblical criticism is another valuable legacy of the liberal theology.

2. HISTORICISM

Although the application of critical methods to the gospel tradition about Jesus was the most poignant issue for the Christian community, the matter did not and could not end there. Historicism, as a new style of thinking and a new form of consciousness, began to dominate every aspect of our interpretation of the human situation. The total phenomenon of christianity was now seen in a historical context.

Troeltsch
Ernst Troeltsch's (1865–1923) *The Absoluteness of Christianity* was a landmark on this trail. The success of empirical science had established, in a manner which could not for the time being be effectively resisted, that nature was best explained in terms of efficient causality and scientific law. Since Darwin it had become apparent that this applied to biological as well as physical nature. Explanation in terms of final cause or purpose was no longer part of science. This was already widely recognised. What Troeltsch saw more clearly than others was the extent of its implications for theology. For most people all that the scientific transformation involved was the elimination or re-interpretation of those aspects of the biblical tradition which had become incredible – mainly the miracle stories and the creation myths. Troeltsch, however, saw that it involved far more than this. It was the beginning of a new form of consciousness and a new age of humanity. All that had gone before he regarded as part of the Middle Ages.

Principles of Historical Interpretation
He recognised that, for theology, it was in historical consciousness that the new scientific spirit came to focus. The habit of mind fostered in the natural sciences spilled over into the human sciences. In history this involved the methodological elimination of all appeals to supernatural intervention or supernatural authority. It involved three principles each of which was at odds with the traditional attitudes of faith. The first principle was that of criticism. This involved not only the critical assessment of sources. It also meant that all conclusions must be regarded as tentative and open to revision in the light of fresh evidence. This was at odds with the certitude of faith. The second principle is that of analogy. Past events are understood by analogy with our own common experience. This is at odds with the absolute uniqueness ascribed by faith to the major events of salvation history. The third principle is that of correlation. This means that historical events are inter-related in a causal nexus and are sufficently explained thereby. This is at odds with the affirmations of faith about supernatural agencies.

The Threat of Relativism
However, Troeltsch saw an even more disturbing implication in these principles. For Schleiermacher and Hegel, despite the novelty of their interpretations, the Christ-event remained *the* event determining the meaning of the whole of history. This is what, for them, made Christianity the final and absolute religion. Under the impact

of rigorous historicism, however, such a stance seemed no longer possible. By the principle of analogy, the significance of the Christ-event could be only relative to that of other comparable events. By the principle of correlation, its significance could be only relative to its role within the total nexus of events of which it was a part. Thus the absoluteness of Christianity was under the severest attack it had as yet faced.

This was just at the time when detailed and accurate information about the other religions of the world was beginning to become available. e.g. Max Müller's fifty-one volumes of translations, *The Sacred Books of the East*, began appearing in 1875. Each religious system seemed to have its own degree of validity within its own historic frame of reference. Even within the Christian tradition, each phase in the development of doctrine appeared to be conditioned by the cultural circumstances of its time.

Troeltsch had no intention of allowing this to drive him into an empty and normless relativism. He saw the seriousness of the problem, however, and recognised it as the major problem of modern theology. He never quite found the solution, but he did have some suggestions.

Beyond Relativism
Firstly, the mere fact that we can form, by the principle of analogy, some understanding of times and cultures very different from our own and of the religious beliefs in which they were nurtured implies some shared element of common humanity between us. Secondly, we can and do form judgments setting a higher value on some religions than others. Such judgments are not entirely arbitrary, even though we cannot give wholly objective grounds for them. Thirdly, he saw in modern trends a movement to transcend the ecclesiastical and theological absolutism characteristic of both the sect and the church type of christian association. This opens the way to a more serious recognition that there is no absolute but God. 'The final ends of all humanity are hidden within His hands'. As historical beings we can never escape the task of theological revision. In every age we must work it out anew in order to display its perpetual relevance to 'the final ends of all humanity'. It was to this task that the liberal theology of the following decades set itself.

FOR FURTHER READING

Braaten, Carl E., and Harrisville, Roy A., (eds.), *The Historical Jesus and the Kerygmatic Christ*, New York, 1964.

Clayton, J. P. (ed.), *Ernst Troeltsch and the Future of Theology*, Cambridge, 1976.
Harris, H., *David Friedrich Strauss and his Theology*, Cambridge, 1973.
Harvey, Van Austin, *The Historian and the Believer*, New York, 1966.
Robinson, J. M., *The New Quest for the Historical Jesus*, London, 1959.
Schweitzer, A., *The Quest of the Historical Jesus. A Critical Study of its Progress from Reimarus to Wrede*, London, 1910.
Troeltsch, E., *The Absoluteness of Christianity*, London, 1972.
Zahrnt, H., *The Historical Jesus*, New York, 1963.

7

LIBERAL THEOLOGY

1. THE SPIRIT AND FORMS OF LIBERAL THEOLOGY

The term 'liberal' has been used to describe the theology which dominated the end of the nineteenth and the beginning of the twentieth century up to about 1920. At that time, in the wake of the terrible trauma of the First World War, it came to a fairly abrupt end in continental Europe. It was replaced by a variety of radically new theological departures often lumped together under the name 'dialectical theology'. In Britain and America it survived alongside the influence of this dialectical theology until the end of the Second World War.

The Liberal Spirit
Essential to Liberalism was an element of optimism and confidence which these wars, the evil of their causes and the relative futility of their outcome, did much to destroy. The further disillusionment of the Vietnam War was the final nail in its coffin. In its day, however, it was an extremely powerful and effective attempt to express and re-interpret Christianity in terms appropriate to the times.

It is by no means easy to say what was comprised in this liberal theology. The term has been loosely applied to a wide variety of theologians of quite diverse views. The liberal theology flourished in a period of rapid social and cultural development. It was a period of intense theological adjustment to modern science, modern history and above all to the new sense of emancipated humanity which pervaded the emergent social democracies. It therefore called for a wide variety of tentative and experimental rather than dogmatic approaches. It was a style of doing theology rather than a school of thought.

It was not merely modernist in spirit. It also sought to conserve and recapture the past. It sought to recover the essential simplicities of the gospel. Thus, in its own way it was a 'back to the Bible' movement. For this reason it did tend to be severely critical of the heavy doctrinal overlay that had been imposed in post-biblical times. It also involved an attempt to gather together the theological achievements of the whole nineteenth century.

Adolf von Harnack

The prince of liberal theology was unquestionably Adolf von Harnack (1851–1930). His *What is Christianity* became one of the most widely read theological works ever written. Basic to the whole liberal development was moderation in historical criticism. The grand manner in which Harnack establishes this is typical. 'Sixty years ago David Friedrich Strauss thought that he had almost entirely destroyed the historical credibility not only of the fourth but also of the first three Gospels as well. The historical criticism of two generations has succeeded in restoring that credibility in its main outlines.' The strong emphasis which some critics continued to place upon apocalyptic, other-worldly elements in the teaching of Jesus he dismissed as merely perverse. The eschatological element in the teaching of Jesus may be interpreted simply to mean, 'Time is getting short'. The miracle stories are a simplistic way of saying that the spirit of God becomes wonderfully apparent in some events. Thus interpreted they do not conflict with either the spirit or the results of modern science.

The Essence of Christianity

The essence of Christianity is the teaching of Jesus and the perfect exemplification of its spirit and principles in his life. This teaching may be summarised under three main heads. Firstly, the kingdom of God is at hand. Secondly, the Father sets an infinite value on every human soul. Thirdly, there is a higher righteousness of love which transcends, but does not destroy the law. The kingdom of God is not to be looked for as an outward phenomenon. It has its reality within the hearts of men. It is experienced as the supernatural gift of grace, as the inward blessedness of communion with God and as consciousness of the forgiveness of sins. The practical proof of the truth of Christianity is in its power to generate love and mercy. Its essential inwardness does not, however, imply other-worldliness. Jesus specifically rejected other-worldly asceticism. The gospel, therefore, has social implications, though it is not itself a social programme.

The incarnation, therefore, should not be interpreted in terms of Greek metaphysics. It should be understood in spiritual and moral terms. We call Jesus Son of God because he perfectly lives out the filial relation appropriate to the loving Father whom he reveals. We adore him as God because he truly embodies the love of God.

Harnack therefore questioned strongly the authority accorded to the traditional creeds of Christianity. They are dominated by Greek, metaphysical concepts. Contrary to the account often given of him, Harnack did acknowledge that it was natural and inevitable that the Greek-speaking Christians should express themselves in this way. However, he saw no reason why this should carry authority for us, who neither think nor speak in that way any more. Every age must express itself in its own way; but the only norm is the gospel itself. A sensible historical criticism which is not perversely radical makes that essential gospel available to us. To that we must return. Harnack developed this theme in detail in his great *History of Dogma*.

The influence of Ritschl in all this is obviously strong; but it is unfair to both men simply to call him a Ritschlian. Indeed, it may fairly be said that the sources of much of the liveliest liberal theology were neither as Ritschlian nor as Germanic as has sometimes been suggested.

2. RELIGION WITHOUT DOGMA

In Britain and America, from the mid-nineteenth century onwards, there flourished a lively and mainly indigenous strain of thought, fundamentally Christian in inspiration but also wholly rational in habit and intention. It was quite different from the rationalism of the eighteenth century, which had banished God into a purely external relation with a clockwork universe. It aimed rather at completing the process, begun by Schleiermacher and Hegel, of bringing God back into the heart of a spiritual universe. It was profoundly disillusioned with the crude supernaturalism of conservative christianity. Romanticism seemed to have degenerated into aesthetic sentimentality and to have lost its practical vigour. This new movement had a special concern with both human affairs and the interpretation of the findings of natural science.

Though initially a minority movement, Anglo-Saxon liberalism was a stirring in the best minds of the mid-nineteenth century, creative in their originality and prophetic in their insights. They have been much maligned in the general reaction of the twentieth against the nineteenth century – a reaction which is now mercifully beginning to respond to treatment.

Carlyle

Thomas Carlyle (1795–1881) represents the more negative side of this movement in its early stages. The traditional church he regarded as beyond all hope of reformation. He said of it, 'When the brains of the thing have been out for three centuries and odd, one does wish that it would be kind enough to die'. The inhumanity of the French Revolution showed that religionless rationalism offered even worse prospects, however. He remained, therefore, convinced that the true quality of human life did have a religious foundation which no single tradition represented adequately. Without that foundation our universe becomes 'one huge, dead, immeasurable steam-engine rolling on in its dead indifference to grind me limb from limb'.

Matthew Arnold

A more positive expression of this spirit is to be found in Matthew Arnold (1822–88). He expressed the mood of the growing number of people fundamentally sympathetic to but intellectually uncomfortable with traditional Christianity. He said that there are two things certain about Christianity, 'One is, that men cannot do without it, the other that they cannot do with it as it is'. For Matthew Arnold, both the dogmatic superstructure and the mythological substructure of Christianity had become an embarrassment.

It is clear that for this growing body of critical and selfconsciously modern thinkers, Christianity had become an aspect of religion in general and religion a function of culture rather than culture the temporal by-product of religion. For Arnold religion was 'morality touched by emotion'. The Bible, he held, was to be read like any other work of literature. Such authority as it has is intrinsic to its ideas and power of expression. It does not depend on dogmas about its supernatural origin. The permanent validity of religion in general and of Christianity in particular is its moral power. Its dogmas and its stories are to be valued primarily for their capacity to undergird moral attitudes. Yet he was not a complete reductionist. He acknowledged the reality of an 'enduring power, not ourselves, which makes for righteousness'. In Jesus he saw the finest representation of this reality.

Emerson

Another important branch in the roots of this movement towards a theology free from all ecclesiastical restraints was Ralph Waldo Emerson (1802–83). America became one of the most vigorous centres of the liberal theology. Emerson was one of the first self-consciously American theologians. In a manner which was to become characteristic of much liberal theology, he totally rejected the traditional doctrine of original sin. In our souls we continue to be the bearers of divinity. Christ is one of us. He is *primus inter pares*. The truth to which he points us subsists in all religion and all nature. Life and not tradition is the vehicle of revelation. Emerson's main ideas are summarised in his famous 'Divinity School Address' (1838)

He was too radical for even the Unitarians of his day. He resigned from the ministry of the Unitarian Church in which he had begun his career.

Channing

American Unitarianism made an important contribution to the early development of liberal theology. In retrospect one can see that the most important thing about the early unitarians was not their unitarianism. Many of them would pass today for modernist trinitarians. What they affirmed was more important than what they denied. Among them William Ellery Channing (1780–1842) was of consequential significance. His Baltimore sermon, 'Unitarian Christianity', was widely regarded as a kind of credo of unitarianism. He did not deny the unique significance of Jesus Christ; but rejected the vulgar tritheism into which latter-day trinitarian theology had degenerated. He recognised the reality of divine revelation, but insisted that it must be interpreted in terms of current knowledge and rational judgment. He acknowledged an atoning work in Christ, but insisted that it must be interpreted in accordance with moral insight.

Another significant figure among the Unitarians was Theodore Parker (1810–60). His emphasis on the teaching of Jesus over against church doctrine – especially in his influential essay, 'The Transient and the Permanent in Christianity' (1841) – was a portent of things to come.

This spirit soon spread to the more lively intellects in other denominations. The mainstream of American protestantism remained evangelical and revivalist in spirit for some time to come; but it was theologically uncreative. The growing point was liberal.

3. THE REVIVAL OF IDEALISM

In Britain, the main philosophical influence in the background to early liberal theology was a revival of interest in the Idealism of Kant and Hegel. It was largely Scottish in origin and theological in motivation. Its aim was to combat both mechanistic materialism in science and supernaturalism and dogmatism in religion.

It was of fateful significance for theology that there took place, in the later nineteenth century, a reversal of philosophical roles between Britain and Germany. Traditionally Britain had been the land of empiricism – of Locke, Berkeley and Hume. Germany had been the land of theological idealism. Quite suddenly these roles were reversed. Empiricism became rampant in Germany. Hegelian idealism was reborn in Britain. (The empiricist strain of philosophy became virulent in Germany. It was eventually to re-infect British philosophy as a withering blight.)

Theological Motivation
The theological motivation of British Idealism is apparent in its initial development in J. H. Stirling's *The Secret of Hegel* (1865) and even more so in Edward Caird's *The Philosophy of Kant* (1877) and in his brief but significant *Hegel* (1833).

This new Idealism was not contemptuous of empirical science. It welcomed its results. However, it emphasised the limitations of its perspective. Science abstracts certain aspects of reality from the whole. Reality is greater than the objective 'given' of science. Consciousness and thought are the primary data. The whole realm of our mental and spiritual aspirations is involved. God is the focus of these aspirations. Whether it is recognised as such or not, this is a universal feature of human awareness. The ultimate aim of all rationality is to know reality not only as it appears but in its essence, its wholeness and its coherence. Since the primary datum is consciousness and thought, our account of reality must not only include, but even give precedence to the mental, the voluntary and the spiritual. The relation of this philosophy to the new science is perhaps best suggested by T. H. Green, one of the most influential of the first generation of British Idealists. He wrote, in his *Prolegomena to Ethics* (1883), 'In the growth of our experience, an animal organism which has a history in time, gradually becomes the vehicle for an eternally complete consciousness'.

In his day, this mode of philosophy was a powerful influence on both moral attitudes and theological opinion. It not only disciplined the minds of its students. It inspired a generation.

Some of the next generation of idealists, such as F. H. Bradley (1846–1924), could find no room for a personal god in their conception of the Absolute; but they remained on the whole respectful of religion and especially of Christianity as a near approach to truth – perhaps as near as a finite mind can come. The relation between

philosophy and theology remained as sympathetic as it had ever
been. There is a hint of wistful regret in some of those idealists who
found that the gap could not be entirely closed – e.g. in William
G. Maclagan's splendid *The Theological Frontiers of Ethics* (1961)
and C. A. Campbell's fine Gifford Lectures, *Selfhood and Godhood*
(1957).

Others, like H. D. Lewis continued to find in this style of philosophy a sufficient and compelling ground for adherence not only to
personal theism but also to a broadly traditional Christian faith. This
brand of distinctively personal idealism was an important counter to
the Utilitarianism of J. S. Mill in the philosophical base of liberal
christianity. It is in the lineage of Andrew Seth's (Pringle-Pattison)
Hegelianism and Personality (1887) and *The Idea of God in the Light
of Recent Philosophy* (1917) and of James Ward – especially his
Realm of Ends (1911).

Idealism and Personalism

The influence of this type of personal Idealism is seen, for example,
in one of the most profoundly systematic of the liberal theologians
of the early twentieth century – John Oman (1860–1939). His *Grace
and Personality* (1917) gives the key to the theological centre of his
thought. The apparent contradiction between the doctrine of divine
grace and the ethical principles of the freedom and responsibility of
the individual had become a great source of vexation. It was the
modern version of the ancient Augustinian-Pelagian controversy.
With new insights into the nature of person and personal relation,
Oman went far towards resolving this dilemma for modern Christianity. The interplay between grace and freedom, he suggested,
corresponds to a universal structure in human experience – the
interplay between dependence and freedom. Grace, is not a limitation but an enhancement of freedom and autonomy. This becomes
the key to understanding the relation between God and the whole
of creation. The relation between God the Father and Jesus Christ
the Son is at its heart.

There are echoes of Schleiermacher here; but there are also anticipations of the crucial role played by the cateogry of 'person' in the
theology of the later twentieth century. Oman raised the personal
to the level of an irreducible metaphysical category. His more
comprehensive work, *The Natural and the Supernatural* (1931),
though a difficult book, deserves wider appreciation than it has as
yet received.

The recovery of a theological understanding of 'person' (never
adequately grasped in the West since its elaboration by the Greek

Fathers in the fourth and fifth centuries) continues as an on-going feature of contemporary theology. For this, liberal theology must be given some of the credit. Oman's treatment of it was developed by H. H. Farmer (1892–1981) in *The World and God* (1935). He elaborated Oman's theology of personal existence through analysis of the 'I-Thou' relation. In this he was immediately indebted to the Jewish philosopher Martin Buber (1878–1965) whose beautifully written *I and Thou* was a seminal contribution to the development of the theology of person in recent decades. The concept of the irreducibly distinctive I-Thou relation was severely brutalised by E. Brunner in his philosophically incompetent and spiritually obtuse *Truth as Encounter*. It was rescued, restored and sensitively developed by R. Gregor Smith in *The Doctrine of God*.

This tendency to interpret the traditional concepts of doctrine in the light of personal values is also apparent in the work of John Baillie (1887–1954), especially his *The Interpretation of Religion* (1929) and *Our Knowledge of God* (1939). Latterly he was somewhat influenced by some of the anti-liberal tendencies of post-war dialectical theology – especially its rejection of belief in progress – but he never really lost his liberal stance. He interprets the Christian tradition in the light of its relevance to the moral and spiritual health of man and society. He found in religion the fulfilment rather than the contradiction of the historic human condition. In Christianity he found the fulfilment of religion. This was even more strikingly true of his less prolific and less philosophical, but spiritually more penetrating brother, Donald Baillie (1887–1954). His *God was in Christ* (1948) was one of the very great books of the period.

This style of interpreting doctrinal tradition in terms of its significance for personal wholeness and spiritual recollection was one of the permanent achievements of the often maligned liberal theology. This was one of the many respects in which it contributed a growing point for the theology of today.

4. GOD AND NATURE

The External World

It must be admitted, however, that this liberal habilitation of the category of the personal as a touchstone of theological interpretation showed a strong bias towards the subjective. This was largely due to its affinities with idealist philosophy, which treated mind as the primary reality. The physical world was treated as little more than the stage on which the spiritual drama was played out. The reality of spirit was thought to consist ultimately in the subjective, the conscious and the mental. But there was another wing of the liberal theology which was inclined to resist this Platonic bias.

Many Christian thinkers of the liberal cast of mind which prevailed in the early decades of the twentieth century thought that this Platonic bias was mistaken on two main counts. Firstly, it did not take sufficient account of the significance accorded to the physical in Holy Scripture. Secondly, it did not take sufficient account of the insights generated by the remarkable advance of modern science – particularly of biological science.

We noted in Chapter I that, from the outset, the nineteenth century faced the problem of a God who had become remote from the world and the affairs of men. Hegelian idealism, qualified by Schleiermacher's theology, had appeared at first to offer a solution to this problem. However, both Hegel and Schleiermacher (at least as they were widely understood) emphasised the indwelling of God in human subjectivity. This tendency was reinforced by Ritschl's disjunction of theological value judgment from objective judgments of fact. This set up the major problem of the latter years of the nineteenth century.

Theology and Science

Natural science, in its preoccupation with the factual and the physical, was left for a time to go its own way. Theology, in its preoccupation with the mental and the subjectively spiritual was left equally free. This truce of non-interference between theology and science was feasible, however, only so long as science remained primarily a matter of Newtonian, mechanistic physics and the biological sciences were almost wholly preoccupied with taxonomy and classification. The publication of Darwin's *Origin of Species* in 1859 and his *Descent of Man* in 1871 changed all that.

For the most part the ensuing debate between science and theology was no debate at all. It was more a confrontation. The main issue for theology was where it should set up its perimeter defences. The biblicist conservatives set them up in enemy territory. They simply refused to accept the results of science where these contradicted biblical teaching. (To a surprising degree this strategy persists to the present day in conservative, evangelical circles. Even within the Roman Catholic Church, as late as 1909, a decree of the Biblical Commission affirmed that the account of the special creation of man in Genesis was to be understood literally and historically.) The more scientifically minded tended to retire within a steadily shrinking perimeter to defend the citadel of God within the gaps in scientific knowledge.

As the gaps in scientific knowledge narrowed, God was forced more and more out of the world of objective fact and physical nature. This, however is the world which modern man instinctively feels is the real world. If God or the tokens of his presence are not to be found in that world, then his relevance for modern Western man is diminished to vanishing point. God's relevance to our understanding of the natural world has become for increasing numbers of people a condition of the credibility of his transcendent existence. This may, in the end of the day, turn out to be an unreasonable, naturalistic prejudice. Certainly, it is very different from presuppositions which seem equally self-evident in some highly sophisticated oriental cultures. Nevertheless it remains a fact of the dialogue between theology and the modern world which cannot be ignored.

Thus the initially successful attempt of the theologians of the early nineteenth century to bring God back into lively presence within the world began to fail. Doubt became widespread about the adequacy of Idealist philosophy, with its stress on mind and subjective consciousness, to meet the apologetic demands of the new situation.

The pressure of the new situation was also felt within philosophy. It responded with a new style of philosophical thinking. Inevitably this had repercussions within theology.

The New Realism
Throughout most of the nineteenth century the only radical alternative to Idealism was a very crass kind of mechanistic materialism. A fresh approach was needed. New developments in philosophical psychology contributed significantly toward this. Fundamental to Idealist philosophy had been the belief that what we know *immediately*, by direct acquaintance as it were, is restricted to our own ideas and sensations – i.e. determinations of our own consciousness. F. C. Bertrano (1838–1917), in Vienna, followed by his pupil A. von Meinong (1853–1920), strongly resisted this view. They argued that we do not infer the existence of the world of external objects from our subjective mental states. We have direct and immediate awareness of them. This was the beginning of a philosophical revolution. Its consequences for theology were as momentous as those of a similar shift in late mediaeval philosophy which played a major part in the Realist/Nominalist debate.

In America, the philosophical psychologist William James (1842–1910) developed and popularised this new psychology of knowledge. The philosopher Charles S. S. Peirce (1839–1914) also contributed significantly to the partial eclipse of philosophical idealism in America. The conviction grew that it is the world that informs our minds, not our minds that shape the world.

In England the philosophy of J. S. Mill was prominent among the influences turning attention from the subjective and mental towards the wordly and the scientifically observable. Cambridge, especially under the influence of G. E. Moore, became a centre of this new style of philosophy. It acquired the name of 'The New Realism'. For some, such as Bertrand Russell, this new philosophical perspective pointed the way to a naturalistic atheism. Others, however, saw it as opening doors to a new style of liberal theology. This new theology sought more than mere co-existence with modern science. It sought a positive, co-operative relation of mutual aid and illumination.

F. R. Tennant (1866–1957) saw the role of theology not so much as the complement but rather as the completion of the task of the special sciences. Like theirs its task was essentially descriptive. Its task was to describe the whole of reality as it is disclosed by all the sciences and to elicit its meaning. This meaning he found best expressed in ethical theism. Like most of the liberals, he rejected the doctrine of original sin as the needless perpetuation of a myth appropriate only to the period of Judaeo-Christian infancy. Man's moral problem is not that of inherited guilt. The destiny of man is to realise moral values in the face of the moral indifference of his natural origins and biological inheritance.

Part of the difficulty was that the sciences themselves had not yet reached a degree of sophistication such as would enable them to co-operate with one another, much less with theology. Biology, psychology, anthropology and medicine still tend, even today, each to plough its own lonely furrow. Thus the liberal-minded theologian who sought a co-operative relationship with science had to fight a battle on two fronts – one for the reform of science, the other for the reform of theology. Canon C. E. Raven was a man of destiny in this respect.

Incarnational Theology
Being himself learned in the biological sciences, Raven found himself, at the beginning of his Gifford Lectures, obliged to say to scientists,

Many of us who insist upon the continuity of nature and supernature cannot approve, indeed strongly resent, the process which has first abstracted from the natural world certain elements in it susceptible to quantitative study and mechanistic interpretation, and then has proceeded to claim that these elements do in fact constitute the whole of the natural order.

On the other front he had to say to theologians,

If nature is so corrupted as to be the antithesis of grace, then the Creator must be, as the Arians supposed, of a different substance from the Redeemer – unless of course He has, as some suggest, ceded His control of the world to the successful rebellion of the devil. If grace is radically contrasted with the beauty and truth and goodness of the natural order, then any belief in a real Incarnation is impossible – unless the Christ be, as the Gnostics maintained, a divine intruder totally other than mankind.

The reference here to the Incarnation is significant. It was a weakness of much of the liberal theology that its appreciation of this doctrine was limited to its moral and personal significance. It is, however, a feature of that strand of the liberal theology which initiated a courtship between theology and modern science that it recovered some of the classic, patristic understanding of the Incarnation. This made the incarnate Christ the pivot of the relation not only between God and man, but between God and the whole of creation.

A similar incarnational emphasis is to be found in William Temple (1881–1944) – particularly in his *Nature Man and God* (1934). He said, 'The World-Process itself is the medium of God's personal action'. In accordance with the Chalcedonian Creed, he affirmed both the unity and the distinction of the divine and human natures in Jesus Christ. He saw in this the wider implication that, though there is a distinction, there is no ultimate separation between the life of God and biological life as we know it in the world. Thus,

Creation and Redemption are, indeed different; but they are different aspects of one spiritual fact, which is the activity of the Divine Will, manifesting itself in love through the Creation, and winning from the Creation an answering love.

So Christ, in his substantial identity with the life of God is also 'the first-fruits of the Creation – the first response from the Creation to the love of the Creator'. Thus the whole World-Process is seen in the light of the Incarnation and as sacramental.

Teilhard

During the same period, the Jesuit priest Pierre Teilhard de Chardin (1881-1955) was pursuing an independent – remarkably independent – line on the integration of theology with a modern, scientific world-view. As a geologist and palaeontologist he was vividly conscious of the emergence of life from a physical basis through the development of increasingly complex molecules. He argued that this emergence – particularly the emergence of higher forms of life and man – could not be adequately explained or understood in terms of natural selection alone. We require the concept of a spiritual 'milieu' in which the creative response of the creature is evolved. This is the universal and dynamic presence of God.

In the evolution of man the spiritual goal of the cosmos begins to emerge. All creation is drawn towards a final consummation in love and communion. This he calls the Omega-point. It is already anticipated and disclosed with enabling power in Jesus Christ.

It must be admitted, however, that there was a vagueness in his thought at crucial points that makes it difficult to determine exactly what he was saying. In view of this and the daring novelty of his proposals, it is hardly surprising that the Roman Catholic Church hesitated to give permission for the publication of his work till after his death. The main outline of his position is to be found in his *The Phenomenon of Man* (E. tr. 1959).

Process Philosophy and Theology

However, perhaps the most consequential development bearing upon efforts of liberal theologians to construct a Christian world-view consonant with modern science was the philosophy of Alfred North Whitehead (1861-1947). He began as a mathematician. His interest in generalisation drove him into formal logic on the one hand and theoretical physics on the other. In each of these fields he made substantial contributions. The same impulse finally drove him to search for a unifying metaphysical theory. He was appointed to his first Chair of Philosophy at Harvard at the age of sixty-three. It was after that that he published his main metaphysical works.

His main work in this field is *Process and Reality* (1929). It cannot be fairly summarised in a few sentences. Yet account must be taken of it. It is the main philosophical resource of what came to be known as 'Process Theology'.

Whitehead saw weaknesses in both Idealism and the New Realism. In particular:

a. Idealism gives undue priority to the subjective and the mental.

New Realism gives undue priority to the objective and the physical.

b. Idealism is too preoccupied with the inter-relatedness of the whole of reality.

New Realism is too preoccupied with discrete facts.

c. Idealism tends towards pantheism in identifying God with reality as a whole.

New Realism, in so far as it finds room for God at all, tends to exclude him from the natural world.

Whitehead attempted to overcome the first of these antitheses by stressing the polar unity of subjective and objective elements in experience. He further suggested that mind is an internal factor at every level of nature down to the humblest atom; though it is only at the human level that it is sufficiently intense to emerge as self-consciousness.

The second antithesis he overcame by a doctrine of the inter-relatedness of all space-time instants in the flow of events. Process, not substance, is the basic metaphysical category.

The third antithesis he overcame by distinguishing between what he called the 'primordial' and the 'consequent' nature of God. In his primordial nature God is above and beyond the actualities of space-time. He is the source and ground of its potentialities. In his consequential nature, however, God is intimately involved in every space-time occurrence.

It is this last point, as much as the base in space-time science, which has fascinated the numerous followers of Process Theology. There is in modern man a yearning for a god in whom absolute transcendence is reconciled with intimate participation in the joy and the pain, the glory and the shame of the world. Whitehead's philosophy of process seemed to hold out the promise of this.

His influence on American theology has been particularly strong. Charles Hartshorne (1897–) was much influenced by him in his own rigorously rational theology. Daniel Day Williams has employed him in the service of a more sensitive and spiritual theology. In more recent times, W. Pannenberg has declared affinity between his theology and Process Theology. Interest in Process Theology, subject to various modifications, is still growing. This too must be regarded as part of the legacy of the liberal phase.

5. THE KINGDOM OF GOD AND THE SOCIAL GOSPEL

The doctrine of the Kingdom of God played a central role in the various liberal theologies. The influence of Ritschl is plain to see in this. But too much has been made of this influence. The roots of the liberal, 'worldly' theology of the Kingdom reach down into the New Testament itself – especially the teaching of Jesus. It was to this that appeal was most frequently made. The pervasive conviction of liberal Christians was that our Christian responsibility to God involves the up-building of a juster, fairer, more charitable society. In England its roots are to be found in J. M. F. Ludlow (1821–1911), F. D. Maurice and the novelist clergyman, Charles Kingsley (1819–75). This was later taken up by people like Charles E. Raven and William Temple.

The Social Gospel in America

It was in America, however, that the liberal Social Gospel really thrived. An emphasis on the Kingdom of God had always been characteristic of American theology – e.g. in the days of the New England theocracy. The pragmatism of philosophers like C. S. Peirce and William James reinforced this. Out of Germany the influence of Adolf Harnack became prominent at the turn of the century. The lively sense of the promise of a brave new world following upon the Declaration of Independence in 1776 still persisted. Rapid social and cultural change had become so intense in America that a renewed stress on the social implications of christianity became inevitable. The way had already been paved by such men as Emerson, Channing and Bushnell.

The Social Gospel was never, in its best representatives, guilty of the naive optimism of which it is so often accused. It was certainly a hopeful movement; but that is another matter. It hardly deserves the downright condemnation which it received at the hands of H. Richard Niebuhr (1894–1962) in *The Kingdom of God in America* (1937) where he says, 'A God without wrath brought men without sin into a kingdom without judgment through the ministrations of a Christ without a cross'.

The best known of the theologians of the social gospel movement is Walter Rauschenbusch (1861–1918). He saw Jesus primarily as a social, moral and religious reformer. However, Jesus was no ordinary reformer. 'By his profounder insight and his loftier faith he elevated and transformed the common hope.' Rauschenbusch did underplay the element of judgment in the teaching of Jesus, saying of him, 'He postponed the divine catastrophe of judgment to the dim distance and put the emphasis on the growth of the new life that was now going on'. On the other hand, he was one of the first to realise that modern society and culture were entering a phase of acute crisis. This he attributed to the sinful condition of the heart of man and his economic and social institutions. He acknowledged the need for conversion of the heart under the power of divine revelation in Jesus Christ. But he equally acknowledged the need for a reform of institutions and proposed an alliance of the church with the labouring and downtrodden classes. More than any other theologian of the period he anticipated our contemporary 'theology of revolution'.

Washington Gladden (1836–1918) was another significant theologian of this movement. Politically he was less radical than Rauschenbusch. He was, however, one of the first to recognise in the trades unions a possible instrument of christian action.

Shailer Mathews (1836–1941) was the most inventive of this group of theologians. He stressed the universal connection between religious ideas and social structures. In *The Growth of the Idea of God* (1931) he drew attention to the fact that our commonest symbols for God are drawn from the social and political sphere – king, judge, father, etc. This provided him with a broader base for his social theology of the Kingdom of God. If the theologians of the social gospel failed to realise the full seriousness of the human situation and the moral bankruptcy of christendom, this was due as much to a deficiency in their social perceptiveness as in their theological insight. The lessons of two terrible wars, totalitarian politics and bondage to market forces had still to be learned.

Reinhold Niebuhr: Theological Realism

It fell to Reinhold Niebuhr (1892–1971) to sound the alarm in America. As a pastor in industrial Detroit for thirteen years he brought as much social concern to his ministry as did any social gospeller. But he also learned that the harsh realities of industrial and political life did not readily yield to good intentions and high-minded programmes. His reading of the Holy Scriptures and his interpretation of the industrial and political scene illuminated one another. He clearly saw the awesome significance of the fact that not only individual men but society and culture themselves are fallen and enslaved to sin. His *Moral Man in Immoral Society* (1931) remains one of the major landmarks of modern theology. He became a member of the distinguished faculty of Union Theological Seminary, New York in 1928. He soon showed himself to be as opposed to doctrinaire socialism as he was to *laissez faire* capitalism as an appropriate base for a Christian society. The first need, he affirmed, was for a recovery of the Augustinian/Reformed doctrine of the moral depravity and spiritual bankruptcy of fallen man. Only on the basis of this recognition and confession could society become open to grace and the renewal of community. The main statement of this is in his Gifford Lectures, *The Nature and Destiny of Man* (1941–43). The radical criticisms of social christianity in Søren Kierkegaard had a considerable influence upon him as did also European Dialectical Theology (of which we shall speak in the next chapter). Niebuhr, however, never lost interest in the direct application of Christian theological insights to social problems. His later work on the theology of history and the theological critique of political power remains as relevant today as it was at the time of writing. It makes at least as much sense to see Niebuhr as the continuation and correction of the social gospel as it does to see him as its antithesis.

FOR FURTHER READING

Niebuhr, H. R., *The Kingdom of God in America*, New York, 1937.
Reardon, B. M. G., *Liberal Protestantism*, London, 1968. *Liberalism and Tradition*, London, 1975.
van Dusen, H. P., *The Vindication of Liberal Theology*, New York, 1963.
Williams, D. D., *Interpreting Theology, 1918–1952*, London, 1953.

8

THE TIME OF THE THREE GIANTS

We have seen that the main thrust of nineteenth century theology was to bring God back into worldly relevance. This was against the false transcendence of rationalistic deism on the one hand and the crass supernaturalism of Protestant orthodoxy on the other. This had to be done in a manner compatible with the spirit and achievements of modern, rational autonomy. It had, at the same time, to distinguish the essence of the gospel from the transitory forms in which, from time to time, it has found expression.

That this was an operation fraught with danger is beyond question. The true and essential transcendence of God could be lost. The gospel could be displaced by the presuppositions and predilections of our own modernity. The theology of the nineteenth century, despite its considerable achievements, did not survive these dangers unscathed.

The rise of modern theology was concomitant with the rise of the modern nation state. These nation states became self-conscious about their own distinctive culture and spirit. This was one of the less fortunate by-products of the romantic movement. This gave an ominous aspect to the tendency to identify faith and culture. There was grave danger that the aspirations of national culture be idolatrously identified with the absoluteness of God.

A portent of this is to be found at the very beginning of our period. In the first of his *Speeches* Schleiermacher had suggested not only that our understanding of religion should be informed by our spiritual awareness, but also that the German people were the true bearers of this spirit. The English he dismissed as too immersed in commerce and the French as materialistic atheists. This was innocently enough said at the time. It was a thought widely current in German romanticism. It came to have its counterpart in the alliance of missionary enthusiasm with British imperialism and of the American spirit of liberty with the freedom of the gospel. The consequences of this close association of faith with national cultures were tragic to a degree that could not be imagined before the catastrophe of the First World War.

Although this sanctified chauvinism was the most tragic, it was by no means the only regrettable aspect of the inadequacies of the marriage of faith and culture which culminated in the liberal theologies of the turn of the century. Other aspects of modern European culture were given an absolute significance beyond their deserts. The bourgeois family, the social virtues of respectability and conformity, the commercially useful aspects of the doctrine of secular vocation and work were idolatrously absolutised.

Kierkegaard

Much of this unfortunate aspect of the new theology had been foreseen and condemned with prophetic passion by the Danish writer Søren Kierkegaard (1813–1855). We might well have considered him in his nineteenth century context. However, in his own day he made little impact. It was not until the twentieth century that he was recognised as a prophet born out of due time. In that sense he belongs more significantly to the history of theology in the twentieth century. He reacted violently against what he saw as the attempt of Hegel to assimilate the individual into the universal, the finite into the infinite, the human into the divine. This, he contended, ignored the infinite qualitative difference between God and man. He rejected the notion of Christendom with its attempt to marry revelation and reason, faith and culture, holiness and ethics. Christianity is not about building a civilisation in which we can take pride. It is first and foremost a judgment on all such concerns. It is essentially other-worldly.

Existence as a responsible subject is a condition which can be acknowledged only in anxiety and dread. Existence as a finite subject has its meaning truncated and eliminated by death. Neither rationalism nor romanticism had succeeded in overcoming the antithesis between the subjectivity of authentic spirit and the objectivity of the world. The objectification of human subjectivity in social institutions is a betrayal of man. The objectification of divine subjectivity in institutionalised religion and academic theology is the ultimate idolatry. In this respect Kierkegaard was one of the fathers of twentieth century existentialism.

The only point of contact between God and man is in Jesus Christ, in whom God became man. This is the ultimate paradox. Even to attempt to make it comprehensible is to blaspheme against it. It is the contradiction of all the aspirations of our finite reason. Its centre is the suffering and death of Jesus Christ. Its only resolution is his resurrection.

It follows, therefore, that these things can be acknowledged only in faith – a faith which is totally discontinuous with autonomous, finite reason. So it is discontinuous with culture, which is the creation of finite reason. Culture is at best an irrelevance, at worst an expression of the sinful and false autonomy which alienates us from God and betrays our true subjectivity.

This sharp critique fell largely on deaf ears; but it lay like a seed in the ground until the new situation, which began with the First World War, released its fertility.

The new and desperate spiritual situation of Western man emerged into conscious recognition around 1920. There ensued a period of remarkable theological creativity. It was dominated by three theological giants. Each in his own way owed and acknowledged some debt to Søren Kierkegaard. They were Karl Barth (1886–1968), Rudolf Bultmann (1884–1976) and Paul Tillich (1886–1965). But all three were more immediately influenced by the holocaust of the First World War and the consequent shaking of a formerly confident Western civilisation to its very foundations.

The period of the early church, when the formerly confident Hellenistic civilisation had fallen into a state of virtually total collapse, has been aptly described as the age of the failure of nerve. The middle decades of the twentieth century have been another such age. This had a considerable bearing on the kind of theology they produced.

1. KARL BARTH

Origins of Dialectical Theology
Barth came out of the liberal stable. He was a pupil of Harnack's. From the start, however, he sensed crisis and sought more theological depth. By his own confession, the immediate occasion of his break with liberalism and all forms of mediating theology was the sanctified chauvinism to which we have already referred. Barth came to see this as the true and monstrous progeny of the unnatural mating of faith and culture. The crux came when, in 1914, ninety-three German scholars, several of Barth's former teachers among them, signed an open letter supporting the Kaiser's war aims in the name of Christian civilisation. Barth's disenchantment with the liberal theology became total.

However, the determining factor in bringing him to a radically

new theological stance was not such merely sociological considerations. Nor was it the existentialism of Kierkegaard or Dostoievsky,
nor the political theology of Franz Overbeck (1837–1905) or J.
C. Blumhardt (1827–91), nor the post-Hegelian theology of P. K.
Marheineke, to all of which influence upon Barth has rightly been
ascribed. The crucial factor in the formation of his basic theological
stance was the reading of Holy Scriptures in the context of parish
ministry. He became pastor of Safenwil in Switzerland in 1911. His
correspondence with his friend Eduard Thurneysen (1888–1974)
during that period is revealing. The burning question for him was
what to preach. It was clear to him that little improving homilies
would not do. If we are to preach at all, it must be a Word which
God has given us and not a mere effervescence of our own
spirituality.

The Epistle to the Romans
This led to his publication of his theological commentary, *The
Epistle to the Romans* in 1919 – re-issued in a heavily revised edition
in 1921. The powerful impact of this small book was immediate.
The Word which God speaks to us through his apostle Paul can be
appropriated by us, in the first instance, only as judgment – upon
ourselves, upon our culture and upon our religion. But the heart of
the message is not judgment. It is the self-disclosure of God in his
holy love. His wrath and judgment are not a contradiction of this
love. Nor are they mitigated by it. They are, rather, the reverse
side of the same coin. In the cross of Christ, both the judgment and
the love of God are disclosed in terrible and awesome majesty. The
resurrection of Jesus Christ discloses and in effect *is* the triumph of
the positive over the negative, of grace over judgment in God. In
God act and being are one. He is as he does in Jesus Christ.

This is not cheap grace. It is not as though we can now forget or
diminish the judgment of God – not any more than the resurrection
makes the cross of Christ as though it had never been. It is only in
the shadow of the gallows cross that we stand in the light of the
resurrection. We are in a state of sin. In the light of God's holiness
our depravity is total. It is only by the miracle of God's grace in
Jesus Christ, and nothing else, that we are saved.

This ran directly counter to the major trend of creative theology
in the past two centuries. This trend was to bring God back into
rational credibility and worldly relevance by establishing some kind
of continuity between the 'self-end' of God and the moral and
spiritual aspirations of mankind. Barth could find only discontinuity
– a discontinuity which could be overcome only by the sovereign

act of God himself. God's intimate relevance to every worldly situation does not rest upon his pervasive immanence in human affairs but upon his utter transcendence and 'otherness'. His credibility rests upon his own faithfulness, not upon our perceptiveness or sensitivity.

The Word of God

There is perhaps some continuity between Barth and the rather uncreative conservative evangelical theology of the nineteenth century. But this can easily be exaggerated. The evangelical theology emphasised religious experience and the inner light – especially conversion experience. Barth set his face against all such subjectivism. Furthermore, in common with later protestant orthodoxy, the evangelicals had fallen prey to a crassly simplistic view of the inspiration of Holy Scripture. There was a tendency to identify the words of Scripture unambiguously with the Word of God. Barth's position on this issue is subtle to a degree which defies summary description. He acknowledged the legitimacy of historical and textual criticism of the Bible – though he deplored as futile the liberal attempt to derive the substance of the faith from such exercises. There is a human element in Scripture which is totally human. There is therefore a sense in which it is a book like any other book. But it is also the Word of God in that it is through these very words and none other that God addresses his own Word of judgment, promise and grace. The mystery of the relation between the human words and the divine Word in Scripture is to be understood – in so far as divine mysteries can be understood – in the light of the greater mystery of the union of the divine and the human in Jesus Christ. The two natures are united; but they are neither mixed nor changed.

This was a complete departure from the naive biblicism of the evangelical conservatives.

Confessions and Creeds

However, if Barth's theology was in these and other important respects discontinuous with the main theological development of the previous century – a discontinuity which he explicitly acknowledged, especially in his *Protestant Theology in the Nineteenth Century* – he also restored to theology its larger continuity. More than any other modern theologian he restored the abiding relevance of the great protestant Confessions, the Fathers of the reformation and the Fathers of the earlier Catholic tradition, as well as the ancient creeds. Thus, without the deliberate intention of so doing, he became a major force in initiating a new phase in ecumenical theology. He opened the way for Roman Catholic and Protestant theology to enter into a more positive relationship.

Theological Objectivity

Although he rejected as folly the effort of the theology of the Enlightenment to establish continuity between autonomous human reason and the revelation of God, Barth was not irrationalist in intention. Theology, he maintained, is a science. The hallmark of scientific objectivity is that each science allows the nature of its object to determine its methods and conceptual structure. The proper object of theology is the self-revelation of God in his Word. Such revelation can be appropriated only in the response of faith. Theology must therefore be written from the standpoint of faith and is a function of the church.

Theology and Church

The application of this understanding of theological method is worked out in detail and at daunting length in Barth's major work, *Church Dogmatics* (1932–1967).

The function of theology is critical. It is to ensure that the church's proclamation remains faithful to the Word to which it witnesses. Barth thus combined the critical and the dogmatic functions of theology. It is a method which bears acknowledged similarities to that of the Reformers. Its context, however, is the modern situation. This is no kind of theological or biblical archaism. Still less is it an obscurantist dogmatism.

It has been suggested, especially by Thomas F. Torrance, that the transformation of theological method initiated by Karl Barth is analogous to the transition within science from Newtonian physics to the principle of Relativity introduced by Einstein. Perhaps the analogy is less exact than Torrance is apt to suggest; but it is certainly illuminating. Newton treated the stance of the observer as absolute. Einstein relativised the position of the observer in relation to the objective space-time continuum. Both Enlightenment and Romantic theology treated the critical standpoint of the autonomous, rational individual as absolute. Barth relativised that standpoint in relation to the revelation and action of God. Many, however, find this analogy unhelpful as an explanation of the obscure through the even more obscure. The essential point is that nineteenth century theology typically criticised the theological tradition of the church in the light of modern culture. Barth perceived a deeper sense in which the Word of God, which comes to us in and through the tradition – particularly the biblical tradition – must stand in judgment over the pride and presuppositions of modern culture.

The Priority of Revelation

God has disclosed himself to us in his Word of revelation. In this revelation the true meaning of the word 'God' becomes cognisible for the first time. This is symbolised in the disclosure of his name. He discloses himself as absolutely sovereign and absolutely free. It is integral to the meaning of this concept that there *can* be no other gods beside him. In his absolute freedom and sovereignty he is in sharp contrast with all the gods of religion who are bound to the nation, the culture, the cult in which they come to expression. This God who creates the world and chooses Israel is bound to none of these.

This free sovereignty in God brings the revelation of his Word into immediate contrast and conflict with the basic presuppositions of typical post-Enlightenment theology. To bring God into harmony with our creaturely reason it sought a *necessary* connection between God and the world. It is the function of natural theology to prove the existence of God on the basis of such a necessary connection. However, this presupposition directly contradicts the freedom and sovereignty of God revealed in his Word. This is why all natural theology must be rejected. Thus there is no *analogia entis* – no way in which we can know God through his likeness in the creature. Least of all can he be known through his likeness in man. This has been totally corrupted by sin. Barth's fellow Swiss, Emil Brunner, argued that there must be some residual point of contact (*Anknüpfungspunkt*) between God and man so that man could appropriate the revelation of God. Barth resisted this. It not only underestimated the seriousness of sin, he argued. It compromised the absolute sovereignty of God. God is not beset by conditions. There is no sense in which he *must* retain a point of contact in man in order to work his will in revelation. God's Word is a creative Word. It creates anew the conditions for its reception. Faith, as much as revelation, is a work of God.

A Cul de Sac?

At first, this uncompromising rejection of all connexion between God and the creaturely world – except that which is unaccountably and ever anew initiated by himself – seemed to take us back to the very problem with which nineteenth century theology had begun. This was the problem of a God who had become remote in his transcendence and arbitrary in his sovereignty. Barth seemed to have destroyed – as indeed he intended – the whole endeavour of nineteenth century theology to bring God back into relevant intimacy with the world.

Then, as he went on to develop his doctrine of the Person and Work of Christ, he surprised everyone. God, in the free sovereignty of his love, enters literally, truly and really into creaturely, finite existence within the world. No connexion between God and the worldly life of men could be more intimate than that. He became and remains one of us. He has the primacy among us only as the one who bore the ultimate humiliation of the human condition upon the cross of sin. He died for us and dies with us. It is truly God who thus becomes our most intimate fellow in Jesus Christ; yet he does this without compromising his absolute, divine sovereignty.

Let God Be God!

How can these things be? How can we accept the sheer irrationality of such a doctrine – that God became a baby and died the death of a condemned man yet still remained the eternal, omnipotent, changeless, eternal God? Barth's answer might be summarised thus: If, before you even begin to listen to the Word of God you imagine that you already know what divinity, transcendence, omnipotence and eternity really are, then you will never make sense of the God who surprises us by being other than we expect. This is where the theologians of the Enlightenment and Romantic movements went wrong. They tried to cut the cloth of revelation to fit a pattern of ideas already laid down. This is neither true rationality nor scientific objectivity. The fundamental irrationality of such a procedure is demonstrable, for instance, from the fact that it leads to a conception of God's sovereign omnipotence which actually restricts what he can do. Because of his free sovereignty he *cannot* become impotent man. To make a restriction out of God's sovereignty is nonsense.

On the other hand, when we are truly confronted by the Word of God and encounter its mysteries, our restricting preconceptions are transcended. We discover a majesty which can incorporate within itself lowliness, a glory which can accept and transcend shame, a constancy which can accommodate change.

This new conceptual structure is not something imposed upon us. It is, rather, something into which we are released. It is true freedom of mind. It is the throwing off of fetters which we did not even know we wore. It is the release of our true rationality from the imperialism of a falsely self-centred autonomy.

The Foolishness of God . . .

In the context of this liberated rationality the mysteries of God have their own inherent credibility. Far from toning them down we must allow them to be the bearers of their own astonishing truth. The virgin birth is the appropriate initiating miracle for the incarnation of God in the person of the Son just as the resurrection and ascension are its appropriate climax. Barth freely admits the inadequacy of the historical evidence for the virgin birth; but denies that the credibility of the mysteries of God's action in the world is dependent on that kind of evidence. The credibility of the mysteries of God's action in the world rests upon his own constancy in faithfulness to his promises and to his own being as love disclosed in Jesus Christ.

Every aspect of theology thus centres upon Jesus Christ. Creation and redemption are indeed different and distinct acts of God. Nevertheless, the Word of God incarnate in Jesus Christ is the Word of creation. The Christ is the fulfilment and the goal of creation. The doctrine of God's election of the redeemed (so long a bone of theological contention) is to be understood in the first instance as God's election of the Christ in love. The elect of the church are chosen in their communion with the Christ in whom God identifies himself with humanity. Whether this implies some kind of universalism is an issue on which Barth never made himself unambiguously clear.

The self-revelation and saving action of God are one. In this revelation three factors are involved – the one who reveals himself, the act of revelation and his communion with those in whom his revelation is received. These three aspects of God's self-revelation correspond to our concepts of Father, Son and Holy Spirit. God, in his faithfulness does not reveal himself as other than he truly is. Therefore we may believe that God is threefold in his very being. Within the unity of his divine being he is Father, Son and Holy Spirit. Thus Barth restored the doctrine of the Trinity to the centre of Christian dogmatics in contrast with, for example, Schleiermacher for whom it was a mere paedagogical device and an appendix to the system of doctrine.

The Analogy of Faith

God the creator, in the sovereign freedom of his transcendence, chooses to bring his three-fold being into the life of the world. In faith we understand our temporal existence in terms of the threefold action of God.

It has often been said of Karl Marx that he stood Hegel upon his head. This could be said even more appropriately of Karl Barth.

Hegel began from an analysis of human consciousness and arrived at an understanding of the triune being of God. Barth began from an analysis of the triune being of God as disclosed in his self-revelation and arrived at an understanding of human consciousness. In this we see both the unity and the disparity of Barth's thought in relation to that of the nineteenth century.

It is difficult to appreciate the tremendous impact of the Barthian theology unless one is old enough to remember the culture shock of the two world wars. He spoke as a prophet in the wilderness – as one through whom God made dry bones live.

In the positive aspects of his theology Barth offered, in his own way, a new solution to the central problem of nineteenth century theology – that of bringing God back into intimate relation with the temporal world. This aspect of his mature theology is clearly set out in his essay *The Humanity of God*.

Barthianism and its Critics

Unfortunately he acquired a following – especially in the English-speaking world – which concentrated mainly on the early, polemical negativities of his theology. It concentrated upon his rejection of 'culture Protestantism' and his emphasis on the otherness and transcendence of God. It could reasonably be classified as *Barthianismus vulgaris*. Barth himself was not unaware of this. He used to say that he did not know what it meant to be a Barthian, but that he was quite sure that he himself was not one.

Thus among both his followers and his opponents he became the victim of his own polemics. It is unfortunate that the sheer volume, verbosity and, it must be admitted, obscurity of his writing has inhibited many from reading him for themselves. He is more widely known by repute than by acquaintance. The stereotype has therefore persisted. Even among his more knowledgeable followers he has been accused by Dietrich Bonhoeffer (1906–1945) of harbouring a 'positivism of revelation' and by Jurgen Moltmann of evacuating the whole meaning of temporal history into the eternal moment of God's saving and revealing act.

He has been accused by his less sympathetic critics of divorcing faith from reason. Thus he left the field wide open for atheistic positivism in both philosophy and science. Certainly his influence was concomitant with a thriving of this tendency in secular scholarship.

He has been accused of divorcing faith from culture. He thus, it is alleged, eliminated its positive bearing on the moral endeavour of mankind (though none could deny the power of his theology in the struggle against Nazi tyranny).

He has been accused of divorcing faith from religion. This, it is suggested, led to an undervaluing of religious experience. It thus opened the way for the theologies of 'religionless Christianity' and the 'death of God'.

Barth intended none of these things. There is, however, no smoke without fire. There are undoubtedly prominent elements in the Barthian corpus which bear such an interpretation. It is not without significance that most of the 'death of God' theologians came out of the Barthian stable. It would be unfair, however, to draw conclusions from this without pausing to ask whether responsibility for this development is to be laid at the door of *Barthianismus vulgaris* rather than the great man himself.

It is also significant that in those countries where the secular authorities claim absolute power – especially the one-party states of the Eastern Bloc – the Barthian theology remains a real power in the land. In the liberal democracies, where there is a more positive relation between Christianity and the social order, Barthian theology has never been a powerful force outside theological seminaries.

Contribution to a Theology of the Future
The more affirmative aspects of his mature theology have yet to be developed to their full potential. His rehabilitation of the concept of revelation, not as privileged information about God, but as the self-disclosure of God in history, has been acknowledged by Wolfhart Pannenberg as a major break-through. His rehabilitation of the doctrines of the Trinity and of Chalcedonian Christology, not as mere metaphors but as fundamental ontological principles, continues to play a seminal role in contemporary theology even where his thought has had to be radically transformed. This is so within the Roman Catholic theological renaissance as well as within Protestantism. A sympathetic appreciation of these aspects of Barth is to be found in such Catholic theologians as Karl Rahner and Yves Congar and even the ebullient Hans Küng, as well as among such leaders of contemporary Protestant thought as W. Pannenberg and J. Moltmann. Eberhard Jüngel's *God's Being is in Becoming* (1966; E. tr. 1976) is a good example of the seminal influence of Barth in a form that is far beyond mere imitation.

Like other giants of the period, Barth has now ceased to be the pied piper whom young men followed as though bewitched. The future of Barth's great work lies with those who do not see his *Church Dogmatics* as a massive pill to be swallowed whole. It is rather a quarry from which some very durable theological building material may be hewn.

2. RUDOLF BULTMANN

The Consequence of Criticism
For a short period Barth and Bultmann moved within the same orbit in the very early days of the dialectical theology movement. However, they soon diverged in quite different – in some respects quite opposite – directions. Bultmann was initially a New Testament scholar of great erudition and disturbingly radical views concerning the factual historicity of the New Testament tradition. He perhaps did his best work as a New Testament critic; but it is not primarily on this account that he attained the status of a giant. This was on account of his theological interpretation of the biblical tradition.

The apparent loss of the historical Jesus at the hands of radical New Testament critics was never a serious issue in the church at large outside academic circles. Certainly the historicity of the New Testament narratives had come to be widely questioned. But this was on ideological rather than historico-critical grounds. The thought-style of modern man, conditioned by the limiting attitudes still endemic in empirical science, had become such that miracles were unthinkable. The central mysteries of the faith – incarnation, virgin birth, resurrection, ascension, Pentecost could be classified only as surviving superstitions of archaic religion. This, rather than the inadequacy of historical evidence was the real problem.

Barth challenged this ideological stance. Bultmann accepted it. He believed the essential Christian gospel to be unaffected thereby. On one thing at least he and Barth were agreed. The Christian faith is not just another ideology. It is something of a quite different order. Ideology conditions and enslaves the mind. Faith is a free act in response to a liberating gospel.

Bultmann saw the possibility – indeed the necessity – to interpret the gospel tradition in terms compatible with the contemporary 'scientific' habit of mind. To do this one must distinguish the essential message from the mythological framework in which it was first expressed. This separation is in no sense a paring down of the gospel to a diminished but credible residue. It is the true gospel, whole and entire, which he believes can be thus separated from its original cultural matrix. This essential message he calls the *kerygma* – the proclamation.

The Kerygma
The proclamation is not simply a message about Jesus. It is an event
in which we meet Jesus and encounter his challenge.
Bultmann accepted that Jesus is unattainable by objective,
historical research. However, in the proclamation which the New
Testament tradition enshrines, he is really and effectively present
to us. In taking this stance, Bultmann was influenced by the work
of Martin Kähler (1835–1912). In *The so-called historical Jesus and
the historic, biblical Christ* Kähler had argued that our approach to
a body of literature must be determined by the intrinsic character
of that literature. The Gospels were written as *gospels*, not as simple
historical chronicles. If we approach them as such we find the Christ
of faith in them. It is, he suggested, inappropriate and ridiculous
that the content of this saving message should be decided upon by
a 'papacy of professors'. In developing this point he made use of
the fact that there are two words for 'history' in German. He used
the rarer word, *Historie*, to describe objective, fact-finding historical
research. The more common word, *Geschichte*, he used to refer to
our living relationship with the interpreted past. Bultmann made
use of this distinction and relied heavily upon it.

History and Myth
It has been suggested by many of Bultmann's critics that he took
this stance because of the failure of the historical Jesus research. It
cannot be too heavily stressed that this is not so. Bultmann's point
was rather that, even if the researches of that kind of purely objective
historical enquiry had been wholly successful and positive in their
outcome, they would still have been a distraction from the proclamation of Jesus as the Christ. Such research could yield only knowledge of Jesus 'after the flesh'. It could not disclose Jesus to us as
the one in whom the Word of God meets us and, with absolute
finality, invites us to the decision of faith.
At the same time it must be understood that Bultmann did not
advocate a flight from history. He totally rejected the view, widespread in the liberal theologies, that the truth of the Christian gospel
consisted in a set of general, ethical and philosophical principles
which could be abstracted from their historical roots. The coming
of the redeeming grace of God into the world is an historic event.
Jesus is the unique bearer of the Word.
Bultmann was far, however, from regarding historical research as
irrelevant. It yields knowledge of the cultural context in which the
gospel tradition came into being. It was an age of mixing cultures,
rich in mythology. It was natural that the life and achievement of

Jesus should be interpreted in terms of the prevailing mythologies. But for us today to identify the gospel with its mythological setting would be to mistake the earthen vessel for the treasure it contains.

'Myth', however, is a slippery term. What Bultmann meant by it is far from clear. Initially he defined myth as 'the use of imagery to express the other worldly in terms of this world and the divine in terms of human life, the other side in terms of this side'. Later, in response to criticism, he defined mythological thought as that which looks upon divine activity 'as an interference with the course of nature, history or the life of the soul, a tearing of it asunder – a miracle, in fact. Thus it objectifies the divine activity and projects it on the plane of worldly happening'.

Three things need to be said about this. Firstly, the second definition betrays a tendency in Bultmann to conflate belief in miracle with belief in the objective truth of allegedly mythological statements. The two problems are related, but by no means identical. Secondly, the definition itself retains elements which many would regard as mythological – e.g. the notions of the other worldly and of the action of God. Thirdly, and following from this, it is quite clear that Bultmann firmly intended to retain the notion of the Acts of God as real events; but as events conceived in a non-mythological sense.

It must be conceded that in precision and analytical clarity Bultmann left much to be desired. We shall see the consequence of this in the subsequent divisions among his followers. It also left him open to unsympathetic interpretation in the hands of his opponents.

Clarity, however, is not all. Perhaps the kind of clarity sought for is not even possible in the existential context of his thought. His main intention was not philosophical but evangelical. To a considerable degree the main thrust of his argument is sufficiently clear. His primary concern was not the analysis of mythological thinking. It was to expose and distinguish the unique character of faith.

Heidegger

To do this he relied heavily on the concepts and terminology of his philosophical colleague Martin Heidegger (1889-1967). Heidegger was no theologian. He was an ontologist who believed that the way to an understanding of the nature of reality was through a perceptive examination of individual, personal existence. He drew a sharp distinction between what he called authentic and inauthentic existence. This became crucial for Bultmann. Each of us tends to hide from the vulnerable chanciness and finitude of our own existence.

We seek absolute security within ourselves through our dominance of the world of objects. In so doing we reduce ourselves to the level of that world. This is inauthentic existence. Authentic existence faces the insecurity of our subjective individuality – particularly in the anticipation of death as its ultimate boundary. We thus escape from shallowness into the only kind of depth of meaning which our existence has.

This is by no means all there is to Heidegger. It is too brief to be an adequate account of even that aspect of his philosophy. It must serve for present purposes, however.

Bultmann did not simply take over the philosophy of Heidegger. He used it selectively and re-interpreted it drastically. He was primarily a biblical theologian and retained more in common with Karl Barth than is commonly recognised. He shared with Barth the post-war reaction against the humanist optimism of the liberal theology. He accordingly re-emphasised the doctrine of the Fall. It cannot fairly be said that he simply identified man's fallen status with Heidegger's inauthentic existence. It is as true to say that he re-interpreted Heidegger's concept of inauthentic existence in the light of the myth of the Fall as that he interpreted the Fall in terms of Heidegger's philosophy. He brought the two together in a way which sheds new light on both. The story of the Fall is the story of man seeking his security within the world of his own dominion. In so doing he in fact subjects himself to the dominion of the elements of this world. He thus loses his true freedom and selfhood. This is the essential nature of sin. It has become endemic in the human situation.

The Word of God comes into this situation from outside and beyond it. It never becomes part of it. Otherwise it too would be subject to the same corruption. It is, in the first instance, a Word of promise that God by his own action will redeem his people from this false and self-destructive situation in which they are imprisoned. Jesus Christ is the fulfilment of this promise. In him God acts. In his death he releases those who respond to him in faith from bondage to inauthentic self and world. In his resurrection he initiates us into authentic freedom and grace.

Authentic Existence in the World

So far splendid! But is not this mythology? No, says Bultmann, not so long as it is understood and interpreted in the context of faith. The act of faith is contrasted in all respects with mythological thinking. Mythological thinking makes the story part of the succession of worldly events upon which in sin and self-delusion we place a false reliance. It reduces the saving acts of God to the level of what is available to us in a worldly way. This has to be rejected in the same way as Abraham had to leave behind the household gods who were available to him in a worldly way. It has to be rejected in the same way as Jesus rejected Jewish dependence on the letter of the law which was available to them in a worldly way.

Faith acknowledges the true and sovereign transcendence of God by acknowledging the absolute discontinuity of the divine action with anything that is available to us in a worldly way. As arising out of the action of God, faith must also acknowledge its own discontinuity with the kind of knowledge that is available to us in a worldly way. It is more than a new form of self-understanding. It is a new way of existing in the world so that we are in it but not of it. From this new standpoint and from it alone it is possible to speak authentically of the action and presence of God in Jesus Christ.

There is no doubt that Bultmann did not intend to deny the reality of God or to reduce the notion of his Word and action to that of a new and authentic form of human subjectivity. His point is, rather, that true recognition of divine reality can occur only within the context of faith thus understood. This existential understanding of faith, he claims, exposes the essence of the New Testament concept. In the context of this faith the truth of the doctrine of the incarnation is recognised in the living presence of God in Christ to us in the Word proclaimed and preached. The reality of his atoning work can be recognised only in the enjoyment of release from bondage to sin, the world and the sting of death. The reality of his resurrection and ascension can be recognised only in his living presence to us in the new life into which he initiates us.

Bultmann: Significance and Assessment

In many respects Bultmann's work is the consummation of a trend which has run through our whole period. This was an attempt to rediscover the distinctive reality of faith as a movement of the divine spirit within the realm of human spirit. It sought to distinguish it from discursive knowledge of transcendent realities on the one hand and belief imposed by crude authority on the other. It began with Schleiermacher and Hegel. It was earthed in social and cultural concern by Ritschl and the Liberals. It was rescued from the danger of total immersion in these concerns by both Barth and Bultmann – each in his own quite different way. For both faith, as an act of the divine spirit within the human scene, is distinguished absolutely from every other kind of perception or knowledge. For Barth it is so distinguished by its origin in the self-disclosure of God. For

Bultmann it is so distinguished by the unique form of its reception in human subjectivity.

For Bultmann this involved an even starker dichotomy between faith and factual knowledge than we find even in Barth. This appears first of all in his absolutising of the distinction between knowledge of historical facts (*Historie*) and interpreted history as it impinges on our present existence (*Geschichte*). It is difficult to maintain this distinction absolutely. Even for interpreted history it is necessary to have something to interpret.

This was recognised by many of his followers. Operating within the Bultmannian ambit, Ernst Käsemann delivered a famous paper in 1953 on 'The Problem of the Historical Jesus'. This led to what has become known (with echoes of Schweitzer) as the new quest for the historical Jesus. Bultmann dissociated himself from this quest despite the fact that there is much in his own writing which is consonant with it. Such scholars as Günther Bornkamm, Gerhard Ebeling, Ernst Fuchs and Hans Conzelmann have contributed significantly to this wing of the post-Bultmannian theology. They distinguish their new quest for the historical Jesus from the old quest. The old quest sought to write a biography of Jesus. It is now generally conceded that that is not possible. However, we can learn a great deal of the quality of his life – his attitude to law and grace, to sinners and sick people, to religious tradition, to civil authority, his faith, his love, his hope, the integrity of his person and so on. Characteristic of the findings of this new quest is the claim of G. Bornkamm in his *Jesus of Nazareth* that while there is a sense in which we can learn only a very little about Jesus from the Gospels, there is another sense in which they enable us to know him better than we know anyone else. One can see the sense in which this is so.

But Bultmann was right in perceiving that this blurring of his absolute distinction between factual knowledge and faith called in question the whole foundation of his system (in so far as it ever was a system). It puts all the fundamental questions back in the melting pot.

Radical Demythologising
It was the left-wing Bultmannians who adhered most rigorously to his fundamental, systematic principles. (It seems to be the fate of every innovative theologian since Origen (c.185–254) to have a following which splits up into a left and a right wing who between them lose the balance of his common sense!). They insisted on a wholly consistent application of his programme of demythologising

the gospel. They applied it to the notions of 'God', 'Act of God' and 'Word of God'. The whole of theology may and must be reduced to existentialist anthropology. Herbert Braun offered the intriguingly full-blooded notion that the essential message of the New Testament is not Christological but anthropological. It is the Christology which is variable. There are different and mutually incompatible christologies of Matthew, Mark, Luke, John, Paul, Hebrews, etc., but throughout there is a consistent, existentialist anthropology, comprising the fallenness of man, his enslavement to sin, bad conscience, alienation, and false, inauthentic consciousness. He is released from this condition through encounter with the life and presence of Jesus Christ.

One can respect the consistency of such a carrying through of the demythologising programme of Bultmann. One can admire the ingenuity of his consistently existentialist, humanist interpretation of the gospel tradition, even if one cannot accept it. It is surprising, however, that he continues to talk about God at all. He used phrases (strongly reminiscent of Schleiermacher) like 'God is the whence of my being in the world' or 'God is the source of the comfort which I receive from my neighbour'. This leaves the heart of the problem precisely where Schleiermacher had left it more than a hundred years before. It makes no real advance.

Fritz Buri is even more thoroughgoing. Using the existentialist theology of his Basel colleague Karl Jaspers rather than Heidegger, he reduces all talk of God and the action of God in Jesus Christ to exposition of the human situation.

The fact is that consistently existentialist philosophy, though it has contributed much to our understanding and analysis of the subjective conditions of faith, does not have the resources to tackle the question of the relation of our finite existence to the essential being of God. Yet there are two thousand years of theology which say that this is the heart of the matter.

This was appreciated by Paul Tillich, the third of our giants of the mid-century.

3. PAUL TILLICH

Paul Tillich was raised a pietistic Lutheran. He served with acknowledged heroism as an army chaplain during the First World War, suffered a crisis of faith and began a period of reconstruction which lasted the rest of his life. He was acutely conscious both of the values of traditional European culture and of its complete collapse after the First World War – particularly as he experienced this in the Berlin of the Weimar Republic. These facts are not merely anecdotal. They have, by his own admission, a direct bearing on the subsequent development of his theology. Because of his resistance to the Nazi movement, he was forced to leave Germany in 1933. The rest of his life – his most creative period – was spent in America. His *Systematic Theology* (1950–1963) is the most thoroughly systematic work which has been produced this century.

Essence and Existence

Tillich recognised that the preoccupation of theology with aspects of existentialist philosophy in the inter-war and post-war period was a phenomenon peculiar to those traumatic times. In none of its forms, therefore, could existentialism be regarded as a new *philosophia perennis* capable of interpreting the whole weight of authentic Christian tradition. He set it in perspective by showing that there has always been an existentialist element in philosophy. But it is only an element and can function adequately only in dialectic relation with the concept of essence or Being Itself. In particular, the Christian concept of God requires for its exposition not only the analysis of the experience of faith within finite existence but also the concept of the essential and eternal being of God. If one is to use the word 'existence' in the existentialist sense, then it is wrong to say that God exists. God does not exist. God *is*. God is Being Itself. Often, to preserve the dynamic element in the concept of God, Tillich prefers the phrase 'Ground of Being'.

The distinction between existence and essence or existence and Being is one that has been recognised as fundamental in philosophy from Plato to Hegel. Thereafter, under the influence of positivism on the one hand and existentialism on the other, it has been virtually suppressed. It has become incomprehensible to us. Tillich engaged in a massive rescue operation designed to recover the proper and indispensable role of this distinction in theology. It must be confessed that his success was only partial at best. The mood of the times was such that the phenomenological and existential elements within his system were taken up avidly by a considerable following – especially in America – but his philosophy of the Being of God was largely ignored. Yet this was the very heart of his whole system.

It could be said that of our three giants of that period, Barth begins from the essential being of God as he discloses himself to us in his Word of revelation. He does this to the virtual exclusion of any discussion of the conditions under which it is possible for man to receive revelation. Bultmann begins from the existential conditions under which man receives revelation in faith. He does this to the virtual exclusion of any discussion of the Being of the God who thus acts towards us in revelation and redemption. Tillich attempts to mediate between these two extremes. He does this by what he called his method of correlation.

The Method of Correlation

Human existence centres upon a question about the meaning of our existence. But this question cannot answer itself out of its own resources. This is our openness to revelation. Revelation answers the question of human existence from beyond human existence. But the question and answer are not independent of one another as though this were some kind of quiz with the answers at the back of the book. When we ask the question of the meaning of life we already do so under the impact of revelation. In the receipt of revelation we deepen our question about the meaning of our existence. This is the correlative relation between finite reason and revelation.

Finite Reason

Tillich's theory of knowledge was more elaborate and complete than that of any of his contemporaries. All knowledge has a correlative structure. It arises within the correlation of self and world. In the act of perception the self shapes the world it perceives. The self is in turn shaped by the world it perceives. (Here Tillich is under the influence of a line of thought which runs from Kant through Hegel up to Gestalt psychology.) There are four main types of knowledge which are distinguishable, but not ultimately separable. There is controlling knowledge which minimises, but cannot wholly eliminate, the factor of correlation. This is typical of laboratory science and technology. There is uniting knowledge, where the correlation is primarily one of communion and empathy. It is typically prominent in art, personal knowledge and devotion. There is dialectical knowledge which typically deals with the polarities of living structures. Finally there is ecstatic knowledge. This is a difficult concept because Tillich has to attempt to rescue the word 'ecstasy' from the shallow, emotional connotation which it has acquired from debased romanticism. Ecstatic knowledge arises from the kind of radically new perception which breaks into and shatters the established structure of our accepted world and our existing self-understanding. It not only shatters, however. It also renews. Ecstatic knowledge is the prominent and distinctive element in revelation. Typical examples would be the illuminating experience of Isaiah in the temple or of St Paul on the Damascus road.

Ultimate Concern

Tillich maintains that there is an element of such *ekstasis* at the heart of all human existence. He calls it 'ultimate concern'. It is sharply distinguished from our everyday or 'proximate' concerns. It is not directed towards a particular object or satisfaction. It is directed towards Being and Meaning as such. We experience our finite existence as threatened by nothingness and meaninglessness. This is the basis of existential anxiety. But it is also the source of the courage whereby we affirm our own existence and significance.

Ultimate concern cannot be identified with any specific, inner-worldly concern. Only that which can determine our being or not-being can become a matter of ultimate concern. This is the meaning of the concept 'God'. God is 'that which concerns us ultimately'. God is Being Itself, the Ground of Being or the Power of Being. The question of God, whether it is consciously recognised as such or not, is the question and the quest at the heart of every life. Religion is its supreme, though not its only expression.

Polytheistic religion is that which identifies the divine with its partial manifestation in the plurality of proximate concerns – the gods of fertility, wealth, family, nation etc. Idolatry is the unambiguous identification of the divine with such limited areas of concern. Such idolatries can take a secular form, as in the Nazi's idolatrous exaltation of state, race, blood and soil, or the communist exaltation of the Party and the destiny of the proletariat, or in the bourgeois preoccupation with success and self-aggrandisement. It can also take the ecclesiastical form of an idolatrous exaltation of the cult or church to the absolute status of God.

Other-worldly religion goes to the opposite extreme. It voids the day to day concerns of both cult and culture of all meaning in order to safeguard the absolute transcendence of God.

The tension between proximate or everyday concern and ultimate concern creates a profound dilemma within human existence. In commitment to the day to day concerns of life we are tempted to seek our security among them. This is an illusory hope. To reject them in favour of a genuinely ultimate concern empties present, temporal concern of genuine meaning. Tillich acknowledges that it was Kierkegaard who pointed up this aspect of the human dilemma most sharply.

Our aspirations outrun the limitations of our finite situation. This leads to the experience of alienation. We are inescapably alienated from ourselves and from God. As soon as we exercise our finite freedom amid the actualities of temporal existence and the ambiguities of daily life we compromise our ultimate commitment to absolute truth, absolute goodness and absolute beauty. This is the meaning of the doctrine of original sin.

Symbols
The possibility of a solution to this dilemma consists fundamentally in the fact that each and any of the finite or proximate concerns of temporal existence can become symbols of that which concerns us ultimately. The marriage relation can become a symbol of the love of God. The bread and wine of the social meal can become the symbol of communion with God. Such symbols are never mere symbols. They participate in the reality which they represent.

The great danger in such symbols is that we are tempted to identify the symbol unambiguously with that which it symbolises and in which it participates. The idolatrous consequences of such an identification in paganism are readily recognised. Christian theologians have been less ready to recognise the same perversion within christian ecclesiastical tradition. Therefore Tillich strongly emphasises the sacramental element in life, but is very guarded in his attitude to the special sacraments of the church.

This dilemma is endemic in every concrete expression of ultimate concern – i.e. in all religion. In Christianity it reaches the acme of paradox. A finite, historical man, Jesus of Nazareth, becomes transparent to or symbolic of that which concerns us ultimately. But Jesus overcomes the dilemma in his own person and life by sacrificing his finite existence to his infinite meaning. This is what drives him to the cross. His overcoming of the dilemma is the meaning of his resurrection. In this paradoxical way, but only in this paradoxical way, he is God with us.

In the achievement of his life, death and resurrection he opens to us the way of life in the communion of the Spirit of God. This is the life of the Kingdom of God. In this way the whole of temporal history is brought into authentic relation with its transcendent ground and meaning in God. The church is both the derivative symbol and the temporal vehicle of this transformation. Existential alienation is transformed into reconciliation.

Conclusion
In this chapter we have dealt with three very great men. It must be emphasised that summary treatment cannot do them justice. Each is worthy of a place among the greatest Fathers of the church. It

must also be acknowledged that, like all great enquiring minds, each raised more problems than he solved. What matters most, however, is that they carried even their residual problems to a level far deeper than that at which they found them.

FOR FURTHER READING

Bromiley, G. W., *An Introduction to the Theology of Karl Barth*, Edinburgh, 1979.
Bush, E., *Karl Barth*, London, 1976.
Clayton, J. P., *The Concept of Correlation: Paul Tillich and the Possibility of a Mediating Theology*, Berlin and New York, 1980.
Kegley, C. W. and Bretall, R. W., (eds.) *The Theology of Paul Tillich*, revised ed., New York, 1982.
Macquarrie, J., *An Existentialist Theology: A Comparison of Heidegger and Bultmann*, London, 1958.
Newport, J. P., *Paul Tillich*, Waco, Texas, 1984.
Schmithals, W., *Introduction to Bultmann's Theology*, London, 1968.
Smart, J. D., *The Divided Mind of Modern Theology. Karl Barth and Rudolf Bultmann, 1908–1933*, Philadelphia, 1967.
Sykes, S. (ed), *Karl Barth Studies in his Theological Method*, Oxford, 1980.

9

THE SECULAR SIXTIES

1. A WORLD COME OF AGE?

From about 1960 the dominance of the three giants crumbled remarkably quickly. This came about primarily because there arose a new generation whose concerns were markedly different from those of their parents. They had missed the experience of two world wars. For them Christendom was not even a memory. It was a thing of the remote past. The new generation had never entertained even the hope of a total view of life which saw it whole and saw it clearly. They did not experience its shattering, so they did not miss it. Alienation they did experience; but it was not through loss of meaning such as their parents had suffered. It was, rather, alienation from any conception of the meaning of life which sought to subordinate its everyday values to holistic ideals. The plural meanings of an open and free society seemed to them sufficient. The loves, the friendships and the interests of the day were for them enough. In Tillich's terminology, proximate concerns were enough and ultimate concern was a corrupting neurosis. Karl Popper's *The Open Society and its Enemies* (1945) anticipated the spirit of these times. Total ideologies, he suggested, are the stuff of which totalitarianism is made.

In these circumstances the question of God could not even be raised, much less answered.

This was confirmed by the prevailing fashion in philosophy. Traditionally it had been thought that, while other disciplines dealt with special aspects of reality, philosophy dealt with questions about the nature of reality as a whole. Such questions came to be regarded as meaningless because there was no known way of answering them. The business of philosophy, it was now suggested, was not to answer material questions, but to clarify their meaning.

There emerged a brief period of curiously adolescent theology.

There is nothing so adolescent as the insistence that one has come of age. The phrase 'man come of age' taken (usually out of context) from Dietrich Bonhoeffer was its slogan.

'Situation' Theology

It is better to begin with the sillier aspects of that season before considering its more serious achievement. In the dialectic between tradition and modernity the modern situation was given pre-eminence. The essential meaning of the gospel was seen as determined by its relevance to the modern situation. Thus there arose a wide variety of 'situational' theologies varying in accordance with one's view of which were the crucial problems in the immediate situation. In the field of Christian ethics we had already been made familiar with the concept of 'situation ethics'. This school contended that moral decisions should be reached more on the basis of understanding of the situation than by application of absolute principles. Analogously, we had theologies of revolution for the economically oppressed, black theologies for the racially oppressed, feminist theologies for the sexually oppressed and even gay theologies for oppressed deviants, and so on. These movements were a significant corrective to a theological tradition which had become captive to an elitist and ecclesiastical camp. They were often little more than that.

'Shocker' Theology

This was also a period of theological shock tactics. 'Secular Theology', 'Religionless Christianity', 'Death of God Theology' and the like made good headlines.

This involves an aspect of contemporary theology which is an entirely new factor – the economics of modern publishing and the other media of communication. The Fathers of the early church wrote for eternity. They often succeeded in informing an age. The theologians of the nineteenth century wrote for an age and usually succeeded in informing a generation at least. The theologian of today writes for a generation but is lucky if his work survives the sale of the first paperback edition. This is not the fault of the publishers. It is a consequence of the stark economics of modern publishing.

The influence of this factor was very great in and around the 'sixties. It was a period of railway-station bookstall theology. Works which were often no more than journalistic comments on the contemporary religious and theological scene were taken up by the media of communication and given a 'whirl' because of their 'shocker' interest. They thus exercised a brief influence out of all proportion to their merit. An outstanding example was John Robinson's *Honest to God* (1963), a work which contained nothing that was new and little that was true. The *Sunday Observer* took it up in Britain and immediately it became a *cause célebre*. In fact, the book did nothing more than present Bultmann, Bonhoeffer and Tillich in a deceptively popularised and homogenised amalgum.

Another example of the pressure of the media of communication upon the theology of that period was the furore over the Dead Sea Scrolls. The discovery of these scrolls in the nineteen-fifties was quite important. Apart from their significance for textual criticism of the Old Testament they confirmed and corrected some opinions which had been circulating about the role of apocalyptic thinking and other related matters at the time of Jesus. The *New Yorker* magazine took up this discovery. Overnight, the whole fate of Christianity seemed to depend upon its interpretation. The whole incident is reminiscent of the story of the famous editor who is alleged to have instructed his staff to report the war in Cuba. When his staff protested that there was no war in Cuba he responded that he, through his newspaper, would see that there was.

Something like this is also true of the so-called 'Death of God' theology of the 'sixties. Various periodicals – especially in America – took up this concept and created a school out of a number of quite diverse comments by various theologians about the prospects for the traditional idea of God in modern society. A school of thought, which did not even know it existed, was thus created.

2. SECULAR CHRISTIANITY

However, behind the popular fascination with the bizarre and shocking in the theological antics of the 'sixties there were a number of important insights. They were diverse in origin and character. Their impact was cumulative.

Origins of Secular Christianity
Firstly, the three giants of the previous decades made their (largely unintentional) contribution. Barth was widely understood to have so emphasised the transcendence of God that he equally emphasised the secularity of the world. In devaluing religion he seemed to emphasise the secularity of the christian faith. Bultmann was understood to have transformed the objective concept of God into one of human self-understanding. Tillich's ontology was ignored. His

concept of ultimate concern was taken up as a reduction of theology to anthropology.

Secondly, a more radical foundation for the edifice of secular theology had been laid by men such as Friedrich Gogarten (1887-1967). He stressed that the prophetic religion of Israel resisted the pagan divinisation of the world and nature. This Hebrew insight, he suggested, is the true origin of modern secularity. The God of Israel is not bound to the nation or the land by ties of nature. He chooses Israel freely. This takes God out of the natural processes of the world. It let the worldly be truly worldly and God be truly God. The life and death of Jesus are the final step in this liberation of the world from its gods. Jesus resisted to the death the tendency of late judaism to turn life into a religious ritual. He thus liberated man for true worldliness and free responsibility.

Thirdly, there were certain voices from the nineteenth century that rang out more loudly in the twentieth. Ludwig Feuerbach has already been mentioned in this connection. In a quite different way Friedrich W. Nietzsche (1844-1900) also became a prophet of the new movement. A maverick in his own day, he now bid fair to lead the herd. He saw the religious, otherworldly Christ worshipped by the churches as Antichrist. The true Christ was an affirmation of the worldly life in all its strength and vigour. The words of Nietzsche's mad prophet in *The Gay Science* (1882) provided both a name and a slogan for the more extreme elements in the secular Christianity movement – 'God is dead . . . And we have slain him . . . What are the churches if not the tombs and sepulchres of God?'

Radical Empiricism
Fourthly, unconnected with all this, but convergent in its influence on theology, was the Logical Positivist movement and its derivatives in philosophy. We have already noted how the kind of sceptical empiricism associated with David Hume was imported into Germany and became virulent just at the time when German Idealism was being given a new lease of life in Anglo-Saxon philosophy in the latter years of the nineteenth century. As the influence of Idealism declined, this virulent strain of empiricism re-infected first British then American philosophy in the 'thirties. Its most extreme form was Logical Positivism. This was a style of philosophy that had been developed by a group of scholars known as the Vienna Circle. They eliminated all metaphysical questions on the basis of the dogma that the meaning of a statement is identical with the method of its verification. i.e. If I say 'There is a table in the

room next door', this *means* 'If anyone performs an appropriate experiment, such as opening the door of the next room and taking a look, they will perceive a table.' This, of course is a trivial example. The Vienna Circle were mainly interested in the philosophy of science. The immediate advantage which the verification theory of meaning appeared to offer was the elimination from science of all questions of fact which could not be answered experimentally. However, its implications were generalised in philosophy. This was the virulent form in which positivism returned from Germany to Britain. It persisted in the English-speaking world long after the fever had abated in Germany.

Empiricist Theology
For a time the negative implications of this fashion in philosophy seriously affected theology. In its strict form the verificationist theory of meaning soon proved to be untenable. It underwent various modifications and transformations. But the tendency to eliminate as meaningless all statements which could not be experimentally verified persisted. This aided and abetted those secular theologians who were inclined to interpret all statements about God and transcendent realities as expressions of attitudes to this world and its concerns. An influential example of this new approach to theology was R. B. Braithwaite's essay, *An Empiricist's View of the Nature of Religious Belief* (1955). His thesis was that in the light of the new philosophical understanding of meaning and language, religious belief should be interpreted as moral commitment supported by stories and images of especially inspiring power. Paul van Buren's *The Secular Meaning of the Gospel* (1963) also applied this principle. He applied Bultmann's demythologising technique with more consistency and perhaps less insight than the master himself. He then went on to argue that Bultmann's residual 'non-objective use of the word 'God' allows of no verification and is therefore meaningless'. Therefore, 'statements of faith are to be interpreted, by means of the modified verification principle, as statements which express, describe, or commend a particular way of seeing the world, other men and oneself, and the way of life appropriate to such a perspective'. This is a typical expression of one strand in the complex texture of what came to be known as secular theology.

Bonhoeffer
Fifthly, there were the remarkable and often enigmatic developments in the later theology of Dietrich Bonhoeffer (1906–45). In his early work Bonhoeffer might fairly be described as a theologian of

the Barthian school. Even in his early days, however, he went beyond Barth in certain respects which opened the way for his later theology. He outdid even Barth in centring all upon Jesus Christ and in stressing the distinctness of the divine and human natures in him. This meant that he stressed the utter humanity of Jesus and the 'hiddenness' of God's presence in him. This pointed him in the direction of a profound interpretation of the work of Christ as the liberation of man to be truly man. This meant his liberation from *every* extraneous, inhibiting power, be it sin, law, demons or gods. In the authoritarian elements in Barth's doctrine of revelation he saw a residual element of such extraneous, inhibiting power. This is why he accused Barth of a 'positivism of revelation'.

When, after much heart-searching, Bonhoeffer became involved in the plot to overthrow Hitler, by assassination if necessary, these insights were intensified. His motives were Christian, but he had to co-operate with people of a variety of views and motives. In an important sense he was on his own as much as they were. His God was not an extra trick up his sleeve. In his famous *Letters and Papers from Prison* he expressed the view that christians were called upon to live *etsi deus non daretur*. What did he mean by this phrase and why did he lapse into Latin at this point? We can be sure that the Latin is not mere affectation. It is a signal that he wants to say something which is not easily communicated in less precise languages. It can legitimately be translated 'as though God were not there'. However, this is not a simple gospel of Christian atheism. What is denied is that the God of Christian faith is present and available to us in the manner of the gods of pagan religion. They are 'there' in their shrine, in their temple, in a special religious sphere. By contrast, there is no special place where we can find the God of Christian faith. In his utter transcendence he is, in this sense, absent from the world. There is therefore no special religious sphere for Christian faith. This is the basis of Christian secularity, Christian worldliness. When Jesus died on the cross the gods of a special religious sphere died with him. However, for Bonhoeffer, this absence or hiddenness of the God of Christian faith is also, in a paradoxical way, the basis of his nearer presence to us.

> The God who lets us live in the world without the working hypothesis of God is the God before whom we are ever standing. Before God and with God we live without God.

This is obviously something very different from the brash and empty secularism of modern man.

The Urban Ideal

Sixthly, this pervasive and rather shallow secularism contributed yet another element to the secular theology movement. It was accorded a measure of theological respectability in Harvey Cox's *The Secular City* (1965). His thesis was that metropolitan life is the dominant and typical form of modern social existence. The Christian faith has made this possible by liberating men to enjoy and exercise their full autonomy. Christianity, however, has yet to adjust to the new ethos of its own creation. Faith must discard its religious form and its subservience to other-worldly interests.

In retrospect there is something pathetic in the optimism of this theology of metropolitan secularity. At the time New York was still booming, London was swinging, Paris was gayer than ever and Berlin was the centre of an economic miracle. It was in fact the sunset glow of the large city. Inner-city areas stood on the brink of becoming social and cultural deserts.

It will be seen from all this that the phenomenon which was known as secular Christianity was not a single movement. It consisted in the convergence of a number of quite diverse strands. There was no coherent, systematic relation between these strands. Some were superficial, some were profound. The most sensitive exposition of the best insights of the period is R. Gregor Smith's *Secular Christianity* (1966). It is significant that when he saw the way in which some of the brasher aspects of the theology of secularity were developing, he immediately began work on his next book entitled *The Doctrine of God* (1970).

3. POLITICAL THEOLOGY

We really need to distinguish two aspects of the secular emphasis in modern theology. There is the secularity of affluence and the secularity of poverty. Many of the shallower types of secular theology which we have so far discussed were associated with a self-consciously affluent society and the confident expectation of a steadily rising standard of living. This included the expectation that the poorer nations could be raised to a similar standard of living in the foreseeable future. The early disillusionment of such expectations rapidly reduced the appeal of such simplistic, secularist theologies. In reaction there developed a secular or worldly emphasis associated with poverty and repression. This came to be known as political or liberation theology.

Moltmann

It should not be forgotten that Marxist dialectical materialism is close kin to Christian trinitarian theology. Hegel's account of the self-realisation of the triune God in history was one of the main sources of Marx's philosophy – though Marx politicised it in a way that Hegel never intended. It could reasonably be argued that Christian theologians and philosophers leant too far in the opposite direction towards idealism. They relied too much on the belief that ideas rather than action would change the world. The brand of secular theology which emerged as political theology sought to correct this. Jurgen Moltmann provided the main initial stimulus in his *The Theology of Hope* (1965).

Like so many of his contemporaries, he acknowledged a substantial debt to Barth. He was, however, critical of Barth's account of the relation between God's time and the fallen temporality of human history. Barth, he maintains, so emphasised the contrast between God's time and the fallen temporality of human history that the divine action in revelation and redemption becomes an eternal moment which breaks into history only at specific points and centrally in the incarnation of Jesus Christ. This devalues human history. He is even more critical of Bultmann who, he argues, reduces concrete history to the existential experience of historicity.

Moltmann does not propose a return to the Hegelian and Liberal historicism which sought to read off the meaning of history from history itself. The meaning of history is determined from beyond history by the action of God. The kingdom of God is not something that can be brought into being by a utopian programme. Being from beyond the world it is not of this world. However, the divine action on which the meaning of history rests is in this world. It becomes concretely temporal in the history of Israel and is completed in the life, death and resurrection of Jesus Christ. The divine Word is a Word of power in action. It has the form of eschatological promise and fulfilment. As such, though it centres on specific times and events, it cuts across every moment of worldly time, determining its meaning in judgment and promise.

Transforming Action

Traditional theology, Moltmann thinks, has taken too lightly the fact that the Word of God is a Word in historical action. It has been too concerned with right belief and not enough with right action. The temporal history in which the Word of God becomes an event of final and decisive meaning is made primarily through political decisions. Christian theology must, therefore, have a prominent political aspect.

In *The Theology of Hope* Moltmann surveys the biblical tradition eliciting this political aspect. The Exodus from Egypt was, after all, the insurrection of an oppressed minority. The message of the prophets was pregnant with political significance. It was primarily on suspicion of political sedition that Jesus was crucified.

Therefore, to be true to the heart of the tradition, theology must be politically involved. Faith must be expressed in doing as well as thinking. Theology must merge into theopraxis. The action of faith must be expressed corporately as well as individually. This involves political action. Moltmann avoids a naive identification of the active expression of faith with the policies of any particular political party. He stops just short of it. But he does insist that the political expression of the faith must be one which identifies unambiguously with the interest of the downtrodden and the oppressed. He develops this at greater length in *The Crucified God* (1975). The distinctive quality of this kind of Christian social and political commitment is brought out in the third volume of his trilogy, *The Church in the Power of the Spirit* (1977). The life of faith in the present power of the spirit permits and involves the enjoyment of liberation from sin, authoritarian law and oppression even in the midst of the fallen structures of the world. But it does not do this in such a way as to distract us from the revolutionary struggle. On the contrary it invites and stimulates us to transform the world.

In Western Europe this theology generated a good deal of enthusiasm among the more youthful members of the Christian intelligentsia. In Europe and North America, however, it was a fashion rather than a movement and its influence soon waned. In fact, much of it had been anticipated in Paul Tillich's *The Socialist Decision*. The German edition of this work appeared in 1933. At the time it made little impact, however, since the first edition was impounded and destroyed by the Nazis and Tillich had to flee the country. He never developed this line of thought further mainly because, though he loved America, the land of his adoption, he never felt able to identify with the political scene as he had done in his native land.

Liberation Theology

However, although political theology in Europe and North America may never have been more than a passing fashion associated with the era of 'student power' in the 'sixties and early 'seventies, the situation in what is now known as the 'Third World' was different.

In the developed world the political parties of the left were, on the whole, only embarrassed by the proffered alliance of an ideology essentially at odds with their own humanistic style. It is in the less developed countries that christian political theology has become a more serious force. This has been particularly so in South America. There a host of extremely able exponents have taken up the theme. Their main criticism of European political theologians such as Moltmann is that they did not go far enough in taking theology out of the academic seminar into the political arena. Prominent among such writers are Gustavo Gutierrez, *A Theology of Liberation* (1971; E. tr. 1973), Jose Miguez Bonino, *Revolutionary Theology Comes of Age* (1975) and Juan Luis Segundo's massive *A Theology for Artisans of a New Humanity* (5 Vols., 1972-4) and *The Liberation of Theology* (1977). These Latin American theologians are mostly Roman Catholic (Bonino is the exception). They are not reductionist in that they do not contend that the whole meaning of traditional theology is exhausted in its political implications. They do, however, hold that the only adequate expression of that theology in the modern world is in practical identification with the poor and the oppressed. Though it has not yet received quite such sophisticated expression in other parts of the world, this type of theology is arousing increasing interest in those countries where the population receives disastrously less than its fair share of the world's goods and services.

In view of the fact that the majority of Christians now live in such countries, this must be regarded as one of the major elements in theological debate for the foreseeable future. Its continuing and increasing influence is evident, for example, in the thinking and policies of the World Council of Churches where Christians from these nations, because of their numbers, have a significant voice. Even in the richer nations, repressed minorities, or minorities who feel themselves repressed, have taken up this style of theology – e.g., in the United States of America, James Cone's *God and the Oppressed* (1975) and *Black Theology and Black Power* (1969).

Perspective

This whole development of political theology has made at least one thing clear. For the past two hundred years we have been trying, rather self-consciously, to construct a Christian theology for modern man. It is now clear that our image of modern man has been far too refined. Schleiermacher began this trend with his significantly entitled *On Religion: Speeches to its Cultured Despisers*. Too little attention has been paid to modern man as he exists in harsh reality rather than in the imagination of a cultured elite. If Christian doctrine is to be reformulated in ways which show its relevance and credibility for modern man, it is this real, economic and industrial man that we must have in mind. It has been the strength of political theology to draw our attention in this direction.

However, it is now becoming clear that a theology whose anthropological base is merely political or economic is equally emaciated and inadequate. It is also becoming pressingly evident that an adequate theological understanding of the human situation cannot remain independent of either the metaphysical or the cosmological. We cannot know man in the wholeness of his being without forming a view of the nature of the universe in which he lives and the reality which underlies its phenomenal appearance. The recognition of this is driving contemporary theology to survey wider horizons than those of either secular or political theology.

FOR FURTHER READING

Bonino, J. M., *Revolutionary Theology Comes of Age*, London, 1975.

Kee, A., *A Reader in Political Theology*, London, 1974. *The Scope of Political Theology*, London, 1978.

Long, E. T. (ed.), *God Secularisation and History. Essays in Honour of Ronald Gregor Smith*, Columbia, South Carolina, 1974.

Newbigin, L., *Honest Religion for Secular Man*, London, 1966.

Ogletree, T. W., *The Death of God Controversy*, London, 1966.

Shinn, R. L., *Man: The New Humanism (New Directions in Theology, vol. VI)*, London, 1968.

Smith, R., Gregor, *Secular Christianity*, London, 1966.

10

THEOLOGY TODAY

To interpret and assess current theological developments will be a task for historians of the future. Only a brief comment can be made here.

Theology has entered a new period of recollection – a gathering together of all its resources. Since 1800 theology has been dominated by one valid but partial insight after another. Each in its day, from Schleiermacher's feeling of absolute dependence to Bultmann's existentialism, has been presented as the key to everything. In fact, each opened only one door in the household of faith. Some systematic unification of these various insights is now called for.

1. HISTORY AND HERMENEUTICS

Coming to Terms with the Past
W. Pannenberg has played a key role in establishing this more balanced approach to theology. He is best known for his handling of the confrontation of critical history with tradition. His *Revelation as History* (1969) was immediately recognised as a work of seminal importance. It established a relation between tradition and history which is the key to the modern situation. Tradition, if it is to deliver its cargo of truth, must be interpreted in its historical context. But such an understanding involves more than a merely positivist approach to history. It involves every aspect of our rational capacities and insights.

As well as the ingathering of the resources of modern theology, there has been the beginnings of a reconciliation of modern theology with its more remote past. Tradition is being rediscovered. But tradition is no longer seen as a changeless body of doctrine – changeless in form as well as substance. It is seen in its historic context as a growing, living thing. Increasingly it is being recognised that tradition is not, like the Tower of Babel, built up brick upon precarious brick. It grows, and like every growing thing, preserves its identity through change. When a living thing ceases to change and grow, it is then that it ceases to be itself. From having first appeared as the enemy of faith, historical consciousness has become its friend.

In the past, the problem of history centred on the question whether the facts as disclosed by historical research were as recounted in the biblical tradition. More recently the question has assumed a broader and deeper form. It has become the problem of how we assimilate our own past. Nicholas Lash expressed the new form of the problem well when he said,

> The past is experienced, not as a rich heritage to be fostered, but largely as a world profoundly 'other' than our own . . . the past tends to be treated as *the* past rather than *our* past.

Contemporary theology has been working towards a solution to that problem; but much more than history is involved. There is taking place an integration of historical consciousness with every other aspect of theology, with philsophy, with metaphysics and with anthropology.

The positivist style of writing history, which was established in the nineteenth century, distinguishes sharply between brute facts and their interpretation. The new style of traditio-historical inquiry recognises that every fact occurs within a context of meaning and that this is part of its historical reality. Schleiermacher, in his lectures on *Hermeneutics*, and after him Wilhelm Dilthey (1833–1911), laid the foundations of this approach to history; but it is only now that their significance in this regard is fully appreciated.

Pannenberg

Pannenberg has set this approach to history in the context of a total theory of knowledge in his *Theology and the Philosophy of Science* (1976). But it was his earlier, *Revelation as History* which constituted the initial break-through. He there illuminated the importance of the transition in our understanding of revelation from that of super-natural verbal communication to that of the self-disclosure of God in the significant events of history. Tradition remembers and reflects these events and their significance. Tradition also provides the context in which each new event of revelation is interpreted. Studies in the development of Old Testament tradition by scholars such as Gerhard von Rad contributed significantly to this.

The God of Israel is depicted as the God and the Lord of history. He is not imprisoned in a timeless eternity. He has a real relation to time. Therefore, says Pannenberg, the self-disclosure of God, through the interlocking history of events and traditions, is also the disclosure of the meaning of history itself. (One can recognise surviving elements of Hegelianism in this suggestion.)

The meaning of history is thus disclosed as pointing beyond history itself. This had to be so because human existence as such points beyond itself. Pannenberg spelled this out in *What is Man?* (1970). Man relates to the 'beyond' of his existence in imagination, in anxiety, in trust and in hope. This is not a relation to a timeless transcendence, but to a transcendence which embraces his future. In this anthropology one recognises surviving elements of Schleiermacher. It is an advance upon the anthropology of the Enlightenment, which saw man's essential relation to transcendence only in his relation to the timeless absolutes of goodness, beauty and truth.

Belief in God thus incorporates a trusting and hopeful expectancy towards the future. But this expectant belief about the meaning of history is inextricably bound up with belief about the meaning of the whole of creation. In its mature development the biblical tradition expressed this in the form of apocalyptic. It was in this context that Jesus presented himself. It was in this context that he was acknowledged as the Christ. As such he anticipates and establishes not only the meaning of human history, but of the whole of creation. His resurrection is the confirmation of this. He anticipates a future consummation which we can still envisage only in apocalyptic symbol. The central symbol is that of the ingathering of all creation and the entire temporal process into God at the end of time. God is the one who in the end will be 'all in all'.

This viewpoint lays the foundation for the re-integration of the historical and existential with the metaphysical and essential. The idealist concept of the 'self-end of God' is re-integrated with the biblical eschatology from which it had become estranged. The transcendence of God is re-integrated with his immanence in history and nature. The positive insights of the nineteenth century have thus been brought to fulfilment in the twentieth; but in the process they have been transformed.

An important element in this transformation has been the replacement of spatial images of transcendence by those of time. Thus, for example, Pannenberg is prepared to speak of the 'futurity of God'. His transcendence is essentially his being for us as the final end and goal of temporal existence. This, however, is qualified by the acknowledgment that God's relation to time is different from ours.

His eternity is not timeless. He has a real relation to time, but unlike finite creatures, he is excluded from neither past nor future.

Pannenberg and Moltmann Compared

There are both parallels and differences between Pannenberg and Moltmann. Moltmann could agree with Pannenberg that faith is centrally an insight into the meaning of history centred upon the Christ-event. But Moltmann, as we have already seen in connection with his contribution to political theology, stresses that the implication of this insight is that faith must break out of the realm of *ideas* about the meaning of history into the making of history through positive action. It could with some justice be said that Pannenberg represents a modified right-wing Hegelianism while Moltmann represents a modified left-wing Hegelianism.

This must be immediately qualified, however, by the recognition that Moltmann is innocent of the kind of reductionism which we found in the left-wing Hegelians of the nineteenth century. While it is true that at one level Moltmann will interpret the doctrine of the Trinity as expressive of the ever open and inviting possibility of new creation, revolution, reconciliation and communion within life and history, he does not reduce its meaning to that level. He acknowledges the transcendent, ontological reality of the triune being of God. He has contributed substantially to the recovery of trinitarian theology currently taking place.

The Recovery of Tradition

For more than a century there has been a strong tendency to accommodate the gospel to the modern frame of mind by reducing its proportions. There is now clear evidence of a turning away from such reductionism – whether humanist, existentialist or political – to a recovery of the full theological structure of Christianity as it has been formed by two thousand years of tradition. This is in no way a return to obdurate, authoritarian conservatism. It is arising, on the one hand, from a development in historical consciousness, and on the other, from a renewed acknowledgment of the continuing relevance of the trans-historical categories of traditional christian metaphysics. This new integration of historical and metaphysical modes of thought is as yet only tentative and exploratory. It is one of the promising and inviting doors into the future.

Behind the current recovery of tradition is the acknowledgment that we have nothing to live out of but our past. The attempt of self-consciously modern man to live only within the confines of his own modernity has proved abortive. Our openness to our future depends on our openness to our past.

This consciousness is accompanied by a theological recollection which inhibits any attempt to go back to biblical inspiration while ignoring everything that has happened between now and then. It sees tradition less as a limiting discipline and more as a liberating resource. It takes what came out of the creative freedom of the past as the indispensable base for the creative freedom of the present.

One splendid outcome of this is that the Fathers of the church – for so long only a hunting ground for theological archaeologists – are again emerging as lively interlocutors in the contemporary debate. Much of the credit for this must go to Karl Barth and after him to W. Pannenberg who, especially in the volumes of his collected papers, *Basic Questions in Theology* (1970–) repeatedly brings to light the lively relevance of the ancient Fathers to contemporary issues.

This feeling after a new relationship to tradition which is both faithful and free cuts right across established ecclesiastical boundaries. One aspect of it has been the splendid new flowering of Roman Catholic theology.

2. ROMAN CATHOLIC THEOLOGY

Very little has been said in this volume about developments in Roman Catholic theology in the nineteenth and early twentieth centuries. This is because, by and large, it had little to say that was radically new. It was backward-looking, inward-looking and, at least in its public expression, disciplined within an inch of its life. The Catholic Modernist Movement around the turn of the century – particularly as represented by A. Loisy (1857–1940) – was more a truancy than a genuine movement of liberation. It was understandably condemned and for a time left a triumphant ultramontanism more firmly entrenched than ever.

But now new things are afoot and there are many indications that the new era of theological creativity will be equally shared by Catholics, Protestants and Eastern Orthodox. A new and more deeply spiritual relation to tradition, dogma and authority is beginning to emerge and is finding theological expression. The Second Vatican Council was an important milestone along this way; though much will depend on how its outcome is used and interpreted.

Karl Rahner

Karl Rahner is the most distinguished representative of this new and flourishing Roman Catholic theology. It is a theology read and valued as much by Protestants as by Roman Catholics. It is a theology both liberated and liberating. At the same time it remains faithful to and informed by church and tradition. Rahner is probably right in his opinion that the present situation is not ripe for the creation of major theological systems. His massive theological output is contained in twenty volumes of essays and papers entitled *Theological Investigations*.

His essay on 'The Development of Doctrine' in the first volume of the *Investigations* is of strategic importance. He revives the best insights of John Henry Newman, but goes further and deeper. He has a better appreciation of the movement of history within the doctrinal life and experience of the church. He is therefore more openly critical of static petrification of doctrine.

True Authority

Near the heart of every theological debate since the Enlightenment there has been a question, either implicit or explicit, about the relation between freedom and authority. In this regard, Protestant and Roman Catholic share much the same problem. They differ only in locating authority in different quarters.

To Barth and Rahner together must go the credit for recalling us to a more adequate vision of the authority of Christ. There are different kinds of authority. There is extrinsic authority of office such as was exercised by Pontius Pilate. There is intrinsic authority of person and spirit such as was exercised absolutely by Jesus and before which Pontius Pilate could only wash his hands. Between this kind of authority and the free response of mind and heart there is no conflict. It is the authority which liberates even as it binds. It is this authority which is vested in the life and structures of the church and in the witness of the Holy Scriptures as a grace. That it has sometimes been confused with the other kind of authority must be admitted on all sides.

That Rahner and Barth could separately have developed Christocentric visions of the truth and authority of revealed doctrine bearing such a remarkable family resemblance is a sign of the times. Ecclesiastically the Roman Catholic Church and the Churches of the Reformation continue to confront one another in attitudes ranging from genteel exclusiveness to open hostility. Theologically, however, there is every sign that the period of Reformation and Counterreformation is coming to an end.

Nowhere is this more evident than in the lively theology of Hans Küng. His criticisms of current interpretations of papal infallibility have attracted notoriety as well as criticism. It is unfortunate that this has distracted attention from the more positive aspects of his theology. He shares with Rahner, Pannenberg, Moltmann and the whole spectrum of recent theology the recognition that saving grace is not a superstructure erected upon nature, but a leaven which is working at the very heart of the whole of creation.

It must not be thought, however, that this recovery of tradition without heteronomy is entirely irenic. Another distinguished Roman Catholic theologian, Hans Urs von Balthasar, is highly critical of both Rahner and Küng; but he shares the same lively experience of renewal in relation to tradition. His work is only now beginning to appear in English.

True Humanity

There is today a shared recognition that the human and the personal must play a more prominent role as normative categories in the interpretation of Christian doctrine. We have broken out of the restrictive confines of existentialism into a more robust and wholesome understanding of our spiritual condition. At the same time, however, there is a shared recognition that humanism and personalism cannot stand alone. In themselves they lead only to an empty autonomy. Human beings must understand themselves in their cosmic setting and in their openness beyond their cosmos if they are to understand themselves at all.

Few of the contemporary theologians who matter would differ from Karl Rahner when he says,

The Incarnation of the Logos . . . appears as the onto-logically . . . unambiguous goal of the movement of creation as a whole, in relation to which everything prior is merely a prep-aration for the scene.

Such agreement is remarkable, for it is a sentence which could just as easily have been written by Athanasius, Irenaeus, Gregory of Nyssa or Basil of Caesarea. Modern theology is finally learning to reclaim its own past and to integrate the living essence of tradition into the present. In so doing it is opening its own future.

We are only at the beginning of this recovery of tradition and its meaning for our own modernity. It has taken two hundred years of searching and heart-searching to get to where we are. What the present signs betoken is not a retreat into tradition as it was before modern theology began. It will be different as children must differ from their parents, no matter how much they have learned from them. But the signs now are that it will not be a diminished tradition. It is not a diminished Christ or a diminished gospel that will take the attention and stir the faith of modern man. Only a Christ who fills the whole created order and is one with the God who will be all in all at the end of time will do.

FOR FURTHER READING

Edwards, D. L., *Religion and Change*, London, 1969.
Galloway, A. D., *Wolfhart Pannenberg*, London, 1973. *Faith in a Changing Culture*, London, 1967.
Robinson, James M. and Cobb, John B. Jr., *Theology as History (New Frontiers in Theology, Vol III)* New York, 1967.
Weger, K. H., *Karl Rahner: An Introduction to his Theology*, London, 1980.

SUBJECT INDEX

NAME INDEX